✳ P

MYSTERIES OF THE NATIONAL PARKS

"A coast-to-coast and rip-roaring ride through the dark, mysterious, and oddball side of America's national parks. A must-read for National Park System lovers!"
—Jeremy Puglisi, coauthor of the bestselling
Where Should We Camp Next? series

"If wonder is the currency of the national parks, Bezemek invites you to double down on the inexplicable. This lively story collection—like the parks themselves—inspires repeat visits and deeper discoveries every time."
—Dave Shively, Sr. Editor at *Outside*
and author of *The Pacific Alone*

"Mike Bezemek digs deep to unearth the histories and mysteries that have shaped our country's national parks. These truly engrossing tales offer even more inspiration to visit these breathtaking landscapes."
—Jedd Ferris, Editor-in-Chief of
Blue Ridge Outdoors magazine

"From Kings Canyon to the Blue Ridge Parkway, these mysteries are often eerie, fascinating, and downright absurd. Mike spent years conducting boots-on-the-ground research, which I learned about first-hand over coffee in Utah when he was tracking Josie Basset."
—Ashley Peel, former longtime
editor of *Duct Tape Diaries*

"*Mysteries of the National Parks* is full of fun and well-researched tales, both historic and modern."
—Cassidy Randall, award-winning author
of *Thirty Below* and *The Hard Parts*

MYSTERIES
✦ OF THE ✦
NATIONAL
PARKS

35 STORIES *OF* BAFFLING DISAPPEARANCES, UNEXPLAINED PHENOMENA, *AND* MORE

MIKE BEZEMEK

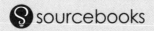

Copyright © 2025 by Mike Bezemek
Cover and internal design © 2025 by Sourcebooks
Cover design by Philip Pascuzzo
Cover image © Don White/Getty Images
Internal design by Laura Boren/Sourcebooks
Map by Laura Boren/Sourcebooks
Internal images © haryadi/Getty Images, sergio34/Getty Images, claudiodivizia/
Getty Images, klyaksun/Getty Images, stockdevil/Getty Images, drmakkoy/Getty
Images, Aleksandr Durnov/Getty Images, GalaChe/Getty Images, anjar suwarno/
Getty Images, Seahorse Vector/Getty Images, ONYXprj/Getty Images

This publication is designed to provide accurate and authoritative information in regard
to the subject matter covered. It is sold with the understanding that the publisher is not
engaged in rendering legal, accounting, or other professional service. If legal advice
or other expert assistance is required, the services of a competent professional person
should be sought. —*From a Declaration of Principles Jointly Adopted by a Committee
of the American Bar Association and a Committee of Publishers and Associations*

References to internet websites (URLs) were accurate at the time of writing.
Neither the author nor Sourcebooks is responsible for URLs that may
have expired or changed since the manuscript was prepared.

Published by Sourcebooks
P.O. Box 4410, Naperville, Illinois 60567-4410
(630) 961-3900
sourcebooks.com

Cataloging-in-Publication Data is on file with the Library of Congress.

Printed and bound in the United States of America.
VP 10 9 8 7 6 5 4 3 2 1

For my mom, whose adventurous spirit and love of
mysteries live within these pages...

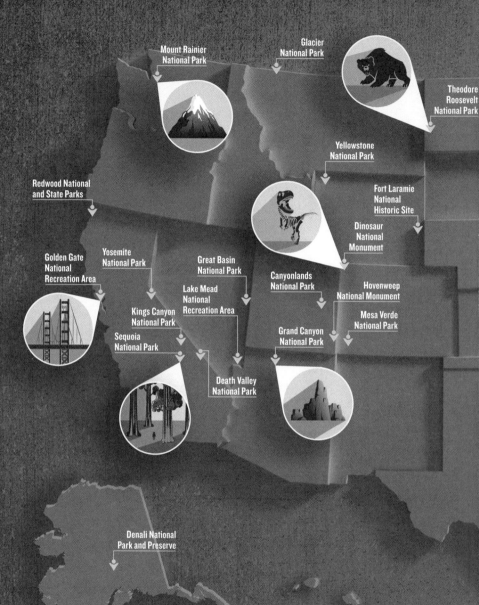

Mount Rainier
National Park

Glacier
National Park

Theodore
Roosevelt
National Park

Redwood National
and State Parks

Yellowstone
National Park

Fort Laramie
National
Historic Site

Dinosaur
National
Monument

Golden Gate
National
Recreation Area

Yosemite
National Park

Great Basin
National Park

Canyonlands
National Park

Hovenweep
National Monument

Lake Mead
National
Recreation Area

Kings Canyon
National Park

Mesa Verde
National Park

Sequoia
National Park

Grand Canyon
National Park

Death Valley
National Park

Denali National
Park and Preserve

Niagara Falls
National Heritage Area

Indiana Dunes
National Park

Ford's Theatre
National Historic Site

Colonial National
Historical Park

New River Gorge
National Park & Preserve

Gateway Arch
National Park

Great Smoky
Mountains
National Park

Blue Rdg Pkwy

Fort Raleigh
National Historic Site

Mammoth Cave

Shiloh National
Military Park

Vicksburg National
Military Park

Cumberland Island
National Seashore

Castillo de San Marcos
National Monument

Big Cypress
National Preserve

Everglades
National Park

MYSTERIES OF THE NATIONAL PARKS

✦ CONTENTS ✦

✦ INTRODUCTION ✦

Follow the Clues, Explore the Parks

What do you think about when you hear the term *national park*? Maybe you see a vast expanse of rugged mountains with scenic views and winding trails. Perhaps you envision iconic scenes from your favorite parks. Geysers erupting above roaming bison and grizzly bears. A granite valley carved by glaciers. A colorful river canyon in the high desert. A vast wilderness with impenetrable forests. Most people hope to visit at least one national park in their lifetime; adventurous travelers may think about visiting every park someday.

Few people consider unraveling a mystery when they visit one of America's protected natural or cultural wonders. Yet some of the world's most puzzling events and strangest discoveries have happened in U.S. national parks. One reason for this is that the National Park Service (NPS) manages around 133,000 square miles of land and water. That's enough area to qualify as the fifth-largest state, slightly smaller than Montana and slightly bigger than New Mexico. In some cases, infamous situations have unfolded within the boundaries of the most famous parks. Other times, NPS units have been established to preserve the sites of legendary occurrences.

That means that there's a lot of wild, undeveloped, and historic territory where something unexpected may have happened. Flying past Mount Rainier, did a private pilot really spot nine shiny objects that spawned the flying saucer craze? Might murder be legal in a small strip of Yellowstone National Park? Did Pocahontas truly save John Smith's life during those early days at Jamestown? Could an eccentric publisher have buried a treasure near the oldest masonry fortress in the United States?

This book presents thirty-five mysteries from across the entire National Park System. Some of these adventurous tales come from famous parks like Grand Canyon, Yosemite, Glacier, Everglades, and Great Smoky Mountains. Other chapters will take you to lesser-known gems like New River Gorge, Kings Canyon, Death Valley, Dinosaur National Monument, Canyonlands, Theodore Roosevelt, Cumberland Island National Seashore, and more.

During the journey, you'll encounter a wide range of mysteries. There are *baffling disappearances*, such as the daring couple who challenged the rapids and vanished on the Colorado River. An alleged spy turned murderer who may have escaped on the Appalachian Trail. A ghost blimp that landed without its crew. Other stories focus on *unexplained phenomena*, such as strange stones that slide on their own, a contorted crater in Utah that was possibly created by a meteor strike, and a seemingly normal sand dune that ominously swallowed a boy.

Enjoy *strange discoveries* such as a stone face carved in the mountains of West Virginia. Unravel *infamous crimes* such as the conspiracy to assassinate Abraham Lincoln at Ford's Theatre, which is now a national historic site. Explore *ancient civilizations* like the abandoned stone cities of Mesa Verde. And consider stories about *hidden history*, including who really was the first to climb Denali. Some of these stories have resolutions, but most mysteries remain unsolved to this day. You can ponder the clues as they unfold before your eyes and develop your own theories. Perhaps you'll be the one who finally unravels the answer.

Throughout the book, keep watch for appearances by *legendary figures* and notorious villains from national park history and America's turbulent past. A mix of riotous characters and beloved conservationists will be stopping by, from Calamity Jane, Hugh Glass, and Al Capone to John Muir, Marjory Stoneman Douglas, and Edward Abbey. Prepare for a sweeping journey through the ages. An unflinching look at forgotten episodes, sometimes violent and disturbing, other times embarrassing, bizarre, or hilarious. Stories will range from the chaotic modern day to the distant past when dinosaurs roamed the Earth and ancient civilizations later arose and vanished.

Hints Worth Visiting

Don't forget that each mystery in this book comes from National Park Service units that you can visit. Learning about these enigmatic stories can deepen your understanding of your favorite parks and enhance your experiences on the ground. Hopefully, connecting the dots will also lead you to new parks to visit and new places within their boundaries to explore. For that reason, each chapter includes travel sidebars about what to expect during a park visit and suggested activities and ways to bring the mysteries to life.

The stories in this book come from a wide range of NPS units found across the country. There are several naming designations for these units aside from *national park*, including *national seashore*, *national preserve*, and *national monument*, among many others. Currently, there are over 430 units, and counting, in the National Park System. As of the time of this writing, only sixty-three of these units are designated as national parks, which tend to receive most of the attention…and the largest crowds. Many outdoor enthusiasts prioritize the best-known national parks while skipping past the approximately 370 additional NPS units. Yet every NPS unit has worthy reasons to visit.

Among these many types of NPS units, you will encounter a greater range of outdoor experiences than most travelers realize. Some are historic sites, which often combine an indoor museum with exterior grounds, like the Spanish fortress at Castillo de San Marcos National Monument. Other lesser-known units can feel very "national park-like," offering similar scenery, wildlife, and recreational opportunities to their more famous cousins. Two perfect examples are Dinosaur National Monument on the Utah–Colorado state line and Cumberland Island National Seashore off the coast of Georgia, both of which have opportunities for hiking, biking, paddling, and more.

Some park lovers have said, "Go west for the nature, and go east for the history."

There's plenty of truth to this statement, but there are numerous outliers as well. Most of the biggest and wildest national parks are found in the mountainous West. Many of the midwestern, southern, and eastern park units can be smaller historical sites. But there are also big and rugged parks in the eastern half of the country, such as Mammoth Cave in Kentucky, Great Smoky Mountains on the Tennessee–North Carolina state line, Acadia in coastal Maine, and Everglades in South Florida. One great way to discover new parks is by checking out the comprehensive National Park System map, which can be found on www.nps.gov.

Today, interest in national parks is at an all-time high. Many of the most popular units are reducing overcrowding by instituting timed-entry reservations. If you don't land a permit, instead of giving up on your national park trip, consider checking out some lesser-known units, including those shared in this book. Perhaps one of the biggest mysteries is why so many excellent NPS units are ignored by travelers. With many of these hidden gems, you'll enjoy fascinating visits and exciting adventures.

In the meantime, you don't have to hop in the car to start discovering the mysteries of the national parks. But buckle up anyway before turning the page. Among the wildlife, there could be secret agents, clairvoyants, ghosts, and bar brawlers. This book is not your typical scenic drive. It's going to be a wild ride.

WEST COAST

CHAPTER 1

DID KENNETH ARNOLD SPOT THE FIRST FLYING SAUCER?

UNEXPLAINED PHENOMENA

MOUNT RAINIER NATIONAL PARK

CASCADE RANGE, WASHINGTON

Through the cockpit windows, the snowy hulk of Mount Rainier dominated the horizon. A private pilot was steering his two-seat prop plane toward the 14,411-foot dormant volcano. Along the way, he studied the southwest slopes for wreckage. The previous winter, a U.S. Marine transport plane carrying thirty-two servicemen had vanished in a storm. When the weather cleared, there was no sign of the plane, which presumably had crashed into the mountain and been buried by snow.

Now, it was a sunny afternoon in late June 1947. The pilot's name was Kenneth Arnold, and he was flying solo on a short hop from Chehalis to Yakima for a business trip. Back home in Boise, Idaho, Arnold was an experienced search-and-rescue volunteer who had learned about a $5,000 reward for locating the lost plane. After two unsuccessful flybys, he was about twenty miles west–southwest of the summit when he banked toward the mountain for another pass.

Suddenly, a blinding flash illuminated the cabin. Arnold scanned the sky, worried he might be on a collision course with another plane. All he saw was a silver DC-4, far off to the southwest, heading toward Seattle. Then he noticed another flash coming from the north in the direction of distant Mount Baker. A chain of nine bright objects was flying south at incredible speed.

As the strange objects approached, Arnold tried to comprehend what he was seeing. They flew in an echelon, a roughly diagonal formation often seen with military planes or geese. But the shapes seemed too big to be birds, perhaps comparable in size to the distant DC-4. They were also moving faster than any aircraft known to man. Despite maintaining the formation, each individual vessel flew erratically. They fluttered and tipped their wings, which flashed reflections of the sun.

As these skittering objects passed in front of Mount Rainier, Arnold noted their silhouettes. Each was shaped like a crescent moon with a convex triangle protruding from the rear, somewhat like a boomerang or the later flying wing. When viewed on edge, they seemed improbably thin. What most surprised Arnold was that he couldn't spot any vertical stabilizers. Were these experimental military jets with camouflaged features?

Using the clock on his instrument panel, Arnold timed the formation as it traveled from Mount Rainier past Mount Adams, more than forty miles to the south. One minute and forty-two seconds. Once the objects were out of sight, Arnold gave up his original search for the plane wreckage and turned toward Yakima. On the way, he calculated the objects' speed. Around 1,700 miles per hour, though he later decreased this estimate by one-third.

Well, that settled it. Yes, there were reports of rocket planes with needle-sharp noses being tested in the California desert. But a human pilot had yet to break the sound barrier, which was typically around 767 miles per hour. Just a few years before, in the latter stages of the Second World War, the Nazis had unveiled a secret rocket. Called the V-2, it hurtled through the sky at 3,500 miles per hour. Arnold decided the mysterious crafts were most likely a new type of guided missile. Hopefully this was a demonstration flight by Americans and not a daring incursion by the Soviets. People had to be on guard, after all. It was the beginning of a new conflict that some were calling a cold war.

A LOOMING PARK

Sixty miles south of Seattle, Mount Rainier National Park protects Mount Rainier, an active stratovolcano considered to be one of the most dangerous volcanoes in the world. Rising to 14,411 feet, Rainier is one of the tallest mountains in the United States. While about 10,000 people attempt to summit each year, the majority of visitors come for stunning views, scenic drives, and day hiking on the many trails.

From One Came Many

After landing in Yakima to refuel, Arnold sought out his friend, the general manager of a local airline. As Arnold enthusiastically relayed his experience, pilots gathered around to listen. The audience seemed skeptical of his descriptions. It was probably just the latest military project. Arnold was inclined to agree. Once his plane was ready, he took off for a short flight to his final destination of Pendleton, Oregon, where he planned to attend an air show. This time, upon arrival, a small crowd was waiting for him. News had traveled by telephone from Yakima. Soon, almost everyone at the airfield was listening to the story.

The next morning, Arnold took his maps and calculations down to the local

FBI branch but found it closed. Instead, he visited the nearby offices of the *East Oregonian*. There, he briefly met with a young reporter named Bill Bequette. When asked to describe the objects, Arnold said their motion was like a saucer skipping across water. The up-and-coming Bequette judged Arnold to be credible. The pilot seemed genuinely puzzled by his encounter. So, the reporter decided to submit a short dispatch to the Associated Press (AP). This might lead to an answer from officials. Bequette's report was only a 150-word summary of the incident, starting with an errant paraphrase: "Nine bright, saucer-like objects..."

When Bequette returned from his lunch break, the receptionist said reporters from across the country had called. Everyone wanted more information about these saucers. Throughout the day, dozens of newspapers published the AP dispatch. Various aviation experts were soon responding with skepticism. An army spokesman in Washington, DC, claimed that there were no high-speed experimental flights being conducted near Mount Rainier.

That afternoon, Bequette went to Arnold's hotel to interview him. The reporter spent the rest of the day writing a longer article, which was phoned into the AP. "Like the tail of a Chinese kite," Arnold reportedly said about the objects' weaving motions. The reflection of the sun off the objects was so bright, it blinded him like an arc light. Regarding the mystery crafts, they were "flat like a pie pan and somewhat bat-shaped." Arnold summed up the whole experience: "It seems impossible—but there it is."

On the morning of June 26, this longer article was picked up by newspapers across the country, many of which ran it on the front page. The *Chicago Sun* offered their own twist with a modified title: "Supersonic Flying Saucers Sighted by Idaho Pilot." Though Arnold hadn't described the objects as *flying saucers*, this soon-to-be-infamous term spread across the country like wildfire.

In the coming days and weeks, there were numerous reports of other sightings. The first was from a private pilot named Byron Savage, who claimed to see a saucer flying high above his yard in Oklahoma City. He offered support for Arnold.

"I know that boy up there really saw them."

Next came a guy in Kansas City who saw nine noisy saucers leaving vapor trails. Then a prospector in Oregon claimed to see five or six saucers over the Cascade Mountains. An advertising man in Hollywood described six silver saucers heading toward Mount Wilson. A coast guard yeoman named Frank Ryman claimed a bright speck in a photograph he had taken was a saucer hovering over Seattle.

When one Chicago man heard an object loudly bounce into his backyard, he naturally assumed a saucer had crashed. A closer inspection revealed a circular saw had fallen from a nearby construction site. The man shared the story with reporters but wisely changed his mind about calling the FBI.

The sightings quickly spanned the country, with reports of saucers in almost forty states, including New York. This caused some consternation from the skeptical *New York Times*, with one journalist noting that saucer colors now ranged far beyond silver to white, orange, and even Technicolor. From Canada to Mexico to Australia and South Africa, saucers were being spotted around the world.

By now, Kenneth Arnold, the instigator of the affair, was back home in Boise, watching dumbfounded as everything unfolded. The outside of his house was besieged by reporters. Letters, telegrams, and phone calls poured in. On July 3, nine days after his sighting, an overwhelmed Arnold was desperate for an escape.

He and a friend, Colonel Paul Wieland, flew out to the isolated tip of the Olympic Peninsula for a holiday fishing trip. Arnold brought along a newly purchased movie camera, hoping to capture proof of what he had seen. Wieland, a career military man, had recently returned from Germany, where he had participated in the Nuremberg trials against Nazi war criminals. Wieland told his friend something he knew firsthand: A wary eye could spot artillery shells whizzing through the air at 700 miles per hour. At the very least, Arnold's claim was visually possible.

A Serious Matter

On Independence Day, United Airlines Flight 105 sat on the tarmac before a scheduled flight from Boise to Pendleton. Before Captain Emil Smith boarded the DC-3, someone asked if he'd ever seen flying saucers.

"I'll believe them when I see them," joked Smith.

Only eight minutes into the flight, the copilot pointed out a loose formation of five flat and circular crafts maybe thirty miles out. Smith and the copilot called in the stewardess to ask what she saw.

"Why, there's a formation of those flying discs!"

The objects were silhouetted against a cloudless sky that was glowing with evening light. They appeared to be smooth on the bottom and rough on top. Smith radioed the control tower in Ontario, Oregon. The operators said they saw nothing. From the cockpit of Flight 105, the crew watched the five objects disappear to the northwest, and then four more followed after them.

A day later, Arnold and Wieland wrapped up their fishing trip and flew east. They stopped in Seattle to refuel on their way back to Idaho. Local newspapers were filled with stories about flying saucers, including the Flight 105 account and Yeoman Ryman's alleged photograph. Hoping to see an enlargement of Ryman's snapshot, Arnold went downtown to the office of International News Services. By chance, Captain Smith was there to provide details about his experience. The two men hit it off over coffee and discussed their sightings. They parted as instant friends. Because the taller captain towered over Arnold, he would come to nick-name him Big Smithy.

Back in Boise, Arnold became increasingly disturbed that the military was not taking the matter of flying saucers seriously. But a week later, an official with the U.S. Army Air Forces invited Arnold to submit a report. He sent off a detailed letter. Despite the ensuing media circus, Arnold insisted that his initial sighting, among others, must be investigated.

A few days later, two members of military intelligence took off in an A-26 bomber from Hamilton Field in California. Their destination was Boise. During dinner with Arnold and his wife, Lieutenant Brown and Captain Davidson said they didn't know what the flying saucers might be. But, like everyone, they were "practically bug-eyed" from watching the sky. After dinner, Arnold drove them all to the Boise airport to meet Big Smithy during his brief stopover between flights. Before flying back to California, the officers asked Arnold to keep them informed of anything unusual.

SCENE OF THE SIGHTING

To see the approximate area where Kenneth Arnold was flying at the time of his encounter, you'll want to head to the popular southern side of the park. Paved highways like Paradise Road from the west and Stevens Canyon Road from the east converge at the Henry M. Jackson Memorial Visitor Center. Along the way, this primary route leads to hiking trails and many scenic views of the mountain. Keep in mind these roads close during winter and inclement weather, so check the park website for current conditions before visiting.

An Amazing Story

As if these events weren't strange enough, the bizarre story was about to take another turn. By late July, Arnold had received several letters from Raymond Palmer, editor of *Amazing Stories.* This long-running pulp magazine was devoted to sensational tales, mostly science fiction, though occasionally stories were presented as factual. Palmer wanted to hire Arnold to investigate a reported saucer encounter in Tacoma. Two harbor patrolmen named Harold Dahl and Fred Crisman claimed to have fragments from one of the objects. After debating for a few days, Arnold agreed to the request in exchange for $200 in expense money.

During his early morning flight to Tacoma, Arnold witnessed another sighting.

Over twenty brass-colored objects were flying over the Grande Ronde Valley toward his plane. They looked like ducks. But the terrific speeds and similar movements to the original nine objects convinced him these were not birds. The pilot-turned-investigator filmed the encounter. Unfortunately, the movie was a failure, only showing a few minuscule dots.

Arnold observed further oddities at the airport. Upon arrival, he was told hotel rooms in Tacoma were hard to come by. After calling around unsuccessfully, he decided on a lark to try the Winthrop, the most prominent hotel in the city.

"Yes, Mr. Arnold," said the clerk. "We have a room and bath for you."

Arnold asked several times how that was possible when he hadn't made a reservation. *Could there be two Kenneth Arnolds?* he wondered. The clerk muttered something about the room and hung up. At the hotel, Arnold demanded to question this clerk, but he'd gone off duty. *Strange*, thought Arnold, as he went up to his room.

He began his investigation by searching the phone book. Upon finding an H.A. Dahl, he dialed. It was the right man who answered, but he seemed reluctant to talk. After some convincing, Dahl agreed to visit the hotel. Upon arrival, he resumed warning Arnold not to get mixed up with this flying saucer business.

When Arnold persisted, Dahl relented and told his story. He was patrolling the bay on a cloudy day with his teenage son and the boy's dog along for the ride. As they approached Maury Island, six strange aircraft began circling overhead. Each was about a hundred feet wide and shaped like a donut. Dahl beached the boat to take photographs of the objects. There was a muffled explosion, and a saucer started spewing metallic materials. One type was thin and white. Another type was darker and heavier. Steam rose from the water where the debris fell. Many pieces landed on the beach. A scrap minorly injured the boy, said Dahl, while larger fragments sadly killed their dog.

After the saucers flew away, Dahl quickly collected some samples and went for help. His superior, Crisman, was skeptical about the whole thing. Then he motored out to Maury Island. His tune changed after spotting another saucer and some twenty tons of fallen debris. The next morning, Dahl was at his home when a nondescript man in a black suit came to the door. The purpose was to issue a vague threat. If Dahl wanted to protect his family, he better not discuss what happened with anyone.

Arnold was speechless. The account seemed unbelievable, yet this man sounded sincere. Feeling vexed, Arnold called up Big Smithy in Seattle. The pilot was so intrigued, he canceled his flights and came down to help investigate. Yet the more they looked into it, the more dubious the story became. When Dahl shared the dark fragments he had collected, Arnold was unimpressed. They looked like lava rocks or slag. When an oddly enthusiastic Crisman showed up, he claimed to have lost Dahl's photographs. Plus, his white saucer fragments seemed to be nothing more than scrap aluminum.

The four men agreed to visit the scene of the explosion. However, shortly before their planned departure for Maury Island, the motorboat conveniently broke down. Strangest of all, a reporter from the *Tacoma Times* began repeatedly calling Arnold, claiming to have an anonymous informant sharing everything about their investigation.

Hoping to force the issue, Arnold suggested bringing in military intelligence. Crisman was all for it, but Dahl was uneasy and disappeared soon after Arnold made the call. Later that day, Lieutenant Brown and Captain Davidson flew north in a B-25 from Hamilton Field. After two and half hours listening to Crisman, the intelligence officers had heard enough. While Crisman did convince them to take a box of fragments back to headquarters, the officers left believing it was all a silly hoax.

Despite being exhausted, Brown and Davidson decided to fly back that night. They'd been running ragged over the past week, chasing saucer sightings. Around 1:30 a.m., they were piloting their B-25 south at about 10,000 feet when the left engine caught fire. The flight engineer and a ride-along soldier parachuted to safety. For some reason, Brown and Davidson never followed. They were still on board as the plane crashed and exploded into flames. Soon afterward, that same reporter at the *Tacoma Times* wrote an article that would spawn countless conspiracy theories. According to an anonymous informant, the B-25 had been sabotaged to prevent analysis of the Maury Island saucer fragments.

SITE OF THE CRASH

To further bring this mystery to life, consider exploring the old Westside Road. The missing military plane that Kenneth Arnold was searching for did indeed crash into the mountain, killing all thirty-two marines aboard. The site was discovered by a ranger about a month after Arnold's search. Today, only the first three miles of Westside Road are paved. Beyond that, this abandoned highway project is a gravel doubletrack closed to vehicles. You can visit the Marine Memorial by hiking or mountain biking just under four miles, one way, along the gravel road, which continues another five miles to Klapatche Point. From near the Marine Memorial, you can view the Tahoma Glacier, where the wreckage and bodies remain entombed in ice. This vantage point also offers views in the same direction as Arnold's 1947 UFO sighting.

UFO or Weather Balloon?

Over the following months, the military would launch a long investigation into flying saucers. The surrounding craze would become a worldwide phenomenon that continues to this day. In the process, a new term would be coined: *unidentified flying object* or *UFO*.

Among those earliest UFO sightings came the most famous incident of all. It happened exactly two weeks after Kenneth Arnold's alleged sighting in the skies above Mount Rainier. The date was July 8, 1947, near Roswell, New Mexico. Some unidentified wreckage was found by a rancher who reported it to the local army base. An official press release described the recovery of a flying disc. Perhaps this was thought to be a clever cover story, a way to conceal a Cold War test project by referencing events around the country. Decades later, it would be revealed that the base was testing spy balloons designed to monitor Soviet atomic tests. But at the time, this offhand comment set off a cascade of media attention.

During a press conference, the U.S. Army would clarify it had recovered a simple weather balloon. But the damage was done. The ensuing conspiracy theories would quickly overshadow the incident that started it all. Kenneth Arnold's sighting would soon be all but forgotten by the general public. In its place came sinister tales of captured extraterrestrials and alien autopsies.

The subsequent U.S. Air Force investigations would eventually be named Project Blue Book. Most cases of UFO sightings were easily dismissed. Some were hoaxes, like the Maury Island incident concocted by Harold Dahl and Fred Lee Crisman. Their story would come to be considered the first UFO incident involving so-called "men in black." These ominous government agents would go on to illustrious fictional careers, as they covered up evidence of extraterrestrials in movies and hit shows like *The X Files*.

Pictured in 1947, Kenneth Arnold looks to the sky while holding the movie camera he hoped would capture proof of his original sighting. AP Photo, 1947/Public Domain

In fact, Crisman would become a repeat character in other major conspiracy theories in American history. In 1963, after President John F. Kennedy was assassinated in Dallas, Fred Crisman would be implicated in his death. The JFK assassination conspiracy investigator Jim Garrison claimed the Tacoma hoaxer was one of the "three tramps" who were arrested near the book depository, the building from where assassin Lee Harvey Oswald shot the president. Though the suspects were later released, some skeptics speculated the three were deep-cover intelligence operatives.

Regarding Project Blue Book, the vast majority of UFO sightings—about 12,000—would be identified as known phenomena, including aircrafts, balloons, or astronomical features like stars or meteors. Though not all investigators agreed, the official determination for Arnold's sighting was a mirage. Later observers would suggest large birds, possibly white pelicans. They fly in formation like geese but have an angular shape and crescent profile when soaring. Regardless, Kenneth Arnold would spend the rest of his life defending his sighting and trying to obtain proof of what he'd seen.

Another Project Blue Book classification did exist for those flying saucer—or UFO—sightings that could not be readily explained. By the time the investigation concluded in 1969, about 700 cases would fall into this category, including the sighting by Big Smithy and his crew on Flight 105: *unidentified.*

CHAPTER 2

WHO WAS THE STAGECOACH ROBBER WHO POSED FOR A PHOTOGRAPH?

INFAMOUS CRIMES

YOSEMITE NATIONAL PARK

SIERRA NEVADA MOUNTAINS, CALIFORNIA

G et down," said a voice.

The open-sided stagecoach lurched to a halt, and a dozing Anton Veith opened his eyes.

Outside, a strange figure was pointing a pistol at the travelers. The man had a comical appearance, more like an opera clown than a highwayman. A ragged linen duster hung from his shoulders in tatters. His face was wrapped in the same material, with two eye holes torn out. He wore a floppy slouch hat and had a rifle slung over his shoulder. Oddly, he'd even disguised his pistol by pulling a glove over the barrel.

It was August 15, 1905, and the stagecoach was on the forested road to Wawona in Yosemite National Park. Veith was the Austrian consul in Milwaukee and a newspaper editor who was making a grand tour of the West. Following the outlaw's instructions, six women stayed aboard while Veith and three male passengers stepped out. The situation felt particularly ironic. Earlier in the ride, the male passengers had discussed how they might react during a robbery.

"You got a gun?" asked the bandit.

"No," replied the driver. His name was Walter Farnsworth, and he was clearly unimpressed. "I would have used it before."

Learning there was no express safe aboard, the bandit robbed only two of the men. He skipped the driver and blacksmiths, saying he wouldn't steal off working men. From Veith, he took forty dollars and a gold watch. The Austrian protested that the watch was a family heirloom. After considering for a moment, the robber surprisingly handed it back.

Next, he stepped onto the stagecoach, where he caught one woman trying to stuff cash inside her box camera. The bandit seemed frustrated by his meager haul. Reaching the last passenger, an Austrian woman, he grabbed roughly for her belongings.

Outside, Veith had been whispering to the other men, trying but failing to convince them to rush the bandit and end the ordeal. Noticing the commotion with the Austrian woman, Veith tried to intervene.

"She doesn't have any money."

The bandit nodded and stepped out of the coach, having only gathered about a hundred in cash. He didn't seem to realize the occupants were seasoned travelers. Most of them had quickly hidden the rest of their valuables.

"You have my money," said Veith. "Now I want a favor of you."

"What is it?" asked the bandit.

Veith explained he wanted to take a photograph of the entire scene.

The bandit paused, considering the request.

"All right," he said, after a moment. "Nobody would recognize me anyway."

Veith walked over to the stage and retrieved his Kodak folding camera. He opened the hinged cover and a lens extended from the bellows. It was a sunny summer after-noon with perfect light. The horses and stage were to his left, with the women and Farnsworth barely visible. A cluster of three men, with hands behind their backs, stood to Veith's right. Wheel ruts followed a bend in the road. Conifers rose overhead. In the middle of the background, yet fairly hard to spot, was the hapless bandit. He half-heartedly brandished his pistol, like he was about to limply fire from the hip.

Anton Veith's 1905 photo of the Yosemite stagecoach hold-up in progress. The robber is wearing a white duster in the center background. Photo courtesy of Anton Veith/Public Domain

An Imperfect Composition

When the so-called victims returned to civilization, and some reporters got wind, the story made the rounds of mostly regional newspapers. Veith joked the forty dollars he lost was a worthy fee for the memory. He described a pleasant scene when the stagecoach pulled away. The bandit had waved goodbye, and the travelers returned the gesture.

The Yosemite Stage and Turnpike Company offered a $700 reward to anyone who could identify the robber. A day after the robbery, the local sheriff led a five-man posse in pursuit. All they found were hoof prints leading away from the scene. The bandit must have hidden a horse nearby. They followed the trail until the tracks petered out on harder ground. Eventually they accepted the search was hopeless. The bandit may have gone in any direction. So, they turned back.

Years later, a local rancher came across a curious find near the holdup site. A makeshift wooden block, shaped like a horse hoof, with a leather strap across the top. One of a pair, it was theorized. The robber had worn these makeshift shoes to create fake tracks pointing the pursuers in the wrong direction. Then he'd simply walked the other way. The clever shoe was later displayed in the Yosemite Museum. Perhaps the clown-like bandit hadn't been so hapless after all.

LANDSCAPE OF WONDER

With over a thousand square miles of stunning landscapes, it's no surprise that Yosemite is regularly found among the ten most visited national parks. Averaging around four million visitors per year, it often jockeys for the fifth or sixth spot with other beloved parks like Yellowstone and Acadia. Due to Yosemite's growing popularity, in recent years the park began requiring entry reservations during peak season to reduce overcrowding. Plan ahead by visiting the park website for updates on this evolving system.

For nearly a century, stagecoach robbery had been both a legitimate peril and a romanticized symbol of traveling through the Old West. The practice peaked around the mid-1800s. It would all but vanish during the first decades of the twentieth century, as automobiles and paved highways replaced wagons on dirt roads.

But before the heyday of stagecoach robbery faded, the practice of photography became widespread with the introduction of roll film and portable cameras. Occasionally, someone would offer up an elaborate photograph that purported to show a stagecoach robbery in progress. Many were perfectly composed images. They might show the broadside of an ornate stagecoach halted in a narrow mountain gorge. Well-heeled travelers would hold their hands high in the air. A few rugged outlaws, wearing immaculate cowboy hats and crisp bandannas over their faces, leveled pairs of six-shooters at their marks. These images were all considered to be fakes, staged to sell postcards in five-and-dime stores.

But the odd photograph taken on the road to Yosemite Valley on that summer day in 1905 would be considered the lone outlier—a belief that lingers to this day. An Austrian newspaperman named Veith had captured the only known image of an infamous crime from a romantic era. A stagecoach robbery in the Wild West. The hapless but affable bandit had gotten away, whoever he was, never to be seen again.

CHALLENGE YOURSELF

Most visitors focus on scenic drives and short walks or hikes to valley waterfalls and nearby giant sequoia groves. Keep in mind that even with the reservation system, Yosemite Valley's roads and trails can be very busy during peak season and weekends. Fewer visitors make the longer drive up to Tuolumne Meadows and Tenaya Lake, where the landscape is surrounded by high-alpine domes and peaks. There you'll find many challenging routes leading into the park backcountry.

The most popular trek, however, typically starts from Happy Isles in the valley. The ascent of Half Dome is a strenuous full-day endeavor involving at least fourteen miles of hiking, round trip, with nearly 5,000 feet of elevation gain. The finale involves scrambling up slick granite on the infamous cable section. Hiking Half Dome requires a permit, which can be obtained online through a pre-season lottery every March.

CHAPTER 3

AN OLD OR YOUNG VALLEY?
A HAUNTED PARK LODGE?

UNEXPLAINED PHENOMENA

YOSEMITE NATIONAL PARK

A VALLEY OF MYSTERY

The sheer-granite landscape in Yosemite makes for some of the most iconic visuals in the National Park System. The looming face of Half Dome. The drama of Yosemite Valley as seen from Tunnel View, framed by the hulking monolith of El Capitan and the Cathedral Rocks. Waterfalls plummeting from the cliffs and sending up clouds of mist.

The geologic story behind the formation of Yosemite and its distinctive valley is a mix of accepted theories and lingering mysteries. During the age of the dinosaurs, around 150 million years ago, the ancestral Yosemite region was very different than it is today. The mountains of that era were likely taller than they are now, created by tectonic subduction of the ancient Farallon oceanic plate under the North American continent. The result was a range of pointy volcanoes similar to the Andes of present-day South America.

Deep within the cores of these proto-Yosemite volcanoes, magma chambers rich in silica were fed by melting continental rocks. Precisely how this buoyant magma coalesced and displaced the so-called country rock already in place remains uncertain. Gradually, these magma chambers cooled into massive plutons of solid granite, some of which had dome-like tops. During the intervening millennia, the upper volcanoes eroded away. Starting about fifty million years ago, these buried granite formations emerged from the Earth. Then around ten million years ago, the Sierra Nevada range was uplifted to near its present heights by renewed tectonic forces. Thus, the valley may have formed anytime during the past fifty million years.

So, how and when did Yosemite Valley obtain its dramatic contours? Based upon the classic U shape of Yosemite Valley, the prevailing theory has long been glaciers. One of the first to recognize this possibility was naturalist John Muir, who is also known as the Father of the National Parks. The sheer cliffs and faces, like those of Half Dome and El Cap, definitely look like they were sharply cut by an invading flow of ice, not slowly molded by rain and runoff. Such a theory points to a fairly recent creation during the ice ages of the past two or three million years, when giant glaciers up to thousands of feet tall filled the valleys and canyons. But did these glaciers do all the work or mostly tidy up the edges of what was already there?

Another theory focuses on a longer time frame. Granite, such as that found in Yosemite, is often subject to something called *exfoliation jointing*. Essentially, fairly flat slabs of rock will flake away from the surface. On the rounded tops of granite domes, this can resemble the peeling away of layers on an onion. On a sheer cliff like El Cap, it might look like a tile falling from a building with shingled siding. Huge slabs of rock commonly fall around the edges of the valley. This happens during winter and spring from freeze–thaw action, where water permeates into cracks and expands into ice. Slabs also fall during summer, when hot, sunny days and cold mountain nights cause the bedrock to expand and contract.

When it comes to the mysterious origin of Yosemite Valley, many geologists increasingly believe it was a combination of mechanisms. Figuring out whether it took fifty million years or only a few will require more time and research.

A Haunted Park Lodge

One of the highlights in Yosemite Valley is the famous Ahwahnee Hotel, a grand lodge built in the NPS rustic style. The hotel is named for the Ahwahnechee people, a group of Native Americans who traditionally lived in the valley before a series of forcible evictions, beginning in the mid-nineteenth century, by the U.S. Army and later the park service.

The Ahwahnee opened in 1927, featuring an interior design blending art deco styles with Native American artwork and tapestries. Soon, the landmark hotel became the setting for a series of hauntings. One of the ghosts was Mary Curry Tresidder, a prominent member of the park's family-run concessionaire. After she died in the hotel, some claim her ghost returned to tuck the living into bed. Others say she roused them to dance in the middle of the night.

Another ghost story relates to President John F. Kennedy. More specifically, a rocking chair he requested for his room during his stay in 1962. After Kennedy's assassination the following year, it was said the president's rocking chair would move around the hotel on its own. Later, the Ahwahnee would provide inspiration for the interior sets in Stanley Kubrick's *The Shining,* a classic horror film about a winter caretaker who loses his mind at a haunted mountain lodge called the Overlook Hotel.

Further tales tell of hauntings in other parts of Yosemite. Galen Clark was the park's first ranger in the nineteenth century, and he relayed an experience during 1857 on a long trek to Grouse Lake, high above Wawona. While stopping to rest on the shore, Clark heard a wailing cry. He assumed it was a puppy lost by Native Americans who were hunting nearby. But when he asked the tribesmen about it, they said it was the spirit of a boy who had drowned in the lake.

Another alleged Native American legend was about Pohono, an evil wind said to inhabit the headwaters of Bridalveil Creek. Several times this spirit supposedly blew hunters and foragers into the rushing waters. They plummeted to their deaths over the edge of Bridalveil Fall.

More recently, a new legend has emerged, coming complete with videos shared online. Caught by surveillance cameras, glowing figures lurch through the park and parts of nearby Fresno. These are the so-called Yosemite Nightcrawlers. Whether actual specters or the work of hoaxers, they make one thing clear: not only is Yosemite hauntingly beautiful, but there are those who believe it's just plain haunted.

CHAPTER 4

ARE BODIES BURIED INSIDE HOOVER DAM?

HIDDEN HISTORY

LAKE MEAD NATIONAL RECREATION AREA

MOJAVE DESERT, NEVADA–ARIZONA STATE LINE

T his morning, I came, I saw, and I was conquered," said Franklin Delano Roosevelt. "As everyone would be who sees for the first time this great feat of mankind."

The president stood before a crowd atop a platform perched on the rim of Black Canyon. Below, a monolithic white wall glowed in the midday sun, spanning a quarter-mile gap between dark cliffs where the Colorado River had previously flowed. It was September 30, 1935, and the speech marked the dedication of a remarkable achievement, the completion of the tallest dam ever built, rising 726 feet. The biggest reservoir in the world was slowly filling upstream. The largest hydroelectric facility in the world would soon operate at its base.

FDR declared this twentieth-century marvel warranted universal approval. A product of brilliant engineering and daring builders. A symbol of American triumph over an inhospitable desert and the Great Depression. Boulder Dam, as he called it, would stop floods and prevent droughts. It would ensure a fair and permanent system of water distribution. Natural disasters would be tamed, and humanity's history of conflicts over resources would soon be coming to an end.

This would be the first in a series of massive public works. Not just dams, but bridges and roads would be built, allowing access to national forests and distant mining districts. An era of big building and intelligent planning had arrived. The modernized future sure sounded like utopia. What could possibly go wrong?

Cracks in the Façade

Hoover Dam was never without controversy. Even its name was a point of contention. Originally, planners conceived it as the Boulder Canyon Project. It was renamed in 1930 to honor the sitting president who authorized it, former mining engineer Herbert Hoover. The decision didn't sit well with some. When FDR won the 1932 election, his administration tried to wipe away all references to their one-term rival by calling it Boulder Dam. That effort never took. After memories of the Great Depression faded, Hoover would rehabilitate his post-presidency image through public service during World War II. In 1947, Congress officially restored the name Hoover Dam.

The naming controversy paled in comparison to other concerns about the dam's effects. As the volume in the reservoir rose during the late 1930s, the ground began to sag. The weight of the water, the trapped sediment, and the dam itself was enormous, estimated at over fifty billion tons. The result was a series of earthquakes in a region not known for seismic activity. The largest was measured in 1939 at 5.0 on the Richter scale. Rocks fell across the desert, sending up ominous plumes of dust.

In hindsight, the bedrock around Hoover Dam was more fractured than previously realized. This situation was underscored when the dam started leaking
from the bottom up. During construction, cement paste had been used to plug
any underground cracks and voids. This was called a *grout curtain*. Hoover Dam
was the first to deploy one of such magnitude, and it was poorly executed. Water
began to fill the lower passageways of the young structure. The drain system was
overwhelmed, and operators had to dispatch bucket bridges. The problem was kept
secret for years, while cramped workers squeezed into tight spaces. They drilled
inside the depths, discovering huge cavities that could lead to collapse. A shocking
amount of cement was pumped in to fill these holes.

Once the interior was secured, new problems arose in the canyon. In 1941,
Hoover Dam's massive spillways were tested for the first time. Dam operators
allowed the reservoir level to rise until water poured into the concrete-lined tunnels that had been blasted through the surrounding cliffs. Below the dam, white
jets of aerated water erupted from the outlets. After the test, inspectors found the
walls of the spillway tunnels were torn to shreds, deeply gouged by the thunderous
flows. Major repairs were completed, but the tunnels went untested for another
four decades.

July 1983 saw record flooding throughout the Colorado River Basin. By now,
another dam had been built upstream in Glen Canyon. Due to poor planning by the
Bureau of Reclamation, both reservoirs—Lake Powell and Lake Mead—were too
full to contain the flood. The surging water was directed into Glen Canyon Dam's
bedrock spillways. The soft Navajo sandstone began to disintegrate from the inside
out, threatening to collapse the cliff face and the dam. Should that have happened,
a catastrophic wall of water would have rushed downstream at twenty miles per
hour, scouring the bottom of the Grand Canyon, rushing across Lake Mead, and
overtopping or collapsing Hoover Dam.

Fortunately, Glen Canyon Dam was saved at the last moment. With the spillways at risk of collapsing, the reservoir operators needed to somehow increase
the capacity of the reservoir. In the end, what might have been one of the worst

disasters in U.S. history was prevented with the same materials found at a local hardware store. Their jury-rigged solution was to raise the height of the dam by lining the top with plywood panels.

SPLIT PERSONALITIES

Hoover Dam is found within Lake Mead National Recreation Area. Located less than an hour from Las Vegas, Nevada, this massive NPS unit covers about 2,300 square miles of reservoir, river, mountains, and desert.

The dam is operated by the Bureau of Reclamation, which charges a fee for guided tours. Otherwise, accessing the visitor center and walking or driving across the dam is free. Averaging about seven million annual visitors, Hoover is the most visited dam in the world.

Meanwhile, Lake Mead is the largest recreation area in the National Park System, and one of its most popular units. Due to declining reservoir levels, annual visitation decreased from a peak of about eight million in 2020 to below six million in recent years. These numbers may rebound should the reservoir refill. Most people focus on motorboating, waterskiing, and fishing on the vast reservoir. Other highlights include campgrounds, paddling routes, and a 35-mile paved multiuse loop for cyclists and pedestrians.

Downstream, the unflooded portion of Black Canyon of the Colorado River offers a classic paddling trip with about twelve miles of class I–II rapids through a volcanic gorge. The trip is particularly popular during the long and hot summer, due to the cold water released from the dam.

But a flood surge was still coming for the overfilled Lake Mead that summer. Once again, water poured into the great spillways of Hoover Dam. Once again, it ripped them to pieces. This time, the high waters continued downstream toward newly built towns and homes. Residents had moved into the floodplain, which was deemed safe after false promises of flood prevention. As these waters receded from the communities, the destruction led to a revelation. Large dams like Hoover could prevent small floods, but not the sudden big ones. The spillways of Glen Canyon and Hoover were rebuilt, this time with a better understanding for the phenomenon of turbulent cavitation. People would have to wait for future floods to see if the dams would hold.

In the meantime, the following decades saw an inverse situation. A prolonged drought descended upon the sprawling Colorado River Basin. Lake Mead dropped to record lows. Numerous politicians had touted the dams and reservoirs, along with a distribution agreement called the Colorado River Compact, as solving water conflicts among the seven states within the Colorado River Basin. Instead, the region would see water grabs, restrictions, and lawsuits that would continue for decades with little resolution.

Clearly, Hoover Dam hadn't kept the lofty promises made on its behalf. In fact, early impressions of its reliability as a water source had been due to chance. The first half of the twentieth century just happened to see several wet decades. After courting a population boom it no longer could sustain, Hoover Dam now was subject to the cyclical droughts that were common throughout the American West. Beyond becoming a source of national pride during the Great Depression, Hoover Dam's first century of operation hadn't gone as hoped.

In the mid-1980s, a country music supergroup of four stars collaborated on a chart-topping single titled "Highwayman." The song told a story in four verses about a daring soul being repeatedly reincarnated. Willie Nelson went first, singing about the original highwayman, a stagecoach robber hanged for his crimes in 1825. Kris Kristofferson told of a sailor killed during a storm in the Pacific. Johnny Cash sang the finale about an astronaut who perishes among the stars. The third story was sung by Waylon Jennings. It was about a dam builder who fell into wet concrete during construction—a soul left to forever haunt the wild Colorado.

It was the latest iteration of a persistent rumor that bodies of fallen workers remained entombed deep inside Hoover Dam. Yes, dam workers had died during the construction in the 1920s and 1930s. This was never in question. Some claimed there was a disturbingly high number of fatalities, but precisely how many deaths would be a lingering debate for decades to come. Regardless, might the murmurs be true. Could there be bodies buried inside Hoover Dam?

Insults and Injuries

"Too thick to drink and too thin to plow," critics said about the Colorado River. The famous river started as a tumbling stream in the Rocky Mountains, gaining volume and sediment from tributaries while meandering through a series of red-rock gorges. After plunging through the rapids of Grand Canyon, it became a muddy watercourse rolling lazily through a barren country of cactus and Joshua trees.

Since the late nineteenth century, there had been talk about building a large dam to tame the mighty river. A vast reservoir would allow the silt to settle out and leave clear waters for the taking. By the 1920s, words had turned into actions. Glancing at the Colorado's 1,450-mile length, a logical target was the lower gorges that were closest to the booming cities and vast farms of Southern California.

The first death typically attributed to the Boulder Canyon Project was a government surveyor scouting possible sites on December 20, 1922. George Tierney's boat bucked in the turbulent waters, hurling him into the river, where he drowned. The man's name would become a morbid bookend for a disaster-filled endeavor.

Nine years later, in April 1931, a consortium called Six Companies began construction at Black Canyon. The no-nonsense foreman was Frank Crowe, the most experienced dam builder in the nation. Almost immediately, accidents began. Early efforts involved building roads and railways into the narrow gorge to transport workers and equipment. Dynamite was used to blast the rocky slopes, often without checking who was below. Most victims in the fall zone escaped with minor injuries, while the unfortunate ones were grotesquely maimed or killed. Other times, the destabilized cliffs would collapse, and workers below were crushed to death under piles of rubble.

With summer, an intense heat wave came to the Mojave Desert, and the dam site averaged daily highs of nearly 120 degrees. While the nearby company town of Boulder City was being built, Six Companies had erected a temporary riverside camp for workers near cliffs at the head of Black Canyon. Exposed to the sun and blocked from the breezes, it was a stifling location with nighttime lows rarely dropping below 90 degrees. Sixteen people died from overheating.

Adding insult to the ongoing injuries, in August 1931, Six Companies made pay cuts between 10 and 25 percent, depending on the job. This was the Great Depression, and a steady supply of desperate laborers was arriving daily in Las Vegas. Those already among the workforce of 1,400 were not pleased. When organizers from the labor union Industrial Workers of the World arrived, these so-called "Wobblies" organized a strike of 600. Six Companies responded with a lockout and shutdown, which the Hoover administration supported. Ultimately, the strikers were evicted from the site. The rest were rehired, along with new recruits, and Six Companies was emboldened to continue its dehumanizing practices.

Bravado Meets Conspiracy

With the arrival of fall came cooler temperatures and new challenges. An acrobatic team called high-scalers took to the canyon walls. They rappelled with ropes, using jackhammers, drills, and dynamite to remove loose rock. Many of them were Apaches, the only Native Americans employed on the project. Their goal was to groom the surface for the eventual dam. Sometimes, one of them was knocked free by falling debris. More than once, a falling worker was saved when they were caught midway by a high-scaler. Occasionally, it was a high-scaler who fell to his death.

Meanwhile, at the bottom of the canyon, tunnel excavation began. One of the greatest challenges was diverting the river from its channel so that the dam could rise. To do this, four massive diversion tunnels, each over fifty feet in diameter, were blasted through the cliffs. The primary method involved what became known as a *jumbo*, a three-story drilling rig mounted on a truck. Once the dynamite was placed, the jumbo drove the men to safety before the charges were detonated.

But as tunnel construction progressed deeper inside solid rock, the workers began to suffer from headaches, nausea, and dizziness. Some fell to the ground unconscious and were taken to the hospital. The reason, once again, was the indifference of Six Companies. Most deep-shaft mining operations of the era used electric vehicles to avoid a buildup of dangerous fumes. To win the largest government contract ever awarded, Six Companies had bid low. Then they cut corners at every opportunity to extract any profit they could find. By using cheaper, gasoline-powered trucks, they had saved about $300,000. The cost to the workers was carbon monoxide poisoning; many of those stricken never revived.

To avoid paying worker compensation, Six Companies concealed the tunnel deaths by listing them as natural causes like pneumonia and heart failure. Then their public relations team went to work. A construction project of this magnitude had never been attempted, they claimed. Fatalities were unavoidable. The men were unaccustomed to the rigors of such work, especially in an inhospitable desert.

In reality, these motivated workers were more than capable, but theirs was a tricky situation. Having any work during the Great Depression, let alone a job on the biggest project in American history, was a godsend. Risking one's life for steady pay was far better than standing in bread lines and living in shantytowns. Not only did the men accept the challenges, they seemed exhilarated by the dangers. An attitude of bravado and competitiveness spread. Work crews regularly raced each other to complete tasks. In fact, the dam site had become a tourist attraction. The death-defying workers—especially the daredevil high-scalers—were the project's heroic stars.

Still, resentment about lax safety regulations and uncaring management boiled up at times. When some workers filed lawsuits alleging negligence, Six Companies's response included denial, legal maneuvering, and even a conspiracy. They arranged for false witnesses to slander the injured. They bribed the juries.

People looked the other way, and all signs pointed to one inevitable outcome: Everyone in America—from endangered workers to unmoved judges to distant citizens reading the papers—wanted this dam to be built more than anything. So, it would be built, no matter the repercussions.

A Burial with Buckets

During June 1933, the dam began to rise. By now, the river had been diverted into the tunnels, and FDR was in the White House. The new interior secretary had briefly looked into improving conditions at the construction site, but due to contracts and politics, little would change. It was business as usual for the final push to completion.

Overhead, huge cableways lowered heavy buckets. Each dropped sixteen tons of concrete into wooden forms, typically fifty-by-fifty-foot squares. Overall, the dam would comprise 230 of these interlocking columns. After the wet concrete plopped out, it was spread with shovels by workers wearing rubber boots. Each bucketload covered about an inch of the form. Temperature and strain sensors were buried by hand for future monitoring. With every five feet gained in height, pipes were laid down to circulate cold water. This would regulate the curing of the concrete, which otherwise would expand from internal heating.

With new methods came new dangers. Occasionally, a crack like a gunshot would echo through the canyon as an overhead cable snapped. A massive concrete bucket might plummet from above, sometimes bouncing off the form and falling toward the riverbed. Several workers were crushed to death or knocked from the rising columns.

A few times, workers were buried in wet concrete, but not within the dam itself. During a night shift, a full bucket tumbled over the edge of the form, somehow ensnaring a signalman and carrying him down the upstream face. Workers searched the scaffolding below but initially found nothing. Then a dim light was spotted flickering midway down. The signalman was found lying on his back, partly covered in slowly setting concrete. One of his hands held up a lit match. Rescuers hurriedly clawed away the cement. Somehow, the signalman survived.

UPSTREAM ENIGMA

Glen Canyon National Recreation Area, which surrounds Lake Powell, is located on the Colorado River in the high desert of Arizona and Utah. Given its remote location and shorter summer season, this NPS unit has historically seen about half the visitation of Lake Mead, though the difference has decreased in recent years.

The construction of Glen Canyon Dam in 1966 remains highly controversial for several reasons. The creation of Lake Powell flooded a wilderness canyon considered comparable in beauty to those found downstream in Grand Canyon National Park and upstream in Canyonlands National Park. Not only is the dam built into friable Navajo sandstone, but the reservoir behind it only reached full capacity for a few years during the early 1980s, when many observers believe it came close to collapsing. Meanwhile, an unknown but growing amount of sediment is depositing toward the northern end of the reservoir, where the remnants of the ill-planned Hite Marina rest high and dry, a half mile uphill from the current channel.

Due to these controversies, many Western environmentalists entirely avoid what some label Reservoir Powell, which has come to be known mostly for motorboating, houseboating, and lake fishing. Other travelers recognize the vast opportunities for outdoor recreation. Paddlers can explore side canyons and the Colorado River downstream of the dam. Road-trippers grab selfies at the iconic Horseshoe Bend. Hikers follow trails leading through slot canyons and rock formations. History buffs wander through ghost towns and Old West ranches, including sites such as Lees Ferry, the famous launching point for river trips through the Grand Canyon. When it comes to controversial places, this enigmatic recreation area in the scorched desert near Page, Arizona, certainly qualifies.

Another victim was not so lucky when a five-foot-high wall of a wooden form broke free. Wet concrete and large cobblestones tumbled down the dam face, gathering pipes and scaffolding as it fell. Standing on the ground, a worker was flattened by the rubble pile. It took nearly a full day to extract his buried body.

A Mysterious Tally

Hoover Dam was completed about two years ahead of schedule. By 1935, over 3.5 million cubic yards of concrete had been poured. The result was a hybrid gravity-arch dam, 660 feet thick at its base, which tapered to a curved top about 45 feet wide. It was the tallest dam in the world, a distinction it held for over two decades before being surpassed by one in the Swiss Alps.

Three months after FDR's dedication speech, an infamous fatality occurred that would be officially declared the last of the project. While working on an intake tower, an electrician named Patrick Tierney fell to his death. This happened on December 20, 1935, and it was thirteen years, to the day, after his father, surveyor George Tierney, had drowned in the Colorado River. But in reality, at least one convenient exclusion was required to concoct the morbid legend that a father and son bookended the construction fatalities at Hoover Dam.

George Tierney was not the first but the second project fatality. Another surveyor had drowned in 1921, a year before the father. Meanwhile, about two months after the son died, construction was declared to be complete when Six Companies transferred management of the dam site to the Bureau of Reclamation. Yet major work continued on the powerhouse until the generators were activated between late 1936 and 1938. Any injuries or fatalities during that time were likely categorized as operational casualties and appear lost to history.

A memorial was erected on the dam crest to honor the workers who had lost their lives "to make the desert bloom." The official number of total fatalities was reported as ninety-six. Yet this sub-hundred number didn't include at least sixteen deaths from heat exposure. It didn't include any of the eighty-eight deaths categorized as from "natural causes," some of which were likely to have been carbon monoxide poisoning. The official tally also excluded those who were injured on the dam project but died in the hospital.

One thing was certain. No bodies had been buried inside Hoover Dam itself. This would have created a dangerous void in the concrete that could lead to collapse. Plus, the methodical approach of spreading concrete a few inches at a time entirely precluded the possibility. It was no mystery that countless lives had been lost. The truth of what happened to these workers had been buried, not by concrete, but by indifference, deception, technicalities, and paperwork. The real mystery was more sinister. No one will ever know how many people died in the building of Hoover Dam.

CHAPTER 5

WHY ARE COAST REDWOODS SO TALL AND GIANT SEQUOIAS SO BIG?

UNEXPLAINED PHENOMENA

SEQUOIA NATIONAL PARK & REDWOOD NATIONAL AND STATE PARKS

SIERRA NEVADA MOUNTAINS, CALIFORNIA & NORTHERN CALIFORNIA COAST

The two strangers came across each other in a mountain meadow surrounded by towering trees. The younger explorer was on foot, leading a pack mule through patchy grass and lingering wildflowers. The older man entered the clearing atop a galloping horse. He pulled to a halt when the explorer called out. It was the end of September 1875, and neither of them had seen another soul in days.

"What are you doing?" asked the puzzled rider, a lean fellow in his late forties. "How did you get here?"

The explorer was a youthful man in his thirties with a bushy beard. He was pleased to encounter someone in such a beautiful and solitary place. He explained that, during the past month, he'd walked well over a hundred miles from Yosemite. He was searching for undocumented groves of what many believed were the world's biggest trees, the giant sequoia. These arboreal towers rose hundreds of feet high, well above the tops of the surrounding forest.

Weeks ago, the explorer had mounted Wamellow Rock and discovered a majestic grove in the Upper Fresno River basin. There he met a mountain hermit, an old forty-niner living in a log cabin, who proudly showed off a giant sequoia with a diameter of over twenty feet. But after continuing his journey, the tree-loving explorer soon encountered even bigger examples. On a branch of Dinkey Creek, a lone shepherd happily led the way to a giant sequoia nearly thirty feet wide. He'd heard it was one of the biggest of all.

"They're whales," said the shepherd about this mysterious species.

Continuing into Kings Canyon, the explorer next found a massive sequoia burned halfway through at its base. Using a lens to inspect the exposed trunk, he found thousands of rings. That would make the tree an equivalent number of years old. Onward he went, crossing tumbling streams and encountering numerous specimens. He passed through a well-known grove of behemoths that had been named for Civil War heroes, including one called the General Grant Tree. Next, the explorer traversed through a series of stunning granite canyons—Redwood Creek, North Fork Kaweah, and Marble Fork. In every direction, the big trees ruled the woods. He was so awestruck that he declared this area to be the finest part of the sequoia belt, and he named it the Giant Forest.

"Oh then, I know," said the older man, with a warm look of recognition. "You must be John Muir."

The Greatest on Earth?

Muir was surprised to be recognized in such a remote place. The Scottish-born naturalist sheepishly admitted he was nearly out of food. The older man's name was Hale Tharp, and he invited his new friend to supper. But first Tharp had to round up some stray horses. Before galloping off, he pointed Muir down a faint track. Muir followed the trail through the woods for a few miles until he reached the upper edge of a narrow meadow. There he found Tharp's home, which was built inside the hollowed log of a fallen sequoia. Around the opening, there was a shingled foyer with a door and stone chimney. Inside this noble dwelling, Muir found the walls were charred from fire. A window looked out on the garden.

Muir stayed for several nights. During the days, he explored outward. He surveyed the boundaries of the sequoia groves. Measured the trunks. Climbed to high points for views of the dome-like treetops that stretched into the hazy distance. Suppertime conversations between Muir and Tharp focused on adventures, animals, and especially the big trees. More sequoias could be found to the south, said Tharp, but how far he knew not.

COASTAL COLLECTIONS

Redwood National and State Parks includes four cooperatively managed units that interweave NPS parcels with three state parks: Jedediah Smith, Del Norte Coast, and Prairie Creek. The result is 217 square miles of towering forests, rolling mountains, and rugged coastline. The park stretches about fifty miles north to south, mostly along the Highway 101 corridor. It's best known for scenic drives and short hikes through old-growth trees. A popular pairing is the ten-mile Drury Scenic Parkway with the mellow paths at Big Tree Wayside. One of the most famous and challenging hiking destinations is the Tall Trees Grove, which requires obtaining a permit in advance.

So, Muir resumed his journey to find out. Between the Middle and East Forks of the Kaweah, he found himself in a spreading forest fire. As the flames crept across the dry duff from sequoia to sequoia, Muir sheltered in a hollow trunk. After dark, he ventured out to watch the show. Occasionally, when the fire reached a trunk, the flames would rise skyward. The treetop would ignite and burn like a candle. Smoking coals fell like snow. A few times a burning branch impacted the ground, shattering into glowing pieces.

Several weeks later, Muir identified the southernmost collection of giant sequoias on Deer Creek in the Kern River basin. All told, there were far more stands than the dozen known at the time. Further surveys would reveal a total of about eighty groves. They occurred in scattered pockets across a 250-mile belt on the western slope of the Sierra Nevada Mountains. These big trees rarely grew below 4,500 feet in elevation. They rarely were found above 7,500 feet. The densest collections were located in the southern Sierras, a fifty-mile swath surrounding Tharp's Log, roughly between the Kings River and the forks of the Tule River. This included the dense region Muir had named Giant Forest. In fifteen years, with Muir's urging, much of this land would be incorporated into Sequoia National Park.

But were these trees really the biggest on Earth? Later in his life, Muir would travel the world on arboreal expeditions to answer that question. He would stare up at colossal eucalyptus in the Great Dividing Range of Australia. He would visit rising deodar cedars in the Himalayas, considered sacred by the Hindu people. In Africa, he saw the iconic baobab trees, with their thick trunks and spreading flattops of foliage. In the Amazon rainforest, it was the spiny crowns of ancient *Araucaria*, also called monkey puzzle trees. Each of these species greatly impressed Muir, yet none could match the grandeur of his beloved big trees, later named *Sequoiadendron giganteum*. He found them to be not only the largest, but also the most majestic on Earth.

To John Muir, the big trees had no equal, save for one. It was yet another monumental being. The closely related *Sequoia sempervirens*, so named for its perennially green needles and everlasting age. The mysterious coast redwood.

These enigmatic trees also lived within an oddly limited range in California.

A narrow band of the Coast Mountains, stretching 450 miles along the Pacific Ocean from roughly Monterrey Bay to near the Oregon state line. In time, the coast redwood would prove to be the tallest tree on Earth. Its mountain cousin, the giant sequoia, was the biggest by volume. Each was found in its own north-to-south strip in different parts of the same state. But why were they found here and only here? And how had they become so large to begin with?

SKIP THE TALLEST

Discovering which redwood is the tallest on Earth has long been tricky, given the challenges associated with surveying and precisely measuring the trees. Currently, it's believed to be Hyperion, which rises about 380 feet. This tree is located off trail in a remote and restricted area of the national park. The park service has forbidden hikers from visiting, given that past pilgrims have trampled the surrounding ground and damaged the roots. Violators risk a fine up to $5,000. One can't really see the top from directly below, anyway, and there are far more scenic tall trees to visit. In an ironic twist, while Hyperion will hopefully avoid being loved to death, it's possible these unauthorized visits will "adore" it into second place. Redwoods grow quickly, and other hidden giants have not been stressed by so many footsteps. One of them will likely surpass Hyperion. Hopefully this "winner" will remain a mystery.

A Commodity Is Found

The Yurok people called the redwoods *keehl*. Using stone hammers, elk-antler wedges, and mussel-shell adzes, they cut lumber from coast redwoods for dugout canoes and plank houses. To explain the presence of the towering trees, various Native American legends considered them sacred warriors, guardians, or gifts created by the spirits. By the eighteenth century, there were several thousand Yurok living in about seventy villages in the area where Redwood National and State Parks would later be established.

In 1769, a Spanish expedition led by Gaspar de Portolá marched north from San Diego into Alta California along a route they came to call the Royal Road. By now, the gold obsessions of earlier conquistadors had given way to a new imperial mandate: colonize the New World and force the native inhabitants to adopt Christianity. In late July, near a river they named the Santa Ana, the party was jolted by a strong earthquake. Aftershocks followed them for days.

In the hilly region between present-day Monterrey and San Francisco Bay, the expedition increasingly encountered trees that were larger, taller, and straighter than any they'd ever seen. They named them *palo colorado* for their color. Subsequent expeditions would return and establish twenty-one missions along El Camino Real, and redwood was often used for the northern constructions.

In the 1820s, trapper Jedediah Smith became the first white American to see the redwoods during an overland foray into Northern California, which was then a territory of Mexico. The redwood stands and piles of fallen trunks were so dense that it took the party ten days to travel twenty miles. Many of their horses and mules died from exhaustion.

During the summer of 1828, French explorer August Duhaut-Cilly was sailing off the California coast on a trading mission. While searching for the Russian colony of Fort Ross, a sailor's telescope spied a settlement on a plateau atop the rocky cliffs. A collection of buildings was surrounded by plank walls. Almost everything was made of redwood. After landing, the trader learned that the commercial colony's original pursuit was hunting sea otters and seals. After decimating those populations, the company had shifted to logging redwoods and sending the lumber to markets across the Pacific.

A new era had begun, and redwood harvesting would soon intensify. After the invasion of Mexico during the mid-1840s, the prevailing United States annexed Alta California. The 1849 Gold Rush led to a population boom and widespread settlement from San Francisco to the Sierras. Coast redwood was found to be among the most valuable species of timber. The lumber was remarkably strong despite its light weight. It resisted fire and decay. The boards rarely warped. It was perfect for buildings, bridges, and railroad ties. Two-man crews spent days pushing and pulling on crosscut saws, and many of the tallest trees that ever lived plummeted to the forest floor with a deafening crash.

The largest of the harvested redwoods to be documented in both photos and verifiable measurements was the Crannell Creek Giant near Trinidad, California, with a diameter approaching 22 feet and a height of 308 feet—three feet taller than the Statue of Liberty. Others were said to be over 350 feet tall, and some loggers claimed to have taken trees longer than 400 feet. In 1893, near Scotia on the Eel River, there were reports of the largest redwood ever felled. Supposedly it had a 77-foot circumference and was 417 feet in height. But was such a claim even possible?

Throughout the latter half of the 1800s, the vast old-growth forests of coastal redwood were shrinking. Without intervention, some feared that the species could be gone before the next century was over.

How Long Can They Last?

Ironically, the very event that revealed the giant sequoias to the modern world would become a symbol that inspired their preservation. Just a few years into the Gold Rush, during the spring of 1852, a major discovery was made in the Sierras. A hunter employed by a canal digging company was on the job near Murphy's Camp in the forests of Calaveras County. After shooting a grizzly bear, Augustus Dowd followed the wounded animal into a shady grove. There he stared up at the biggest tree he'd ever encountered, about twenty-five feet wide and rising over 280 feet.

Back in camp, no one believed Dowd's claim. So, a few days later, he tricked them by asking for help hauling in a grizzly carcass. Doubts turned to awe when the group was led to a specimen later named the Discovery Tree. And Dowd soon came to regret opening his mouth in the first place.

Countless Native Americans and a few European and American explorers had long talked about the presence of the big trees. These reports had mostly been dismissed as exaggerated frontier tales. However, the Gold Rush brought numerous witnesses with a new mindset: economic conquest. Quickly, a few local leaders recognized the potential for a spectacle. Five men spent twenty-two days drilling holes into the trunk with augur pumps and hacking away at the gaps.

Segments of the bark and trunk were put on display in San Francisco and later New York City. Other toppled sequoias joined the circuit and were shipped to distant cities like London. Curious crowds flocked to see these reassembled giants, but the public response was less supportive than expected. Many museum goers were dismayed by the destruction. Back in the Calaveras Grove, the Discovery Tree stump became a tourist attraction. One could stand atop the exposed rings that revealed an age over 1,200 years old. Visitors could have a drink at the bar and a waltz amid the remaining forest.

"The laborious vandals," a seething John Muir later wrote about the loggers. They had cut down one of the world's biggest trees for "a dancing floor."

The legacy of the Discovery Tree and other toppled giants sent round the world to sell tickets represented a shift in public priorities. Why were these ancient trees being exterminated like this? Frenzied searches during the Gold Rush had revealed several sequoia groves near a startling granite valley that also was worth preserving. In 1864, the federal government approved the landmark Yosemite Grant, which ceded the lands of a future national park to the state of California.

Protecting the giant sequoia, despite its far lower numbers, proved some-what easier than saving its coastal cousin. The mountain species was ill-suited for lumber, due to its brittle and fibrous wood. When these whales struck the ground, much of the wood shattered and splintered, leaving only about half for the taking. What made it to the mill was mostly used for scrappy applications like fence posts, building shingles, and matchsticks.

With its mediocre timber confined to remote groves in the rugged Sierras, there was less profit in harvesting the giant sequoia. Even so, around a third of the old-growth stands would be lost to logging before most of the remaining groves were protected. By the 2020s, these preserves would be home to an estimated 80,000 native specimens. Their endangered status was now due to intense wildfires caused by accumulated underbrush from a century of misguided fire suppression.

During the Gold Rush, far more redwoods were found throughout a larger coastal range, reaching five to fifty miles inland. At that time, it is estimated there were up to 3,500 square miles of old-growth redwood forest. This was a total area roughly equivalent to modern-day Yellowstone National Park, with a staggering number of redwoods in the low hundreds of millions.

However, the human population nearby was booming, and the coast redwood's superior lumber incentivized widespread harvesting and entrenched resistance toward preservation. Early hand crews and livestock carts gave way to steam-powered tools and railroad hauling. Vast fields of stumps and smoldering branches appeared across the Coast Range. Around the turn of the twentieth century, an estimated 500 square miles was gone. Twenty-five years later, the lost old growth summed to over 1,000 square miles, or one-third of the range.

===== SEE THE BIGGEST =====

Bring the mystery at Sequoia National Park to life by visiting the famous Giant Forest, the largest unlogged old-growth sequoia grove. Many visitors start at the Giant Forest Museum, before heading out on a series of paths. One highlight is the largest tree in the world, the General Sherman. Over 2,200 years old, it is 275 feet tall with an astounding base diameter of 36.5 feet. Further trails wind throughout the forest, including a mile-long route to the historic hollowed sequoia cabin of Tharp's Log.

A Shifting Approach

When the National Park Service was created in 1916, the first director was a successful businessman named Stephen Mather. He sent several prominent conservationists to Northern California to investigate reports of vanishing old-growth forests. However, opposition from the timber lobby was strong and little would happen at the federal level for many decades.

Instead, these well-connected conservationists established the Save the Redwoods League. The nonprofit objective was to use private wealth to purchase old-growth forests and turn them into public lands. The first was Humboldt Redwoods State Park, established in 1921. It would become the largest old-growth preserve, expanding over the following decades to surround thirty-two miles of scenic highway called the Avenue of the Giants. The busy 1920s saw the creation of further state parks, including Prairie Creek, Del Norte Coast, and Jedediah Smith, with more to follow.

Yet for every conservation success came plenty of defeats. The timber companies owned most of the remaining old growth. Meanwhile, rival preservation groups were increasingly arguing about how to best acquire and protect the remaining trees. The Save the Redwoods League wanted to continue with creating smaller, semi-developed parks for recreation. The Sierra Club, originally founded by John Muir, wanted to protect the larger ecosystem by establishing undeveloped wilderness areas. Meanwhile, the old-growth forests continued to dwindle.

By the time a compromise was reached and Redwood National Park joined the lineup of established preserves in the late 1960s, about 10 percent (or 350 square miles) of the original old growth remained. By the 2020s, that number would be cut in half to just 5 percent. Today, only around 175 square miles of the old-growth forest remains. A vast area about the size of Yellowstone was reduced to remnants smaller than the San Francisco Peninsula.

Around three-quarters of the surviving old-growth redwoods are found in a series of public parks and nature preserves, which continue to expand as private lands are purchased. Though these protected trees represent only a fraction of the towering, 1,000-year-old specimens that once blanketed the Coast Mountains, it is not an insignificant number. Saving these several million old-growth redwoods has allowed for another endeavor—studying them.

MOUNTAIN BEHEMOTHS

Located in the southern Sierras, Sequoia National Park protects around forty groves of the world's biggest trees, the giant sequoia. This quieter park averages between a quarter and a third of the annual visitors that Yosemite sees, despite offering comparable scenery when combined with the adjacent Kings Canyon National Park. Looming in the park's high country is Mount Whitney, the tallest peak in the lower forty-eight at 14,505 feet. The summit is accessible only by strenuous hiking and mountaineering routes. Most people start from the Whitney Portal in the Eastern Sierras, and permits are required in advance.

A Living Fossil

In the late 1930s, paleobotanist Shigeru Miki of Kyoto University in Japan was studying plant fossils found within Mesozoic sediments over 150 million years old. The fossils were clearly from the cypress family, which includes modern conifers like bald cypress, giant sequoia, and coast redwood. While examining the specimens, Dr. Miki recognized a divergent leaf structure. He had discovered a new genus, which he named *Metasequoia*.

By this time, a picture was emerging from the fossil record. Over a period lasting many millions of years, the ancestors of redwoods and, to a lesser extent, the giant sequoia had once spanned the globe. The earliest redwoods were found in China, from Jurassic and Cretaceous rock formations that also yielded fossilized pterosaurs and theropods—the age of the dinosaurs. Further ancestors were found from Asia to Western Europe. Redwoods had grown in the Alps and around the Mediterranean. They were found in Greenland and Canada. Across the United States, redwood fossils were found from the East Coast to the Southwest to Alaska and Mexico.

While most plant fossils are imprints of leaves and stems left in soft sediments, another type of fossilized redwood was found. When a tree is buried in wet sediments or volcanic ash, mineral-rich fluids can permeate the organic material and replace it with silica. Such petrified redwoods, from about fifty million years ago, were found in Yellowstone National Park, on Specimen Ridge overlooking the Lamar Valley.

Another collection from thirty-four million years ago was found in the Rocky Mountains of Colorado. The Florissant Fossil Beds National Monument was established to protect these giant trunks that had been turned to stone. One example was the Big Stump, which had a 12-foot diameter and was estimated to have been up to 230 feet tall. Not only had redwoods once been found across the Northern Hemisphere, but the ancients were giants as well.

By cobbling together geological clues from across the globe, including evidence of past glaciation, a prevailing theory was emerging. Starting several million years ago, vast ice sheets slowly encroached from the north, pushing the redwoods to the south. During warmer interglacial periods, arid conditions slowly spread from the south, further shrinking the range. Eventually, the only place where the big trees remained was a mild climactic oasis called California. The redwoods were restricted to a long strip along the coast. Here, winter rains and summer fogs provided the ample moisture required for the tallest of trees to maintain their height. To the north, they were blocked by steep mountains in coastal Oregon. To the west and south, they were blocked by arid valleys and deserts.

Meanwhile, the elevation-adapted giant sequoias were sequestered in favorable pockets in the Sierras. But only on the west slope, where they enjoyed ample precipitation and granitic soils, and mostly toward the milder southern extent of these mountains. To the north, the mountains became too harsh for the sequoia. To the east, the Sierra Crest was too high for the sequoia to cross. These were the final wild refuges for two survivors from an ancient family of giants.

That's what everyone thought, at least, until one day several botanists in China discovered a third survivor. In the years before and after World War II, a strange tree was spotted by field researchers along the wet slopes of river valleys in the inland provinces of Sichuan and Hubei. At first, it was identified as a Chinese swamp cypress, given both lost their deciduous needles each winter. However, this new tree could reach greater heights, sometimes topping out over 150 feet tall. Upon examining samples in the lab, a shocking match was made to the fossils identified by Dr. Miki. It was a *metasequoia*—a living fossil that would be named the "dawn redwood."

With each passing year, the mystery surrounding this ancient family of big trees was deepening. One unknown was the roots of the sequoia name itself. The Austrian botanist and linguist who identified the genus in 1847 never explained the origin. A few said it came from the Latin word for sequence: *sequor*. Most claimed it was in honor of the early 1800s Native American scholar Sequoyah who had created the Cherokee written language.

Another enigma was the so-called fairy rings, an odd tendency for some groups of redwoods to grow in circles. In the center, there might be only dirt and needles. Other times there was an old stump, either due to a natural fall or, increasingly, logging. It was as if the younger trees had sprouted in a tribute to a fallen relative.

Strangest of all were the albinos, a bizarre type of offshoot that people occasionally found deep within the old-growth stands. They were hard to spot on forest floors, lined with emerald ferns that saw mostly shade at high noon. On rare occasions, growing out of an otherwise normal redwood, there might be a branch or a sprout that was entirely white. The ghost redwoods.

Genetic Secrets

In 2017, the Redwood Genome Project began a multiyear endeavor to unlock the secrets of the world's tallest tree. Cell samples were taken from two living specimens, each over 1,300 years old. One was a coast redwood from the Santa Cruz Mountains, the other a giant sequoia from the Sierras. After extracting DNA from the samples, the fragments were chemically analyzed and processed by super-computers. The goal was to create a genetic map that might explain how the trees evolved to be so tall and so big.

═══ **FURTHER DISCOVERIES** ═══

Numerous places mentioned in this chapter can be visited. Short of traveling around the entire world, here are a few within California. There's a reconstructed Yurok plank-house village at Sue-meg State Park. Many of the missions along El Camino Real are now historic sites. The coastal Russian colony is preserved at Fort Ross State Historic Park. The stump of the Discovery Tree is found at Calaveras Big Trees State Park. And several giant sequoia groves can be found at Yosemite National Park.

By now, much had been learned about the life cycle of these trees. After emerging from the ground, coast redwood seedlings can grow exceptionally fast. With ideal moisture and ample sunlight, they might rise three to eight feet per year. During their first fifty to a hundred years, they can reach 100 to 150 feet or more. At some point, their growth rate will slow, but they will continue to reach new heights throughout their lives. Meanwhile, a young sequoia will grow taller at a slower rate, perhaps two feet per year under ideal conditions. But the bulk of that giant's growth is directed toward establishing an ever-thickening trunk.

Other than logging, very little can kill either tree. The tough wood resists diseases and pests. Theoretically, they might live and grow forever if not for a few limiting factors. Threats to the giant sequoia come from potential extremes found within its mountain environment, such as prolonged droughts and intense fires. Erosion around the base might weaken the trees' hold in the ground, after which windstorms could topple them.

For the redwood, one restraint is gravity. Its theoretical peak height is estimated around 420 to 430 feet, an astounding stature, comparable to the Great Pyramid of Giza in Egypt. Above that, a redwood simply cannot maintain enough water pressure within its fibers to keep the treetop alive. In fact, to support its lofty hydration needs, the redwood grows two types of needles. One of these spindly leaves does the typical job of gathering sunlight for photosynthesis. The other absorbs the dense coastal fog directly into the branches, lessening the need for water to travel internally to the extreme heights of the tree.

The redwood's main natural threat comes from wind gusts. The tree doesn't have a taproot or other deeply penetrating anchors. Instead, it has a shallow root system that spreads out widely and intertwines with the roots of other trees. This creates a strong base, but its towering heights still make it susceptible to windthrow.

When a redwood does fall or is toppled by logging, it has another unique adaptation to maintain the species. The tree not only reproduces sexually, with male cones releasing pollen that fertilizes female cones, but a redwood can also reproduce asexually by cloning itself. Sprouts may emerge from a stump or fallen branches. This ability is what explains the fairy rings. New redwoods rise from the root crowns of their dying relatives.

In 2020, the results of the Redwood Genome Project were released. The tallest tree was one of the most genetically complex beings ever sequenced. It has 26.5 billion DNA base pairs and six sets of chromosomes. Humans, in comparison, have three billion base pairs and two sets of chromosomes. The giant sequoia was also found to be complex, but to a lesser extent than its cousin, with eight billion base pairs. Many of the big tree's genes seem to have uniquely evolved to make it so adaptable and resilient. More study is needed, but perhaps this genetic complexity is what allows these trees to reach such stunning ages, sizes, and heights.

The redwood was the second-longest genome ever sequenced at that time. Just above it was the axolotl, with over 28 billion base pairs—though other beings would later be found to be even more genetically complex. This critically endangered salamander once thrived in the vast waters of Lake Xochimilco before the valley was drained to establish Mexico City. The axolotl is particularly known for some unique regenerative abilities. It can regrow its limbs, gills, tail, and even some damaged organs. It's a miniature redwood of its kind.

The ghost redwoods are seemingly the result of such genetic complexity as well. Some consider the albinos to be arboreal vampires. Not only do they lack pigmentation, but they can't survive on their own. Like parasites, they take water and nutrients from the host tree. One theory is that these white offshoots are dumping grounds for toxins and heavy metals from the host tree.

Other theories suggest that the ghosts are an evolutionary accident. A genetic mutation. An example of the redwood's tremendous ability to adapt and evolve. Yet another baffling feature of the tallest and perhaps strangest trees in the world.

CHAPTER 6

WHAT HAPPENED TO THE CREW OF THE *GHOST BLIMP*?

BAFFLING DISAPPEARANCES

GOLDEN GATE NATIONAL RECREATION AREA

SAN FRANCISCO BAY AREA, CALIFORNIA

The sky was overcast and the winds were light as the patrol blimp *L-8* lifted off from Treasure Island in San Francisco Bay. Inside the noisy control car were two U.S. Navy officers, Lieutenant Ernest Cody and Ensign Charles Adams. After rising to an altitude of 1,000 feet, the airship flew west at a speed of forty knots toward the Pacific Ocean. Below passed the sharp orange towers of the Golden Gate Bridge, which recently had marked its fifth anniversary.

It was shortly after 6:00 a.m. on Sunday, August 16, 1942, and the United States had been at war with Japan for nine months. *L-8* was on a standard four-hour patrol flight, which would take it thirty miles out to the Farallon Islands. Then the

150-foot blimp would turn northeast to Point Reyes, head south along the coast to Montara Beach, and finally return to base.

After the surprise attack at Pearl Harbor on December 7, 1941, the Japanese military had quickly expanded the war across the Pacific. To patrol domestic waters, the U.S. Navy established a series of airship squadrons along the coast. In February 1942, a Japanese submarine had shelled an oil refinery near Santa Barbara. It was the first attack on the U.S. mainland since the British bombarded Fort McHenry in Baltimore during the War of 1812. Four months after Santa Barbara, a Japanese sub fired at Fort Stevens, which guarded the mouth of the Columbia River in Oregon.

As L-8 continued out to sea, the airmen scanned the waters below for signs of enemy submarines. Should they encounter one, the officers had two armaments at their disposal: a .30-caliber machine gun and a pair of 325-pound depth charges—bombs rigged to explode underwater and potentially rupture a sub's hull.

URBAN PARKLANDS

Seeing over fifteen million visitors per year, Golden Gate National Recreation Area typically competes with the Blue Ridge Parkway for the most visited unit in the National Park System. About 128 square miles of disconnected parklands wrap around the San Francisco Peninsula and continue north into Marin County. Established in the early 1970s, much of the rec area's land was formerly used by the U.S. Army. Today it's considered one of the largest urban parks in the world.

Two Solid Airmen

Of the two pilots aboard *L-8*, the thirty-eight-year-old Adams was the more experienced. In recognition of a daring twenty-year career, just the day before he'd been promoted to ensign. Back in 1935, he'd been an enlisted man aboard the USS *Macon*, one of the two largest airships ever built by the U.S. Navy. The other was the USS *Akron*. These were no ordinary blimps, but flying aircraft carriers. Using a swinging trapeze, they could launch and recover biplane fighters from a hangar built inside the rigid hull. At just under 800 feet in length, the dimensions were comparable to an airborne *Titanic*.

While the vessels were certainly innovative, they were also accident prone. Despite being filled with nonflammable helium, both had been destroyed within a few years of service. The *Akron* crashed in a thunderstorm off the coast of New Jersey, killing all but three of its seventy-six-person crew. The *Macon* went down in a storm off Big Sur, south of San Francisco. This time, only two crewmen died while sixty-four survived, floating in life jackets and emergency rafts. Adams was among those plucked from the sea.

Two years later, Adams was stationed at Lakehurst Naval Air Station in New Jersey when the *Hindenburg* arrived from Germany. This Nazi-flagged zeppelin and its twin remain the largest aircraft ever built, and each was filled with flammable hydrogen. Upon approach to the mooring mast, the tail of the *Hindenburg* mysteriously exploded.

"It's fire and it's crashing," wailed a radio reporter who broke into a sobbing ramble. "Oh, the humanity!"

The airship turned upright, and the skin burned away to reveal the frame within. As the flaming wreckage collapsed, Adams and other personnel rushed onto the field to rescue survivors.

Now it was 1942, and Nazi Germany was an Axis enemy, along with Japan, in a second world war that ensnared the United States. The other naval aviator aboard *L-8* was Lieutenant Cody. Only twenty-seven years old, he was an Annapolis graduate known for being a cool-headed and capable pilot.

Back in April, Cody had piloted *L-8* out past the Golden Gate to aid in preparations to retaliate for Pearl Harbor. While the blimp hovered over the seagoing USS *Hornet*, about 300 pounds of custom parts were lowered onto a carrier deck filled with B-25s. Two weeks later, sixteen of these modified bombers attacked Tokyo as part of the surprise Doolittle Raid. Though the damage was small, this symbolic U.S. win paved the way to an even bigger victory at the naval Battle of Midway in June. For the rest of the summer, American fears ran high that a reeling Japan might directly strike the West Coast.

MORE PARKS

Within the Golden Gate National Recreation Area, there are many smaller NPS units. Tour the infamous former prison of Alcatraz Island. Board nineteenth-century ships at San Francisco Maritime National Historical Park. Explore the coastal Fort Point National Historic Site from the Civil War era. Hike beneath redwoods at Muir Woods National Monument.

Suspicious Sightings

About an hour and a half into the patrol flight, Cody made a routine radio call to his base. It was 7:38 a.m., and *L-8* was four miles east of the Farallons. A few minutes later, he radioed again.

"Am investigating suspicious oil slick," said Cody. "Stand by."

It was a clear day, with visibility over three miles. Within sight was the Liberty cargo ship SS *Albert Gallatin*, steaming between ports. Patrol blimps stamped with the words US NAVY had become a common sight along the coast. Thus, for the merchant marines on the *Gallatin*, the mere presence of *L-8* was no cause for fear.

But then several crew members did witness something concerning. As the blimp descended, it dropped a pair of smoke flares. Aboard the *Gallatin,* the general alarm was sounded. The guns were manned.

Nearby, fishermen aboard the trawler *Daisy Gray* pulled in their nets. It seemed possible the Navy blimp might drop a depth charge. The first mate was close enough to spot two men inside the control car. This would be the last time Cody and Adams were ever seen.

For about an hour, little happened. Crews aboard the two ocean vessels watched as *L-8* circled at an altitude of a few hundred feet. Eventually, the blimp descended to only thirty feet above the waves. Just after 9:00 a.m., the airship lifted upward and returned to San Francisco. False alarm.

Back at the naval air station on Treasure Island, the radio operator repeatedly tried to raise *L-8.* After an hour and half of silence, the squadron commander became concerned. He dispatched two Kingfisher float planes to search for the blimp. Meanwhile, an alert was radioed to other aircraft in the vicinity.

The first sighting of *L-8* was by a Pan Am commercial pilot at ten minutes to eleven. It was floating east over the Golden Gate Bridge. Next, an army pilot in a P-38 spotted the blimp. It was above Lands End, near the northwest corner of the San Francisco Peninsula, two miles southwest of the bridge. Soon one of the Kingfisher pilots spotted it a few miles west of the peninsula, rising through the overcast ceiling at 2,000 feet. This was roughly the altitude at which an L-class blimp would reach its pressure limit. Any higher and escape valves would automatically vent helium to prevent the interior gas bags from bursting. A few minutes later, *L-8* reappeared, descending through the underside of the clouds.

So Little Amiss

Around a quarter after eleven, some locals were visiting Ocean Beach near Fort Funston, about four miles south of Lands End. They watched as a partly deflated blimp dipped to only fifty feet above the surf. The typically taut envelope was sagging in the middle from the weight of the control car. The folds obscured the letters *N* and *A,* but the marking was clearly decipherable: US NAVY.

L-8 drifted sideways toward the beach. The control car briefly touched the sand, lifted off, and was blown into the side of an inland hill. A propeller on the starboard engine bent inward with a metallic creak. One of the depth charges dropped free, landing with a thud and rolling down the hill. Suddenly relieved of this 300-pound bomb, the blimp lurched over the hill, moving east with the breeze.

Wherever people stood, they stopped to watch the drifting mass. Drivers braked in the street and craned their heads out car windows. At the Olympic Club's lakeside golf course, players and caddies paused their games. In Daly City, a growing crowd began to follow on foot as *L-8* descended toward a suburban neighborhood.

Richard Johnston was standing at his front window when the blimp appeared overhead. He had just finished waxing his classic 1928 Dodge, and the shiny saloon car sat in his driveway. As the shadow surrounded the house, Johnston rushed his mother out the back door.

First the control car struck a utility pole. The rear fins swung around and impacted electrical wires, which released a shower of sparks. This punctured the helium bag and the intact nose billowed upright. Tail first, the deflating envelope collapsed atop Johnston's classic sedan.

At half past eleven, the control car came to rest, standing upright in the middle of Bellevue Avenue. The first rescuers to arrive were firefighters who had been burning brush on a nearby hillside. Next came the local police.

"The door was open, and nobody was in the cabin," said one firefighter, who was the first to look inside.

Another firefighter noticed the door was latched open. Dangling through the doorway was a corded microphone, used to hail surface ships with exterior loudspeakers.

Soon, response teams from the navy and army arrived. A thorough inspection revealed little was amiss, other than a crashed patrol balloon and missing crew. The radio worked just fine. So did the engines, which had been left running but disengaged. The parachutes and life raft were still aboard. So was a briefcase filled with classified documents. Two life jackets were missing, but this was understandable, as regulations required that they be worn by pilots during a patrol. One of the men had even left his hat hanging atop the control panel.

TRACK THE BLIMP

You can roughly follow the journey of the *Ghost Blimp* across the city. Take the Bay Bridge to Treasure Island, site of the former naval air station in the middle of San Francisco Bay. Today, there are some walking paths with great views and the developing Treasure Island Museum. The museum is housed in the former base headquarters, an art deco building that later served as the Berlin Airport in 1989's *Indiana Jones and the Last Crusade.*

Next, drive or walk across the Golden Gate Bridge, or explore Fort Point underneath, around where *L-8* left the bay and later reappeared. Adventurous travelers can consider a whale-watching boat tour to the Farallon Islands. Next, head southwest along the coast to Lands End, Ocean Beach, and Fort Funston. Along the way there are plenty of scenic viewpoints and walking trails. From there, *L-8* drifted inland and crashed on Bellevue Avenue in Daly City. Don't expect a grand monument or a Chipotle or anything. It's still a suburb.

An Inconsistent Theory

Over the coming days, an extensive search commenced. Planes searched from the air. Ships took to the seas. Authorities scoured the coastline. Nothing. So, the navy convened a weeklong board of investigation. With testimony from over thirty-five witnesses, the precise movements of *L-8* were confirmed.

When it came to the missing crew, the board's findings were inconclusive. They saw no reason that Cody and Adams would have voluntarily abandoned the airship. It must have been an accident, and a corresponding theory emerged. After *L-8* descended to investigate the suspicious oil slick, perhaps one officer latched open the door. Leaning out for a better look, maybe he fell into the water below. Quickly idling the engines, the remaining pilot could have grabbed the loudspeaker mic and stepped into the open doorway. While directing his swimming crewmate, did he somehow fall himself?

Once the derelict blimp was relieved of the two men's weight, it would have risen and floated back toward San Francisco. Upon passing an altitude of 2,000 feet, the pressure valves opened. Now *L-8* sank and caught shifting breezes while its envelope sagged from the reduced pressure. Ultimately, the board found that *L-8* was unmanned and moving randomly for two and a half hours before it crashed.

The theory was plausible but didn't account for several inconsistencies. Should the first man have gone overboard, why didn't the remaining officer quickly radio for help? And then there were the concerned sailors on the two nearby ships. Even if none of them noticed the two airmen fall, what about once they were in the water? Adams had survived worse before. It would have taken several hours to succumb to hypothermia in the mid-fifty-degree water. Their life jackets should have kept them afloat even longer. Yet no bodies were ever found, neither floating nor washed ashore. The navy's official determination was "100% Unknown/Undetermined."

Over the coming months and years, the rumors mounted. Suppose there had been a Japanese sub lurking in that oil slick. Could the two Americans have been captured or killed? Other ideas were proposed, each increasingly far-fetched. Might two dedicated officers go AWOL together, and in such a dramatic way? Both men were married, but maybe one killed the other over a woman and fled. Or an ill-timed rogue wave somehow splashed them both from the cabin. Suppose they were secretly testing an experimental technology that went wrong, and the navy covered it up. There were even murmurs about alien abductions.

Whatever happened aboard *L-8* during the ninth month of World War II never came to light.

Given the gentle nature of the crash, the control car was soon repaired, and the blimp resumed military service as a trainer. After the war, *L-8* was returned to the Goodyear Tire & Rubber Company. When the infamous airship next took to the sky, it had a different paint scheme. The words US NAVY were replaced with new lettering and an iconic wing-foot logo.

What was once called the *Ghost Blimp* became the *Goodyear Blimp*. For decades, it sailed over sporting events across the country, forever holding its secrets.

VISIT VERTIGO

Speaking of mysteries, one of the greatest films of all time, Alfred Hitchcock's *Vertigo* was filmed and set at many locations later incorporated into Golden Gate National Recreation Area. These include Fort Point, the Legion of Honor at the Presidio, and Muir Woods. At the latter location, Kim Novak studies a redwood cross section and utters a famous line: "Here I was born...and here I died."

CHAPTER 7

HOW DO THE SLIDING STONES MOVE ACROSS RACETRACK PLAYA?

UNEXPLAINED PHENOMENA

DEATH VALLEY NATIONAL PARK

CALIFORNIA–NEVADA STATE LINE

During the winter of 1915, prospector Joseph Crook brought his wife Cara to a dry lake bed in the mountains near Death Valley to show her something strange: thousands of stones resting on the playa seemed to have previously slid on their own, leaving behind long tracks in the dried mud.

Joseph had been visiting this roughly oval-shaped basin for years, which had come to be called the "Racetrack." Some old-timers claimed Indians once raced horses across the almost perfectly flat surface, and a large bedrock outcropping near the northern end was called the grandstand. Another reason behind the place name was how the puzzling rocks often moved parallel to one another, as if they had raced each other across the playa.

Cara found it hard to believe that the stones, most of which had traveled from roughly south to north, could have moved naturally. Sure, maybe the smaller rocks, which weighed only a few ounces. But other rocks were large, weighing several hundred pounds. Many tracks were long and roughly linear, extending for hundreds of feet with the occasional wiggle or jog. Some tracks were curved or made sharp turns from one direction to another. She decided to mark the position of one larger stone. Sure enough, when she returned on a later date, the rock had moved away.

A Bewitching Scene

While casual interest in the Racetrack persisted, it wasn't until after World War II that scientists tried to figure out what was happening. In 1948, a pair of geologists from the U.S. Geological Survey office in San Francisco introduced the phenomenon to the Geological Society of America during their New York convention. The two geologists explained that they visited the Racetrack in late spring, after the evaporation of shallow water that had covered the four-square-mile playa during winter.

They described observing many stones and tracks of various sizes, which had zigzagged through dried mud. One narrow track seemed to have been made by a machine gun shell. Their theory was that, when the surface was wet, the stones were moved by "strong gusts of wind blowing consecutively from different directions, such as erratic whirlwinds that commonly produce dust devils."

This initial report spurred interest in Racetrack Playa. In 1952, *Life* magazine sent a photographer, who returned with stunning images. Four small piles of burrow droppings, with tails resembling comets, seemingly frozen mid-race. A three-quarter-ton rock that had skidded 200 feet from several other boulders. A so-called "ghost experiment," in which an amateur sleuth must have hammered a stake into the mudflat surface and tied up a rock with a rope. The weathered rope had snapped, and the boulder skated away.

"Local theories blame this bewitched behavior on the lake bed's tipping back and forth," claimed the unnamed *Life* author. Other theories focused on "flood waters, or on Russian tampering with the magnetic pole."

More and more people came to the Racetrack in the early 1950s, fascinated by the mystery, including Louis and Ruth Kirk. They'd recently moved to Death Valley for Louis to work as a ranger in the national monument. During their first visit, Ruth and her husband searched unsuccessfully for any sign of footprints or human tampering. They determined a sixty-six-pound block of limestone had somehow traveled over a mile from the only limestone slope bordering the playa.

Ruth's theory was that the elevation—3,700 feet above sea level—might be a factor. Perhaps this resulted in more precipitation falling than nearby Death Valley's paltry inch and a half per year? Some geologists had recently suggested ice floes might play a role, but Ruth doubted the desert climate could produce enough ice. With most tracks moving roughly south to north, the same direction as the prevailing winds, the most likely explanation remained storm gusts.

PARK OF EXTREMES

Covering about 5,280 square miles, Death Valley is the largest national park in the lower forty-eight. Despite its scale, it sees less than two million visitors per year. The park is home to the lowest point in North America at 282 feet below sea level, a signed spot you can visit in Badwater Basin. Looming above is the park's highest point, Telescope Peak, at 11,049 feet, which can be reached via a challenging hike. The hottest temperature ever measured on Earth, 134 degrees Fahrenheit, was allegedly recorded here in July 1913. Not to brag, but Death Valley is also considered the driest place in North America. Basically, this aptly named park is best visited from fall through spring.

Why Here and Not There?

One scientist named John Shelton had a plan to simulate this wind. In early spring, the Pomona College geology professor landed on the playa in a light aircraft. After stabilizing the plane, he used the propeller wash to produce winds up to forty-two miles per hour. Near a man-made waterhole on the south end of the Racetrack, a nineteen-ounce piece of limestone was blown about two feet across the saturated playa surface, which rippled from the air blast. Elsewhere on the playa, Shelton noticed a thin film, like tissue paper, which had formed atop the dried mud tracks. Later lab testing revealed this gelatinous film was blue–green algae, which Shelton theorized might act as a lubricant.

As the 1950s came to the close, the frenzy surrounding the Racetrack would wane. By now, there were two prevailing hypotheses: winds pushed the stones through wet, slippery mud, or winter ice floes shoved the stones around. Some geologists, like George Stanley, suggested a combination of the two. In such a scenario, the rocks were encased in an ice sheet, which slightly floated them off the muddy surface. Then the sheet and rocks were blown by the wind.

However, a later study disputed the ice theories. Two scientists named Sharp and Carey encircled several stones with vertical steel rods, each hammered into the playa about two to three feet apart. Twice a stone escaped from this corral, and the scientists concluded a moving ice sheet couldn't be responsible, since it would have been broken up by the rods.

Despite a few attempts, no one had ever witnessed the stones moving. Some observers wondered, *Why here, in this remote mountain basin in the desert?* Yes, sliding stones had occasionally been observed at similar desert locations across southeastern California and into Nevada. But Racetrack Playa was the only known place where sliding stones occurred in such abundance and with rocks of such large sizes.

Given the absence of proof, more outlandish theories proliferated. Could it be a multigenerational prank by some very organized college kids? The work of playful extraterrestrials, possibly related to Area 51, located one hundred miles east? Some people told fantastic tales of wild animals with incredible strength moving the rocks for winter shelters. Others claimed the rocks themselves could magically levitate. Whatever the cause, the mystery of the sliding stones would linger for decades.

REACH THE RACETRACK

Bringing this mystery to life takes some time and effort, either by joining a tour group or driving the rough dirt road yourself. An hour north of the Furnace Creek Visitor Center, the paved road ends at Ubehebe Crater, a volcanic caldera that you can hike into. From there, it's about twenty-seven unpaved miles that typically take another two hours to negotiate. Four-wheel-drive or all-wheel-drive vehicles with all-terrain tires are strongly recommended.

When the Racetrack is dry, you can wander freely around the playa and view the rocks. Sadly, the site has suffered occasional incidents of vandalism. To preserve this natural landmark for future visitors, and to keep the rocks moving, the park service asks that you don't walk on the playa when muddy. It is also prohibited to move the rocks or to drive on the fragile surface. Think of the Racetrack as a living outdoor museum.

A Shift in the Winds

Throughout the latter half of the twentieth century, the Racetrack saw a steady stream of visitors. Tourism grew almost every year, with a significant boost when the monument was redesignated a national park in 1994. Periodically, new scientists arrived. Most observations confirmed that the stone movements clearly corresponded to prevailing wind patterns.

Meanwhile, a boom in college enrollment turned the Racetrack into a popular destination for class field trips. University vans made the bumpy drive along a rough dirt road. At the playa, laughing college students spilled out. Professors lectured about the various theories, and students would wander among the rocks, taking measurements and notes, pondering the puzzle.

FAR MORE THAN DEATH

Some adventurous visitors will hike trails and explore slot canyons, like Golden Canyon or Mosaic Canyon. Meanwhile, many park highlights include scenic drives and viewpoints with short walks.

The famous Artists Drive scenic loop passes through the kaleidoscopic hills of Artist's Palette, a colorful result of mineral oxidation. Zabriskie Point is an overlook on the edge of stark badlands, essentially crinkled ridges free of vegetation. It's a popular area for photography and viewing sunrises and sunsets. The Mesquite Flat sand dunes are usually viewed from afar, but others venture out onto the shifting sands. The Harmony Borax Works are the preserved remains of a sodium borate mining operation that operated for five hellish years in the late nineteenth century.

Finally, Dante's View at 5,575 feet overlooks salt flats winding like rivers through the valley. If the view looks familiar, there's a reason. Before the park stopped allowing movie productions, Death Valley was a filming location for the original 1977 *Star Wars*. These salt flats were the fictional location for the Mos Eisley spaceport, rated by some park visitors, like the opinionated Obi-Wan Kenobi, as a "wretched hive of scum and villainy."

In the late 1980s and early 1990s, a professor from Massachusetts named John Reid brought students to the playa to assist with an experiment. First, they built wooden boxes around some of the sliding stones. Then they flooded the boxes with enough water to mimic the muddy conditions of winter. Using ropes, pulleys, and measurement devices, they pulled on the stones until they slid.

For the wind theory proponents, the results were not promising. A 45-pound rock would require wind speeds around 175 miles per hour. Moving the largest rock, which weighed an estimated 700 pounds, would require winds of about 280 miles per hour. Even the fastest wind speed ever recorded on Earth fell short, 231 miles per hour at the summit of Mount Washington in New Hampshire. This experiment suggested that wind alone couldn't make the stones slide no matter how slippery the muddy surface might be. Something else was happening here.

An Event Finally Seen

Starting in 2011, a team of scientists funded by NASA arrived at Racetrack Playa with vehicles filled with equipment. On the elevated alluvial fan adjacent to the mudflat, they used sand bolts to anchor a weather station. In addition to recording temperature, rainfall, and wind speed, the station's time-lapse cameras would record images throughout the upcoming winters.

Then they unloaded the heavy stuff. With park service permission, the team had visited a nearby canyon to collect fifteen limestone blocks of similar sizes and shapes as the mysterious sliding stones. Into each stone, they drilled a large hole and inserted motion-activated GPS sensors. The stones were placed out on the playa, atop magnetic triggers buried beneath the surface, not far from the largest concentration of natural sliders. When the stones began moving, the entire system would be monitoring. The team waited, but nothing happened for almost two years.

After two relatively dry winters, a storm brought significant rain and snow in late November 2013. When the storm cleared, a shallow pond only a few inches deep covered the playa. Most days were sunny and clear. Meanwhile, nights dropped below freezing, and a thin sheet of ice began to form on the water surface. In early December, the instruments awakened. The stones were moving.

A few weeks later it happened again. This time, two of the team members were standing on shore. It was the first time the sliding stones at Racetrack Playa were known to have been seen in motion. Based on the team's personal observations, and a review of the weather station data and imagery, the mystery was solved.

Overnight, a thin layer of ice—only a tenth to a quarter of an inch thick—formed atop the playa pond. With morning came a sunny winter day and temperatures slowly crept above freezing. With loud pops and cracks, the ice sheet would break apart into large floating panels dozens of feet in size. Mild but steady winds, around two to twelve miles per hour, blew these panels into the rocks. Sometimes multiple panels piled against a single stone.

Slowly, at an almost imperceptible speed of a quarter mile per hour, the stones slid through the slippery mud. Then the ice melted, erasing the evidence of the culprit. The stones came to rest, waiting for the next time conditions were right, when they could move off in a different direction. The occurrence of smaller ice panels seemingly explained how, years before, one of the stones had escaped the corral of steel rods while the other did not.

In the mystery of sliding stones, the answer was a downright pleasant and anticlimactic surprise. There were no levitating rocks. No violent shoving by dense ice floes. No otherworldly gusts of wind. Just thin ice, clear skies, and a gentle breeze.

CHAPTER 8

DID A 1950s AIR FORCE PILOT STAGE A JET CRASH?

KINGS CANYON NATIONAL PARK

SIERRA NEVADA MOUNTAINS, CALIFORNIA

When the fishing party came across him, the disheveled stranger was sitting on a boulder in Granite Basin, eating wild strawberries out of a coffee jar. He had a thin face and bushy beard, like that of a grizzled mountain man. But otherwise, he seemed particularly out of place amid the backcountry landscape of bare rock and scraggly pines. Not only was he a young man of twenty-three, with only a knapsack and no horse, but his tattered jumpsuit bore the name tag of an air force pilot recently declared dead: *Lt. Steeves.*

"I've been up here almost sixty days," said David Steeves. "Have you got any food?"

Over the coming hours, the hungry airman rambled through a most incredible story. Meanwhile, he devoured everything offered by guide Albert Ade and three others: sweets, fruit, and half a loaf of rye bread with peanut butter and jelly.

On May 9, 1957, Steeves had taken off from Oakland Municipal Airport, across the bay from San Francisco, in a T-33 Shooting Star. His final destination was his home station of Craig Air Force Base in Selma, Alabama. While passing over Fresno, on his way toward Bakersfield, Steeves said his plane experienced some kind of explosion, and he was knocked unconscious. When he came to, the cockpit was filled with smoke. He released the canopy and ejected.

After falling through clouds, he discovered he was above snow-covered mountains. With several rips in his parachute, he came down fast. During a hard landing onto a bare ledge protruding from the snowy slope, Steeves rolled both ankles. Gathering his strength, he painfully crawled and slid down the mountain into a basin. He dug a snow cave under a log and wrapped himself in his parachute. Then he built a small fire and prayed for rescue. Meanwhile, his ankles throbbed in his boots, and a late-spring snow continued to fall.

Three days later, a slightly recovered Steeves realized the persistent cloud cover meant no one was coming to rescue him. He believed he was on the west side of the Sierra Nevada Mountains, somewhere above 10,000 feet. He decided to follow a partly visible trail along a nearby stream, which might lead him downhill toward civilization in the San Joaquin Valley. Unable to carry the parachute, he took only what he could wear: his summer jumpsuit, flight jacket, cap, gloves, knife, and a .32 caliber revolver holstered in his boot.

For about two weeks, he limped, scrambled, and slid his way through deep snow and piled boulders. Typically, he covered only a mile per day. When the first stream joined a steep and tumbling river, Steeves followed it through a rugged granite canyon. Water sources were abundant, so hydration wasn't an issue. But without food he became increasingly hungry and weak. Luckily, he had plenty of matches. During the cold nights he made fires and huddled against rocks or logs sticking out of the snow.

MISSING VISITORS

Stretching from the Gold Country foothills to the Sierra Crest, Kings Canyon National Park is comanaged with the adjacent Sequoia National Park. The resulting 1,353 square miles offers a lot to explore. There are majestic groves of giant sequoia, looming granite mountains, rugged trails, and dramatic waterfalls.

The scenery is comparable to Yosemite, which averages around four million visitors per year. Yet Sequoia typically sees just over a million and Kings Canyon only half that. This mystery can be your ticket to solitude, and the reason seems to be the park's remote location in the central Sierras. Kings Canyon has just a single scenic byway winding its way into the high country. It dead-ends in a stunning glacially carved valley. From there, you have to go on foot.

A Way to Escape

After nearly three weeks in the wilderness, a starving Steeves emerged into a scenic valley where he discovered a ranger shed. Using a tree branch, he broke open the door and found some canned and dried foods, including corned beef hash, beans, tomatoes, and gelatin. He drank ketchup from a bottle and ate two-thirds of the hash before forcing himself to ration the rest. He limped to the river to fill a canteen. Then he returned to the shed, where he cleared off a mouse-chewed mattress.

Steeves had been wearing his calf-high boots during the entire ordeal. The moment he took them off, his purpled ankles swelled before his eyes. Just pulling a piece of tent canvas over himself made him cry out in pain. For three days, Steeves feverishly drifted in and out of sleep, while his lower legs radiated heat. Occasionally he woke and snacked on dehydrated soup powder or ate mustard from a jar. When the pain finally receded, he used the outdoor fireplace to cook beans and rice.

In the cabin, Steeves found a map. He'd landed somewhere above the John Muir Trail in Kings Canyon National Park. He was currently at 6,000 feet in Simpson Meadow, with two trails leading out. One went down the river, and the other went high up over 10,673-foot Granite Pass. Eventually, his ankles felt good enough to try the lower route. He stuffed a knapsack with supplies, including a canvas blanket, first-aid kit, signal mirror, kindling, matches, and leftover beans. With the help of a walking stick, he trekked downstream to the valley below a granite monolith named Tehipite Dome.

It was early June now, and the Middle Fork Kings River was running high, engorged from snowmelt. The trail seemed to end at some cliffs, but the opposite shore looked passable. He crammed most of his clothes into the knapsack, strung his boots around his neck, and clenched his underclothes in his teeth. As Steeves waded into the frigid water, he was horrified to see his protruding ribcage.

Plunging into the rushing current, he lost his footing and was swept downstream into a tumbling rapid. Gasping for breath, he lost his underwear but managed to crawl onto the opposite bank. After resting and drying his clothes by a small fire, he continued downstream only to learn this side was also blocked by sheer cliffs.

The next day, he retreated to the shed and spent five days waiting out bad weather. His meager food stores were almost gone. He questioned his sanity, talking aloud to himself constantly. He increasingly prayed to see his wife, Rita, and fifteen-month-old daughter before he starved to death. On the first day of good weather, he tried to hike through Dougherty Meadow up toward Granite Pass, but the snowdrifts were still too deep.

Returning to Simpson Meadow, Steeves turned his efforts toward food. He found a small fishing case with a line and two hooks. He used grubs for bait and dropped the line into the river. In addition to nabbing occasional trout, he caught a few grass snakes around the valley. This was a lot of effort for limited calories, so he set his sights on something bigger. Near a salt lick made for horses, Steeves fastened his revolver to a sapling. Then he tied a string to the trigger and used an old hinge to create an animal trap. On the third morning, he found a buck, shot dead but half-eaten by scavengers. He lugged it back to the shed and, for two days, cooked the meat by using a toolbox as an oven. He re-set the trap. It fired day after day, and he occasionally saw blood on the ground, but took no further prey before running out of bullets.

BRING YOUR BOOTS

Until the park starts issuing skydiving permits for "historical research purposes," there's no way to replicate David Steeves's exact escape from the Sierras. But you can still bring this mystery to life by hiking some of the trails that he followed. The best method would be a backpacking trip starting from the Cedar Grove Visitor Center. Thus, you'll need to unravel the route summarized below in reverse.

The airman landed somewhere below Bishop Pass near the Dusy Basin Trail. He followed this downhill to the John Muir Trail/Pacific Crest Trail in Le Conte Canyon and continued on that trail along the Middle Fork Kings River. Where Palisade Creek joins the river, he hung a right onto the Upper Middle Fork Kings Trail and followed it to Simpson Meadow. His next escape attempt took him downstream on the Lower Middle Fork Kings Trail to just past Tehipite Dome. His final and successful attempt to escape took him up the steep Granite Pass Trail and down the Granite Basin Trail to Zumwalt Meadows and the Cedar Grove Visitor Center.

A Hero Returns

One day, Steeves awoke to an earthquake violently shaking the shed, like the world was ending. Enough was enough. The deer meat was gone. His ankles felt stronger. The snow was melting. Steeves was ready to try again for Granite Pass. He packed the knapsack with a few fish and wild strawberries. That morning, he started at daybreak, walking up Dougherty Meadow, mounting the pass, and reaching Granite Basin by midday. That's where he was resting when the fishing party arrived.

While telling his story, the airman chain-smoked his way through the offered cigarettes. The four-person audience was astonished by his tenacity. They made camp nearby and gave Steeves a feast: two steaks, fried potatoes, four pieces of cake, and three cups of coffee. The next morning, Steeves awoke to that strange shaking, once again, and he learned the cause. Atomic bomb tests at Frenchman Flat, 150 miles away in Nevada. The guide Albert Ade and Steeves rode out on two of the party's horses to the park service station at Cedar Grove. The rangers were equally shocked, calling it a scenario that even the most experienced mountaineer might not have survived.

Steeves called Connecticut, and his mother answered with a gasp. After they spoke, the phone rang. It was Steeves's wife Rita, who only three weeks before had received a U.S. Air Force death certificate. According to Steeves, they immediately made plans for a family trip to Florida. Throughout the rest of the day, he gorged himself in the park cafeteria and smoked a pipe he bought in the gift shop. When reporters began arriving, Steeves gave interviews and posed for photos. Eventually, military staff whisked him away to nearby Castle Air Force Base in Merced.

The next morning, Steeves limped into a packed press conference, still wearing his soiled jumpsuit. His ordeal soon made headlines across the country. The six-foot-tall airman had lost forty-five pounds in fifty-four days. Though he spoke in a halting and exhausted way, the handsome and charismatic survivor seemed a natural hero. Someone asked how his pretty wife had reacted to the news he was alive?

"Happy," responded Steeves, which a reporter from the *San Francisco Examiner* joked must be the understatement of the day.

Two days later, the high school sweethearts were reunited on a crowded tarmac at La Guardia Airport in New York. When David disembarked, Rita put her hands to her mouth.

"How horrible!" she blurted, before clarifying for observers. "The beard looks horrible."

The coming days were a whirlwind of autograph seekers and media attention, with appearances in newspapers, radio programs, and television shows. Steeves sold the exclusive rights to his story to the *Saturday Evening Post*. He would receive $10,000 for a two-part article and $5,000 more for a subsequent book, to be written by associate editor Clay Blair Jr.

A Story in Doubt

A week later, Steeves and a small party returned to Kings Canyon. With him was his wife, the writer Blair, and Steeves's rescuer, the guide Albert Ade. Their goal was a horse-packing trip to retrace the airman's harrowing journey. Everyone seemed in friendly spirits when the rangers bid them farewell at Cedar Grove. But four days later, the party emerged from the backcountry in a far different state, noticeably tense and seemingly at odds with one another.

By early August, things took a drastic turn. Newspapers reported Rita wanted a divorce. The *Saturday Evening Post* canceled the article and book, citing discrepancies in Steeves's story. Journalists across the country, who had previously lauded Steeves as a hero, now speculated wildly. Had it all been a hoax?

The skeptical Blair referenced several inconsistencies in Steeves's story. For one, he claimed the boots Steeves wore upon emerging from his ordeal seemed to be in remarkably good shape. Another concern was the remnants of a large forest fire, found by rangers across the river from the shed Steeves occupied in Simpson Meadow. Blair said Steeves repeatedly denied starting the fire. Later, he admitted that he'd done it to attract a rescue party. In hindsight, the airman said he felt ashamed. Soon new articles raised further doubts about the survival story.

Life magazine interviewed the packtrain driver who had found Steeves's abandoned belongings in Dusy Basin, where he claimed to have landed. *Why*, the packer wondered, *would Steeves leave behind valuable items like the parachute and a book of matches? Why were the singe marks from Steeves's first fire only one foot off the ground, when the snow depth was supposed to have been six feet in early May?* Then there was the *Life* photographer who had snapped an up-close photo of a deer in Simpson Meadow. If they were so easy to approach, why had Steeves needed such an elaborate trap?

The local sheriff suggested it was all a staged event. Maybe Steeves did eject, sure. But suppose he landed in Simpson Meadow and hiked up to Dusy Basin to plant the items and enhance his tale? *Time* magazine raised a puzzling issue. Why had U.S. Air Force searchers failed to locate Steeves's crashed plane? Perhaps there never was an explosion. Maybe Steeves bailed out on purpose and let the T-33 fly on autopilot out to sea. Amid the pervasive espionage fears of the Cold War, other skeptics theorized that perhaps Steeves flew the jet to Mexico where he could have sold it to the Soviets. Then he hiked into the national park for an alibi.

SURVIVE THE STORY

Anytime you venture into a wilderness as rugged and remote as Kings Canyon, you need to be prepared. Only experienced backpackers in excellent physical condition should attempt the backcountry trails discussed in this chapter. These are steep hikes at high elevations, with altitude sickness being a legitimate concern. That said, easier options do exist, including several flat trails through Zumwalt Meadows.

A Chance at Redemption

Meanwhile, more troubling news came out about Rita and David's relationship. Supposedly, it had been severely damaged long before his disappearance. When she gave birth to their baby girl, the new father was said to have cried for not having a son. After withdrawing from their family life, he confessed to having a mistress in San Francisco. Earlier that year, he'd spent over half a year's salary on a Jaguar convertible. This left little money for his wife and daughter, who lived in a trailer in Alabama.

Other people defended Steeves and his story. His strict evangelical parents noted how their athletic son, at age eighteen, had managed similar adventures. After hitchhiking and working his way to Alaska, he later returned south as a crewman on a salmon ship.

The superintendent of Kings Canyon National Park said rangers retraced Steeves's path only ten days after he emerged from the wilderness. Everything checked out. In addition to finding the parachute in Dusy Basin, they found the pilot's monogrammed handkerchief. In Simpson Meadow, they saw the remains of his animal trap and deer bones near the shed. The air force was so convinced, they sent Steeves to work at their survival school in Reno.

Albert Ade was in full agreement. Upon rejoining his fishing party, he'd even followed Steeves's tracks back to the shed. The guide wondered if the field journalist was the problem.

"Every step his horse took," Ade recalled about Blair, "he looked as if he were going to fall off."

In fact, in the coming years, Blair would be sued numerous times for slander. Ultimately, he would lose a multimillion-dollar case to a popular football coach after falsely accusing him of throwing a game. The scandal would put the beloved *Saturday Evening Post* out of business. In fact, Steeves himself would sue the publication, which paid him a settlement out of court.

Repeatedly, Steeves defended his story. In January 1958, he got a chance to thoroughly reply in an exclusive feature in *Redbook* magazine. The airman admitted the truth. He was a horrible husband to his wife. A terrible father to his daughter. He had realized this, with a shock, during that first night in an icy hovel in Dusy Basin. He was selfish, cruel, shallow. But he wasn't lying about what happened to him in the Sierras.

"How does *Life* know the depth of the snow in Dusy Basin in early May?" he asked. "Do they have a correspondent there?" Snow drifted, he explained, and was therefore thicker in some places and thinner in others. It all depended on the topography, after all. And about the matches? Steeves had been panicking and he simply dropped them.

The *Redbook* article ended on a bittersweet note. The subject was a physically strong but emotionally stunted airman whose story had been harshly judged by society because of his inexcusable flaws. Upon publication, a remorseful Steeves said he agreed with every word. One of his main motivators during those fifty-four days in the wilderness was making it out and setting things right. He still held hope that he and Rita could reconcile and rebuild their family.

PARADISE IN A DAY

For a more reasonable hike with breathtaking scenery, one of the best trails in the park leads to Mist Falls, which cascades steeply over ledges and slides. Starting from Road's End, the out-and-back hiking route is eight miles round trip, requiring about 900 feet in elevation gain. For your efforts, you'll follow a tumbling river through the stunning South Fork Canyon to the lower end of Paradise Valley. There's no mystery behind the name. It's well earned.

A Disgraceful Discovery

Before the end of 1958, the divorce was finalized. In her filing, Rita revealed new details about Steeves's behavior. Once, he had forced his reluctant wife to meet his mistress, face to face. Other times, Steeves drunkenly hit Rita.

The story of the 1950s jet pilot who survived the wilderness of Kings Canyon vanished from the papers. Public opinion remained split. A few still believed the troubled airman's tale, while a much greater number didn't. Steeves requested a discharge from the air force. He moved to Fresno, down in the valley west of the national park, where he worked a variety of jobs in the aviation industry.

For years, it was said the disgraced pilot would fly over Kings Canyon, always searching for his lost plane. He unsuccessfully tried to sell his story to Hollywood. He briefly tried his hand at acting in local theater. A lone newspaper critic was not kind. Steeves died in a plane crash in 1965, never having found the wreckage and the redemption he hoped it would offer.

In 1977, a group of Boy Scouts were hiking off trail around the Citadel. This 12,000-foot peak overlooks the Middle Fork Kings River. It's just west of Dusy Basin, where the airman claimed to have landed, twenty years before. At the scouts' feet, they came across the wreckage of an aircraft.

The next season, park rangers returned to the spot. They found a jet canopy stamped with the serial number 52–9232. A records search revealed it was part of the plane that David Steeves ejected from. A twenty-one-year-old mystery was solved. It was the perfect survival story—one that had been lived by a very imperfect person.

CHAPTER 9

WHO WAS THE FIRST TO CLIMB DENALI?

DENALI NATIONAL PARK AND PRESERVE

ALASKA RANGE, INTERIOR ALASKA

The steamer *Hans Egede* arrived at Lerwick, capital of the Shetland Islands in the North Atlantic, on a clear morning in early September 1909. A skiff was lowered into the water, and Dr. Frederick Cook and the ship's mate rowed over to the docks where the herring boats delivered their catches for curing. After tying up, the men walked through a historic village of sandstone buildings to the hilltop telegraph station. When Cook handed over his handwritten message, the operator glanced up in surprise.

"Reached North Pole April 21, 1908," began the telegram to the *New York Herald.*

The message went on to describe Cook's discovery of land in the far north, and the promise of an exclusive report on the historic expedition for a fee of $3,000. The American would claim that in February 1908, he set out from the hunting settlement of Annoatok in Greenland. With him were nine Inuit, eleven sleds, and over a hundred dogs. About 360 miles from his goal, he sent most of the party back and continued onward with two top men, Ahpellah and Etukishook. The trio spent twenty-four days making a final push to the Pole.

During the return journey, disaster struck when the pack ice broke up and their path was blocked by open water. They were forced to shelter in a cave on Devon Island until the following winter, desperately hunting for game to avoid starvation. When the sea refroze, they finally returned to Annoatok after fourteen months of hardship. There they learned that everyone assumed they had perished.

The lesser-known arctic explorer—the conqueror of Mount McKinley, called Denali in Alaska at the time—had surprised everyone once again. For decades, explorers had tried and failed to reach the elusive North Pole. Several infamous expeditions had ended with boats trapped or crushed by the drifting pack, with survivors setting out across the ice and often freezing to death. Now Cook's party had braved the elements to achieve the crown jewel of exploration.

By the time the *Hans Egede* reached Copenhagen three days later, Cook was being hailed worldwide as a hero. Adoring fans and reporters gathered at the harbor, waiving their hats and cheering. The smiling Cook wore the suit of a gentleman sailor and a mariner's cap. He certainly looked the part of a rugged but aloof adventurer. For one thing, the forty-four-year-old had lost his front teeth during the expedition, though he soon had them replaced in the Danish capital.

Over the coming days, there were celebrations and banquets. Cook gave well-received lectures to packed houses. Various authorities in Europe and America had no reason to doubt Cook's claim. They said they looked forward to examining the explorer's data when he was ready to share his journals. Documentation of daily mileages, compass bearings, and astronomical observations was expected from record-seeking explorers to verify their discoveries.

WILDERNESS PARKS

The nation's largest state is home to the most preserved lands in the National Park System, an astounding 87,500 square miles. Among Alaska's twenty-three National Park Service units, there are a variety of monuments, historical parks, preserves, and eight designated national parks. Only three of those can be reached by road, with the others requiring a boat trip or travel on foot. The state's most popular NPS unit is Glacier Bay National Park.

A close second is Denali National Park, which sees about a half-million visitors per year. Most people come during the short summer season, from June to August. It's important to know that private vehicles are only allowed on a short section of the park road. Most visitors reserve a seat on a private bus to fully explore the park. Once arrived, highlights include wildlife viewing, photography, and enjoying scenic views of the mountains. Hiking is also popular. There are only a few marked trails, mostly found near the park entrance, and each is three miles or less. Another option is to join a ranger-guided outing. For hikers and backpackers venturing off trail, experience with backcountry navigation is strongly recommended.

Thoroughly research this park before visiting to make sure it's right for you. Upon arrival, speak to a ranger about realistic options, weather forecasts, and current conditions. Understand the risks and techniques for wilderness travel in grizzly bear territory. This park is remote, but by no means is it impossible to experience. Be prepared and stay safe.

Competing Claim

"Peary Discovers the North Pole After Eight Trials in 23 Years" was the headline in the *New York Times* on September 7, 1909. The article described how, five days after Cook's declaration, the famous explorer Robert Peary emerged from the Arctic. He walked into a telegraph station at Indian Harbour in Labrador, Canada, and sent his own triumphant announcement.

"I have the pole, April sixth," Peary had wired, with subsequent messages elaborating upon his claim. Peary was a fifty-three-year-old U.S. Navy officer who was frequently sponsored by the National Geographic Society. He had spent decades developing the sledging practices and frozen routes to reach the North Pole. In the process, he'd lost all but two toes to frostbite. Yet he always trudged onward, never abandoning his dream of being first to reach ninety degrees north.

Upon returning to the edge of civilization, Peary was shocked to receive so little attention for what he expected would be the news of the century. When he learned the reason, he was furious. Peary considered Cook to be a trivial explorer with little chance of winning the prize. As a younger man, the latter had been a field surgeon for Peary during a lengthy Greenland campaign in the early 1890s. Peary was initially impressed by Cook, whom he judged to have a calm temperament, positive attitude, and the requisite physical endurance.

However, the two men had a falling out when Cook sought permission to publish a book about the expedition. The domineering Peary refused. Lacking the influential backers that Peary had long cornered, Cook embarked on his own series of shoestring expeditions to the far north. After completing an impressive first circumnavigation of Denali in 1903, he returned three years later to bag the summit of the tallest mountain in North America. With this feather in his cap, Cook found enough notoriety to line up a single benefactor for a longshot bid at the Pole.

To investigate Cook's claim, Peary arranged an interview with Ahpellah and Etukishook. With a damning transcript in hand, Peary felt satisfied enough to wire a rebuttal to the *New York Times*.

"Cook's story should not be taken too seriously," Peary wrote. "The Eskimos who accompanied him say that he went no distance north. He did not get out of sight of land."

The public response was, once again, not what Peary expected. Most of the establishment, including wealthy businessmen and esteemed members of the National Geographic Society, stuck with the celebrity explorer. Everyone else was firmly on the other side. The general public viewed Cook as a plucky underdog competing against a sore loser who belonged to the elites.

Cook particularly helped his case by maintaining a congratulatory and professional demeanor toward Peary. As the controversy deepened, and Peary's wrath grew, Cook refused to publicly criticize his rival.

"I believe him!" Cook once said. "There is glory enough for us all!"

Scandals Abound

"We Believe in You" read a banner in Brooklyn. A hundred thousand spectators lined the parade route welcoming home Frederick Cook in late September. He was a native son, the child of German immigrants. After falling into poverty at age five, when his father suddenly died, the tenacious Cook had worked his way through medical school. He was a self-made man who epitomized the American Dream, and every one of his fellow citizens seemed to have an opinion on the matter. Several newspapers conducted polls, including one by the *Pittsburgh Press* that reported 73,238 voters sided with Cook. Only 2,814 believed Peary.

Adding to the controversy was the fact that neither explorer had yet shared any proof of their polar accomplishments. Cook claimed he'd left his documents in the far north, for safekeeping, where they'd been lost. Peary said he was withholding his data so that the impostor Cook couldn't steal the figures. As a result, the issue devolved into a debate about which one of them made it that was based upon the character and pedigree of each man. So, Peary and his allies launched a new front in their discreditation campaign.

In October 1909, Edward Barrill arrived in New York City with a wild story to share about the Denali expedition three years before. After failing to find a southern route up the mountain, the main party had been retreating toward the Pacific Coast during late summer of 1906. Along the way, Cook suddenly decided he wanted to split off and perform some foothills reconnaissance for next season's attempt. He invited Barrill to be his lone partner. When Cook returned to civilization, he announced to the world that the two men had reached the top of the continent. Barrill went along with the ruse in hopes of making some money. Now the remorseful accomplice signed a sworn affidavit admitting it had all been a lie.

Regarding Denali's summit at 20,310 feet, Barrill said the two men never got closer than fourteen miles, nor did they ever climb higher than 8,000 feet. The dramatic summit photo that Cook had published to great acclaim? Staged on a minor outcropping that would come to be called "Fake Peak." During their homebound journey, Cook had borrowed Barrill's journal and doctored the entries that later were used as proof.

Supporters of Cook seethed that Barrill could not be trusted. They correctly surmised that he was being paid by the Peary camp to offer his testimony. However, other members of Cook's 1906 Denali attempt soon came forward to corroborate Barrill's account. The expedition photographer said that Belmore Browne emerged as the strongest mountaineer in the party, serving as de facto leader when Cook kept leading them astray.

Browne and other members insisted the nature of the mountain made Cook's claim impossible. Called the "High One" in local Athabascan, Denali was a massif that rose 18,000 feet above the surrounding tundra. Though there were taller mountains in the world, Denali had the greatest rise on land from base to peak. There was no way Cook and Barrill could have reached the summit during the brief time they were alone.

"I knew it in the same way that any New Yorker would know that no man could walk from the Brooklyn Bridge to Grant's Tomb in ten minutes," Browne later wrote.

Cook's response was a mix of surprise and denial. He was given several opportunities to defend himself from both scandals, with invitations to testify before the

Explorer's Club and the National Geographic Society. Not only did Cook refuse to appear, but he soon claimed exhaustion and left the country. He was later spotted in Copenhagen, where he failed to renew any support from the Danish authorities who had once extolled him.

The public backlash against Cook was swift and severe, at home and across the world. Only the occasional diehard fan continued to defend him. Most observers begrudgingly admitted that Peary was right after all. He'd been first to the North Pole. However, the adulation that the connected explorer sought never materialized, due to unfavorable impressions that formed during the scandal. The whole affair was dismissed as a farce. Numerous editorial cartoons lampooned both men, sometimes depicting them as children or brawlers slugging it out on pack ice.

When Peary agreed to submit his records to the National Geographic Society, the quick confirmation seemed almost perfunctory. A few observers raised concerns that Peary's claims seemed equally improbable. One critic was Roald Amundsen, the daring but fastidious Norwegian explorer who would successfully ski to the South Pole in 1911. However, few people seemed to care anymore. Not about the North Pole and not about Denali. Of course, if Cook had faked the first ascent, that meant the continent's tallest mountain was still waiting to be climbed.

Sourdough Expedition

By December 1909, the mood inside the smoky Washington Saloon in Fairbanks had turned bitter. Gold harvesting was in sharp decline, and all anyone talked about was yet another scandal involving a *cheechako*. Locals used this Chinook word to describe inexperienced outsiders from the south who came to the remote Alaska Territory. They fancied themselves adventurers and posed for photographs. They renamed Alaskan mountains like Denali after distant and irrelevant presidents.

The cheechakos were an embarrassment, both to themselves and to the local sourdoughs who worked for a living and had no time for spectacles. That's what the locals called themselves: *sourdoughs*. They were prospectors and trappers who trekked through northern wilderness carrying pouches of fermenting sourdough starter around their waists. They used the yeast to make bread and donuts that could withstand the harsh subzero temperatures.

The sourdoughs knew from the beginning that Frederick Cook didn't climb Denali. Now the world had finally caught up. Of course, this meant that more cheechakos would be coming. Instead, they felt, the first people to summit Alaska's tallest mountain ought to be sourdoughs.

So, a few days before Christmas, a crowd of locals cheered as six sourdoughs rode sleds out of town. These rugged frontiersmen had no formal experience with mountaineering, but they did have plenty of grit, whiskey, and hard-earned survival skills. To preserve their sled dogs, they took turns on foot, breaking trail through the snow ahead or running behind. Along the way, they hunted and smoked the ample meat needed to fuel their mission. They used canvas tents and caribou-fur bedding to survive nights that fell to sixty degrees below zero. Going in winter meant short days with just four hours of sunlight. It also meant they would cross frozen rivers and, hopefully, avoid melting crevasses and seasonal avalanches.

In Kantishna, thirty-five miles from Denali, they were joined by a crucial seventh member, an accomplished outdoorsman and surveyor who would document their climb with altimeter readings and photographs. Of course, soon a drunken brawl broke out and the surveyor and two others returned to Fairbanks. The four remaining sourdoughs pushed on, hoping to figure out the camera as they went.

The method to their madness was actually quite rational. Their endeavor would become one of the earliest examples of expedition mountaineering. After building a base camp, they slowly probed Denali for a safe climbing route, eventually establishing two more advanced camps higher up the mountain. As the short days lengthened, they spent the months of February and March hauling downed trees up the Muldrow Glacier, building bridges across open crevasses. Then they carried backpacks filled with food, firewood, and equipment up to the higher camps.

At the end of the glacier, they shoveled snow and chopped steps into the ice until a 1.5-mile stairway ascended 3,500 feet up Karstens Ridge. They believed their final camp sat around 15,000 feet. Without an altimeter reading, they were vastly mistaken. They began their summit push from just 11,000 feet.

What happened next would be debated for over a century. Two days after their first summit attempt was aborted by a storm, the weather cleared. They started shortly before dawn on April 3, 1910. They wore duck-down snowsuits and massive fur mitts that were soon encrusted with ice. They carried no ropes, but they did wear homemade crampons welded from sheet metal. At least one of them carried an alpenstock, a long wooden staff with a spiked tip that was commonly used before the adoption of ice axes. To make sure they received credit for their climb, one of them carried a fourteen-foot spruce flagpole to mark the arrival on top.

Denali has two summits. The southern summit is the highest at 20,310 feet. The northern summit is nearly nine hundred feet lower at 19,480 feet. Not realizing which was higher, three of the sourdoughs claimed they reached the northern summit. They said they completed this ascent of 8,000 feet and returned to their highest camp in only eighteen hours.

The route they later described, with some variation between members, took them up the Harper Glacier, where they turned north and scaled a precipitous 2,000-foot chute, later named Sourdough Couloir. On the northeast ridge, at about 18,500 feet, the man carrying the spruce pole said he anchored it upright in rocks where they believed it could easily be seen from below. Years later, he changed his story to say he turned around there as well. But earlier on, all three of them said they jogged up the final ridgeline to the summit. It was later revealed that the fourth sourdough, the eldest leader, had not gone higher than 11,000 feet. However, upon returning to civilization, he told everyone who would listen that all four sourdoughs had conquered both the south and north summits.

Their changing stories, and a few other key details, caused most observers to doubt they had summited either peak. One reason to doubt was that they described no problems with altitude sickness, despite their sprint into thin air. Their photos were mostly out of focus, though one successfully developed image showed that they reached at least 16,500 feet, at roughly the base of Sourdough Couloir.

A third reason to doubt was that only a single climbing party, three years later, reliably claimed to have seen the erected spruce pole. Rumors spread that other people below the mountain saw the pole, too. Seeing the sourdoughs' flagpole became something of a mountain myth, like spotting a yeti. No other climber ever saw the pole again, though given the howling winds, it could have been knocked down. Yet even if the indomitable sourdoughs had accomplished their claimed ascent of the north summit, the higher true summit of Denali remained untrodden.

Epilogue of Explorations

On June 7, 1913, a climbing party led by local Alaskans Hudson Stuck and Harry Karstens trudged atop the south summit, completing the first verifiable climb of Denali. They followed a similar route as the sourdoughs, up the Muldrow Glacier, and established a higher camp at a more opportune elevation of 17,500 feet in the Grand Basin.

They ticked all the boxes, making atmospheric measurements to document the altitude and obtaining grainy but decipherable photographs on the peak. Everyone in the party suffered, to some extent, from altitude sickness. The exhausted team leader, Stuck, collapsed and briefly fell unconscious upon reaching the highest point.

After he revived, he put binoculars to his eyes and spotted a surprising detail. He passed the field glasses to several climbing partners, and each concurred with the assessment. On the northern ridge, around an altitude of 18,500 feet, there was a vertical pole rising into the air. Though it would never be seen again, members of the Stuck expedition were convinced their fellow Alaskans made it. Had the Sourdough Expedition reached the south summit after all?

Frederick Cook's two claims as an American hero of the romantic age of exploration were debunked as hoaxes. Ironically, the explorer had accomplished several impressive and verifiable feats, including expeditions to Greenland and Antarctica and the first circumnavigation of Denali in 1903. But most observers believe he faked the ascent of North America's tallest mountain so that he could fake his claim on the North Pole. Where he was during those fourteen months in the Arctic Circle never came to light, but if he did spend them on icy Devon Island, this was no small endeavor itself.

Before Cook died in disgrace in 1940, one final scandal enveloped him. During the 1920s, he became an oil promoter in Fort Worth, Texas, where he sold shares in a crude field that didn't yield. He pled not guilty and was convicted of fraud, with a sentence of fourteen years. While in prison, the Fort Worth oil field proved to be part of the Yates Pool, one of the largest and most profitable oil finds in U.S. history. Cook was released after seven years and later pardoned by President Franklin Roosevelt.

After Cook died, a small but dedicated movement formed to restore the explorer's legacy. If he had been railroaded for the oil hoax, perhaps he was unfairly slan-

dered by Peary as well. Maybe Frederick Cook had reached the North Pole and the summit of Denali? But most observers remain unconvinced that he ever stood at either spot.

One place Cook clearly reached was Fake Peak, which became an infamous outcropping in Denali National Park. It's located at an elevation of 5,338 feet, nineteen miles southwest of the mountain's true summit. This key site was found and photographed by the incensed Belmore Browne in 1910. It later became something of a pilgrimage site for mountaineering skeptics whenever a partisan of Cook claimed the man had summited.

The staged summit photo taken by Frederick Cook in 1906 shows Edward Barrill standing atop Fake Peak, a 5,338-foot outcropping nearly twenty miles away from the peak of Denali. Photo by Frederick A. Cook, 1906/Public Domain

The Haunted Pole

In time, Robert Peary's 1909 claim on the North Pole would also be mostly debunked. After seven expeditions over two decades had come up short, the fatigued and aging Peary knew his eighth attempt would likely be his last. On April 1, 1909, he found himself out on the pack ice. He was the closest he'd ever been, but still 133 miles south of the Pole. Each day, they managed to sledge about ten miles, at most seventeen. Sometimes it was less, given how often they had to navigate around pressure ridges of jagged ice or dangerous gaps of open water.

Then Peary made a particularly suspicious decision, sending back his second-in-command and strongest sledge driver, Bartlett. He was the only other expedition member capable of using instruments to verify the leader's distances, bearings, and astronomical observations. Once Bartlett was gone, Peary, along with a personal assistant and four Inuit, made an improbable dash to the Pole in two and a half days. Then he was back at Indian Harbour in Labrador four and a half days after that.

To accomplish this incredible rate of travel, Peary's small team would have had to cover a total distance of 429 miles in a week. Sledging an average of sixty miles per day, across the rough terrain of drifting pack ice, would have been a feat that had never been accomplished before. Nor has such speed been repeated since, though some Arctic adventurers have tried.

For pointing out these concerns, Roald Amundsen and other contemporary skeptics were mostly dismissed by the exploring establishment of the era. The Norwegian shrugged off the criticism, skied to the South Pole, and then became the first explorer to verifiably reach ninety degrees north as well. Only a few days before Amundsen arrived, yet another explorer had claimed to fly over the Pole in a propeller plane. His unverified claim was later debunked, whether due to mistaken navigating or purposeful fraud.

On May 12, 1926, Amundsen and a party of American and Italian adventurers floated over the North Pole in an experimental blimp. Because Peary's claim remained widely accepted at that time, they didn't know for certain that they were the first. They didn't seem to care. They went because they wanted to see what was there.

The North Pole was a beautiful but obscure point that generations of brave explorers had sought to reach. There was no continent nor land of any kind. It was a frozen region that became the final resting place for many lost souls—including Amundsen. He would disappear in the Arctic two years later during a failed rescue mission to save other explorers.

The northernmost point on Earth was a serene expanse of drifting ice with an uncertain history of haunting lies.

MOUNTAIN
WEST

CHAPTER 10

IS MURDER LEGAL IN THE ZONE OF DEATH?

INFAMOUS CRIMES

YELLOWSTONE NATIONAL PARK

ROCKY MOUNTAINS, WYOMING

The crime seemed particularly brazen. The rangers were standing in the snow next to the headless body of an elk. Other than the bloody decapitation, the bull's winter coat didn't show signs of distress. In fact, the carcass still seemed warm, giving off steam that rose into the cold air.

The kill had been found along the mountainous upper Gallatin River, near the northwest boundary of Yellowstone National Park. Less than a hundred yards away was Highway 191. During summer, tourists often stopped a few miles up the road to take photos at the park's entrance sign. Now it was late December 2005. The area was mostly empty, except for sparse local traffic and the occasional explorer venturing into the winter backcountry.

Hunting season had closed the month before, but poaching was common throughout the region. This was likely the work of illegal hunters, who wanted the head and antlers for wall mountings. To aid an investigation, rangers collected tissue samples from the carcass. But the likelihood of catching the culprit was slim. Most poachers around Yellowstone were never caught.

A Latest Offense

The morning before, Mike Belderrain had set out on a horseback ride along the upper Gallatin River. All was quiet. Just mountains and trees and wildlife. In the snowy distance, Belderrain saw a herd of elk. As he approached, one in particular caught his eye. *It is beautiful*, he thought. The biggest bull he'd ever seen, with massive antlers spreading into fine points. The trophy he'd been chasing his entire life.

Sitting atop his horse, Belderrain felt a buzz of adrenaline mixed with apprehension. Despite all the reasons not to, he decided then and there to kill that elk. Having reached his mid-thirties, the man was known for numerous run-ins with the law. He'd been cited for alcohol-related offenses, public violence, and firearms infractions. Sometimes, he went to bars and sat near the biggest asshole in the room, just to bait the guy into starting something. Belderrain had even been caught serving as an unpermitted hunting guide. Thus, he knew exactly what he was doing.

Belderrain pulled out his rifle and got the elk in his sights. His aim was to shoot it behind the shoulder, in the flank. That way, the injured animal would bolt into the trees and die. The crack of the rifle filled the valley. The bull dropped right where he was struck. An accidental head shot.

"*Oh no*," thought Belderrain, his stomach turning. "*Not good. Not good at all.*"

Belderrain was standing a hundred feet inside the federal boundary, while the dead bull had fallen just outside. Both were within sight of the road, which was empty—for now. Moving quickly, Belderrain hacked away at the head until it was severed. Then he dragged it back to his truck, where it was parked on a nearby side road. After trailering his horse, he sped down the highway and hoped things didn't catch up to him.

A BUSY PARK

Geysers and grizzly bears. Rivers and bison. Lakes and mountains. Yellowstone National Park has a bit of everything. It's the second-largest national park in the lower forty-eight, after Death Valley. Averaging over four million annual visitors, it's typically among the top five most visited national parks. Given the high elevations, primarily above 6,000 feet, the area has long winters. Most people come between May and September, with visitation peaking during July, when it can feel quite crowded. Aim for the spring and fall shoulder seasons for a somewhat quieter time.

Many visitors' favorite activity is viewing the abundant wildlife, including bison, moose, bighorn sheep, and much more. Two popular areas for large mammals are Hayden Valley and Lamar Valley. Other beloved highlights include the many geysers, with the most famous being Old Faithful, which typically erupts every ninety minutes to heights of 150 feet. Found in the Midway Geyser Basin, the rainbow-rimmed Grand Prismatic Spring is the largest hot spring in the United States.

Hiking is popular on over 900 miles of trails winding through park wilderness, wildlife viewing areas, geyser basins, and surrounding mountains. There's also paddling in the park and rafting opportunities outside. Given lodgings and campgrounds usually fill up, plan ahead by making reservations far in advance.

A Surprising Objection

Back in town, Belderrain began to regret what he'd done. It was considered poor form to harvest an elk head and leave the carcass to rot. Then again, he didn't feel that bad. This was the biggest kill of his career, and nothing would have stopped him from taking the shot. So, he brought the head to a local taxidermist to have it stuffed and mounted.

Belderrain's cover story was that the bull had been harvested legally, during the November season, up in the Buffalo Horn Drainage. But the timeline didn't add up, and word got around that the head may have been from a poached animal. Soon state wildlife officials were asking questions. Hoping to settle things quickly, Belderrain admitted he'd shot out of season but maintained the location was well outside the park. In March 2006, he pled no contest to poaching in state court and agreed to pay a fine.

Meanwhile, the federal investigation into the decapitated carcass continued throughout the year. Eventually, the local taxidermist told the feds that the elk head he'd preserved came from the Yellowstone kill. Search warrants were executed, and a tissue sample was taken from Belderrain's trophy. DNA tests confirmed a match. For once, a poacher would answer for his crime.

The stakes were high. The case would be tried in federal court in Cheyenne, Wyoming, which had jurisdiction over the entire park. Word was the government hoped to make an example of Mr. Belderrain by seeking a felony conviction with a lengthy prison sentence. They wanted to send a message to the many brazen poachers around the edges of the park: *stay away.*

The case slowly progressed until the summer of 2007. That's when the public defender filed a motion to dismiss, with a surprising twist. The objection was related to Belderrain being tried in a Wyoming court. After all, the shooting had occurred in Montana. The U.S. Constitution guaranteed the defendant the right to be tried in the state of the crime and before jurors from the judicial district where it happened.

In the brief, the public defender referenced a loophole in the justice system, an exception that only applied to two small portions of land within the boundaries of Yellowstone National Park. One was a narrow strip of the park just inside Idaho. The other was a roughly L-shaped parcel extending into Montana, where Belderrain's crime had occurred. Inside these two areas, due to a judicial error made over a century before, crimes were supposedly legal—even murder. The so-called *zone of death.*

A Gate Thrown Open

Several years before, law professor Brian Kalt was contemplating a possible article about the minutiae of the Sixth Amendment to the U.S. Constitution. He was a legal scholar at Michigan State University who would be going up for tenure in a few years, and his interests included obscure legal situations and loopholes. This time, he was thinking about the oft-forgotten topic of *vicinage,* a defendant's constitutional right to a trial by a jury drawn from the same state and district where the crime was committed. While searching for a suitable case study, Kalt discovered a unique situation in the country's first national park.

When Yellowstone was established by Congress in 1872, over 90 percent of what would become the 3,472-square-mile park fell inside Wyoming territory. The remainder spills over into two adjacent territories, which today is about 35 square miles in Idaho and 105 square miles in Montana. When all three territories were given statehood in the 1890s, legal jurisdiction of the entire park was exclusively ceded to the federal government, more specially, the U.S. District Court of Wyoming. As a result, two small slivers of Idaho and Montana now fell under the jurisdiction of another state's district, the only such instance across the entire nation. The Idaho part of the park was uninhabited, while the Montana portion had just a few dozen residents. As a result, it would be nearly impossible to form a jury in the event of a trial.

This jurisdictional phenomenon violated the rights guaranteed to citizens by the Sixth Amendment. In Kalt's opinion, it created a theoretically lawless zone where no major crime could be successfully prosecuted. At first, the professor didn't seem too worried about his discovery. He wrote a somewhat satirical journal article that mixed humor with a discussion of constitutional law.

"Say that you are in the Idaho portion of Yellowstone, and you decide to spice up your vacation by going on a crime spree," wrote Kalt, who described a cartoonish state-line crook. "You make some moonshine, you poach some wildlife, you strangle some people and steal their picnic baskets."

Titled "The Perfect Crime," the article was accepted by the *Georgetown Law Journal* for an early 2005 issue. Prior to publication, Kalt sent a letter and copy of the essay to the House and Senate Judiciary Committee, the Department of Justice, and the U.S. Attorney's Office in Cheyenne.

"The courts may or may not agree that my loophole exists," wrote Kalt. "If the loophole described in this Essay does exist it should be closed, not ignored."

Kalt was quite satisfied by his "carefully crafted arguments." As he later admitted, he was also naïve. He figured, in short order, the 109th Congress would see the wisdom of his claims and enact a simple fix. But as the months dragged on, and Kalt received no replies, he began to worry.

After his article revealed a so-called "zone of death" to the world, would ruthless lawbreakers flock to the roadless wilds of Yellowstone? Disregarding the fact that most career criminals don't read academic journals, there was some precedence here. In fact, over a century before, America's national park experiment had gone from idyllic preserve to shockingly lawless almost overnight.

A Landscape Like No Other

In 1805 and 1806, the Lewis and Clark expedition passed through the Northern Plains and Rocky Mountains on their way to and from the Pacific Ocean. Along the way, they encountered tribal members and French trappers who told of a great southern tributary to the Missouri. Supposedly the name came from a Minnetaree expression meaning "yellow rock" or "yellow stone." This possibly referred to the color of bluffs on the lower river or a dramatic place near the headwaters. That region was said to be filled with wonders, rich stocks of wildlife, and, incredibly, a fuming volcano. In this area, a gushing river plunged over a 300-foot water-fall between brightly colored cliffs. Later it was named the Grand Canyon of the Yellowstone.

For decades after the Louisiana Purchase, this region remained little explored by Americans. The occasional mountain man might return with mystifying tales about a hidden plateau surrounded by peaks. Abundant wildlife grazing amid a landscape of fire and brimstone. Boiling springs. Steaming vents gouged into the Earth. Geysers erupting high into the sky. The stories were dismissed as tall tales, and few investigated until after the Civil War.

By the early 1870s, word had gotten out. Yellowstone was a landscape like no other. Geologist Ferdinand Hayden led the first government survey to investigate a growing proposal: a national park to preserve this remarkable landscape for the people of a reunified nation. Among the team of fifty was a promising landscape painter named Thomas Moran, whose dramatic illustrations would galvanize the movement.

Hayden and his surveyors were equally awed by what they saw. With limited time in the field, they were uncertain about the full extent of the geothermal features. So, in his report to Congress, Hayden estimated a rectangle, without regard to territorial lines, that hopefully contained all the geothermal features. The northern boundary was where the Gardner River entered the Yellowstone River. The western edge was ten miles past Shoshone Lake. The southern and eastern lines were ten miles from the edges of Yellowstone Lake.

While the precise boundaries would later be amended to better follow the terrain, it was Hayden's original arbitrary borders that would give rise to a twenty-first-century obsession called the *zone of death*. But first, the Wild West came to Yellowstone.

Haven for Crime

Due to the lean federal budgets following the Civil War, the Forty-Second Congress was willing to establish a public park in the headwaters of the Yellowstone River, but they weren't willing to fund it. The bill presented a tract of land, withdrawn from settlement, that could be managed at no cost to the federal government. Any future operating expenses would come from fees paid by park concessions, such as restaurants, hotels, and tour companies who served the guests.

The one exception to congressional frugality was the authorization of a second Hayden survey to better map and inventory the new park. Yellowstone's first superintendent was essentially an absentee volunteer who would enter the confines just twice. But at least he was allowed to tag along with Hayden. In the superintendent's few reports to the government, he offered a series of recommendations. Regulations were needed to protect the wildlife from poachers and the forests from logging and careless fires. A series of access roads, laid out like a figure-eight, could take visitors to the park's natural attractions. Eventually, he proposed a federal agency or service should be created to protect this new national park. All requests were declined.

Meanwhile, the remote Yellowstone remained almost inaccessible, save for jolting stagecoach trips across unimproved paths. During the first five years, less than 500 annual visitors made it to the park. Those who did found themselves the occasional targets of highway robbers. A new message got out: Yellowstone was a great place to get away with things.

In those early days, the most common crimes were vandalism and poaching. In pursuit of souvenirs, tourists might take a hammer to a sparkling mineral formation surrounding a hot spring pool. Fishermen tossed dynamite into Trout Lake and collected the cutthroats that floated to the surface. Elsewhere in the park, sport hunters indiscriminately shot anything they came across—birds, antelopes, bighorn sheep, bears. Hide hunters slaughtered elk by the thousands, taking only the tongues and skins. Left behind were vast fields of carcasses and branching antlers.

The Secretary of the Interior, who now oversaw the park, was slow to react to the alarming reports from the West. In the late 1870s, Congress authorized a meager park appropriation. Now a salaried superintendent lived on-site, overseeing an ambitious road building campaign on a shoestring budget. In the early 1880s, a lone game warden was hired to protect the wildlife. This first national park ranger resigned after a year, reporting that an entire police force was needed for the task.

Then the Northern Pacific Railroad arrived in 1883, and the bad situation worsened. A spur line was built to Cinnabar, a town twelve miles north of Mammoth Hot Springs. Petty outlaws began to gather. Most had been run out of nearby rough-and-tumble towns by vigilance committees. Others had heard about the lawless opportunity. Tourist luggage began to go missing. Visitors' horses vanished, only to be returned by suspicious characters seeking rewards. Accusations of cheating caused card games to erupt into violence. Some miscreants took up residence in park buildings during the offseason. Other squatters built illegal ranches in the northeast corner of the park. Their hope was that growing criticisms of Yellowstone, both regionally and in Washington, might lead to a repealing of the national park and a reopening of the tract for settlement.

Due to the railroad, visitation steadily increased during the final decades of the nineteenth century. Not all tourists behaved themselves. Red hot embers flew with the wind from unattended campfires, and blazes spread through the forests. Illegal specimen collecting was common throughout the park, including fossils, petrified wood, sulfur crystals, and volcanic glass. To test the power of geysers like Old Faithful, tourists tossed trash, soap, and timber into the cone and waited for the eruption. When the rising fountain sent the foaming debris sky high, the spectators let out a cheer. Park staff, now expanded to a meager ten assistants, shuddered. Signs were erected that forbid these deeds, but, without enforcement, the rules were meaningless.

Send in the Cavalry

The first attempt at imposing law and order failed. Late in the summer of 1884, with the superintendent's support, the Territory of Wyoming assumed jurisdiction of the park. The governor appointed two justices of the peace, two constables, and a force of deputies. But the way the enforcers were paid proved to be a major problem. Half of all fees assessed against offenders would go to the territorial treasury. The other half went to the arresting officers. The result was selective enforcement of laws against those who were easy to catch and could pay the most fees. Wealthy tourists might be hauled before the judge for leaving a single warm coal in an otherwise extinguished fire pit. Meanwhile, most bigger crimes went unchallenged. After two years, the plan was abandoned.

That's when the U.S. Army marched in. Fifty cavalry soldiers established a fort at Mammoth Hot Springs, and the captain took over as superintendent. Change, however, took time. A pair of wildlife conservation acts, in 1894 and 1900, were critical steps to stop the poachers, thieves, and vandals. But Yellowstone was a big park, and the army couldn't be everywhere at all times.

In 1908, a single bandit held up a string of tourist wagons during their trip along Grand Loop, about five miles from Old Faithful. Cavalry soldiers were sent in pursuit, but the thief escaped on foot through dense forest and was never found.

"The entire United States Army would be needed to assure travelers in the Yellowstone National Park against any possibility of a holdup," said General Edgerly.

The act was described in newspapers as the most daring robbery in criminal history, and this unofficial title lasted for six years until an even bigger robbery in 1914. A clever crook positioned himself at a bend in the Grand Loop Road, near Shoshone Point, where the drivers of twenty-five tourist wagons couldn't see one another. Reports indicated nearly two hundred tourists lost several thousand dollars in money and valuables. This time the mastermind was caught. Ed Trafton of Teton Valley was called the last of the stagecoach robbers.

Except, the same thing more or less happened again in 1915. Twelve stages were robbed near the Firehole River. This time it *was* the last. Only because, in 1916, the park banned stagecoaches to pave the way for automobile travel. After twenty-two years of U.S. Army occupation, control of the park was handed over to the newly created National Park Service.

DON'T BECOME A TOURON

Throughout its 150-year existence, Yellowstone has developed a reputation for bad tourist behavior. Every year, foolish visitors are injured after approaching wildlife too closely, increasingly to take selfies with these creatures. This is not a zoo, and there are no cages. Sometimes these wild animals defend themselves by charging or kicking the person invading their space. Occasionally, these animals have to be euthanized, meaning what seems like a goofy prank is actually leading to a protected animal's death. The park service requires that visitors stay at least one hundred yards away from bears and wolves and twenty-five yards away from all other animals, including bison. For the best views, bring a pair of binoculars or a camera with a telephoto lens.

In recent years, car accidents in the park have increased. Some drivers speed along park roads in an effort to see it all. Other drivers slam on the brakes in the roadway upon spotting wildlife. Please drive cautiously and only stop if there's a suitable pullout. To protect both visitors and the fragile hydrothermal features, no swimming or soaking is allowed in park hot springs. The water in these springs often reaches boiling temperatures and can be highly acidic and contain dangerous microorganisms. Every year, several park visitors ignore these warnings and become severely burned or even die due to illegally entering hydrothermal features.

The popular Instagram account Tourons of Yellowstone collects photos and videos of dangerous behavior from throughout the park. Sadly, they never seem to run out of something to post. Perhaps the greatest mystery at Yellowstone is why so many tourons keep supplying new material.

Tabloid Hypothetical

During the spring of 2005, while Professor Kalt eagerly awaited replies from government officials, he instead received a different type of response. After posting "The Perfect Crime" on the Social Science Research Network, an online repository for scholarly papers, the article earned a favorable review on the *Volokh Conspiracy*, a libertarian legal blog. Suddenly, a swell of interest from bloggers and journalists briefly elevated Kalt's article to the most downloaded constitutional law paper in SSRN history.

Next came news coverage and interviews with the *Washington Post, BBC News, All Things Considered* on NPR, and local media. Kalt was invited to give a public lecture in Brooklyn, hosted by comedian John Hodgman, a future correspondent for *The Daily Show with Jon Stewart*.

"I've concluded that there are two kinds of people who think about how to commit the perfect crime," said Kalt, in the opening line of his monologue. "There are sociopaths, who worry about how to do it, and there are neurotics, who worry about the sociopaths... I come at this subject from the neurotic's point of view."

Six months after the *National Enquirer* tabloid newspaper covered "Yellowstone's Perfect Crime Spot," Kalt received an email from a bestselling Wyoming author. C. J. Box was planning to use the zone of death as a plot device in the seventh installment of his Joe Pickett detective series. The story opens with a smug lawyer walking into a remote Yellowstone ranger station and surrendering his still-warm firearms. He flippantly confesses he just murdered four campers at Robinson Lake, in the Idaho portion of the park. The lawyer is freed by chapter three, due to Kalt's loophole. Published in May 2007, *Free Fire* was a major hit among readers.

By now, Kalt had received some mixed responses to his 2005 government inquiries. The Department of Justice (DOJ) and Senate Judiciary Committee never replied, while the U.S. Attorney claimed that he was powerless to amend the law. But a staffer for the House Judiciary Committee started a discussion by email, until the address became invalid. The staffer had been a summer intern instructed to hunt for counterarguments.

So, Kalt sent more letters to over thirty U.S. representatives and senators, including his local Michigan delegation. He even attended a talk by one senator on the Judiciary Committee. Afterward, as Kalt describes it, he "handed the senator a copy of the article and muttered something about people getting killed and downloads on the Internet." The senator thanked him and turned away.

The lone reply came from a staffer for a U.S. senator for Michigan, who said the office of a U.S. senator from Idaho was investigating. Kalt never learned if they did. Meanwhile, an Idaho Falls reporter obtained comments from Idaho Congressman Mike Simpson. He was skeptical, believing the judicial system would prevail.

The only meaningful correspondence on the topic came in 2007 from a fan of C. J. Box. After learning about the issue depicted in *Free Fire*, U.S. Senator Mike Enzi of Wyoming inquired with the Department of Justice. The senator's assistant invited Kalt to respond to the DOJ's position that the jurisdictional situation amounted to a "harmless error." No federal court, they claimed, would allow an accused murderer to simply go free due to a minor jurisdictional issue. Clearly, officials were not concerned by an obscure hypothetical. What was needed was a real case that tested the so-called zone of death.

A Loophole Remains?

That summer, Kalt got his wish in the form of poacher Mike Belderrain. He was caught red-handed in the illegal killing of an elk, not a person. But the federal charges still warranted a jury trial to decide the verdict and punishment. Given the media attention surrounding the now-infamous zone of death, plus Yellowstone's history of crime, it seemed only a matter of time before a defense attorney played the card and a criminal walked free.

"While Mr. Belderrain acknowledges that standing on his Constitutional right to Montana vicinage makes it inconvenient to prosecute him..." read the lawyer's motion. "If the only practical solution is for the Court to dismiss the charges, so it must be..."

The judge studied the motion, and afterward Kalt studied the case. The legal scholar believed the court had limited options to let the action continue: (1) order a trial somewhere in Montana; (2) order that the jury must come from the few dozen residents inside the Montana portion; (3) do both; or (4) declare that a Wyoming trial and jury somehow did not violate the Constitution. Such a decision would set a precedent for future cases, and hopefully close the zone of death forever.

"For practical purposes, any cause of action occurring within Yellowstone National Park, whether in Wyoming, Idaho, or Montana, must result in a jury trial in the District of Wyoming," wrote the judge, in a simple decision. "To adopt a different position would create a virtual no man's land. Since there is no case law that states otherwise, this Court must dismiss Defendant's objection to a Wyoming jury panel."

According to the judge, Kalt's article was "interesting" but "esoteric" and of "little practical value."

Well, that was that. A contrite Belderrain went to federal prison for three years, saying that he deserved it. In his plea deal, he agreed not to appeal his sentence based on the so-called "zone of death" loophole. Kalt claimed this verdict simply kicked the can down the road. Someday, the theory might reappear and be used to free a killer. This time, the victim could be an unlucky person on the outskirts of Yellowstone.

The Zone of Death Lingers

Throughout the following decades, the legend proved firmly established. During the pandemic year of 2020, an attractive young woman named Gabby Petito went missing while documenting her van life on social media. As a ground search commenced, homebound internet sleuths launched a campaign of viral posts. Why wasn't anyone looking in the zone of death? Sadly, Petito's strangled body was recovered near a dispersed camping area in Bridger-Teton National Forest, southeast of Yellowstone.

As the law closed in, the decomposing corpse of her suspected murderer was found in a flooded wildlife refuge in Florida. Her fiancé, Brian Laundrie, had shot himself. His waterlogged journal dubiously claimed a mercy killing, but those reading between the lines saw a guilt-stricken attempt to exonerate himself.

And so, the zone of death is still out there. The tales continue to circulate, from late night campfires and mountain hiking trails to numerous podcasts and online articles. The claims are no longer qualified maybes. Now people confidently declare, with a mischievous smirk, that this lawless land definitely exists.

A sinister place in the first national park where murder is legal. Or maybe it isn't.

CHAPTER 11

HOW WAS *HEAVEN'S GATE* NAMED ONE OF THE WORST *AND* BEST FILMS OF ALL TIME?

HIDDEN HISTORY

GLACIER NATIONAL PARK

ROCKY MOUNTAINS, MONTANA

Rain was turning to sleet as the limousines lined up along Third Avenue in New York City. Umbrellas flapped as celebrities hustled inside Cinema I and II. It was the evening of November 19, 1980, and the marquee outside the theater announced the long-awaited premiere of Michael Cimino's *Heaven's Gate*.

Just like the chaotic Montana production of this Western epic, the event was not without incident. Earlier in the day, actor Kris Kristofferson ducked inside a dressing room to change and discovered he had no suit pants. Like all things with *Heaven's Gate*, a minor issue quickly spiraled into the latest crisis until a pair was

retrieved. Now the lead actor sat with covered legs next to his co-stars Isabelle
Huppert, Christopher Walken, and Jeff Bridges.

Suddenly, there was another commotion in a nearby row. Some guy had hit
his girlfriend. In an instant, the abuser was being pummeled by the burly Richard
Donner, who recently had directed Christopher Reeves in *Superman*. Ushers in
tuxedos dragged the mangled boyfriend outside, and the event began.

The film opens with a prologue set during Harvard graduation day in 1870.
Naturally, the fortysomething actors depict their twentysomething selves. There
are speeches. There are drunken celebrations. There is a beautifully choreographed
sequence with waltzing and a marching band.

This went on for seventeen minutes, during which the audience grew increasingly restless. The film was not landing well. Before the first act was over, usher
Don Winslow passed through the lobby. He later claimed to witness a lone man
with his face in his hands.

"What am I going to do?" the man supposedly muttered. It was director
Michael Cimino.

On screen, the film shifts to Montana in 1890. The story loosely follows a
highly fictionalized version of the Johnson County War, set amid the stunning
landscape around Glacier National Park. In Cimino's version, an association of
wealthy cattle barons hire mercenaries to murder 125 poor Eastern European settlers for encroaching on the public range and occasionally stealing livestock to feed
their starving families.

Kristofferson plays a hard-drinking U.S. marshal who sides with the common
folk against his fellow Ivy-League kind. Walken is an eccentric hired gunslinger,
who wears a distracting amount of eyeliner while assassinating the occasional
homesteader. Eventually, Walken's character begins to tepidly question the moral-
ity of his employers. Huppert is a frontier madam in love with both men, who
constantly vie for her attention. Finally, Bridges runs a social hall and roller-skating
rink named Heaven's Gate.

Much of the film's first two hours—out of a total running time of three hours and thirty-nine minutes—is about establishing the characters and building the love triangle. The setting is the frontier town of Sweetwater, amid a beautiful background of snow-covered mountains, grassy meadows, and alpine lakes. There's also a real cock fight, a five-minute roller-skating sequence accompanied by a skilled teenage fiddler, and a game of old-timey baseball with little bearing on the plot.

For the audience, about halfway through the premiere, there was a ten-minute intermission. While a group of executives argued in the lobby, the subdued attendees mostly skipped the free champagne. When Cimino wondered why they weren't drinking, the publicist supposedly gave a pointed reply.

"Because they hate the movie, Michael."

Some guests slipped out the door before a diminished crowd filed back to their seats and the film resumed. In one scene, as the mercenary army slowly approaches the town, the marshal gathers everyone at the social hall to share the kill list. Kristofferson doesn't read all 125 names during this four-minute scene, but many in the audience sure felt like he did. On screen, the equally enraged townsfolk then rush off to fight back against the invaders, which occupies the final hour or so.

During a somber epilogue, a lone person laughed. As the credits rolled, the sound of people rushing for the exits was louder than the few polite claps. When the disappointed viewers emerged onto the sidewalk, they discovered the theater manager had already removed the director's name and movie title from the marquee.

An "Unqualified Disaster"

Almost immediately, critics eviscerated the film.

"A series of unconnected, hopelessly confusing scenes," wrote Kathleen Carroll for the *New York Daily News*. Given the soundtrack's street noises and mandolin-heavy score, she found it nearly impossible to hear the dialogue.

"I thought it was easy to see what to cut," wrote Pauline Kael in the *New Yorker*. "But when I tried afterward to think of what to keep, my mind went blank." She pointed out that the actual number of casualties in the historical conflict were limited, but Cimino turned it into "a shoot-'em-up holocaust."

STARING AT THE SUN

Glacier National Park doesn't mess around when it comes to blinding scenery. Towering peaks dominate this remote 1,600-square-mile landscape. Rugged forests and valley meadows are home to wildlife such as elk, bighorn sheep, grizzly bears, and the iconic white furry mountain goats. Nestled in rocky basins are alpine lakes with turquoise waters due to glacial till.

Regarding the park's namesake feature, the glaciers are sadly disappearing due to climate change. Researchers believe that during the century prior to the park's designation in 1910, there were around eighty. Today, about two dozen named glaciers remain.

Most visitors focus on a driving tour along the famous Going-to-the-Sun Road. This scenic mountain road traverses the park's interior for fifty miles, crossing the Continental Divide at 6,646-foot Logan Pass. An alternative to private vehicles is a guided Red Bus Tour in the popular "Jammers," classic 1930s motor coaches.

Also popular is hiking on over 700 miles of trails, with easier options around the park villages and harder routes leading high into the backcountry. Various whitewater rafting trips can be found on the Middle and North Forks of the Flathead River. There's camping, backpacking, horseback riding, fishing, and more. Located in a remote corner of Montana, this is a classic national park that feels far from civilization.

In the *New York Times*, Vincent Canby called it "pretentious" and an "unqualified disaster" that felt "like a forced, four-hour walking tour of one's own living room." Canby went on to reference Cimino's previous film, which had won

Academy Awards in 1979 for Best Director and Best Picture. "*Heaven's Gate...* fails so completely, that you might suspect Mr. Cimino sold his soul to the Devil to obtain the success of the *The Deer Hunter*, and the Devil has come around to collect."

The film became a laughingstock in newspapers and TV programs across the country. A week later, Michael Cimino placed a full-page letter in the *Hollywood Reporter* apologizing to United Artists's president, Andy Albeck. The disgraced director requested *Heaven's Gate* be withdrawn from theaters so he could reedit the film. The studio agreed. Though a revised film did return to theaters in April 1981, at a more palatable running time of 149 minutes, the damage already was done.

Few moviegoers went to see the recut picture, and the production lost nearly $40 million. A financially struggling United Artists had to be sold. Hollywood soon shifted away from director-driven projects toward an era when producers would dictate the types of formulaic movies that were made. Receiving nearly universal condemnation, *Heaven's Gate* would come to be called one of worst films ever made.

Only a few critics protested, many of them in Europe.

Cimino's effort was unfairly judged, some said.

A cult classic, said others.

A forgotten masterpiece, was an eventual claim.

In 2015, thirty-five years after its original release, BBC Culture named *Heaven's Gate* number 98 on a list of the 100 greatest American films. This wasn't the typical simplistic Hollywood story. How had the same film been named one of the worst and one of the best of all time?

An Outright Lie?

In the early 1970s, after years of making TV commercials and writing scripts, Michael Cimino got his first big break with *Thunderbolt and Lightfoot*. Clint Eastwood agreed to star, and he wanted Cimino to direct. The film was a hit. A raucous and comedic crime caper mixed with a scenic Mountain West road pic. A charismatic newcomer named Jeff Bridges stole the show.

Cimino's next stint as writer and director came with the 1978 epic *The Deer Hunter*, starring Robert De Niro. The film follows three Russian–American friends, steel workers from a Pennsylvania town, who enlist for the Vietnam War. A lengthy opening act includes compelling factory and bar scenes, the pageantry of an orthodox wedding, and a deer hunting trip to some gorgeous mountains that look much more like Montana than Pennsylvania. Then the story shifts to Vietnam. There, the trio is captured by the Viet Cong and forced to play Russian roulette against each other. They escape, but this traumatic experience disrupts each of their lives in unique and haunting ways.

Audiences were floored by the emotionally wrenching scenes and graphic depictions of violence. Critics compared it to acclaimed films like *The Godfather* by Francis Ford Coppola. *The Deer Hunter* won five Oscars, and Cimino was heralded as the newest motion picture auteur.

But not all reactions were positive. Many viewers assumed the story was based on real events from the controversial war, which had ended in defeat only a few years prior. Perhaps the brutal events had been uncovered by the director. After all, he'd claimed in interviews that during his military service he was a medic attached to a Green Beret unit. The characters, he said, were based on people he knew. Some observers debated whether the film was anti-war and ironic, as many first assumed, or earnestly pro-war. Others complained that depicting Vietnamese soldiers as sadistic torturers was racist. Veterans said there was no evidence the Vietnamese forced American POWs to play Russian roulette.

The mercurial director didn't help his case much. Known for providing inconsistent personal information, including changing details about his upbringing and true age, he responded with a mix of qualifications and defensiveness. No, he had not been deployed to Vietnam during his six-month service. He was stationed in New Jersey and Texas. But almost anything that could be imagined about the Vietnam War might have happened. It wasn't ironic, nor racist. It was a film of the heart. A film about the courage of ordinary people. The specific details of the war were unimportant because the film is fictional, not meant to be realistic but surrealistic. Many of the critics who had been so enamored now felt embarrassed or duped. A central element of the film was an outright lie, some critics complained. Others began to regret their effusive praise.

Bigger than Lunch

By this point, Cimino was already hard at work with United Artists on his next film about the Johnson County War. Principal photography began in mid-April 1979 in Montana with a budget just under $12 million. Given his recent success, Cimino basically had been given free rein, and his typical perfectionist tendencies intensified. Almost immediately, the production became legendary for chaos and controversy.

With permission from the park service, the frontier town of Sweetwater was constructed on the eastern shore of dramatic Two Medicine Lake in Glacier National Park. Once built, it was said Cimino found the main street too narrow. He insisted it be entirely torn down and both sides moved back three feet each to maintain symmetry with the scenery.

Cimino personally oversaw the costuming of hundreds of extras, often arranging them in scenes as if he were painting with people. He required dozens of takes, around thirty per scene. For one story beat in particular—when Kristofferson is woken from a drunken stupor by townsfolk and responds by cracking a whip—the director demanded fifty-two takes.

By the sixth day, the production was already five days behind schedule. Cimino had spent nearly $1 million to shoot 60,000 feet of film, of which he deemed only a minute and a half to be usable. After two weeks, they were ten days behind. When the young executives at United Artists did the math, they realized the film wasn't just going over budget. It was on track to become the most expensive picture ever made, surpassing 1963's *Cleopatra* starring Elizabeth Taylor.

When these young execs saw the raw footage, they did agree that it was breathtaking. But they also recognized the financials were unsustainable. They had recently been elevated during a studio shakeup, and reining in the intense director proved a challenge. They repeatedly pleaded with and threatened Cimino, who reluctantly agreed to speed up the shoot and reduce costs. Yet, much like the nineteenth-century steam locomotive that Cimino rented from a museum in Denver, the production rolled onward with furious momentum.

The actors called it "Camp Cimino." They took horseback-riding lessons. Gun-shooting lessons. Slavic dialect lessons. Dancing lessons. Roller-skating lessons. Cockfighting lessons. Most of them seemed impressed by the director's fanatical attention to detail. He cared about getting it right.

Those on the crew didn't always feel the same. Though they were earning plenty of overtime, the demands were exhausting. During one morning shoot, the cameras lost the sunlight when overcast clouds drifted overhead. Cimino decided to wait it out. By 3:00 p.m., people were hungry, so one assistant bravely asked about lunch.

"Lunch?" a dazed Cimino supposedly said. "This is bigger than lunch."

In mid-June, the NPS superintendent of Glacier kicked the production out of the park. He referenced numerous violations of the permit. At Two Medicine Lake, the crew had covered the parking lot with soil containing non-native weeds. They brought in trees to use as props without the park's knowledge. They trampled sensitive areas that had been roped off. Staining oils, used to give the constructed buildings a weather-beaten look, had washed into the lake.

At Many Glacier, an area known for dangerous grizzly bear encounters, a ranger caught crewmembers slaughtering three live cows so cameras could capture the blood and guts. Actions such as these would later lead to protests of *Heaven's Gate*. As a result, the Screen Actors Guild would require that future film productions be monitored by welfare experts and include the disclaimer: "No animals were harmed in the making of this film."

With permission withdrawn to shoot inside the park, including a baseball sequence next to the North Fork Flathead River, the production shifted to private lands nearby. Meanwhile, the NPS superintendent issued a list of required restorations. A defiant Cimino publicly disputed the accusations, yet still ordered and paid for the cleanup. The locals seemed split, with some decrying the environ-mental damage and others appreciating the economic boost to the nearby town of Kalispell.

The extras, who numbered over 1,200 by the end of the picture, also had complaints. One man from Whitefish, Montana, wrote a letter to the *Great Falls Tribune*. He and his wife and children had joined the production on day one. His letter referenced fifteen- to seventeen-hour days and dangerous conditions. Extras rode atop the historical train cars without restraints. Extras were left standing for hours in blowing snow. Extras regularly begged for bathroom breaks, refreshments, and better conditions. Extras were thrown from horse-drawn carts or run over by the wheels. Extras were quitting in disgust, including the Whitefish man's entire family, after he and his wife were hit by a runaway horse.

SLICE OF HEAVEN

If you want to visit places that appear in the movie *Heaven's Gate*, your best option is to make your way to Two Medicine Lake. The fictional town of Sweetwater was built atop a parking lot on the eastern shore, to the south of the historic general store. Other scenes were shot around the stunning Many Glacier region of the park. Important to note, both of these areas can be reached on entirely paved roads.

The climactic battlefield sequence was shot in the far north-western corner of the park, somewhere southwest of Kintla Lake. This is a remote area reached only by rugged dirt roads along the North Fork of the Flathead River. If you manage to get out there, it may be best to forget about the movie and just focus on the adventure.

An Undercover Extra

That's around the time that freelance journalist Les Gapay took an interest. After a career at the *Sacramento Bee* and *Wall Street Journal*, he'd left behind the newsroom grind to run his own cherry orchard in Montana. Since the film was closed to the press, Gapay hired on as an extra to observe. He discovered that the director had earned a nickname on set. Ayatollah Cimino—a perfectionist obsessed with every detail.

"That extra had a cigar yesterday," Cimino might say.

"That woman needs a wedding ring."

"Get that guy some glasses."

Wearing jeans and a scarf, Cimino would quietly relay his orders to an assistant who used a megaphone to call "Action!" During the roller-skating scene, the heat inside the social hall tent got so bad, one extra hid ice packs under his hat. Amid the weeklong shoot of the cockfighting scene, the crew wore surgical masks to combat the smoke. Supposedly, the roosters got more breaks than the humans.

"Cimino interviewed 300 horses for this film," one extra joked.

Even Gapay got trampled by a horse. The X-ray showed a crushed toe, and his days as an undercover extra were over. The journalist's article came out in early September. "An Unauthorized Progress Report on *Heaven's Gate*" was read in earnest around the country. The fickle public was on notice. *Heaven's Gate* wasn't just an expensive Western by a cocky newcomer. It was the costliest shit show in history.

Recuts and a Cult

Production ended in Montana on the second day of October. Since Harvard had refused permission to film the prologue there, Cimino traveled to Oxford the following March. Against the English university's wishes, one night his folks from Hollywood secretly laid down dirt over the asphalt. At dawn, they filmed Kristofferson running across the courtyard for the film's opening scene.

By the end of shooting, about $30 million had been spent. The budget was on its way to five times the original estimate. Cimino had shot over 220 hours of film, which had to be reduced to about three hours in length. He locked himself in the editing room and posted an armed guard outside. In late June, the United Artists execs arrived at the MGM theater for a private screening.

"The final version will probably be fifteen minutes shorter," said an exhausted Cimino, before rolling the film.

The first cut ran for five hours and twenty-five minutes. While much of the footage was certainly beautiful, the final battle scene alone ran for around ninety minutes. At the producers' insistence, Cimino worked with editors over the next five months to shorten the length to five hours, then four and a half, and eventually the three hours and forty-five minutes that were shown at the New York premiere. After that version flopped, Cimino kept cutting it down to about two and half hours. But the April re-release performed no better with a public that had already made up its mind.

For all intents and purposes, Michael Cimino's career was over after three films. Many observers said that he deserved the comeuppance, given his perceived untruthfulness with regards to *The Deer Hunter*. A scant few supporters claimed it was a case of savage mob mentality sinking an imperfect but otherwise rewarding delight. While Cimino would go on to make the occasional smaller-budget film, these rarely received much attention.

In the late 1990s, even the title *Heaven's Gate* would be further tainted when it was co-opted by a bizarre cult from Southern California. The choice in name seemed unrelated to the film, but the parallels felt about right. Led by a strange bald man with wide eyes named Marshall Applewhite, the cult members believed they could shed their corporeal bodies and allow their souls to ascend on an extrater-restrial UFO to a heaven amid the stars. In San Diego, during March 1997, thirty-nine of the cult members committed mass suicide by taking phenobarbital with applesauce and vodka. Then they put plastic bags over their heads and asphyxiated.

The cult's timing coincided with the nearest approach of comet Hale-Bopp, which they believed would carry them to the next level in human evolution. A few weeks later, the TV show *Saturday Night Live* parodied the dead cult members in a skit that imagined them reaching outer space. Henceforth, the term "Heaven's Gate" would evolve as a term of ridicule. Now it wasn't associated with a maniacal movie director but with a maniacal cult leader and his band of sheepish and oddly smiling followers.

Michael Cimino died in 2016 at the age of seventy-seven. During the final decade of his life, the film *Heaven's Gate* underwent a radical reappraisal.

"Time has been kind," declared the *New York Times*.

"A masterpiece," agreed others.

Perhaps the greatest Western of all time? Well, let's not get ahead of ourselves.

Four years before he died, Cimino oversaw the release of a remastered version of *Heaven's Gate,* which he said restored his original vision. The long-banished director was invited to attend a showing at the Venice Film Festival. As the credits rolled on this unique film—oddly touted as one of best *and* worst of all time—the audience rose to their feet. Michael Cimino finally received what he'd hoped for decades before: a standing ovation.

CHAPTER 12

WHY DID THE CLIFF DWELLERS ABANDON THEIR STONE PALACES?

BAFFLING DISAPPEARANCES

MESA VERDE NATIONAL PARK

SAN JUAN BASIN, SOUTHWEST COLORADO

Snow was falling in large flakes as the two cowboys rode north across the mesa. Visibility was poor, so they followed some tracks winding through powder-dusted stands of scraggly pinyon and juniper. Stray cattle belonging to the Wetherill family's Alamo Ranch had wandered off with wild cattle typically hunted by the Utes. It was December 18, 1888, and their horses were panting from breaking trail through snowdrifts and prickly underbrush.

Coming upon a precipice, the men dismounted to rest their animals. Richard Wetherill and his brother-in-law Charlie Mason walked out on a bare bluff. The snowfall was thinning, which afforded them a stunning view of the Mesa Verde country. To one side was a narrow ravine, which joined a larger chasm with sheer cliffs of gray and gold sandstone. A half mile across the wider canyon was a vast alcove with overhanging bedrock streaked by desert varnish.

"Look at that," blurted Wetherill, grasping his partner's arm.

Inside the massive alcove, bathed in overcast light, the ruins of a stone village stood out from the shadows. There were dozens of buildings with angular shapes and black voids for windows. Multistory towers rose toward the cave ceiling. Most walls were intact while others had crumbled. Both men were used to spotting smaller ancestral ruins throughout Mancos Canyon, which wrapped around the eastern and southern edges of Mesa Verde. Those sites had been known to trappers and government surveyors for decades. During their spare time, the cowboys often hunted for relics in the debris mounds.

But this village was much larger than any cliff house they'd ever seen. Forgetting the strays, the men rode around the head of the canyon to a spot overlooking the alcove. After assembling a makeshift rope ladder using tree branches, they climbed down to explore. As they moved throughout the empty village, they left footprints in a thick layer of dust that had accumulated for centuries.

The clues suggested to them a possibly violent end. The roofs were long gone, and the wooden floor beams were mostly missing. Perhaps they'd been used as firewood during a siege? Pottery vessels, including large jars and bowls, rested on ledges and floors. Valuable items like woven sandals and stone hatchets had been left behind. Spotting just a few human bones, the cowboys surmised that the residents had fled in a hurry. With well over a hundred rooms, this was no ordinary village. It was a wealthy enclave, a fortress or castle. So, Wetherill suggested a name that stuck: the Cliff Palace.

Before making camp, the excited cowboys decided to search for more ruins to the north. Splitting up, Mason turned east and found nothing. Wetherill turned west, and, near the top of a wooded gulch, he spotted an alcove. Inside was another dwelling, slightly smaller than Cliff Palace but in even better condition. In front of the cave opening, trees had grown, including a towering one that rose from a stone wall. Wetherill called the ruin Spruce Tree House.

An Unheeded Warning

After camping for the night, Wetherill and Mason resumed searching the next morning. At the edge of Navajo Canyon, they looked down upon a smaller set of ruins with an impressive four-story structure rising against the cliff face: Square Tower House.

On the ride back to town, intent on sharing the news of their find, the incredulous cowboys pondered their discovery and who might have lived in these cliff dwellings. The thirty-year-old Wetherill had some ideas after working the Alamo Ranch for eight years. During the two decades before that, his father Ben had led their large Quaker family across the American frontier, zigzagging from Pennsylvania, through Kansas and Missouri, to Southwest Colorado.

Unlike the majority of white settlers who viewed the Indians as enemies, the Wetherills maintained friendly relations with the native people who were forced onto ever-shrinking reservations. The Alamo Ranch was always open to the Utes, who occupied the lands around Mesa Verde and the lower Mancos River. In return, the Wetherills alone were allowed to graze their cattle unmolested throughout the Utes hunting range.

After a few years, Richard and his four younger brothers built a winter cabin near the junction of Johnson and Mancos Canyons. Nearby was the home of a Ute man named Acowitz, whom they asked about the smaller ruins they'd seen. The stone houses were not built by his ancestors, Acowitz explained. The Utes were a nomadic tribe, who had traveled on horseback and slept in tepees while hunting deer, elk, and antelope. When his people arrived in the region, the ruins had already long been abandoned by an ancient tribe of farmers who cultivated the mesa tops.

One day, Acowitz was visiting the winter cabin when he shared a secret. Hidden deep within the canyons of Mesa Verde, there were stone villages built by the ancient ones, far bigger than those seen by white settlers. Wetherill asked how to find them, but Acowitz shook his head.

"Utes never go there," he said. "It is a sacred place."

Riding away from the cliff palaces, Wetherill now understood. He'd finally seen what Acowitz had been hinting at several years before. Wetherill felt certain that an ancient civilization had vanished, and he wasn't about to let superstitions get in the way of his curiosity. Wetherill had asked more questions, but Acowitz only shook his head. He'd said too much already. Instead, Acowitz offered a final warning.

"I could tell you, but I warn you not to go there. When you disturb the spirits of the dead, then you die too."

Perhaps, in time, Wetherill would regret ignoring the advice. The cowboy was now on a path to becoming a controversial figure—a self-taught archaeologist who would meet a grisly end.

The Relics Rush

News of the Cliff Palace spread quickly from the false-front boomtowns to coastal cities. Eking out a living on the western frontier had always been a tough endeavor. The spreading drifters, the prospectors, the entrepreneurs were always on the lookout for new schemes to get rich. Any commodity was worth a venture, whether it was furs, gold, or ancient pottery. Meanwhile, wealthy tourists were coming by rail, hoping to experience the Wild West before it was gone. Back East, museum curators, university scholars, and private collectors all wanted authentic artifacts to show around.

Due to the timing of their discovery, the Wetherills found themselves at the center of a relics rush. The remote location of Mesa Verde, at the end of an unmarked route across rugged Ute lands, provided the ranching family with a monopoly at the outset. Within days of the discovery, Wetherill, Mason, and several brothers returned to the Cliff Palace with shovels. During that first year, when their ranching obligations allowed, the family explored over 180 cliff dwellings, carefully collecting anything of value. Among the best finds were intact pottery with a characteristic black-on-white design of geometric lines and shapes. In one ruin, they found numerous mugs, including three hanging from a yucca rope, so they named it Mug House.

Other relics included buckskin clothing, woven blankets, and baskets. Pieces of shell jewelry that must have come from the coast. Arrows with knapped stone tips. Bows with strings of twisted sinews. Grinding stones. Refuse mounds with corncobs and squash rinds. Whole and broken pottery—the smallest pieces would be called *sherds*. The more they looked, the more human bones they found. Some skulls were intact while others had been bludgeoned with stone weapons. On occasion, the Wetherills unearthed complete mummies, with weathered skin and frayed clothing preserved by the dry air and cool temperatures inside the alcoves.

Like all settlers in the region, the Wetherills' goal was to turn a profit. Yet they recognized the cultural significance and scientific value of a place like Mesa Verde. So, they sought to conduct their business differently from the typical tourists and pot hunters who were scavenging the Southwest. Sunday picnic parties regularly visited the ruins for souvenir hunts. More destructive looters would ravage a dwelling, knocking down walls, tossing aside building stones, and crushing more artifacts than they recovered. After hurrying back to town for a quick sale to the highest bidder, they went out to do it again.

Instead, the Wetherills wanted to protect the relics from private scavenging by selling their collections to public museums. Then citizens could view the artifacts, and experts could study them to unravel what had happened to the cliff dwellers. In late 1889, Ben Wetherill began sending letters to the director of the Smithsonian Institution. The family hoped to continue their collecting under an official partnership with the national museum, seeking direction in proper practices. Furthermore, the letters referenced a growing movement. Since the creation of Yellowstone Park in the 1870s, observers increasingly proposed that the ancient ruins of the Southwest be protected in some type of national preserve or outdoor museum. Mesa Verde should become such a national park.

The response from Washington bureaucrats was not what the family had hoped. William Pierpont Langley, director of the Smithsonian, sent a supportive reply about the Wetherills' efforts, but he didn't have the budget to act. He forwarded the letter to John Wesley Powell, the director of the Bureau of Ethnology.

Powell forwarded it to his assistant, who forwarded it to William Henry Holmes, the director of the Smithsonian's nascent division for field archaeology.

In his reply, Holmes explained he'd been part of the U.S. Geological Survey expedition to the San Juan country in 1875, so he was thoroughly acquainted with the Mesa Verde. It was a pity the ruins could not be saved in time, but it would be a Herculean task to preserve the multitude found across the Southwest. If the Wetherills knew how to collect properly, by making descriptive notes and maps about the "place and manner of discovery," then there would be less need for scientific supervision. Perhaps Holmes would send his own party in the near future. In that case, he might desire their services.

In reality, the 1870s government surveyors hadn't come close to the well-concealed Cliff Palace, just like the Wetherills had missed it for years. During the surveys, Holmes had been a young artist and mapmaker who often worked with William Henry Jackson and his photographic division. Each time they passed through, the crews found impressive but smaller dwellings in Mancos Canyon before moving on to other locations.

Ben Wetherill sent several more letters to Holmes and other officials, but no partnership materialized. The father insisted they had kept records of all discoveries, including taking photographs. They could create maps for all prior and future excavations. The family had become quite skilled at finding sites and recovering relics, wrote the father. But without government intervention, they feared the other great ruins of the Southwest would be overrun within a few years.

According to the Wetherills, they never received another word from Holmes. The embittered family was done with the government, and they moved forward by approaching private organizations. Richard Wetherill sold the first Mesa Verde collection to the Colorado State Historical Society, including the mummy of an ancient child, for $3,000. A later collection went to two Minneapolis businessmen who put it on display at the 1893 Chicago World's Fair. Afterward, the exposition was donated to the University of Pennsylvania. Another collection was sold for display at a museum in Denver.

Of course, not all of the Wetherill relics went into these larger collections. Some artifacts were put on sale in a makeshift gallery in their barn near Mancos. Richard and the brothers became famous guides to the ruins for tourists, newspaper reporters, and aspiring scholars. During those early years, the Alamo Ranch became the unofficial hub of archaeology in the San Juan Basin.

Proper Techniques

One memorable visitor was a twenty-three-year-old Swedish aristocrat named Gustaf Nordenskiöld. After taking a university degree in the natural sciences, he'd been diagnosed with tuberculosis. So, in 1891, he embarked upon a world tour to more arid climates, including the American Southwest. Upon learning about the ruins of Mesa Verde, he diverted from Durango to the Alamo Ranch in early July. He planned to explore for a week or so but ended up staying four months.

While the Wetherills showed the visitor the cliff dwellings, the budding scientist shared with his enthusiastic guides the proper techniques for excavation. Start by thoroughly documenting and photographing the untouched scene. Then proceed to excavation using a smaller trowel instead of a crude shovel. Keep track of everything, including the smallest details, whether fire coals or pottery sherds.

The visitor was impressed by the speed at which the Wetherills improved their methods. They led Nordenskiöld to Long House, suggesting that he conduct the initial excavation of the second-largest cliff dwelling at Mesa Verde. He showed his gratitude by naming the area Wetherill Mesa. Nordenskiöld's attention to detail was evident in his field notes, photographs, and interpretations of the ruins. Sadly, the young man would succumb to his illness just four years after leaving. However, before he died, his place in Mesa Verde history was secured by two events.

In 1893, Nordenskiöld published a remarkable book, *The Cliff Dwellers of Mesa Verde.* It would be considered the first scholarly work on the subject, offering generations of archaeologists a glimpse into the past when some major ruins remained untouched. Like other early archaeologists in the Southwest, Nordenskiöld recognized that the cliff dwellers had not vanished without a trace, as many Americans said. Instead, the cliff dwellers seemed to have migrated several hundred miles south. Using a similar architectural style, they built stand-alone pueblos in the Rio Grande Valley of northern New Mexico and around the Little Colorado in Arizona. Other evidence included pottery designs and oral traditions that closely matched the discoveries around Mesa Verde. However, the reason the cliff dwellers left so suddenly and never returned remained elusive.

A second event involving Nordenskiöld inadvertently launched a national movement to preserve Southwestern archaeology. During his excavations, he collected over 600 artifacts for transport to Scandinavia. His shipment was intercepted in Durango, and the visitor was arrested for theft. Yet no law existed to prevent relic collecting on U.S. public lands. The Swede was released, and his artifacts ultimately went on display at the National Museum of Finland.

Americans who had failed to act when their fellow citizens ransacked Southwestern ruins were now incensed that a European had done the same. Calls to save the cliff dwellings and protect ancient artifacts would increase dramatically in the coming years.

A Women's Park

In 1877, an eastern author and newspaper correspondent named Virginia McClurg moved to Colorado Springs. Early the following decade, she began visiting the ruins of Mancos Canyon. Her 1886 party explored north into the lower canyons of Mesa Verde, where they came across several smaller cliff dwellings. Less than a mile southeast of the hidden Cliff Palace, in nearby Soda Canyon, they became perhaps the third known group to enter the medium-sized Balcony House. The memorable experience caused McClurg to devote herself to saving the cliff dwellings. When the state of Colorado gave women the right to vote in 1893, her efforts intensified.

McClurg published numerous articles about the ruins. She traveled the nation, giving lectures about preservation. Ultimately, she enlisted the support of a quarter million members of the General Federation of Women's Clubs, who funded the activist's efforts through numerous small donations. At the turn of the twentieth century, McClurg created the Colorado Cliff Dwellings Association, leading the organization as regent-general until she passed away in 1931. McClurg was an indomitable advocate whose fierceness was legendary, but her idealism and self-righteousness often worked against her.

One of the biggest obstacles to a federal preserve was that the larger cliff dwellings were located on the Ute reservation. So, McClurg met with two tribal leaders, an elder named Ignacio and the prophetic Acowitz. She offered a thirty-year lease on the land surrounding the cliff dwellings, paid to the Utes in annual installments of $300. Such a deal meant yet another removal. At one time, the Utes held legal title to nearly all of western Colorado, but broken treaties had reduced the reservation to several smaller parcels. Trying to assuage her guilt, McClurg offered several concessions that never happened. The Utes could retain grazing and hunting rights, she said, and appoint their own police force to patrol the park.

Ignacio had heard such empty promises before, so he made a counteroffer. Pay the entire $9,000 rent up front. The stunned McClurg left without a deal and slowly pivoted to a new plan. Instead of a Ute park, she began envisioning a park run by women. When congressional support didn't materialize for any type of protection, she partnered with Lucy Peabody, an activist and socialite with Washington connections.

As vice-regent, Peabody offered a much-needed pragmatic approach. The association renewed their offer to the Utes. Now, the stumbling blocks were the men in Washington, where officials refused to consider any concessions made in an unofficial treaty. To rally support, McClurg and Peabody arranged for VIP tours of Mesa Verde. Eastern scientists, archaeologists, journalists, and wealthy donors were awestruck as they explored the ruins with the Wetherill brothers and a new guide named C. B. Kelly. But Washington debates over the details would delay the proposed park for years, as the pillaging of Mesa Verde continued. While Peabody lobbied Congress, McClurg approached the new President Teddy Roosevelt, who was supportive.

By mid-decade, the creation of a national park seemed eminent. Then McClurg made a stunning reversal and withdrew her support for federal control. She insisted that Mesa Verde be transferred to the state of Colorado and the park be managed by her organization, the Colorado Cliff Dwellings Association, and 125 female members who enjoyed hereditary membership. A dismayed Peabody strongly disagreed. An internal rift soon exploded into an estrangement, with all accusations and insults reported in the papers. The vice-regent resigned from the association, and other members followed as they focused their efforts on salvaging the national park movement.

McClurg was furious. Her pursuit bizarrely shifted from women saving the ancient cliff dwellings of Mesa Verde to privately constructing her own fake ruins near Colorado Springs. First, McClurg and partners found an unexcavated site in McElmo Canyon of the San Juan Basin. It wasn't a cliff dwelling, but a freestanding ancestral pueblo. They crated up the entire ruin, stone by stone, relic by relic. The materials were shipped east to a private parkland acquired in the resort town of Manitou Springs. A rock face was dynamited to create an alcove, and then a fabricated ruin was installed. With clever wording, the attraction would present itself as an authentic cliff dwelling, a scientific reproduction that was relocated to the Front Range. A convenient alternative for the masses, far more accessible than the remote Mesa Verde.

Appalled by the swirling scandal, many of the remaining members abandoned McClurg's association. After a congressional vote prevailed in 1906, Mesa Verde would come to be praised as a women's park in honor of its essential supporters. But the original leader of the cause would not be part of the celebration.

Fifteen years later, the park superintendent received a heavy shipping crate. Inside was a white marble marker commemorating the efforts of two parties: Virginia McClurg and her Colorado Cliff Dwellings Association. Though no one else agreed, McClurg insisted that the marker be erected in the most visible spot at Balcony House. At some point, the regent-general began claiming she'd been first to discover the famous ruin. Later investigators would claim she'd looted the ruin, taking a valuable ancestral loom and intact blanket.

Virginia McClurg's early and essential championing of the ruins would mostly be forgotten until after she died, and her controversial downfall faded from memory. For her role, Lucy Peabody would be cheered as the mother of Mesa Verde National Park.

TRIP THROUGH TIME

Located in far southwestern Colorado, Mesa Verde National Park protects some of the most intact and impressive Ancestral Puebloan ruins in the United States.

Joining a guided tour is necessary for exploring the largest ruins complexes, including Cliff Palace, Long House, Balcony House, Mug House, and others mentioned in this chapter. These highly popular tours are offered from roughly mid-spring to mid-fall. Tickets must be purchased up to fourteen days in advance through recreation.gov. Most tours are considered strenuous, given the need to negotiate steep trails, stairs, or ladders at an elevation around 7,000 feet. There are usually two self-guided tours, one through Spruce Tree House and another through Step House on Wetherill Mesa. Note that tours rotate each season, so check the park website for updates: www.nps.gov/meve.

Other highlights include driving the twenty-one-mile main park road, which passes numerous scenic vistas and ends at the Chapin Mesa Archeological Museum. Another area worth exploring is the Mesa Top Loop, a six-mile drive leading to early pit houses and pueblos, with the Far View Sites being particularly impressive. There are around thirty miles of hiking trails in the park. Many options are a mile or two in length and lead to fascinating archaeological sites. The Long House Loop, located on Wetherill Mesa, is a five-mile paved multiuse trail open to bikers, hikers, and pets, which leads to many ruins and overlooks.

Anasazi and a Vanishing Myth

Much like the relics rush era that followed the revelations at Mesa Verde, the first decades at the new national park were not without controversy. Recreational needs often took precedence over field research. Rough dirt roads were built to rustic park buildings and accommodations. Artifacts and debris were cleared from the cliff dwellings, which were stabilized and reconstructed for the benefit of guided tours.

Early archaeological efforts were mostly directed by Jesse Fewkes, a Smithsonian ethnologist who first visited on a VIP tour sponsored by McClurg's association. Now the scientist seethed about the condition of the Cliff Palace, which he believed might be the most looted site in the Southwest. Much of his ire was directed at his former guides, the Wetherills, who had lost their status as the de facto chaperones at Mesa Verde.

After father Ben Wetherill died in the late nineteenth century, the mother and younger brothers carried on for several years. But stiff competition from new guides like C. B. Kelly meant the family's monopoly was finally over. Their guided trips for McClurg had been something of a last hurrah. Ranching had always been a tough endeavor, even when it was their family's sole focus. After they fell behind on the mortgage, the Alamo Ranch was foreclosed and sold at auction. Some of the brothers turned to other pursuits, while a few joined Richard, who had moved south and become an excavation foreman leading relics expeditions for prominent institutions.

Fewkes seemed particularly incensed by Richard Wetherill. However, later scholars would direct their ire toward both Wetherill *and* Fewkes. While the latter man was excellent at public relations, he was criticized for poor practices. His notes were limited. His maps were inaccurate. Many of his stabilization efforts at Mesa Verde would fall apart and require reconstruction. In general, Mesa Verde was a poster child for the chaotic state of early Southwestern archaeology. To an extent, the so-called experts were all self-taught. Thus, ignorance compounded with arrogance led to endless mistakes, and finger-pointing was the typical method for deflecting the blame.

Despite the growing animosity toward him, Richard Wetherill's influence was widespread during the early decades of Southwestern archaeology. Noticing a pattern across excavations, he'd made a simple but important observation. A more primitive type of pit-house ruin was buried below and therefore older than the more advanced masonry structures. The stone cliff dwellings and freestanding pueblos had kiln-fired pottery, a technological innovation. The pit-house sites had woven baskets.

So, Wetherill coined the term *basket people* for the older culture, which academics later modified to *Basketmakers*. When it came to discussing the cliff-dweller culture, Wetherill chose an infamous name that would gradually capture the imagination of everyone—the scholars, popular writers, regional entrepreneurs, and the American public. He likely overheard some Navajo workers describing the ancient cliff dwellers as *Anasazi*. This compound word can have several meanings, depending on the context, including *ancient others* or *ancient enemies*.

Pleasing and enigmatic to the ear, the name Anasazi would come to be generally defined in white society to mean the *old ones*. And the prevailing story would come to include another disputed claim, namely that the old ones had vanished without a trace. This made for great advertising copy, and so a campfire mystery became a widespread promotional campaign to lure wealthy tourists to struggling towns on their way to a remote park.

Most people who looked closely at modern Pueblo architecture in New Mexico and Arizona could see the similarities. The square interlocking buildings and protruding roof beams closely resembled the ancient cliff dwellings and freestanding ruins of the San Juan Basin. When Native Americans living in those Pueblos pointed out that their ancestors didn't vanish but migrated just a few hundred miles to points south, their claims were mostly dismissed. Oral histories weren't proof to the scholars and tour guides who sold themselves as the experts of a lost civilization. Occasionally, a magazine article or museum display about the vanishing Anasazi might include a small qualification—that some of the cliff dwellers may have migrated south.

The dismissal of the modern Puebloans was only one example of the park's poor relations with neighboring Native Americans. The Utes were also unhappy.

A so-called trade forced them to give up the vegetated Mesa Verde in exchange for more arid and exposed lands toward Sleeping Ute Mountain. Later, it was revealed the lands traded had already been set aside for the Utes. What park supporters insisted was a two-for-one land swap in the Utes' favor was yet another land grab. Meanwhile, once the national park was established, the management avoided hiring Ute workers, opting for members of the Navajo Nation, with whom relations were less contentious.

While the Navajo workers needed the jobs, the positive feelings may not have always been mutual. On a bluff above Spruce Tree House, the Mesa Verde Museum housed a collection of artifacts excavated throughout the park. Among the exhibits were human remains. In the late 1930s, a perfectly preserved mummy went on display, a twenty-year-old female unearthed from Basketmaker ruins. Nicknamed "Glamorous Esther," her desiccated face was described in park literature as having a "hideous grimace" that often startled the visitors.

Occasionally, Navajo workers and their families might visit the museum. They came from a culture with a tradition of hypersensitivity toward the dead. Some members could experience frightful shocks when encountering human remains. In October 1939, a group of elder Navajo dance performers stepped inside the museum. Upon spotting the mummy, they rushed from the museum in horror. The museum staff who witnessed the encounter shared the story, which spread throughout the park to great amusement and mockery.

Ancestral Puebloans of Mesa Verde

With time, the park cleaned up its act. Esther was removed from display in the early 1970s. In 2013, the ancestral woman's remains were reburied by members of the Hopi Tribe and Pueblo Acoma. More repatriations followed, including human remains and funerary objects from Gustaf Nordenskiöld's collection. In 2020, the National Museum of Finland returned the ancestors' remains to the twenty-four associated tribes of Mesa Verde, with representatives including the Zia and Zuni.

Along with shifting mindsets, science became a priority. Within the park's 82 square miles, over 5,000 ancient sites were found, including around 600 cliff dwellings, plus many mesa top ruins and irrigation structures. This made Mesa Verde the largest archaeological preserve in the nation.

Interpretation became less about selling a good mystery and more about accurately and respectfully interpreting the faint traces from an enigmatic past. The name Anasazi was supplanted by the term *Ancestral Puebloan* to acknowledge that the cliff dwellers had migrated south to New Mexico and Arizona. Native Americans were asked to share their beliefs and oral histories, and some became park rangers and anthropologists.

A more comprehensive theory emerged about the reasons behind the cliff dwellers' permanent departure. Now, the story didn't rely on the earliest speculations made at the most disturbed sites. New excavations at ruins throughout the Southwest benefited from improving practices. Dendrochronology, the analysis of tree rings, yielded data about paleoclimates. Pollen analysis offered clues about ancient crops. Wooden materials, including structural ceiling beams, were radiocarbon dated, which offered a time frame for the constructions.

Current theories suggest nomadic ancestors arrived around 10,000 BCE, following herds of big game, including mammoths. By 3,000 years ago, members of the Basketmaker culture were living in small villages on the mesa tops, where the pit houses were made first from mud and later stone. During this time, farming gradually surpassed hunting and gathering as the main sources of food.

The era of the Ancestral Puebloans was theorized to begin sometime around the year 600 CE, characterized by the increasing complexity of their masonry structures. One evolving type of structure was the *kiva*, a circular depression used as a ceremonial space. Inside, there was often a *sipapu*, a hole on the north side of the chamber, which symbolized the people's place of emergence from the underworld. Tunnels leading between kivas and interior rooms were concealed deep within the cliff dwellings. Often a tower was built above the kivas, which may have had several uses, including observation and defense.

Gradually, Mesa Verde and the San Juan Basin became a major population center in the ancient Southwest. But cycles of regional drought and rain had always plagued the region, and the population growth rose and fell accordingly. For half a millennium, the Ancestral Puebloans at Mesa Verde lived near their fields and carried vessels to and from water sources in the alcoves below the cliffs. Sometime around the year 1150 CE, the situation changed. The residents began to construct their hidden cities of stone, the cliff dwellings. Now they lived by their water sources and walked to their fields.

The reasons for this dramatic move are uncertain, but the paleoclimatic data suggests a thirteenth-century shift from a warmer and wetter period to numerous decades of drier and increasingly colder conditions. Combined with natural resource depletion, this may have caused failed crops and societal stress. Signs of violence and cannibalism were discovered in some human remains, including smashed skulls and cut marks on the bones. This implies conflicts between hungry groups, whether neighbors within the region or invaders from afar. Newly unearthed weapons included spears, clubs, and shields made with woven baskets and hides. Times were always tough, but then they'd become much worse.

So, the Ancestral Puebloans gradually migrated south to warmer climates at lower elevations where the conditions were more tolerable. The youngest wooden beam found in a cliff dwelling was felled around the year 1280. Conditions were so bad around that time that archaeologists called it the Great Drought. By the end of the thirteenth century, Mesa Verde was abandoned. Ancient travelers continued to pass through from time to time. But there was no evidence of major attempts to reoccupy the cliff dwellings. For five hundred years, the stone palaces were covered with layers of falling dust.

The Death of Anasazi

Before the turn of the twentieth century, Richard Wetherill knew better than anyone where to find unexcavated ruins in the Southwest. To fill their archaeology halls with the best artifacts, many top institutions turned to Wetherill to guide their field scientists to the best spots. Meanwhile, newly appointed professors were looking to establish their careers and build anthropology programs at universities. Those who could hired Wetherill to lead them to the goods.

Wetherill's work for the American Museum of Natural History, the esteemed institution across the street from Central Park in Manhattan, began in 1893. The partnership was funded by two museum benefactors, wealthy brothers who gave their name to the Hyde Exploring Expedition. Their first joint venture was excavating Grand Gulch in Utah over several seasons. Then they went to the Keet Seel ruins in Tsegi Canyon of Arizona Territory, which later was included in Navajo National Monument.

Next, they set their sights on a massive set of ruins in an obscure part of northwest New Mexico Territory. Later, the ancestral great houses in this desert valley would be considered of comparable importance to the more famous cliff dwellings of Mesa Verde. But at the time, few people other than Wetherill knew much about the remote Chaco Canyon.

It was important to maintain appearances during the era of Virginia McClurg's lecture tours and rising public backlash to the relics rush. So, the museum sent along a twenty-three-year-old archaeologist to direct the expedition. He'd previously focused on New York City digs and never been to the Southwest. Everyone recognized that the real field leader was Wetherill.

In a clever but underhanded move, the former rancher filed a 161-acre homestead claim for the land surrounding the great houses. The largest was Pueblo Bonito. Built in the shape of a half-circle, the structure had around 800 rooms, including over thirty kivas, with several of great size. Chetro Ketl had half the rooms, but they were found around the edges inside an even larger walled structure. Pueblo del Arroyo had 300 rooms, including fourteen kivas.

Employing a workforce of local Navajos, Wetherill led the efforts to excavate one of the most impressive collections of Southwestern artifacts ever assembled. In an ironic twist, his Navajo workers gave Wetherill a familiar nickname. They called him *Anasazi*.

Before their work was halted by federal intervention after six years, Wetherill

and his team excavated nearly 200 rooms in Pueblo Bonito. The resulting collection included 10,000 pieces of ancient pottery. Thousands of tools and weapons made from stone, wood, and bone. Artistic sculptures and stunning jewelry.
Fourteen human skeletons. And 50,000 pieces of turquoise, which hinted that
Chaco Canyon, long ago, was a major trade center of the Ancestral Puebloan world.

Chaco would mark the end of Richard Wetherill's excavation career. Not
because he'd gone too far this time, but because his efforts didn't stretch widely
enough. Wetherill could only collect for so many interest groups. Now there were
aspiring academics, curators, administrators, tour guides, federal land managers,
and civic-minded preservationists. Everyone wanted a piece of the ancient past.
Issues of how to properly preserve a ruin and collect artifacts were still years from
being addressed. Securing access for the professionals of a nascent field came first.
The powerful parties that hired Wetherill and gobbled up the best artifacts were safe
from political attacks. Wetherill was just an old cowboy who could be dealt with.

A series of federal agents came to investigate the Chaco Canyon operations.
They generally found the excavations to be professionally handled, but that point
was moot. The prevailing attitude had shifted toward ancient artifacts on federal lands being treated as public property. A new preservation law, called the
Antiquities Act of 1906, would soon be enacted. The New Yorkers agreed to stop
work, but someone continued to excavate, and all signs pointed to Wetherill. Next,
the Government Land Office rejected his homestead claim to the ruins, which was
a violation of the act's agrarian intentions.

Wetherill walked away from the great houses but won an appeal to keep his
adjacent land, where he'd established a small ranching operation and trading post.
With the ruins now under federal protection, Wetherill, with several brothers and
associates, worked to establish a franchise of Southwestern-style trading outposts.
At the peak, they had about ten affiliates, mostly at travel junctions around the
Colorado Plateau, including Monument Valley and Albuquerque, plus a satellite
store in New York City.

Unadvertised backroom sales were rumored to include authentic relics, no questions asked. But mostly the outposts sold goods made by local Navajos, includ-ing colorful blankets, pottery, jewelry, and trinkets. Payments to the Navajos for their merchandise were often made in credit for goods and foodstuffs. Another item that was rumored to be available at some remote outposts was bootlegged whiskey.

It's uncertain if Wetherill's trading post at Pueblo Bonito sold whiskey, but plenty found its way to Chaco Canyon all the same. Putting bottles in the hands of laborers was common practice throughout the West. Doing so on credit often indebted alcoholics to the store owner. Drunken dustups and fights were common in Chaco Canyon, just like everywhere else—whether between whites, Navajos, Mexicans, or others passing through.

Further rumors about the controversial Wetherill suggested he had a harsh side to him, as did many aging cowboys who lived out their days in the Wild West. One story claimed that one night, Wetherill became angry with some Navajo men, who may or may not have been drunk on the very whiskey he sold them. Knowing about their fear of the dead, Wetherill supposedly locked them in a dark room inside Pueblo Bonito with several skulls unearthed from the ruins. In one version, he illuminated the skulls with candles. Some defended it as a dark joke that few would get.

One summer evening in June 1910, Wetherill and another cowboy were riding horseback on the main wagon road through Chaco Canyon. From the shadows at a bend in the road, a Navajo man named Chiishchilí Biyé stepped out. He leveled a rifle at Wetherill. The first shot knocked the cowboy from his saddle. The man was dead when he hit the ground.

"Are you sick, Anasazi?" taunted Biyé standing over the body. Then he shot off half of Wetherill's head.

Later, Biyé would say that he deeply regretted killing his friend. Others noted that the convicted killer had owed Wetherill a great deal of money, due to a long line of credit being extended at the store. Some said Wetherill got what was coming to him, while most said an execution outweighed any crimes he'd committed. Those who knew Biyé claimed he was never right in the head, at least not since witnessing his father being killed by white cowboys. Another theory was that one of Wetherill's enemies—perhaps the local Bureau of Indian Affairs agent—convinced the troubled Navajo man to do the job. Many people felt the full story never came to light.

Regardless, the long-forgotten prophesy of the Ute chief Acowitz had finally come to pass. Yet only in part. When it came to the Southwestern relics rush, countless people had plundered the ruins, collected the artifacts, and disturbed the dead. Except for a cowboy archaeologist named Richard Wetherill, the vast majority of the offenders walked away.

CHAPTER 13

WHAT WAS THE PURPOSE OF THESE ANCIENT TOWERS?

STRANGE DISCOVERIES

HOVENWEEP NATIONAL MONUMENT

CAJON MESA, GREAT SAGE PLAIN, UTAH–COLORADO STATE LINE

It seemed a particularly inhospitable place for a townsite. The small party from the U.S. Geological Survey (USGS) was exploring a shallow valley filled with rubble. They'd found few signs of water on this windswept mesa of sagebrush. Just the occasional spring trickling out from sandstone ledges near the head of small canyons. There was little shade too, other than scattered junipers and pinyon pines that were mostly wider than they were tall.

The nearest break in the desert basin was Sleeping Ute Mountain, about twenty miles distant. This distinctive and sacred range was named by the local Utes for its resemblance to a chief with arms folded, lying on his back beneath the sun-bleached sky. It was mid-September 1874, and the four members of the USGS photographic division had come from the San Juan Mountains to the east. Days before, they'd captured the first wet-plate photograph of a cliff dwelling, a two-story tower built inside an alcove in Mancos Canyon near the Mesa Verde.

DESERTED MONUMENT

Despite being home to some of the best-preserved Ancestral Puebloan towers and ruins in the Southwest, Hovenweep National Monument is one of the least visited NPS units. Due to its remote location far from major towns and highways, only about 35,000 people make the journey each year. While you can reach the visitor center on a paved route, most of the area's roads are rough and unpaved. It's easy to get lost in this confusing desert landscape, and navigation apps can send drivers the wrong way. The park service strongly recommends you download or print directions and a map from the monument website at www.nps.gov/hove. Cell service may be limited or nonexistent. Pay attention as you drive and watch closely for NPS road signs.

The place they were now exploring was called Hovenweep, a Ute word meaning *deserted valley*. Despite the barren landscape, the numerous piles of stones gave rise to remarkably intact structures unlike any documented across the American Southwest. There were multiroomed buildings with jagged walls, resembling castles atop the bluffs. Even more impressive were the towers. Some were round. Some were square. Some rose several stories high.

Yes, there were architectural similarities with other sites being revealed, particularly those in the Arizona Territory. This suggested that Hovenweep was once part of a larger ancient civilization. But the Hovenweep ruins were not leaning against cliffs, nor were they sheltered in defensible canyon alcoves. These towers and castles were out in the open, exposed to the elements, where whistling winds carried tumbleweeds and whipped up dust devils.

The most surprising aspect was how some towers were situated, built atop large boulders that had long ago split away from the bluffs. A few of these boulders offered nearly flat foundations to work with. Other boulder tops rested at improbable angles. Regardless, the masonry of each wall had been meticulously crafted to conform with the underlying topography.

Perhaps every inch of suitable building space had once held a structure. This hadn't been the hovel of starving villagers struggling to survive in an impoverished desert. The towers of Hovenweep seemed to represent the heights of an advanced and thriving populace.

PROTECT THE PLACE

The stone towers, ruins, and landscapes found at Hovenweep are very fragile. To protect these resources, the park service asks that visitors follow several guidelines. Please do not sit, stand, or climb on rock walls nor disturb any rock art sites and artifacts, such as pottery sherds or arrow points, which must be left in situ. Please remain on marked trails and avoid trampling sensitive biological soil crusts, an important formation of living organisms that grows on the desert floor, providing plants with nutrients and protecting the ground from erosion.

Little Ruin Canyon

Enthralled by what they saw, William Henry Jackson and the members of the USGS photography division dismounted from their horses. They began the involved process of setting up for a shot. Tripods were erected, one for the collapsible camera and another for a portable darkroom, essentially an unfolding supplies cabinet with a small tent hanging over it. To prepare the heavy glass plate, the first step was coating it with collodion solution. Inside the darkroom tent, the dampened plate was next dipped in silver nitrate, which rendered it sensitive to light. The now-dripping plate went inside a lightproof case, which was attached to the rear of the camera.

When Jackson removed the lens cap, the wet plate was exposed to the ambient light. The subject matter began to imprint as a negative image. Depending on the brightness, this might take anywhere from twenty seconds to several minutes or more. When complete, the case was returned to the darkroom, where the plate was removed and treated with developer solution, followed by a fixing agent and a rinse in a water bath. After the wet plate dried, the final step was to apply a varnish to protect the negative. Suffice it to say, there was usually time to shoot only a few locations each day.

These ruins, described as being at the mouth of Hovenweep canyon, were photographed by William Henry Jackson on his return visit in 1875. Photo by William Henry Jackson, August 1, 1875, National Park Service/Public Domain

The famous photographs taken by Jackson between 1874 and 1877 would prove essential for convincing the American public and the U.S. government to protect Southwestern ruins from vandals and pot hunters. Among the images was one titled *Ruined Fortress on the Hovenweep*, capturing a survey guide leaning against a sizable wall while further structures stretch along a ridge.

═══ HIKE THROUGH HOVENWEEP ═══

For those looking for an adventurous park unit to explore, Hovenweep delivers with a range of trails leading through the ruins. Due to the high desert climate, summers are scorching hot and winters are cold, so the suggested seasons for hiking are spring or fall. Whenever you go, it's important to carry enough water and use suitable sun protection.

The 785-acre monument preserves six groups of ruins, or ancestral village sites, that are found on dispersed parcels of NPS land in Utah and Colorado. The highlight is Square Tower Group near the visitor center, where a moderate two-mile hiking trail loops around Little Ruin Canyon.

The remaining units—Holly, Horseshoe and Hackberry, Cutthroat Castle, and Cajon—are each impressive in their own way. Some can be reached with longer hikes from the visitor center or by driving on rough dirt roads for which four-wheel or all-wheel drive is recommended. Stop by the visitor center to learn more about these options.

Another photograph showed surveyor horses and a pack burro standing in front of a square boulder, about twenty feet tall, with a large ruin perched

on top. The most impressive image captured the Square Tower, three stories
tall and made of perfectly fitted stones. This one, in particular, would remain
surprisingly unchanged from its initial discovery to when Hovenweep National
Monument was established in 1923 to how it would continue to look into the
twenty-first century.

With time, excavation and stabilization efforts would further reveal the complexity of the Hovenweep towers. No two were exactly alike, and the best examples were found in what was named Little Ruin Canyon. Stronghold House stands
like a watchtower atop a the thirty-degree slab of rock. Eroded Boulder House is
built into a pocket in the heart of one fallen rock, while on top were signs of an
upper-level structure. On a bluff above Square Tower, the Hovenweep Castle is
one of the monument's largest ruins, with numerous walls, rooms, and windows.

The most baffling are the Twin Towers, perched on either side of a boulder
that had long ago cracked apart. One tower is oval-shaped, the other has a footprint
like a horseshoe, and only a two-foot gap separates its exterior walls. They are two
of the most intricate buildings ever constructed by the Ancestral Puebloans.

A consensus eventually developed about the community that once existed at
Hovenweep. They were clearly successful farmers during an era of wetter climate.
Small check dams excavated throughout the monument were used to impound
water and irrigate crops. Archaeologists found evidence the inhabitants grew corn,
beans, squash, amaranth, and possibly cotton. The Hovenweep time frame closely
matched nearby Mesa Verde, with the structures built during the mid-1200s and
abandoned before the start of the next century.

Theories behind the purpose of the towers ranged widely. Some were used
as granaries to store surplus food during the cold winters and hot summers. The
windows in the taller towers implied defensive fortifications to some observers.
Others saw astronomical observatories. The presence of kiva ceremonial chambers
at the bottom of some buildings suggested religious purposes. Many scholars came
to believe the towers had a variety of uses. Beyond that, why such creative designs
were built here and how their creators lived among them remains a mystery.

CHAPTER 14

WHO WAS THE REAL CALAMITY JANE?

LEGENDARY FIGURES

FORT LARAMIE NATIONAL HISTORIC SITE

PLATTE RIVER VALLEY, WYOMING

C alamity Jane is dead," declared newspapers across the country.

The legendary frontierswoman passed away on August 1, 1903, near the mining town of Deadwood, South Dakota. Obituaries correctly reported her full name, Martha Jane Canary, but otherwise mixed half-truths with outright lies. For the past three decades, she'd been called the wildest woman of the West. One of the High Plains's most celebrated and eccentric characters. A crack shot with a rifle and a feared killer of men.

During the Indian Wars of the 1870s, as the story went, she donned male attire to serve as an army scout under Generals Custer and Miles. While passing through the foothills of the Bighorns, her captain was shot in an ambush. Riding into gunfire, she was said to have whisked the injured soldier away on horseback, thus earning the nickname Calamity.

Later, she supposedly rode for the Pony Express on a dangerous mail route through the Black Hills, dodging war parties and swimming important dispatches across swift rivers. When her compatriot Wild Bill Hickok was murdered, peace to his ashes, it was claimed that Calamity led the posse through Deadwood. She cornered the notorious assassin Jack McCall in a butcher shop, grabbing a meat cleaver for her weapon.

Famous frontiersman Buffalo Bill Cody, creator of the Wild West Show, recalled her fondly. A product of the old days, who drank as hard as she lived. When a lawless camp became a civilized town, it was generally time for Calamity to move on. Her later years were spent sharing adventurous tales in dime shows and saloons, while dipping dangerously in and out of poverty.

It was claimed she'd gone through twelve husbands, with the latest one still alive. For now. Some said she asked to be buried next to her long-lost love, Wild Bill Hickok. In mid-August, a massive funeral was held at the Methodist Church in Deadwood. Afterward, a hearse took her body to Mount Moriah Cemetery, where she was laid for eternal rest next to Hickok's grave. Yet even in death, Calamity Jane would not go quietly. To start, there were the inconsistencies in her background. Some said she was an orphaned pioneer from Missouri. Others called her a wealthy heiress from a family in Virginia City, Nevada. Her age at death was reported as anything from mid-forties to early seventies—even her tombstone would prove to be wrong.

Less complimentary journalists sought to dispel what they claimed were fabricated myths about Calamity Jane. She was never a soldier or a scout, they countered. She'd never killed anyone, nor had she ridden for the Pony Express. She'd never even met Wild Bill Hickok, or Buffalo Bill Cody, for that matter. She was a drunk. A liar. Possibly a prostitute. She lurked around whiskey dens and dance halls with rough men. One small-town paper jeered that, by dying, she'd finally done the proper thing.

"The whole story of this strange woman never has been told," wrote one correspondent. "And now that she is dead, the curtain of mystery will probably never be lifted from certain chapters of her checkered life."

A Prelude to Calamity

"Martha Canary, 4," read a census ledger for northern Missouri during the summer of 1860. She was the oldest daughter of Robert, thirty-five, a farmer from Ohio, and Charlotte, twenty, his wife from Illinois.

Three years later, the family joined a wagon train heading west. For five arduous months, the party followed a rough trail, sometimes using ropes to lower the wagons over ledges. Along the way, Martha learned to ride and shoot. She swam with horses across swollen streams. Their destination was the mining boomtown of Virginia City in the Rocky Mountains of Montana.

During the disastrous winter of 1864 to 1865, the town was snowed in, and food became scarce. While Martha's father gambled, some speculated that her mother turned to prostitution. Meanwhile, Martha took her younger sister and infant brother begging. The next year, the struggling family followed the boom south to Blackfoot City on the Snake River, where Martha's mother died. Seeking charity from the Mormons, the distraught family continued south to Salt Lake City, where the father died in 1867.

Orphaned at age eleven, Martha found spaces for her siblings in boarding homes. Her sister would later marry and move to Lander, while her brother became an errant cowboy and went to prison. Meanwhile, Martha followed the Union Pacific to the railroad town of Piedmont just north of the Uinta Mountains. Martha tended children and worked at a boardinghouse, but her evening antics around town caused a rift with the motherly innkeeper.

Shortly after the Golden Spike was nailed at Promontory Summit, completing the Transcontinental Railroad in 1869, Martha began bouncing among mining camps and boomtowns in Wyoming. By 1875, she was living near Fort Laramie. Some said she worked as an entertainer or prostitute at a nearby "hog ranch," a rough district of brothels and saloons frequented by soldiers from frontier forts.

The year before, General George Custer had been leading a scouting expedition through the Black Hills when soldiers found traces of gold in the streams. Soon scores of prospectors were illegally descending upon this mountainous region of Dakota Territory that had belonged to the Sioux since the 1868 Fort Laramie Treaty. The U.S. government was split about how to respond, with increasing pressure to break the treaty and reap the wealth.

Come late May 1875, a large expedition of soldiers, mining geologists, and packtrain teamsters set out from Fort Laramie, heading north for the Black Hills. Rumors quickly spread that among them was a young woman called Calamity Jane. As the story went, after being turned away once in women's clothing, the nineteen-year-old Martha dressed like a male soldier and slipped into the ranks. Discovered after a few days, she was sent away, only to repeatedly reappear. Eventually, she joined the teamsters, proving to be a valuable addition. She was always willing to help with any tasks, from cooking to sewing to nursing.

When another expedition was sent the following March, Calamity Jane was present once again. This time her role included bull-whacking mules with the teamsters. One leader later claimed he briefly hired her to scout in advance of the party during a vacancy. Off duty, when the men got into their cups, Calamity easily kept pace. After the expedition, she was jailed in Cheyenne for stealing clothes. Acquitted after a short trial, she paraded through the streets in a borrowed gown.

That summer, she was back near Fort Laramie when a half dozen wagons stopped on their way to the Black Hills. One leader was Wild Bill Hickok, who sought a gold strike to support his new wife, a circus performer in Cheyenne. With him were the Utter brothers, who planned to start a delivery service. At nearby Government Farm, a drunken Calamity had been locked in the guardhouse after over-indulging with the recently paid soldiers. The officer of the day asked the wagon party if they might take this wild spirit away. By chance, Steve Utter was a friend. As the party departed, their ranks had swelled with the addition of thirty wagons and a hundred people, including a soon-to-be-infamous American figure.

A CROSSROADS

Located at the confluence of the Platte and Laramie Rivers, Fort Laramie was originally established in the 1830s as a High Plains fur trading post. In 1849, the fort was purchased by the U.S. Army, which stationed a garrison of infantry and cavalry to protect white citizens traveling on the various overland trails. Gold seekers, wagon emigrants, and frontier settlers heading west were increasingly coming into violent conflicts with regional Native American tribes. The fort, itself, saw mostly minor skirmishes but became a launching point for several campaigns during the so-called American Indian Wars. With the completion of the Transcontinental Railroad in 1869, the overland wagon routes were mostly abandoned. Gradually, the fort became obsolete and was decommissioned in 1890. Over the years, most buildings decayed into ruins though about a dozen survived.

A Town Becomes a Legend

"Calamity Jane has arrived," announced the *Black Hills Pioneer* in mid-July 1876.

Their entrance to Deadwood was called spectacular. Members of the Hickok–Utter party paraded on horseback down Main Street in buckskin suits with swinging tendrils of fringe. Along the way, they greeted people who came out from rowdy false-front establishments. Just beyond town, Hickok and the Utters built tents near a creek. The party fanned out to seek their fortunes.

"Boys, I wish you would loan me twenty dollars," said Calamity upon visiting the men's camp a few days later. "I can't do business in these old buckskins. I ain't got the show the other girls have."

The loan was made, and Calamity spent the following days transforming herself. Gone were the clothes of the frontiersman. Away washed the trail grime with a bath in the creek. Jane was soon dressed toe to head in the outfit of a frontier maiden. New shoes. Stockings. A dress wrapped tight around the waist. A fine scarf and hat.

At the age of twenty-one, Calamity Jane went to work for the notorious Al Swearengen at the Gem Variety Theater. She was part hostess, waitress, and dancer. A few claimed she was also a prostitute, like some of the house girls. Others considered her one of the boys who drank and cussed with the best of them. One day, Calamity strolled into the Hickok–Utter camp, rolled down her stocking, and extracted two greenbacks to repay her loan.

While Calamity tore up the town, her new friend Wild Bill spent his time at a poker table in the No. 10 Saloon. On the night of August 1, he won sizable pots off a seedy drifter named Jack McCall. The next afternoon, an incensed McCall returned to the saloon and slid down the bar to where Hickok was playing.

"Damn you, take that!" shouted McCall. He lunged toward Hickok with a pistol, shooting him in the back of the head. Wild Bill went limp, allegedly holding a pair of aces and eights—later called the *dead man's hand*. McCall tried to shoot his way out, but the gun backfired. A crowd cornered the fleeing murderer at a nearby butcher shop, but Calamity was not among them. Upon hearing the news, some claimed she rushed to the No. 10 and cradled Wild Bill's head in her arms. Later, a distraught Calamity was seen leaving flowers on Hickok's grave on Mount Moriah.

Calamity Jane stayed in Deadwood for several years. During the 1878 smallpox epidemic, she risked her life by volunteering as a nurse to help the sick. More selfless acts of frontier nursing would follow in subsequent years. In the early 1880s, she left Deadwood and ranged around the neighboring towns and territories. Sometimes she camped. More often she worked in the wild saloons of rising boomtowns, dealing cards, dancing, and sharing drinks. Occasionally, she protested her nickname, declaring that she'd taken a husband and was going straight. Without fail, she would later return to her hell-raising ways.

HIGH PLAINS HISTORY

The national historic site was established in 1931. Today, this small NPS unit preserves the sprawling grounds of Fort Laramie, which lacked a palisade and was more like a frontier town. Visitors can wander the thoroughfares and enter about a dozen restored buildings, including a powder magazine, bakery, guardhouses, officer quarters, and barracks. Elsewhere, foundations and partial ruins remain.

A Star Is Made

"That's Calamity Jane," said a man from Montana, according to journalist Horatio Maguire, in his 1877 book *The Black Hills and American Wonderland*. They were about a mile outside of Deadwood, watching a horse rider who, on first glance, appeared to be a daredevil boy with long hair. In fact, it was a daring young woman who spurred her horse and rode off toward town.

In just two paragraphs, the journalist describes a new heroine of the West. An orphaned heiress from Virginia City, Nevada, he wrote, who disguised herself in men's clothing to survive the mining camps. A woman of the world. A reckless mistress of her own destiny.

Immediately, Maguire's descriptions of Calamity Jane were picked up by newspapers from the West to New York. The portrayal inspired the reclusive dime novelist Edward Wheeler. That October, he released *Deadwood Dick, The Prince of the Road; or, The Black Rider of the Black Hills*. This instant bestseller featured a daredevil character named Calamity Jane, who dressed like a cowboy and bore a striking resemblance to Maguire's depiction.

Over the coming eight years, Wheeler went on to release thirty-three short novels in the series. As a fearless sidekick, Calamity Jane would gallop on scene, brandishing pistols. She'd run off the villains and rebuff the hero's romantic advances. Other times her name and image graced the title and cover, and occasionally she was the de facto protagonist. Eventually this fictional Calamity married Deadwood Dick, only to meet her end right beside her husband while fighting back against an angry mob. Audiences ate it up, and Calamity Jane became a household name around the country.

A portrait of Calamity Jane in an outfit similar to what she would wear during her dime store performances, taken by photographer C.E. Finn circa 1880s. Imprint of C.E. Finn, Livingston, Mont., 1880s/Public Domain

A Nickname Is Earned

"Calamity Jane!" declared the dime show poster, announcing her debut at the Palace Museum in Minneapolis on February 2, 1896. She stepped on stage wearing cowboy boots, buckskin pants and coat, and a slouch hat. She clutched a rifle by the barrel and had an ammo belt strung around her waist. The audience included many women, along with the usual men, which suggested a growing role for heroines in the male-centric Wild West.

"My maiden name was Martha Canary," she began, reciting a memorized version of her life story. She had recently published an eight-page autobiography for sale—most likely it was dictated, given she was mostly illiterate. This mix of truth and fiction included most of the dramatic embellishments that would later populate her obituaries. She omitted certain facts, including that she gave birth to a baby boy who died in the early 1880s. But she did mention her eight-year-old daughter, whom she sought to financially support through her performances.

Over four months, Calamity toured cities across the Midwest and East. By June, she returned to the Black Hills to tend to her ill daughter, Jesse, who was in a boarding school in Sturgis. From there, the mother and daughter began their own tour, with Calamity selling photographs and copies of her autobiography in towns across the West. One of her new haunts became the young national park called Yellowstone, where she obtained a permit to entertain tourists.

Calamity repeatedly expressed intentions to reform and serve as a traditional mother to Jesse. But wherever Calamity went, so followed the drinking. One might see her warmly reminiscing about the old days with friends, only to soon switch into a drunken rage. She'd ramble on about the lying newspapermen who called her a rustler, a highwaywoman, or worst of all, in her opinion, a minister's daughter. Eventually, one of Jane's unofficial husbands took Jesse away to be raised by his mother.

Over the final years of her life, Calamity lived up to her nickname. She wandered from place to place, drinking on friends' tabs and credit until getting tossed in jail or ushered out of town. She was briefly in the Yukon. Back in Yellowstone. At Niagara Falls. Appearing in the Pan-American Expo in nearby Buffalo. There she visited with her friend Buffalo Bill, who gave her money for a train ticket west, back to the only home she'd ever really known. Next, she was stranded partway across the country in Chicago. She had sold her onward ticket for drinks. Finally, she made it back to the Black Hills, where she eventually worked for madam Dora DuFran in Belle Fourche.

Some nights, Calamity would hallucinate, believing she was in a battle with Indians. Other nights, she howled along with the coyotes. Occasionally, she turned violent, shooting up a saloon or robbing a shop with a hatchet. She went on week-long benders, slept in box cars, shacks, and saloons.

"Short Pants!" she slurred late one night while clutching a lamppost. "Can't you tell a lady where she lives?"

"Show me where the lady is and I'll try," retorted passerby Lewis Freeman, who later wrote about his encounter for *Sunset* magazine.

"She's me, Short Pants. Martha Canary…better known as Calamity Jane."

The night ended with a crowd carrying Calamity up a fire escape and shoving her through a window into her room. The next morning, she was drinking beer with Freeman at breakfast.

In late July 1903, Calamity Jane boarded a train for Deadwood, telling the conductor she was going there to die. During her final days, she refused all medicines prescribed and visited the grave of Wild Bill Hickok at Mount Moriah Cemetery. Less than a month later, her body would occupy the adjacent plot. Some said her final resting place was arranged on her request. Others claimed it was a practical joke on Wild Bill, who never actually liked her. As did most observers, her tombstone judged her to be older than she really was, reading fifty-three. The enigmatic Martha Jane Canary died after forty-seven years of hard living. An infamous and tragic life overflowing with calamity.

CHAPTER 15

WHAT HAPPENED TO GLEN AND BESSIE HYDE ON THE COLORADO RIVER?

BAFFLING DISAPPEARANCES

GRAND CANYON NATIONAL PARK

COLORADO PLATEAU, ARIZONA

It looks like a floating coffin," said Harry Howland.

He was standing on shore with a friend, watching Glen Hyde hammer together a wooden sweep scow from fresh lumber. It was October 18, 1928, in the high desert town of Green River, Utah. Both observers were experienced river runners, more so with flatwater than rapids. When they tried to warn Hyde about the folly of his ways, the twenty-nine-year-old Idaho rancher scoffed. Glen explained that he had navigated the challenging rapids of the Salmon River in a sweep scow. He could run anything.

The two locals gave up and left, assuming that some other foolhardy man would be joining Glen's voyage, not his twenty-three-year-old wife, Bessie. Ever since meeting eighteen months before, on a steamship traveling from San Francisco to Los Angeles, these two bohemian souls had become nearly inseparable. They had already traveled east to meet Bessie's parents, the Haleys. Then they returned west to meet Glen's. They went camping in the Sawtooth Range. Their only time apart was when Bessie moved to progressive Elko, Nevada, for the mandatory five-month waiting period before filing for divorce from her estranged high school sweetheart.

The day after the divorce was finalized, Glen and Bessie were married in Twin Falls, Idaho. While working the summer planting season together on the Hyde Ranch, Glen suggested a daring honeymoon. The year before, two partially successful but haphazard whitewater expeditions through the Grand Canyon had received national attention. Wooden rowboats had been portaged, smashed, and sunk. Such upsets had become common among the roughly dozen groups to try since John Wesley Powell's historic first descent in 1869.

Glen believed that he and Bessie had a better shot with the faster and nearly unsinkable Salmon River sweep scow. They would float around 800 miles on the Green and Colorado Rivers. Not only might they set a speed record for boating through the Grand Canyon, but they would make Bessie the first woman to complete the harrowing journey. Between the dark chin-length locks of her flapper haircut, Bessie's face broke into a mischievous smile.

Champions of Cataract

On October 20, 1928, with Glen manning the bow oar and Bessie handling the stern, they pushed off into the current. After a hot desert summer, the autumn water level was low. But the season was late, and the cooling weather meant the young newlyweds were bundled in warm clothing. Wool pants. A knitted jacket for the tall and slender Glen. A fur-lined leather coat for the compact Bessie, who stood just under five feet tall.

The first eight days took them 120 miles through calm waters, which gave

Glen a chance to teach his wife about their boat. About twenty feet long by six feet wide, and with three-foot gunwales, the scow was basically a barge that barreled downstream with the current. Fully loaded—with food, supplies, a makeshift kerosene stove, and even bedsprings—it weighed an astounding two tons. The two oars were each twenty feet long and weighed over a hundred pounds. They were counter-balanced with logs, which helped the river runners handle them while angling the craft through riffles and rapids.

Through the winding meanders of Labyrinth Canyon, the pair floated between cliffs of Navajo Sandstone. At a spot later called Register Rock, they stopped to carve their names among those of past explorers. They passed through a widening basin of spires and buttes, called Tower Park by the Powell expedition. Next came the deepening gorge of Stillwater Canyon, followed by one of the most remote spots in canyon country, the confluence where the Green River joins the Colorado River.

Here the flow doubled to about 7,000 cubic feet per second. The extra water proved helpful as they cruised toward their first real challenge, the violent rapids of Cataract Canyon. Some called it the graveyard of the Colorado. Cataract Canyon was known for rocky falls and smashed rowboats, which often had to be portaged around the worst rapids. However, due to the heaviness of the sweep scow, plus the challenges of stopping, portaging would be nearly impossible. The Hydes would have to run everything.

Only a few rapids into Cataract, Bessie dropped her sweep oar into the tumultuous river. The current wrenched the oar, and her ninety-pound frame was flung through the air into the river. Glen grabbed her foot and pulled her back aboard. Below the tenth rapid, the scow was pushed into an eddy where it spun amid swirling waters. After running up onto a mid-river rock, they called it quits and made camp.

During their second day in Cataract Canyon, they made it past another eleven rapids. The third day, October 30, they navigated through twenty more. This included some of the most challenging whitewater yet, with later names including Mile-Long Rapid, the Big Drops, and Satan's Gut. The next day was Halloween, and they floated out from the canyon exhausted but triumphant. They were the first river runners to pass through Cataract without portaging.

The Hydes' reward was another long stretch of flatwater before large rapids resumed in the Grand Canyon. Such impending challenges now seemed far less intimidating given their recent success. That night, a massive thunderstorm hit their camp. While holing up under a leaky tarp, they laughingly named their sweep scow *Rain-in-the-Face*. Partly this was for the Lakota warrior who helped defeat Custer at Little Bighorn. Partly it was for how water would splash up from their boat's massive bow when plunging through rapids.

The Colorado's flow soon doubled from the storm runoff. The Hydes sped onward with the swift current, past the sheer walls of Narrow Canyon and through the sandstone domes and cliffs of Glen Canyon. One day, Glen shot a deer with his rifle, supplementing their canned and dried goods with venison. Another day, strong headwinds forced them to turn the scow sideways and row through calm pools.

A String of Successes

On November 8, they reached Lees Ferry, near the head of Marble Canyon at the edge of Grand Canyon National Park. During highwater the previous spring, the crossing had shut down after the ferryboat sank and drowned three men. The ferry operator's family, who had remained to ranch the Paria River bottoms, tried to talk the Hydes out of continuing. The grandson, Owen, had been a boatman on the sloppier of the two expeditions the year before. They had abandoned the endeavor at Hermit Rapid and hiked out. Owen was impressed by Glen's rowing skills but not by the scow itself. It didn't seem adaptable to the coming rapids, Owen later noted. Plus, the bigger danger was going through with only one boat.

"Bessie is feeling fine and eating everything but the boat," wrote Glen in a letter to his father. "The cataracts were rather fierce. I don't think…any worse than some places on the Salmon…but they are faster and the waves dash higher… I'd quit the river here, (not on my own account tho) but from what they tell us we are over all the worst water…"

After pushing off from shore, the undeterred Glen lost his balance in Paria Riffle and nearly fell overboard. A few miles downstream, he and Bessie stopped at the construction site for Navajo Bridge, soon to become the highest in the world, rising 470 feet above the river. They scrambled up a steep slope to reach the trading post, where they bought some food and supplies. An hour later, they were floating deep within the walls of Marble Canyon. The first obstacle was Badger Rapid. After running onto a rock, Glen labored to pry the scow loose. They called it a day and made camp.

The next morning, they reached Soap Creek Rapid. For decades it had been considered unrunnable due to the funneling current plunging over a huge boulder, creating a massive hole, where the water violently recirculated upstream. The first successful run had happened only the year before and by accident. Those boatmen hadn't realized where they were. After a quick scout, Glen grabbed both sweeps and maneuvered the scow cleanly down the right side of Soap Creek.

For the next few days, the Hydes met with nothing but success. They glided through the Roaring Twenties, stopping to scout and take photos at some of the frequent frothing rapids. They sailed beneath Vasey's Paradise, a mossy waterfall bursting from a mid-cliff spring. Near Nankoweap Canyon, they passed an ancestral granary built into the canyon wall high above. They ran aground in the braided shallows below but soon worked free. At night, they camped on beaches and bedrock shelves, while steady winds covered everything—including Bessie and Glen—with sand. Twice they saw bighorn sheep along the banks, which watched, curiously, as these odd visitors floated by.

On November 12, the couple passed the Little Colorado River, with its typically milky blue inflow. This marked the end of Marble Canyon and the start of Grand Canyon proper. The next day, they reached Hance Rapid, the first major obstacle since they had left Cataract Canyon two weeks before. Fortunately, the couple found a line through this lengthy minefield of boulders, holes, and crashing waves.

Just downstream, the scow entered Upper Granite Gorge, an ominous gap between cliffs of black schist rising 1,000 feet overhead. The next rapid was named

Sockdolager by Powell's men for its knockout wave crest. Sure enough, Glen was cracked under the chin by an oar. He flew feetfirst into the river. Bessie grabbed both oars and managed to keep the scow straight. Glen sank beneath the waves twice before grasping the scow, and Bessie pulled him aboard. In the pool below, a rattled Bessie said she was ready to climb the canyon walls right then and there. Glen only laughed.

Onward they went, through the steep wave trains of Grapevine Rapid. On the morning of November 15, they passed beneath the Kaibab Trail suspension bridge and tied up on the beach at Bright Angel Creek. They were several days ahead of schedule, well on their way to setting the speed record. Needing to restock their rations, they began the steep hike to the South Rim.

Mistaken Assumptions

The sky above the Grand Canyon was darkening by the time Glen and Bessie Hyde reached Yaki Point. Throughout the afternoon, they had hiked up the grueling seven-mile Kaibab Trail from the Colorado River, 5,000 feet below. Along the way, they passed through a brief snowstorm before emerging above the clouds and admiring the colorful cliffs in the changing light.

After walking a few miles along the road, a passing motorist gave them a lift to the village. Glen and Bessie had dinner in the luxurious El Tovar Hotel, but they were not the typical wealthy tourists who visited the country's burgeoning national parks. Mindful of their budget, they opted for cheaper lodging in a nearby tent cabin. The next morning was a flurry of errands. They bought groceries and arranged for them to be transported by mule to the river. Visits were made with the park's assistant superintendent and a *Denver Post* reporter. The resulting story was soon reprinted throughout the country, quoting the slight Bessie, who told of close calls in foaming rapids between sheer canyon cliffs.

"I have had the thrills of my life," she said. "I've been thoroughly drenched a dozen times, but I'm enjoying every minute of the adventure."

The Hydes next called on Emery Kolb, the famous photographer who had boated the canyon with his brother back in 1912. These days, he operated a studio perched on the rim. The trio of adventurers swapped river stories over lunch. Kolb tried unsuccessfully to convince the couple to take life preservers, but they just looked at each other and smiled. Sweep boaters in Idaho never used life preservers. Before departing, they wrote letters to their families. In the correspondence, Glen and Bessie relayed a belief that they were past all the bad rapids. They claimed that they would reach Needles, California, in about three weeks. Both assumptions would prove to be drastically incorrect.

That afternoon, Kolb's wife and daughter drove the Hydes to the top of the Kaibab Trail.

"I wonder if I will ever wear pretty shoes again," mused Bessie. She glanced between the daughter's nice shoes and her own worn hiking boots.

This would be one of the last times the couple was seen alive.

An Unimpressed Passenger

The next afternoon, the Hydes returned to the river. They made a quick detour up Bright Angel Creek to the under-construction Phantom Ranch. "Going down the river—Nov. 16–28 in a flat-bottomed boat," one of them wrote in the guestbook. Back at the beach, they found a portly tourist peering through his eyeglasses at their scow. Adolph Sutro was a wealthy businessman from San Francisco. In his twenties, he'd learned how to fly airplanes from some well-known instructors, the Wright brothers. Now approaching forty, he still craved new adventures. After hearing about their impressive journey, Sutro asked the couple if he might join them for a few days of running rapids. He could depart at the next trail. In exchange, he'd pay for their groceries.

The following day, this motley crew of three shoved off into Bright Angel Riffle. Almost immediately, challenges arose. A mile downstream, strong headwinds pushed the scow into a swift eddy, swirling them in circles. They pulled the boat with a rope from shore and eventually got free. Next came a sharp violent drop at Horn Creek Rapid. Slamming through the waves and cliffs terrified Sutro and Bessie.

Dripping wet, they made camp nearby. An increasingly skeptical Sutro began wondering how these broke, under-equipped kids had made it this far. Around a campfire, Glen explained they hoped to make money after the trip by sharing their tales on the vaudeville circuit. Glen seemed decent but irresponsible, thought Sutro. He later wondered if young Bessie really wanted to stop but kept going along with her husband's obsessions.

On Sutro's last day with the Hydes, the scow bounced through the cliffside waves of Granite Falls. By the time they reached Hermit Creek on November 18, Sutro had experienced more than enough.

"Better to be a live coward than a dead hero," he later wrote about his brief trip with the Hydes.

Bessie and Glen hiked with Sutro a mile up to Hermit Camp. They had lunch at the cabin resort, where the businessman's guide was waiting with mules and the promised groceries. Over the past few days, Sutro had taken several excellent photos of the Hydes and their sweep scow on the river. Now he took one final portrait of the couple standing together at Hermit Camp, their faces grim and unsmiling. At some point they hiked back down to the river. They swapped hiking boots for the grippy tennis shoes they wore while running the river. Untied the scow. Plummeted through the waves and troughs of Hermit Rapid. Glen and Bessie Hyde turned the corner and were never seen again.

A Murderous Falls?

Rollin Hyde had been told by his son Glen to expect a telegram from Needles, California, on December 9. After three days with no word, the concerned father boarded a train for Las Vegas. For two months, he'd anxiously followed this latest and most daring exploit by his son and new daughter-in-law through letters and the occasional news dispatch. Over the coming weeks, the Idaho rancher would telegraph numerous authorities. Afterward, he'd often arrive at the authorities' offices in person by automobile or horse. Bessie's family would quickly join the push. Telegraphs were sent to regional governors begging for an aerial search by planes. Other telegraphs went to river runners, including Emery Kolb at the South

Rim, asking if he might help. Perhaps by searching the inner gorges by boat? As the days turned into weeks, multiple parties set out overland and down the river in search of the long overdue couple. Meanwhile, stories of the disappearance appeared in newspapers across the country.

On December 19, a pair of army biplanes took off from Las Vegas, heading east. They flew between the 4,000-foot walls of the Grand Wash Cliffs at the downstream edge of the Grand Canyon and proceeded upstream. After thirty miles, they saw the whitecaps of large rapids in the river below. A few minutes later, they spotted a boat adrift. Circling, they saw no people, so they made a beeline for the landing strip at the South Rim.

Rollin Hyde and Emery Kolb were waiting when they landed. After listening to the airmen's descriptions, Kolb hopped into the rear seat. They flew through snow flurries to the spot of the sighting, near river mile 237. During a close pass, Kolb recognized it was a scow, seemingly stuck in calm water. He even spotted bedsprings. No question, this was the Hydes' vessel. But the couple was nowhere to be seen.

A few days later, Emery Kolb, along with his brother Ellsworth and their friend Brooks, arrived at Diamond Creek, a rough access point about twelve miles upstream of the derelict scow. After patching an abandoned rowboat, they took to the river on Christmas Eve 1928—thirty-six days since Glen and Bessie were last seen at Hermit. The water level was shockingly low, only 4,000 cubic feet per second, perhaps half the level it had been a month before. This turned the rapids into exposed rock gardens, and the pools between them were like lakes without current.

As Emery rowed downstream, the three men hollered out for the Hydes and scanned the shore for footprints. Ellsworth hadn't been on the oars in years, but he convinced his brother to swap places above 232 Mile Rapid. In later years, it would acquire the nickname Killer Fang Falls. After coming around a sharp turn, the current bounced off a left-side cliff, creating a series of cresting waves that pushed their boat to the right. In the runout below were the bedrock fangs, a series of water-smoothed teeth bursting from the surface. Like many rowers, both before and after, Ellsworth botched the run. Their boat impacted the fangs. Fortunately, the current was slow enough that they were able to push off the rocks and reach the shore. The day was late, so they made camp nearby and built a driftwood bonfire.

The next morning, they reached the scow, still floating empty in the same placid pool. The sweep oars were in their locks. One end of the boat was floating slightly lower, with about a foot of water in the bottom. While Emery filmed the event from shore, Ellsworth and Brooks boarded the scow. They inventoried the gear, which all seemed properly secured. There was a full sack of flour and an untouched baked ham. The couple's hiking boots and warm coats. Blankets. Glen's rifle. Bessie's camera and film. On the gunwale, they found forty-two carved notches, one for each day of the trip. A quick glance at Bessie's journal found the last entry dated November 30. Taken together, this meant the Hydes made it twelve days past Hermit before whatever had happened to cause their disappearance.

The searchers tugged unsuccessfully on the scow's bowline, which ran tautly underwater, seemingly caught on something below. Eventually, Emery cut the line to free the boat. It was a decision he would later regret, and one that would be widely criticized. What if a body was at the other end? Or what if the Hydes were alive? Perhaps they'd been separated from the scow, somewhere upstream. Suppose the derelict craft had drifted downstream, and the couple was still scrambling around the sheer cliffs in search of it? Missing for twenty-seven days, in a cold canyon wilderness, this seemed unlikely, but it wasn't impossible.

Ellsworth guided the scow downstream through a riffle, but when he suggested they take it further, Emery balked. It was the middle of winter with temperatures hovering around freezing. They needed to play it safe. After unloading as many of the Hydes' possessions as they could fit in their rowboat, the party set the scow adrift. Sweeping into the next rapid, it wedged amid rocks, where they left it.

Soon, the search party was struggling to get out themselves. The first challenge was the massive Separation Rapid, which they stopped to scout. Here three members of Powell's 1869 expedition had left the river and hiked north up a side canyon, never to be seen again. After Emery dropped their over-loaded rowboat into the maelstrom, he couldn't pull away from a big rock. The boat flipped, and the men went into the water. They were carried a quarter mile before righting the boat and reaching shore. Their clothes began to freeze amid plummeting temperatures, so they gathered driftwood for a life-saving fire. The next day they rowed about six miles to Spencer Canyon, where they joined a ground party and rode horses out on a pack trail.

THE TRIP OF A LIFETIME

One of the best ways to bring this mystery to life is to join a guided raft trip down the Colorado River through the Grand Canyon. The wait can be long, with prime dates often booking up a year or two in advance. The price can be high as well, with trips often running from a few thousand dollars to over $5,000. Motor-rig trips are typically faster and cost less, as do partial trips, where you hike in or out at Phantom Ranch.

But if you want to experience the river like the daring Bessie and Glen, minus the going missing part, then consider doing the full river in oar boats. These longer trips move at a gradual pace, with more days and nights spent on the river. Such a trip is a commitment in both money and time, around two weeks on the river. The benefit is a complete break from society and a full immersion in what the canyon offers. More stunning views, more campsites, more side hikes, more hidden creeks, more secret waterfalls.

River running is safer now, with decades of lessons learned about how to navigate the river. A guide will row the rapids in either a rubber raft or hard-sided dory. Some trips may take along a paddle raft for the adventurous souls willing to put a blade in their hand and take their chances with the rapids.

Clues from the Canyon

The search continued for weeks and then months, directed and funded by a relent-less Rollin Hyde. New clues were found, including one of the couple's camps, near mile 206, with trash such as a fruit can and lima beans from the Hyde farm in Idaho. Footprints belonging to the Hydes were noted on shore in several places, includ-ing the scouting paths at Ruby Rapid, Bass Rapid, and the long, snaking 217 Mile Rapid. This meant the Hydes had become only the second party to successfully run through infamous Lava Falls, near mile 180, with its cauldron of crisscrossing waves.

The Kolb brothers felt particularly moved by Rollin Hyde's quest. They devel-oped the couple's film and studied Bessie's journal, which suggested the couple was in over their heads yet resourceful in a pinch. At notorious Bedrock Rapid, mile 130, their scow had been pushed left into a churning eddy above a rocky mazelike channel. One sweep oar was smashed, and Glen stayed up all night to keep the trapped scow off the rocks. Somehow, the next day, the couple managed to portage their two-ton vessel over boulders along the shore. Below the rapid, they repaired the scow and resumed their journey. The couple's photographs confirmed the epi-sode but offered little new information. Each of them had taken turns shooting the final images, showing the scow floating below Tuckup Canyon at mile 165, while the other grasped their oar.

The final journal entry was made on November 30. Bessie's brief notations suggest they made it past Diamond Creek and Travertine Creek, floated through a riffle, and navigated one rapid without incident, possibly 231 Mile Rapid. Most observers would later believe the journal ends shortly above 232 Mile Rapid, a.k.a. Killer Fang Falls.

The prevailing theory became that Glen and Bessie Hyde were separated from the scow around here. Maybe they tried to scout the rapid, a particular challenge given the steep gorge and water-polished bedrock. Could one or both have fallen in? Then, suppose the other dove in after them. Perhaps the scow pulled free during the scout. They may have tried to climb out to the north, only to vanish like Powell's men had, fifty-nine years before. After dying from hypothermia, the Hydes' bodies could have been devoured by scavengers. Their bones may have been dispersed by a later flash flood.

More likely, the Hydes ran through the 232 Mile Rapid without scouting. From upstream, it would seem like a simple riffle since the worst part is hidden behind a cliff. The scow barreled around the bend and smacked into the fangs. Somehow, they both ended up in the icy water, where together they drowned. Seeking closure, Rollin Hyde spent three years and every cent he had searching for the bodies of his son and daughter-in-law.

A Campfire Confession?

In October 1971, the members of a two-raft commercial trip were sitting around a campfire near Three Springs Canyon. Since World War II, the introduction of rubber rafts had created a bustling whitewater rafting scene in the Grand Canyon. It was known to paddlers as the trip of a lifetime. The head guide had just finished telling the tale of Glen and Bessie Hyde, concluding that, to this day, no one knows what happened.

"I know," said a small woman in her mid-sixties.

"Well, what happened?" asked one of the boatmen.

"I'm Bessie Hyde," she said, staring at the flames. After some prodding, the wiry woman with white hair continued. "Somewhere along here we had a real bad fight and he beat me up. So late that night, I got a knife and stabbed him."

The woman gravely claimed she dragged Glen's body to the river and set the boat adrift. She walked downstream to Diamond Creek, and then hiked up the wash to the highway. She took a Greyhound bus back east.

The others laughed and grinned at one another, figuring she was pulling their legs. But this new twist to the mystery would be repeatedly told around riverside campfires at the Grand Canyon. Many began to wonder. Years later, a curious author tracked down the old woman in Ohio. She said she'd never heard of Bessie Hyde. Some found this reply to be particularly strange, given the missing river runner had grown up only forty miles away.

Other theories and new leads emerged. After Emery Kolb died at age ninety-six, in 1976, a skeleton was found in an old canoe suspended from the rafters of his garage. A bullet was found in the skull. Had Emery shot Glen to save Bessie? The skeleton's height seemed about right for Glen Hyde, but the facial structure, clothing fragments, and belt buckle didn't match the photos taken during the trip. Plus, Kolb had openly showed these remains to people for years, claiming he'd found them below the rim before the park was established in 1919.

Two Legends Meet

In 1992, at the age of eighty-one, celebrated river guide Georgie White Clark died at her mobile home in Las Vegas. During World War II, she had trained as a pilot and ferried planes between bases for the military. In the 1950s, she became the first woman to run a Grand Canyon rafting company. Not long into her thirty-five-year career, she began strapping three thirty-three-foot bridge pontoons together into a monstrous vessel called the G-rig. Georgie would sit at the back, with a beer in one hand and the tiller in the other.

Shortly after her death, friends were cleaning out Georgie's trailer when they found her birth certificate. Her name at birth was actually Bessie DeRoss. Nearby they found a certified copy of the marriage certificate for Glen R. Hyde and Bessie Haley. Even before this discovery, some river runners had wondered. Might Georgie be Bessie Hyde? But the mischievous Georgie was five inches taller, with blue eyes. She was exactly the type who might leave around a red herring as a practical joke.

Besides, everyone knew that Bessie Hyde's eyes were dark brown—penetrating eyes unmistakably captured in dozens of photos taken in the days and weeks before her disappearance. She was the first woman to run all but the final few rapids of a mighty river. An impressive feat that ended in a mystery that forever since has haunted the depths of the Grand Canyon.

CHAPTER 16

WHO LEFT BEHIND THE FORGOTTEN WINCHESTER?

STRANGE DISCOVERIES

GREAT BASIN NATIONAL PARK

SNAKE RANGE, NEVADA

O h, my gosh!" exclaimed Eva Jensen.

The staff archaeologist was walking along a rocky hillside near the northern boundary of Great Basin National Park when she spotted something extraordinary. Partly illuminated by the midday sun, a weather-beaten nineteenth-century rifle was leaning against a juniper tree. Jensen went silent, stunned by the discovery.

Several fellow archaeologists glanced at Jensen, worried she'd fallen off a ledge. It was early November 2014 and the team was searching for Native American artifacts and petroglyphs in a remote area scheduled for a prescribed burn.

WILD NEVADA

The Silver State isn't usually associated with the words *national park*. This sparsely populated western region is best known for hot spots like Las Vegas and Reno, tourist cities filled with blinking casinos. But there's a natural side to Nevada, with miles of pristine desert, rising mountain ranges, and one of the least visited national parks. Despite a large size of roughly 120 square miles, Great Basin National Park sees only about 150,000 people per year. The reason is the remote location on U.S. Highway 50, over a hundred miles from the nearest interstate.

Jensen circled the find as the other archaeologists gathered around. Given its earthy colors, the old rifle looked like just another split of the juniper's trunk. The barrel was dark brown from rust, and the faded wooden butt was buried several inches deep in soil and fallen needles. The rifle had clearly been exposed to the high desert elements for a long time, with only limited shelter coming from the overhanging branches. An engraving on the mechanism indicated it was an 1873-model lever-action Winchester. "The gun that won the West," as the saying went. Could this abandoned rifle have been resting here for over a hundred years?

"Why do you set your gun down and forget where you put it?" pondered one team member.

More conjecture followed. The spot was at over 8,000 feet of elevation in the remote Basin and Range Province, a region with steep mountains rising between arid valleys. During the days of the Old West, the Snake Range was mostly known for mining, particularly tungsten, but also silver, lead, and copper. What if an excited prospector thought he'd struck the mother lode and misplaced his gun?

FORGOTTEN MOUNTAINS

The few who make the trek are often pleasantly surprised by this park. The high-elevation Wheeler Peak Scenic Drive winds its way up to over 10,000 feet. From there, hiking trails lead to stunning alpine lakes, the mountain summit at 13,065 feet, and an ancient bristlecone pine grove where some specimens are over 4,000 years old. Be sure to acclimate and pace yourself to avoid altitude sickness. Other highlights include ranger-guided tours through the impressive speleothems in Lehman Caves and five NPS campgrounds.

Of course, the area also saw sporadic grazing with cattle and sheep. Maybe a cowboy or shepherd had come up here to gather stray livestock.

One also couldn't rule out a gun battle involving outlaws. Perhaps the rifle jammed or the shooter ran out of ammo. That said, the upright positioning suggested casual placement, not a chaotic abandonment during a firefight. It was as if the owner had leaned it against a tree during a lunch break. Perhaps a big-game hunter tracking a buck had lost the forgotten Winchester.

Jensen used a small spade to clear the duff from around the butt. Carefully, orange tape was applied to the rifle to keep it intact. Back at park headquarters, the investigation began. Shining a light at certain angles revealed a serial number. So, Jensen contacted the Firearms Museum at the Buffalo Bill Center of the West. Located in Cody, Wyoming, their archives contain the manufacturing records for Winchester firearms.

The forgotten rifle was made in 1882, the same year that the infamous Jesse James was assassinated—shot in the back, while hanging a picture in his home in

Missouri, by new accomplice Robert Ford. The .44–40 caliber Winchester was first released in 1873, at a cost of fifty dollars, and could fire fifteen shots without reloading. By 1882, the price had come down to twenty-five dollars, equivalent to about $750 in the 2020s. Around 25,000 total were manufactured. This particular one had shipped from the company warehouse in Connecticut, but the destination and recipient were not listed in the records.

SEARCH THE SPOT

To further bring this mystery to life, stop by the visitor center to learn more about the remote north end of the park, near Strawberry Creek, where the Forgotten Winchester was found. There are a few trails and primitive campsites out there, but no services or water. Keep your eyes peeled, and, who knows, you might even spot another artifact from the Old West. That said, please remember that any artifacts, whether rifles or Native American relics, cannot be disturbed or removed from the park. Inform a ranger if you find anything.

Road Trip for a Rifle?

In January, park staff posted photos of the Forgotten Winchester on Facebook, which quickly went viral. For a few days, the item went on public display in the visitor center. One hope was that someone might come forward with clues—perhaps a local with a family tale about their great-grandfather losing his favorite rifle in the mountains. While curious folks did visit, none could offer information about the rifle's origins.

So, the artifact went on an adventure. Jensen put it in a case and drove to

Wyoming. At the Cody Firearms Museum, experts began by making sure it wasn't loaded. Since the action was frozen, they inserted a wooden dowel into the barrel, which encountered some type of blockage before reaching the breach.

They took the rifle next door to the local hospital. An X-ray revealed the mechanism wasn't loaded. The blockage was probably organic matter—juniper needles, bark, and dust—that had fallen into the barrel over time. However, while examining the X-ray, they noticed something curious on the edge of the image. A second X-ray of the stock revealed a cartridge concealed within the trap, a small storage space in the butt that's typically used for cleaning supplies.

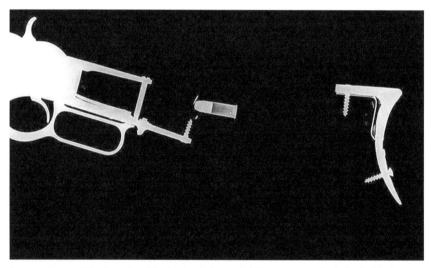

An x-ray image of the Forgotten Winchester that revealed the presence of a bullet inside the trap. Courtesy of the National Park Service

Opening the trap door, the experts found a live .44–40 Winchester center-fire cartridge manufactured by the Union Metallic Cartridge Company. This type of ammunition was produced between the years 1887 and 1911, a period roughly considered the final decades of the Wild West.

Perhaps the rifle was left by an infamous outlaw? The 1890s saw the rise of Butch Cassidy and the Wild Bunch. In the early 1900s, the gang robbed a bank in

Winnemucca, about 250 miles to the northwest. Their typical roundabout escape might have led a few of them through the Snake Range on their way toward a meetup in Texas. Regardless, the days of the Wild Bunch were numbered. The early 1900s saw the spreading of law and order throughout the American frontier. The abandoned rifle most likely belonged to a law-abiding citizen trying to eke out a living in the high desert.

In 2016, the famous artifact was returned to the Great Basin Visitor Center, just in time for the park's thirtieth anniversary. It was placed inside a permanent display case that simulates the spot where Eva Jensen found it. Now, visitors file past while pondering the scant clues available. Beyond that, the story behind the Forgotten Winchester remains a mystery.

MUSEUM TRIP

An hour east of Yellowstone National Park, in Cody, Wyoming, the Buffalo Bill Center of the West includes five museums on topics primarily related to the Old West. The Cody Firearms Museum, mentioned in this mystery, houses over 10,000 firearms from across the centuries. The Plains Indian Museum explores the lives, cultures, and traditions of Native Americans from the Great Plains. The Buffalo Bill Museum documents the life and exploits of controversial Buffalo Bill Cody, creator of the vaudeville Wild West Show, and performers like Wild Bill Hickok, Annie Oakley, and Sitting Bull. The Whitney Western Art Museum displays numerous works from acclaimed Western artists like Thomas Moran, Albert Bierstadt, and others. And the Draper Natural History Museum offers child-friendly exhibits about the plant and animal life of Yellowstone.

CHAPTER 17

WAS UPHEAVAL DOME CREATED BY A METEORITE IMPACT?

UNEXPLAINED PHENOMENA

CANYONLANDS NATIONAL PARK

COLORADO PLATEAU, SOUTHEASTERN UTAH

t was still dark when the seasonal ranger awoke to the familiar sounds of dawn. The howling of coyotes and the wild chirps of circling nighthawks. Each time these nocturnal birds plunged through the star-filled sky, there was a roaring buzz, like a truck blowing past on a highway. But the ranger, along with his wife and one-year-old son, were living in a tin house trailer eight miles down a dirt road inside Arches National Monument. It was mid-August in 1957, and as streaks of light rose from the horizon, there wasn't a paved road in sight. Just a bare landscape of rock and sand, desert shrubs, and strange formations of stone.

Once the sun was up, the ranger said goodbye to his family and went to work.

With a staff of only five, each day was different at this little-known backcountry park. Everyone, including the superintendent, spoke with visitors, picked up trash, and cleaned the outhouses. Compared to the famous destinations like Yellowstone and Yosemite, which welcomed over a million visitors per year, the dusty Arches might see 30,000.

Today the ranger had been asked to join the search for a missing man. The hiker had disappeared beyond the unit boundary in a rugged part of Bureau of Land Management (BLM) land. Outside his trailer, the ranger tossed his canteen and rucksack into the step-side government pickup, painted in park-service green. Overhead rose a shadowy formation, which resembled a Moai statue from Easter Island, called *Balanced Rock*.

The ranger drove west through Willow Flats and the sandy Courthouse Wash, which fortunately was passable despite the recent rains of monsoon season. His destination was up on Dead Horse Mesa. Because it stood 1,000 feet above the surrounding landscape, some folks called it an island in the sky.

The Dead Man at Upheaval Dome

The Sunday before, a U.S. Geological Survey (USGS) geologist named H. R. Joesting had noticed a car parked off the dirt road to Upheaval Dome. Growing magazine coverage was turning the mesa into a minor tourist destination, and the bizarre crater was considered one of the more spectacular features. For decades, it had been interpreted as an eroded salt dome. In this scenario, a deeply buried salt formation would have pushed up from below, which slowly upheaved and deformed the surrounding rocks. Then the top and interior of the structure eroded away. Whatever created Upheaval Dome, the result was a circular depression, three miles wide, that looked like a crater. Down inside, a contorted inner peak rose up from a trough-like basin that was surrounded by a huge ring of outward-tilting and highly deformed sedimentary rock.

Joesting was investigating some magnetic and gravity anomalies coming from beneath Upheaval Dome. When he returned on Tuesday, the abandoned car was still there. So, the geologist contacted Bates Wilson, the superintendent at Arches. Bates had joined the county sheriff in a quick search for the car's owner that first afternoon, but they found no one.

The next morning, the sheriff gathered a larger party near the abandoned vehicle. They had learned that the missing man was a sixty-nine-year-old hobby photographer. Now his adult son was present for the search. Bates had brought his own college-aged son to help. Plus, a seasonal ranger named John Abbey had come up from Natural Bridges National Monument. Then the other seasonal ranger from Arches pulled up in a green pickup. It was John's brother, Edward Abbey.

With everyone assembled, the searchers divided up the area and fanned out. Johnny hopped in with Ed, and they drove to the end of the road and split up. For four hours, Ed looked in the shade of juniper trees and overhanging ledges. He wandered along the mesa rim from vistas to gullies to fissures to massive potholes scoured into the bedrock. Mantraps, he figured. Then again, given the number of days the tourist was lost in the desert, this was more likely a body search. With the hot sun high in the sky, Ed found himself out of water. So, he returned to the truck. There he found Johnny waiting with a lost expression on his face.

Johnny had found the missing man under a shady pinyon pine with a spectacular view. The searchers deduced that the man had left his car and walked along the edge of Holman Springs Basin before crossing over to the rim above Trail Canyon. He'd briefly descended into a ravine. At some point, he retraced his steps in an increasingly frantic manner. Perhaps he panicked as the heat rose, and he realized he had forgotten his water in the car. Feeling ill, he stopped to rest in the shade and expired with his camera in his lap. To die in such a splendid landscape was a stroke of enviable luck, Ed later wrote. "The brink of the unknown."

However, carrying the dead man to the road was particularly unlucky for the searchers. The mourning son was spared the task, and he was soon out of earshot. This allowed the stumbling and overheating stretcher bearers to let off some steam. During the agonizing mile back to the road, few insults were spared at the expense of the bloating body inside the coroner's black bag.

"You'd think he'd float like a balloon," joked one of them—possibly Ed. "Maybe the old fart would walk if we let him out of the bag."

A Moneymaker or a Park

As a seasonal ranger, the thirty-year-old Ed Abbey was a source of irreverent amusement among the Arches staff. For one thing, his head was too big to fit the typical flat-brimmed hat of a park ranger. At first, he wore a black cowboy hat around the monument. Bates didn't like the look, so the jovial super made Ed wear a safari pith hat with an NPS emblem. The cantankerous Ed definitely didn't like that look.

Bates was a popular boss who made it a point to work in the field with his staff. After hard days of trail building, he'd cook up a Dutch oven meal, and they'd all camp out under the stars. Bates had big plans for not just Arches but the very island in the sky they now marched across. Each shouldn't be just a monument and BLM land but large national parks, he believed, with paved roads and better facilities for the American public to enjoy.

"Arches National Moneymint," ribbed Ed, who felt differently about the increasing numbers of tourists. To him, they were nuisances who couldn't appreciate a majestic place that should be left undisturbed. About the dead man atop island in the sky? "We are well rid of him," Ed later wrote.

Had he known the man, Ed admitted, he might have mourned. Instead, he saw him from a great distance, through the same eyes as a circling vulture. Huddled under a pinyon, succumbing to the heat, near the most contorted formation in Canyonlands.

The competing views of Bates and Ed were particularly relevant in the booming postwar period. Which way the forty-one-year-old National Park Service would continue during the second half of the twentieth century was still a mystery. Everyone—the rangers, staff, visitors, critics, and fervent supporters—seemed split about how to proceed in wild and hidden places like Southeastern Utah.

The irreverent Ed had described himself to his colleagues as a writer and poet, but they had not realized the reach of his words. His book about two seasons spent at Arches, *Desert Solitaire*, would become a classic work of conservation literature. For the memorable chapter "The Deadman at Grandview Point," the crafty Ed would shift the morbid setting from near Upheaval Dome to a few miles southeast for more resonant scenery.

Ed's vision of the West would win the hearts of many wilderness conservationists. Bates's vision of accessibility for the masses would win the future. Arches would become one of the more popular national parks in the nation. Island in the Sky would become the most popular of three districts in the remote Canyonlands National Park. For many pragmatic conservationists, the alternative was far worse. There were plenty of critics who didn't want the parks at all. They wanted the land for mining or ranching or reservoirs. Bates was already hard at work making sure that didn't happen.

A few years later, the new Secretary of the Interior Stewart Udall was flying over Southern Utah. With him on the plane was a man who would soon live in infamy. Some would call him notorious, while others defended him as necessary, depending on their points of view. As the commissioner of the Bureau of Reclamation, Floyd Dominy would be the driving force behind dozens of public dams, including Glen Canyon.

As the two officials looked down on the confluence of the Colorado and Green Rivers, each had very different visions. Dominy saw a chance for another massive dam. Udall saw what Bates was proposing.

The rising spires and jointed grabens of the Needles. The tortuous canyons and colorful ridges of the Maze. The White Rim cliffs that framed a twisting river below Island in the Sky. And the contorted crater of Upheaval Dome, which would soon have an improved road and a string of scientists competing to unravel its uncertain origin.

To Udall, the Canyonlands region looked to be one of the most magnificent places in the United States. So, he said a few words that would change the course of history in Southeastern Utah.

"That's a national park."

SOUTHWESTERN ORBIT

Many places mentioned in this chapter can be visited, and here are a few from around the Southwest. Arches National Park is a great place for scenic drives and desert hiking during milder weather, including fall and spring. During summer, the sun and heat are oppressive, though early morning hours around sunrise may work. Some of the top hikes are on out-and-back trails leading to famous formations. Round-trip distances are one mile at the Windows, two miles at Landscape Arch, and three miles at Delicate Arch, which is particularly nice at sunset.

Canyonlands is the least visited of Utah's five national parks, averaging around 750,000 visitors annually. Most people head to the Island in the Sky District, where the highlights include views and hikes around Grand View Point Overlook, Green River Overlook, and White Rim Overlook. Watching the sunrise over the La Sal Mountains through Mesa Arch is a classic Moab-area experience. The White Rim Road is a challenging 100-mile unpaved backcountry loop for four-wheel-drive vehicles and mountain bikes.

A Meteor Crater After All

About 250 miles south, in Flagstaff, Arizona, Eugene Shoemaker spent much of the early 1960s establishing the USGS Astrogeology Research Center. The space age was less than a decade old, and much had already been accomplished. While Soviet cosmonauts and U.S. astronauts were rocketing into space, Shoemaker was contributing major breakthroughs on the ground in the nascent study of impact craters.

With increasing talk about sending astronauts to the moon, attention had turned to studying the target. Most craters on the moon, and those found on Earth, had long been considered the result of volcanic eruptions. To understand this outdated view, imagine a typical triangular volcano, spewing ash from its summit vent. When the magma chamber inside drained out, the peak above typically sank into the hollow interior. This could leave behind a caldera, with an upraised rim around a sunken circular floor.

The result was that two very different geological processes created surface craters that looked very similar. Sometimes, however, a terrestrial crater might not show any evidence of volcanism. At first, these mysterious voids were attributed to hypothetical crypto-explosions caused by some yet unknown phenomena—a theory that was later abandoned. Occasionally, scientists had suggested that both terrestrial and lunar craters might, in fact, be caused by meteorite impacts.

Shoemaker not only revived the lunar impact theory, but he began to ponder another mystery. Our planet and its lone natural satellite are essentially a binary system. Thus, if the smaller had been struck so regularly, then so had the larger. Yet where were the impact structures on Earth? Due to a variety of factors, they would not be easy to find. Terrestrial forces like water, wind, and ice would slowly erode a crater. Vegetation could obscure it. Humans might flatten a crater for farming or construction.

One of the first places Shoemaker looked was Barringer Crater, forty miles east of Flag. It was a squarish bowl carved into the high desert plain, about three-quarters of a mile wide and 500 feet deep. The USGS had previously linked it to the cinder cones and calderas of the nearby San Francisco volcanic field. But back in the early 1900s, a mining engineer named Daniel Barringer believed it was produced by an impact. After all, meteorite fragments had been found on the surrounding plains. Barringer hoped to extract the valuable remnants of a massive iron impactor he believed was lodged beneath the rubble on the crater floor.

Over the coming decades, several scientists, including meteorite pioneer Harvey Nininger, continued to study the question. To produce a crater of that size, a hypothetical meteorite likely would have to weigh 300,000 tons. It would have mostly vaporized on impact, leaving no deposit to mine and also no evidence.

But some tiny pebbles buried around the crater yielded intriguing clues. These pebbles had a rounded shape, were partly melted, and contained magnetic iron–nickel minerals that were sometimes fused with native rock types. Yet nature had other ways of metamorphosing stone, and not all observers were convinced by the meteorite theory.

In the early 1960s, Shoemaker brought samples from Barringer Crater to USGS geologist Edward Chao. Looking under a high-powered microscope, Chao identified two rare minerals, altered forms of quartz named *coesite* and *stishovite*. These transformed minerals could only be created by the intense heat and pressure found in a few situations. One was beneath Earth's crust, in the semi-molten depths of a subduction zone. Another was at ground zero of atomic explosions. And if coesite or stishovite were found in unmetamorphosed rocks, like the sedimentary units at Barringer Crater, it meant one thing: an impact structure.

Barringer, Nininger, and a few other prescient scientists had been right. It was an impact structure after all, and a nickname became official: Meteor Crater. Scientists now had a diagnostic criterion for identifying a terrestrial impact site, a rare phenomenon called *shock metamorphism*.

Medieval Meets Extraterrestrial

The next place that Shoemaker went looking for evidence was Germany. On the western edge of Bavaria, in the mountains of the Swabian Alb, there was an oddly circular medieval town, ringed by a fortress wall built in the fourteenth century. Nördlingen was located inside the shallow Ries Basin, a roughly circular depression a dozen miles wide that had been long attributed to an ancient volcano. Many of the stone buildings, including St. George's Church, were made with local suevite from the nearby Otting quarry. This grayish stone with small black flecks was long believed to be some unique type of compacted volcanic tuff.

Then Shoemaker showed up at the Otting quarry with a pick and rock hammer to collect samples. On his way to the post office, he stopped by St. George's Church and pulled out his hand lens. Just peering at the exterior seemed to show melted minerals and shocked quartz. Back in the States, when Chao received the shipment of rock samples, his microscope analysis confirmed the discovery. This medieval town had been built from impacted stone. In less than a year, Shoemaker was two for two. Nördlinger Ries was an impact crater.

With this paradigm shift, scientists fanned out across the globe to find more impact craters. When the samples collected during NASA's Apollo missions confirmed the frequency of impacts on the moon, the search on Earth only intensified. By the early 1970s, over fifty terrestrial craters had been found. During the 2020s, that number would exceed 200. From studying craters across the solar system, including those on Earth but especially those on the moon and later Mars, a new discipline emerged: the field of impact science.

SEE THE UPHEAVAL

Bring this mystery to life at the Island in the Sky District with a stop by Upheaval Dome, where a popular trail leads about a half mile to a first lookout and another half mile to a second overlooking the crater. Adventurous hikers can circle the crater on the 8.5-mile Syncline Loop Trail, which is considered the hardest hike in the district due to steep switchbacks and boulder scrambling. Once inside the crater, an additional three-mile out-and-back detour leads to the central peak. This all-day endeavor should only be attempted in mild weather by experienced hikers.

How Do Impact Craters Form?

Imagine a fiery meteorite speeding through the atmosphere and striking a desert region of sand and stone like the American Southwest. Instantaneously, the impactor and target rocks compress downward. As these materials violently shrink into a smaller space, their density increases. The pressure and temperatures rise exponentially. Shockwaves spread outward. Suddenly, the rock depressurizes and explodes into the sky, leaving behind a cavity.

The ejected material is a mixture of vaporized, melted, shocked, and fractured rocks that flies outward in ballistic arcs. Much of this ejecta immediately lands just outside the crater, forming the uplifted rim. Meanwhile, the remaining debris blankets the surrounding area and thins out downrange. Those shockwaves that were initially directed outward and downward, into the bedrock surrounding the cavity, create a zone of breccia. Basically, this is a compacted region of metamorphosed rocks. Beyond that is a fracture zone of shattered, faulted, and cracked bedrock.

Once the dust settles, there are two primary types of impact craters left behind. Smaller impactors create *simple craters*, which have rounded cavities and a single elevated ring encircling the feature. Larger and more powerful impactors create *complex craters*. These usually have an uplifted peak rising from the center of a shattered crater floor that extends broadly outward. The walls of a complex crater are often terraced. This is due to the surrounding bedrock developing listric faults that roughly parallel the curvature of the cavity walls. These listric fault blocks resemble the bottom portion of a crescent moon cut in half. Imagine them sliding downward while rotating inward. This is what creates the upturned terraces. And the weight of this inwardly slumping material causes a rebound effect that uplifts the central peak.

Sometimes, in particularly large impacts, a complex crater may develop a series of rings encircling the inner peak. Called *peak ring craters*, these structures look like a bull's-eye target. Almost as if a pebble was dropped into water, and the resulting circular waves were frozen in stone.

An Alarming Reason to Look Up

Once people went looking for them, Earth turned out to have a wide array of crater types. The well-preserved Wolfe Creek impact structure in Australia's Great Sandy

Desert is an example of a small and simple crater, created only a few hundred thousand years ago. It has a sharply elevated rim, and a sunken floor resting eighty feet below the ground outside the crater. The largest terrestrial site found so far is Vredefort Dome in Free State Province, South Africa. The theory is that nearly two billion years ago, a massive meteorite about fourteen miles in diameter created a crater up to 200 miles wide.

Across the United States, around thirty impact structures have been recognized, with more likely to be discovered in time. A crater was even identified beneath the waters near the mouth of Chesapeake Bay. The current theory is that thirty-five million years ago, a massive meteorite nearly two miles wide slammed into the coastline of North America. The resulting crater was up to fifty miles wide. This triggered a towering tsunami that swept inland, perhaps reaching as far as the Blue Ridge Mountains.

The most famous impact structure was found off the coast of the Yucatan Peninsula in the Gulf of Mexico. Chicxulub crater is believed to have formed about sixty-six million years ago from an impactor six miles wide. After it struck, a cloud of glowing dust and fiery ash circled the globe, igniting the world's forests in flames. The hulking dinosaurs never had a chance.

With this growing awakening to the threat of impact strikes came an alarming incentive to look up. Now astronomers turned their telescopes and observatories toward watching the skies for approaching asteroids and comets. One such observer was Eugene Shoemaker, inspired to join the field after his discoveries in impact science. His wife, Carolyn Shoemaker, took up the call as well. After changing careers in midlife, she went on to discover thirty comets and over 500 asteroids. Their friend David Levy was a prolific science writer who also searched between the stars.

Together the trio would make a famous discovery, out in space, beyond the asteroid belt. Comet Shoemaker–Levy 9 had broken apart due to tidal stresses in orbit above Jupiter. Earthlings were watching in 1994 when the string of impactors slammed into the swirling clouds of the gas giant, sending up fireballs and leaving behind brown scars that lingered for months.

MORE PARKS

Many travelers knock off Utah's so-called "Mighty Five" national parks during one or a few sweeping road trips. The most visited is Zion, followed by Bryce Canyon, Arches, Capitol Reef, and Canyonlands. While these big-name destinations get most of the attention, several lesser-known parklands offer comparable experiences, including Natural Bridges National Monument. This smaller NPS unit protects three impressive sandstone archways, which can be viewed from the scenic drive or up close via hiking trails through the rugged canyons.

Looks Can Be Deceiving

During the decades surrounding the comet impact, Shoemaker and some colleagues began studying Upheaval Dome to see if they could put an extraterrestrial twist on the origin story. When these impact scientists looked at the contorted feature, they interpreted it as the best exposed complex crater on Earth.

To them, Upheaval Dome was the visible remnants of what potentially happened beneath the cavity rubble during post-impact collapse. They saw a central peak surrounded by a ring structure. They noticed that the normally horizontal sedimentary rock units comprising the crater walls were tilting outward; in other words, they were sloping downward away from the center. This was just what one would expect from the listric faulting that followed a larger impact.

In this case, the theory became that an impactor with a diameter of around one-third of a mile struck the previously overlying rock units, creating a crater between four and five miles wide. Millions of years of erosion had carried away the overlying rubble, revealing the structure underlying the impact zone.

When examining aerial photos of Upheaval Dome, its outward appearance certainly resembled other complex peak ring craters being discovered on other worlds. By now, space probes had fanned out from our planet to capture images of craters throughout the solar system, including craters like Tycho and Bürg on the moon and Eddie and Yuty on Mars. Further examples were found on Mercury and the rocky moons of Jupiter and Saturn. Other complex craters were found on Earth, including Mistastin, a crater lake with a central peak in far northeastern Canada.

But as volcanic calderas had already shown, looks can be deceiving in geology. There wasn't another crater nor salt dome on Earth that closely resembled the bizarre Upheaval Dome. Theoretically, the enigmatic structure could have been created by either process.

Inside the Upheaval

So, the impact scientists trekked inside Upheaval Dome, where they examined the exposed rock units composing the central peak. These included the famous White Rim sandstone, which otherwise should have been buried here. Instead, these beds of White Rim sandstone were jumbled together with several rock units that would normally lie flatly above. Each unit was highly faulted and turned nearly vertical in places. Something must have forced the buried White Rim and other rocks upward. But was it a violent impact or the gradual flow of salt?

By now, the salt dome theory had evolved. Buried deep beneath the bedrock of the Canyonlands region was the widespread Paradox Formation. The weight of the rock units above sometimes squeezed this buoyant, plastic-like salt sideways and upward into weaker spots. The resulting salt tectonics could warp and crack the surface rocks in strange ways. When combined with erosion, this led to the dramatic landforms found in the surrounding national parks like rock arches, joints, fins, and spires.

The one thing that wasn't present at Upheaval Dome was exposed salt from the Paradox Formation. If it was responsible for pushing the White Rim rocks upward, one might expect some salt to remain, like fingerprints left by the deforming culprit. Furthermore, when researchers used various geophysical surveying methods, like seismic refraction, the results did not seem to support the salt dome theory. The uppermost surface of the underlying Paradox Formation was mapped to start about 1,500 feet below the bottom of Upheaval Dome. And that upper surface of salt appeared to be flat. There did not seem to be any disturbances or protrusions rising upward toward the crater.

A preeminent geophysicist and expert in salt tectonics offered a compatible solution. A salt diapir, or bubble, could have pinched off from the underlying Paradox Formation. It would have risen upward like a drop of oil rising through water, upheaving the dome, and then eroding away without leaving a trace of evidence. This was certainly possible, though it would mean that Upheaval Dome was the most eroded salt structure ever found.

What Shoemaker and the impact scientists needed was that same slam-dunk evidence that had won the debate at Meteor Crater and Nördlinger Ries. They needed to find signs of shock metamorphism.

During their 1990s fieldwork, the team believed they found some. Near the center of Upheaval Dome, in the thin sandstone beds of the Moenkopi Formation, they spotted some potentially faint shatter cones. These conical features are created by shockwaves radiating outward through bedrock. The results are metamorphic rocks with a fanlike pattern of grooves that records the stresses from impact. However, the shatter cones they identified at Upheaval Dome were rare and far more subtle than those found at many other impact structures.

The team continued searching. In the depressed trough on the east side of the crater, they came across some rounded quartzose cobblestones. They initially theorized that these were formed by impact melting and cooling. However, a follow-up study conducted by geochemists determined the nodules were not, in fact, impactites. These rocks had been altered by hydrothermal processes. The theory remained unproven, and Shoemaker might have continued his search around the crater, but he never got the chance.

NORTHERN A TO Z

Check out the sites around Flagstaff, including Lowell Observatory, which blends night-sky telescope viewing, star shows, and museum exhibits. Learn about the region's eruptive past at Sunset Crater Volcano National Monument and explore the Ancestral Puebloan great houses at adjacent Wupatki National Monument. In nearby Winslow, Arizona, at Meteor Crater & Barringer Space Museum you can learn about meteorites and view the iconic crater from several viewpoints connected by paved paths along the rim.

A Lingering Debate

In 1997, Gene and Carolyn Shoemaker were driving a rented Toyota Hilux through the Australian Outback. It was a sunny winter day on the red dirt Tanami Track, which wound through a rolling desert of yellowed grasses. They came to this southern continent regularly to explore its ancient interior. Over billions of years, about forty impact craters had been preserved within the bedrock cratons. This time their destination was the remote Goat Paddock crater in the Kimberly Region.

As Gene drove around a curve, an oncoming Land Cruiser appeared without warning. The head-on impact killed the scientist at the age of sixty-nine. A severely injured Carolyn was airlifted to a hospital. She fortunately survived and later returned to Flagstaff and her work at Lowell Observatory.

The best-known proponent of the meteorite theory was gone, and the Upheaval Dome debate lingered for decades. Occasional new studies were published that leaned one way or the other. Eleven years after Eugene Shoemaker died, in 2008, a pair of German geologists declared they had confirmed the impact origin of Upheaval Dome. In the northeastern corner of the crater, within the Kayenta

Formation, they had found impactites. But not many. From the 120 samples that they prepared for microscope analysis, they counted only two shocked grains of quartz.

It wasn't enough to sway the meteorite critics in the salt diapir camp. The argument may have swung toward the impact side, but it remained far from settled. More field studies, more rock samples, more microscope analysis, and more evidence will be needed. In the meantime, a few things are certain. There is a strange and uniquely contorted crater atop the Island in the Sky District in Canyonlands National Park. No one has definitively proven what created it. Upheaval Dome is unlike anything else found on our planet.

CHAPTER 18

WAS JOSIE BASSETT A CATTLE RUSTLER, BOOTLEGGER, AND MURDERER?

LEGENDARY FIGURES

DINOSAUR NATIONAL MONUMENT

UINTA MOUNTAINS, UTAH

Turning off the highway, a young reporter drove nervously along a dirt road winding through remote Dinosaur National Monument. Nearby, the Green River lazily meandered through the desert.

In the dry hills above rose an impressive structure of steel and glass. A new visitor center completed two years before enclosed a rock wall of fossilized bones. Yet the purpose of the reporter's visit had little to do with the monument. It was a sunny summer day in 1960, and the twenty-year-old aspiring author was on his way to interview the notorious Josie Bassett Morris.

Many locals considered the eighty-six-year-old Josie to be a living legend.

She'd grown up in the infamous Browns Park, during the days of the Wild West, as the oldest daughter of the vigorous Elizabeth Bassett and sister of Queen Ann of the Cattle Rustlers. Josie was also said to be a livestock rustler and a close friend to dangerous outlaws, including Butch Cassidy and the Wild Bunch. She was a witness to frontier lynchings and murders—perhaps even a participant in them. Rumors said she shot one husband, poisoned another, and nearly killed a third with a frying pan, but that one got away. In recent years, Josie had become somewhat of a celebrity, particularly after *Life* magazine visited her Cub Creek homestead for an article in the late 1940s.

After crossing a small bridge over the river, the reporter followed the road past cliffs filled with ancient petroglyphs. These images of lizards, bighorn sheep, and human figures had been carved into rock by members of the mysterious Fremont culture a thousand years before. He parked at a locked gate and anxiously climbed the fence, unsure what to expect. A five-room log cabin stood in a grove of cottonwood trees below a sharply upturned ridge of cream-colored cliffs extending north from Split Mountain.

As the reporter approached, he saw an old woman pulling on a rope running through a pulley in a tree. On the other end of the rope was the carcass of a freshly slaughtered yearling calf rising into the air. The woman had short, silvery hair and a slight frame clad in ranching attire, including baggy blue jeans, a western shirt, and a brimmed hat. Josie Bassett.

"Mrs. Morris?" he called out.

Josie glanced up, startled. She darted for her porch and grabbed her Winchester rifle.

"Who are you? What do you want?"

He mentioned a mutual friend who had arranged the interview.

"Was that today?" said Josie. "Mercy, I must have forgotten all about it."

The reporter helped hoist the beef into the shade, and Josie wrapped it in a sheet. She leaned the rifle against the doorframe as they went inside her kitchen. Josie excused herself to change and soon returned wearing slacks and a floral-print shirt, rolled up at the sleeves to reveal forearms speckled from decades of sun and wind exposure. Being interviewed was nothing new to Josie. In recent years, numerous journalists and historians had made the trek out to Cub Creek to hear the tales of her incredible life and allegedly villainous deeds.

WHAT'S IN A DESIGNATION?

Dinosaur National Monument is one of those amazing NPS units that gets overlooked simply for not being designated a national *park*. It's also worlds away from other, better-known destinations like Zion or Yellowstone. Often called simply Dino, the monument spans 330 square miles of river canyons and twisted rock formations, like the improbable Split Mountain. Organized into two units, most of the roughly 300,000 annual visitors head to the Utah side. There, the focus is on dinosaur fossils at the impressive Quarry Exhibit Hall. Short hiking trails lead throughout the rugged landscape, and there are several campgrounds.

A Wild Woman Gang

"It was the most beautiful place I ever saw," said Josie during that summer of 1960 about Browns Park.

She was only four years old, perched atop a wagon, when the family arrived in 1878. The picturesque valley was surrounded on all sides by mountains, filled with grassy meadows and cottonwood bottomlands. On the eastern side were the dramatic Gates of Lodore, named by explorer John Wesley Powell, where the Green River plunges between cliffs into the northeastern Uintas.

The family had come at the invitation of Josie's rugged uncle Sam, one of the earliest white homesteaders in the valley. Sam helped Josie's hapless father, Herb, build a log cabin—at first two rooms and later expanded to five. A few months after arriving, the youthful Elizabeth gave birth to Anne. Among Josie's earliest memories was playing with native Ute children in Vermillion Creek, where they used wet sand and clay to form little houses. Only a year later, this peaceful coexistence was shattered by news of the Meeker Massacre. This was one of the final atrocities of the American Indian Wars, a violent series of military campaigns by the U.S. Army and retaliations by native tribes. The result was the forced relocation of all Utes to the south, where they were confined to a reservation in the Uinta Basin.

This left Browns Park in the hands of mostly white families running small ranches and grazing their herds on the open range. With the wave of Western settlement came powerful cattle companies that coveted the fertile lands of the valley. Given the isolated location, at the three-way border of the state of Colorado and two territories, Utah and Wyoming, Browns Park developed a reputation as a particularly lawless place.

When the vast herds of company cattle passed through the valley, it became common for the territorial residents to defiantly pilfer a few and doctor the brands. While the bookish Herb occupied himself with more domestic concerns, becoming postmaster and justice of the peace, the spirited matriarch Elizabeth was counted among the rustlers. Her so-called Bassett Gang included wild daughters Josie and Anne, plus a motley assortment of ranch hands. A young Texan cowboy named Matt Rash. A fiery Scotsman, Jim McKnight. And a former slave, an African American named Isom Dart, who, like the family, was originally from Arkansas.

Though Browns Park was remote, it was no more violent, and perhaps even less so, than other rough-and-tumble regions across the American frontier. One counterintuitive reason was that the valley was a stop on the so-called outlaw trail, offering shelter to an equally defiant band of misfits plaguing the stagecoaches and false-front banks of the invading gentry. While the outlaws were often violent by occupation, they mostly behaved themselves in the welcoming valley hideout, and their presence helped keep the petty ruffians at bay. One noted visitor was Butch Cassidy, an affable twenty-year-old who raced horses at the rowdy Crouse ranch.

"I thought he was the most dashing and handsome man I had ever seen," said Josie. "I was such a young thing, and giddy as most teenagers are."

At first, Butch seemed more interested in his horse than the pretty girl with curly copper hair and faint freckles. After being snubbed, Josie went home and stamped her foot on the floor in frustration. But Cassidy came to visit the Bassetts regularly. Their ranch was located where the main road entered the eastern valley, and it became an unofficial guest house and dance hall. The latter purpose was the result of a rather unique feature. Unlike the typical dirt ground of most valley homes, the Bassetts had an actual wooden floor.

One evening, the Bassetts let a fleeing Butch hide in their hayloft. When the outlaw asked Josie for a book from Herb's study, she told him it wasn't safe to light a lantern.

"He said, 'What am I going to do to keep from being bored?'" recalled Josie. "Well, all I can say is, I didn't let him get bored."

An Infamous Killer?

When Josie was sixteen, her parents sent her to Catholic finishing school in Salt Lake City. Two years later, her mother suddenly died at age thirty-seven from a mysterious illness. Josie later theorized it was appendicitis. Devastated, the daughter returned home to stay with her distraught father. Soon after, she realized she was pregnant with cowboy Jim McKnight's child. They married in March 1893 in Green River City, Wyoming. She was nineteen; he was twenty-four.

An ailing Uncle Sam gifted Josie some ranchland, up on Beaver Creek, in exchange for helping him after a stroke. By now, Isom Dart was like a member of the family. He moved with the young couple to work as a cowboy, and he helped raise their sons, Crawford, born that July, and Chick, born in 1896. While Josie was content with ranching life, the mercurial Jim was not. He drank heavily, spent hours at Crouse's ranch, and talked constantly about selling Josie's land and opening a saloon in Vernal. Josie, who rarely drank, wasn't having it. Not long after Uncle Sam died from a second stroke, the valley rumor mill reported that Josie and Jim's marriage had turned from argumentative to violent.

Herb took Josie to a judge in Hahn's Peak, Colorado, to file a restraining order. Jim flew into a rage, absconding with the boys to Salt Lake City before leaving them with an aunt near the Idaho border. After retrieving her children, Josie's next challenge was serving the divorce papers. The trap was set at a friend's ranch in early April of 1900, with Josie sending word to Jim that she was ill and wished to "fix up matters."

Jim entered the house, and things began cordially enough. But when the local sheriff presented the divorce papers, McKnight threw them on the table and stormed out. The sheriff followed, demanding the defendant pay a bond to appear in court. The alternative was arrest, with the means of persuasion being the sheriff's aimed revolver. Jim refused to halt, and one of two shots struck him in the back. The sheriff declined the injured man's demand to finish the job.

Then an enigmatic character entered the scene. A ranch cook, going by the name Tom Hicks, had recently arrived in the valley. He rode on horseback forty-five miles to Vernal to summon McKnight's brother to care for him. Hicks was a suspicious man, according to Josie, with "something wrong about him."

This tale would go on to take several bizarre turns when Hicks was later revealed to be the infamous frontier assassin Tom Horn. He'd been hired by a cattle company baron to retaliate against the rustling residents of Browns Park. Horn would soon embark on a murderous sweep, and two beloved members of the Bassett Gang would fall dead. One was Isom Dart, whom Josie would help bury in an aspen grove on Cold Spring Mountain. The other was Matt Rash, Ann's fiancé. A few months later, Josie's sister and two brothers were playing cards in the Bassett home when shots splintered through the door. They extinguished the lamps and hid on the floor through the night.

Jim McKnight would survive being shot by the sheriff in 1900, but early news reports of his demise would blend with another rumor: that Josie Bassett McKnight shot, and perhaps even killed, her hot-tempered husband. This myth would be amplified decades later by the 1938 book *The Outlaw Trail* by Charles Kelly, a controversial historian and the first superintendent of Capitol Reef National Monument. Three X-rays never found the bullet that struck Jim McKnight, who said he carried it for the rest of his life. Kelly claimed it was Josie who gave him the "leaden souvenir."

"The most ridiculous fool things I ever read," said Josie. "That Charles Kelly said I shot him. Well, he was quite an active man for a dead man." When the rumors persisted, despite the facts, Josie later remarked: "No, I did not shoot him. If I had, I wouldn't have missed."

A Search for Herself

The relatively peaceful Browns Park that Josie had known for over two decades was descending into murder and chaos when she decided to sell her land on Beaver Creek. Her father felt a remote ranch in an increasingly dangerous valley was no place for a single mother with two children. Though Josie accepted her father's advice, she later came to regret the move to the nearby city of Craig, Colorado. She enrolled the boys in school and took over the lease of the Elmo Hotel, with the trio making their home on the second floor among the guest rooms.

Charles Ranney, the owner of the town drugstore, took an interest in the young woman. He seemed undeterred by her circumstances, despite living in an era when divorce for any reason was harshly judged. They went fishing and took buggy rides out into the high desert that Josie missed so much. They were married in April 1902. Josie Bassett Ranney was twenty-six. Charles was thirty-three.

Josie and the boys moved into a stately residence with the wealthy Charles. Yet domestic bliss would once again prove elusive. Before running the drugstore, Ranney had been the principal when Josie attended grade school in Craig. As a stepfather, he was a strict disciplinarian. The mild-mannered Crawford simply hated Ranney. The younger Chick, a strong-willed Bassett like his female elders, outright rebelled. After a whipping at age eight, Chick saddled a horse and rode for Browns Park. Howling coyotes at dusk turned him back, but Josie recognized her son was too wild for town life. Fortunately, her sister Ann and new husband welcomed Chick to come live on their ranch in the park. But the damage to Josie's second marriage was done. Charles's attempt at a remedy, by moving the remaining three of them to a country ranch, didn't take. After three increasingly tumultuous years, he returned one evening to find the home empty.

Forty miles north, in the town of Baggs, Wyoming, Josie opened a hotel called the Ranney House. In the summer of 1906, the twice-divorced renegade gave marriage a third try, with Charles Williams. Josie was thirty-two now. Charles wasn't around long enough for anyone to learn his age. This Charles was also a drugstore owner, and a part-time prize fighter, with little interest in the countryside other than passing swiftly through on his way to boxing matches. Four months was enough time for the mistake to manifest, with the cause for divorce being "desertion."

Josie spent the next four years moving around the region. She ran boardinghouses in Rawlins, where the boys finished high school, and in Rock Springs, where Crawford spent a year at a university.

"I wanted to do something, to get away off somewhere," Josie later explained. "I wanted to be in the hills—I didn't know what I wanted. I didn't want to be in town."

RIVER TRIP

One of the best ways to experience Dino is a whitewater rafting trip on the Green River. The most common is a day trip on the Split Mountain section, while a more adventurous option involves a four-day trip through Lodore Canyon. During springtime, trips are also possible on the undammed Yampa River.

A New Year's Eve Death

With her sons grown, Josie got her wish in the summer of 1911 when she returned to Browns Park with her fourth husband. Emerson Wells was a ranch foreman ready to step out on his own. Josie was thirty-seven. Emerson was forty. Though known for being a "peach of a fellow," Wells regularly slipped into stuporous whiskey binges followed by nasty withdrawals with sweats and tremors. The couple rented the old Davenport Ranch, and Josie set about trying to change his ways. She purchased the "Keeley Cure," a popular product that claimed to end liquor addictions. As indicated, Josie added the concoction—which included tartar emetic, a chemical with effects similar to arsenic—to her husband's coffee. This produced the desired vomiting but didn't curb his alcoholism.

For a Christmas dance in 1912, Josie and Emerson drove their horse-drawn buckboard through falling snow to Linwood, near where the Green River entered the colorful cliffs of Flaming Gorge. A reluctant Josie wanted to stay just a few days, hoping to minimize her husband's inevitable bender. The other reason for her reluctance was that the town's boardinghouse was run by Minnie Crouse Ronholde, whom Josie had clashed with since they were kids in Browns Park. Matters only worsened when a blizzard snowed them in. Josie spent the week at the hotel and her husband at the saloon.

By New Year's Eve, Wells was in fine form. A family friend of the Bassetts lifted his watch and brought it to Josie. To prevent it from being stolen by some gamblers, he said. Early the next morning, another friend woke Josie. Wells was in the living room, curled up and twisting in agony.

"I feel like hell," said Wells.

Snow be dammed, Josie decided they would leave at sunup. She helped him dress for the open-air ride. Washed his face in a basin of warm water. Combed his hair. Her husband refused breakfast and drank only a few sips of coffee. The friend suggested a sip of whiskey, which he took. Yet, the man continued to writhe in misery. After some time, his body convulsed. Wells foamed at the mouth and died.

Josie was not a woman prone to crying, so she quietly went about the sad business. She spoke to the town constable, and friends helped her take the body to Browns Park for a funeral. But the regional rumor mill once again began turning. This time, the tales came from Josie's old rival. Minnie Crouse Ronholde's version of the story involved a terrible argument the night before Wells died and a mysterious glass of milk. She claimed Josie prevented another woman from drinking this milk before delivering it to her perfectly healthy husband. Could the convulsions have been strychnine poisoning? Why, what else could have caused them? Regarding the constable, Minnie said the devious Josie had wrapped him around her little finger, just like she always had done with men from Butch Cassidy on.

The story took hold, and grew with wild variations, some of which Minnie would repeat into her nineties. When Josie was summoned for questioning, it was said she appeared with a six-shooter and a rifle. When the sheriff exhumed Wells's coffin, it was said to be empty. Presumably, Josie dumped the body into a ravine for the vultures. Supposedly, Josie killed every husband she ever had, including forcing one to march to his demise atop thin ice on the Green River. Josie shrugged off the stories while perhaps wondering, could the Keeley Cure have played an unanticipated role in Wells's demise?

CABIN TRIP

Bring this mystery to life with a visit to the Josie Bassett Morris cabin at Cub Creek. Along the way, stop to look at (but please don't touch) several panels of Fremont culture petroglyphs, including iconic lizards etched onto sandstone. After touring Josie's cabin, a pair of short trails lead into nearby side canyons.

A Ranch or Roadhouse

In the summer of 1914, Josie once again said goodbye to Browns Park. With her was a fifth and final husband. Ben Morris was an Oklahoma cowboy hired by Wells to work the Davenport ranch. Josie was now thirty-nine. Ben was thirty-four. Together, they herded fifty head of cattle and fifty sheep over Diamond Mountain to a homestead at Cub Creek. They built a cabin, corral, and chicken coops. Josie planted a vegetable garden and fruit tree saplings for an orchard.

With Morris, Josie's luck was no better than the rest. An early argument between her sons and Morris, about him stealing local sheep, led to a fistfight and falling out. After two years of marriage, Josie caught Morris abusing a feisty horse, causing its mouth to bleed from a spade bit. Enraged, Josie grabbed a frying pan from the kitchen, and that was that.

"She gave me fifteen minutes to get off her property," Morris would jokingly tell people. "And I only used five of them." When he showed back up at Cub Creek, saying he had ten minutes left, Josie may have laughed, as they remained friends in the years to come. When Utah introduced statewide Prohibition in 1917, two years before the Feds passed the Eighteenth Amendment, Morris turned moonshiner. He built a rock cabin with a still in what came to be called Firewater Canyon near the Green River.

With Morris gone, Josie's sons resumed coming to visit and helping out. For a time, Crawford, with his wife and children, lived in an expanded cabin at Cub Creek. But the relationship between Josie and her daughter-in-law was always strained, so the family eventually moved to Vernal. Josie's father Herb died from a stroke in 1918. During the Great Depression, her brother Ebb fell deep into debt and committed suicide.

Increasingly, Josie found herself alone at Cub Creek. This was both challenging and rewarding for the independent woman. She was finally living the life she'd long sought at the age of fifty. In the mid-1920s, according to some stories, Josie's skirt became caught while clearing brush. In one fell swoop of her ax, she severed the dress. Hence forth, she wore pants around the ranch. Another story told of the time her long hair was caught in branches. Once again, there was a swing of the ax. She kept her hair short for the rest of her life.

The Depression was felt hard across the region. To make ends meet, Josie got creative. She hid a still in a nearby gulch and began experimenting with corn whiskey. Soon she specialized in apricot brandy, using fruit from her orchard, which became famous around the region. Sometime in the early 1930s, her grandson came galloping into the yard. Revenuers—treasury agents who rooted out illegal bootleggers—were planning a raid. The two of them carried the mash vats down to the gulch and covered everything with vines.

When the revenuers arrived, a confused Josie glanced up from tending her garden and offered these nice gentlemen coffee. After a search found no distilling equipment or broken bottles, the typical signs of a roadhouse, the embarrassed men conceded the error and accepted the coffee.

A Granny and a Thief?

A few years later, an adversarial neighbor named Jim Robinson accused Josie of rustling his cattle. Throughout the Depression, Josie had been sharing what she could with hungry families around the area—and not just the chickens, vegetables, and butter from her homestead. Josie shared cuts from stray cattle with the brands conveniently removed. Other times she sold an occasional cut of beef when she needed cash to keep her place running. Whether these came from her own herd was often unclear, but other area ranchers suspected theft.

Robinson's sworn complaint in 1936 alleged that his branded hides could be found on Josie's property. He even described the exact spot to dig. When a sheriff's posse arrived, Josie suspected a setup. In fact, her own sister, who was known as Queen Ann of the Cattle Rustlers, had faced the exact same situation twenty years before, orchestrated by a rival cattle baron who coveted the Bassett lands in Browns Park. Sure enough, the posse at Cub Creek conveniently unearthed, from the frozen January ground no less, eight tidy Robinson hides. Each was wrapped around wild hay from Josie's nearby stack. Loyal friends paid Josie's bail, and the trial was held in Vernal.

"Good morning, judge," said the sixty-two-year-old Josie upon entering the courtroom with her family, including a gaggle of grandchildren. She wore a frilly dress, sensible shoes, and had her gray hair neatly done up. When she got her chance to speak, she did not disappoint. "Your Honor, do you seriously believe that a little old lady could kill and butcher even one beef cow by herself?"

Josie was tried not once but twice for cattle rustling. Both times, the result was a hung jury.

RIDE ONWARD

Few visitors venture out to the monument's remote Colorado side, which is reached from Browns Park. The highlight is a short hike to view the Gates of Lodore, where the river plunges into the mountains. Nearby, check out the John Jarvie Historic Ranch and the Browns Park Wildlife Refuge.

Queen of the Cattle Rustlers

Sitting in Josie's kitchen in the summer of 1960, the young reporter glanced at the yearling carcass hanging from the tree, wondering if it was stolen. When *Life* magazine had visited Cub Creek in the late 1940s, Josie had demonstrated how she *might* steal a cow.

"*If* I were a rustler," she teased.

The resulting article called her "Josie, Queen of Cattle Rustlers." This was a title typically associated with her sister, Ann, ever since the time of her own rustling career and trial during the first decades of the twentieth century. Queen Ann was enraged. Queen Josie just smiled.

The young reporter and Josie spoke further about Ann, who had died in 1956 at the age of seventy-nine. They talked about the outlaw era, with the reporter claiming that Josie told him Butch Cassidy didn't die in a shootout in Bolivia as was commonly thought. Cassidy's demise was yet another lie reinforced by Charles Kelly, according to Josie. After returning from South America, Butch had come to visit her in Rock Springs in 1920.

The question that most interested the reporter, the one he left for last, was about murder. Specifically, if Josie had killed any of her husbands. This would prove a particularly ominous inquiry, given that over two decades later, this reporter would be convicted of second-degree murder for killing his own wife. It was an incident that would later call into question his reliability in reporting his 1960 interview. Supposedly Josie's reply came with a wry grin.

"Let's just say some men are harder to get rid of than others."

Josie was the last surviving member of the notorious Bassett Gang of Browns Park. A legendary figure from the Wild West, who died in 1964 at the age of ninety. She most definitely was a moonshiner. Quite likely a cattle rustler. But probably not a murderer. Whatever else she may have been guilty of, the indomitable Josie never said.

GREAT PLAINS AND MIDWEST

CHAPTER 19

HOW COULD A SAND DUNE SWALLOW A BOY?

UNEXPLAINED PHENOMENA

INDIANA DUNES NATIONAL PARK

LAKE MICHIGAN, INDIANA

The Woessners and another family from their church were spread out on towels and blankets at the beach. It was a sunny afternoon, July 12, 2013, and they had come to the shore of Lake Michigan for a camping trip. Behind them was the iconic Mount Baldy, one of the tallest freshwater sand dunes in the world.

After the kids splashed in the waves for a few hours, someone suggested a race up the dune. Soon the two dads were leading the way. Behind them was Nathan Woessner, an adventurous six-year-old boy known for catching frogs and fishing for catfish in the river behind their Illinois home. Alongside him ran his best friend, Colin. Midway up the mountainous dune, Nathan diverted to examine a small hole in the sand. In an instant, the boy plummeted feet first into the void and was gone.

"Nathan fell," cried out Colin.

The two fathers circled back, spotting only a perfectly round hole about a foot wide. Colin's dad Keith was the taller and thinner man, so he laid down on the sand and reached inside with his long arm. Nothing. The two men sent Colin back down to the beach to get help.

"I'm scared," called a distant Nathan from somewhere in the depths.

"We'll get you out," said his dad, Greg.

But when the two dads began to frantically dig with their hands, the hole collapsed. All that remained was powdery sand. Greg ran down the slope, covered in sand and dripping with sweat. Midway he encountered Colin leading his distraught wife, Faith, uphill.

"He's gone," said Greg. "He's gone."

LAKE MEETS PARK

In 2019, the Indiana Dunes National Lakeshore was redesignated as the state's first national park. The twenty-four square miles of parklands includes a series of semi-connected parcels of dunes, woods, and beach that span a twenty-mile stretch along Lake Michigan. The park averages a bit under three million visitors per year, with most coming in the summer for beach days, swimming, and short hikes.

A Dangerous Dune?

For thousands of years, the southern shore of Lake Michigan has been lined by huge sand dunes. As water levels fluctuated, particularly during glacial periods, sand deposits on the lake bottom were exposed and blown by prevailing winds to form the dunes. Over time, most of these dunes were naturally stabilized by grasses and trees. Yet for some reason, Mount Baldy remained an outlier, perhaps due to a violent storm that blew down any larger vegetation. As a result, it's mostly bare sand with occasional shoots of grass.

During the industrialization of the nineteenth century, the adjacent Michigan City built a harbor with a breakwater. This reduced the movement of sand along the shore, which otherwise would have replenished the beachside dunes that once protected Mount Baldy. Simultaneously, a growing population brought more visitors to the lakeshore. The steady stream of eager footsteps up Mount Baldy helped keep it bare by preventing new vegetation from establishing.

The result is that Mount Baldy began to migrate inland, with the soft sand blowing up the windward face and depositing upon the leeward side. Each year, the dune shifted anywhere from a few feet to as much as twenty. Between the 1930s and early 2000s, the dune moved a total of nearly 450 feet. As Mount Baldy lumbered inland, it covered anything in its path, including a cottage, a walking path, a staircase, and trees in the surrounding forest.

By the time young Nathan disappeared, most visitors to this popular hiking area thought of Mount Baldy as nothing treacherous. Just a big pile of sand. Instead, it was actually a highly dynamic and ultimately dangerous place. Though no one had noticed, for years strange holes would appear in the sands of Mount Baldy only to quickly collapse and vanish.

A Rescue or Recovery

People dug with their hands until their fingers bled. They took turns hurling sand with shovels and buckets. Once exhausted, they moved aside, and the next person stepped forward. Anxious observers glanced at the distraught parents nearby, who waited for any sign. An hour passed as arriving firefighters, police officers, and bystanders worked frantically. Some expressed doubts that the child was buried at all, so others began to search the nearby forest. On Mount Baldy, the digging continued, but the mood became somber. The effort increasingly felt less like a rescue and more like a body recovery.

"I found a hole!" yelled a deputy.

Someone aimed a flashlight down a round chute that went so deep, they couldn't see the bottom. The boy must have fallen much further than anyone realized. The police chief pulled out his cell phone.

About two hours after Nathan disappeared, a local construction worker arrived with a backhoe. The loose slope was so steep, he had to drive in reverse, using the sharp-toothed bucket to pull the machine up Mount Baldy. The site was now a five-foot alcove dug into the side of the dune. Before using the backhoe, rescuers used metal rods to probe the sand. One wrong scoop and the boy could be killed. Two excavators arrived an hour later to join the operation, with the heavy machines removing tons of sand to aid the rescuers.

Around 8:00 p.m., four hours into the search, the sun hovered just above the horizon of the lake. One of the equipment operators noticed a dark discoloration in the sand. When a rescuer plunged his metal rod down, he struck something. A firefighter fell to his knees and clawed at the sand, revealing the dirty blond hair of Nathan. The boy had fallen twelve feet deep. He was unearthed in a standing position, pulled cold and limp from the sand. The party fell silent. Firefighters strapped the boy to a backboard and loaded him into a lifeguard pickup, which bounced down the dune toward an ambulance. Rescuers collapsed onto the sand, exhausted. They stared at the lake surface reflecting the colorful horizon. Tears fell to the ground. They were certain it was too late.

A Remorseful Mistake

At a nearby restaurant, a local geology professor was eating with her fiancé and father. Earlier that day, she'd been at Mount Baldy, conducting fieldwork about wind speeds with park service staff. Witnessing a commotion, the team had come upon the scene of a father desperately digging with his hands. A shocked mother praying to God. Their son, they said, had fallen into a hole that disappeared.

"He's here," Greg Woessner had said. "He's right here."

The professor considered herself an expert on dunes. Solid piles of sand, without sinkholes or caverns, which simply did not collapse. They definitely did not snatch people, despite what Hollywood might have you believe. For decades, scientists loved to ridicule the 1962 film *Lawrence of Arabia*, which depicts a Bedouin boy being swallowed by a sand pit. Can't happen, they'd laugh. Quicksand doesn't form in sand dunes because, as everyone knows, they're too high above the water table. The skeptical professor scanned the area on Mount Baldy for signs of recent digging.

"This doesn't make any sense," she said to the park service fieldworkers. The boy was probably hiding somewhere. She watched distantly for a while as the rescue began. Then she carried her wind meter to her car and drove home.

Now sitting in the restaurant, the professor stared wide-eyed at a TV screen showing a news report from Mount Baldy. After a four-hour search with fifty rescuers, a boy was pulled from the sand. Cold to the touch with no pulse.

The professor sobbed on the car ride home. She hadn't even tried to help. She had dismissed the frantic parents and walked away. Everything she thought she knew from books and classes had failed her. If the rescuers had listened to her, they wouldn't have even tried.

SCENE OF THE DUNE

Since the near-fatality in 2013, access to most of Mount Baldy has been restricted to ranger-led hikes. These short and steep scrambles lead to the summit with beautiful views of Lake Michigan. Daytime and sunset hikes happen on weekends throughout the summer, plus other times of year. Visit the park website for hike dates and times.

MORE WALKS

The rest of the park's trails are unrestricted and open for self-guided hikes. For a glimpse of the mystery, one option is the eponymous Beach Trail, which leads 0.75-mile, one way, along the edge of the dune with a steep scramble down loose sand to the beach. A more challenging hike is the 4.7-mile Cowles Bog Trail, which leads through diverse park ecosystems, including marshes, savannas, dunes, and beaches. For a visit with some variety, consider the West Beach area. The Dune Succession trail is only a mile in length, with stairs leading to a viewpoint. Or combine three loops into one hike, about 3.5 miles in length, through a variety of park landscapes.

A Memory Resurfaces

Nathan's parents, Greg and Faith Woessner, were sitting in a private room at the hospital, still wearing their swimsuits under T-shirts and shorts. Suddenly, the door swung open.

"He's alive," gushed the paramedic.

In the ambulance, the paramedic had noticed the boy's head was bleeding where a searcher had hit him with a tool. Bleeding was good. Bleeding meant a pulse, however faint it might be.

"Mommy, Mommy," Nathan had moaned as they carted him into the emergency room.

He was placed under sedation while the doctors went to work. Sand was under his fingernails and toenails. Sand was in his ears and his mouth. Nurses suctioned sand from his lungs. Three days later, they revived him. People called it the Miracle at Mount Baldy. No brain damage, no trauma. He didn't even remember what happened.

On a news report, a ranger speculated that maybe an air pocket saved Nathan, perhaps from a buried tree that had rotted away. Mount Baldy was closed to the public—a seemingly wild and unstable place within sight of smokestacks and factories. Now that people were looking for them, more holes were observed, empty pipes in the sand that would collapse and disappear within a few days.

The Environmental Protection Agency sent a team to survey Mount Baldy with ground-penetrating radar. They found sixty-six anomalies. The once-skeptical professor sought redemption by studying the mystery, and other scientists joined her. They named the phenomenon *dune decomposition chimneys*. First, the sand dune covers the trees. With time, ground water and tree fungi rot away the wood. At the contact between bark and sand, a natural calcium–carbonate cement forms through biomineralization. Later, when the sand blows away and the chimney top is revealed, the weak cement gives way, collapsing the hole.

Other observers pointed out that the phenomenon had been known about for a long time, at least colloquially. Some people called them sinkholes, others devil's stovepipes. Author Ken Kesey described the exact process using the latter term in his 1964 logging novel, *Sometimes a Great Notion*.

Was the sand dune that swallowed a boy a case of modern society simply forgetting about a recurring danger of the natural world? During the age of pervasive media, the viral nature of Nathan's close call seemingly led to a cultural rediscovery. Might there be more of these hidden pipes lurking underfoot at beaches and dunes around the country? Perhaps more voids would soon be revealed, wherever there exists a similar set of circumstances. One part human alterations to a natural world. Another part unconquerable forces—like wind, sand, wood, and water—marching onwards, undeterred. The third element being complacent people filing past, who had forgotten to tread cautiously. One mystery was solved, with others yet to be revealed.

CHAPTER 20

DID HUGH GLASS TRULY SURVIVE A GRIZZLY BEAR ATTACK?

LEGENDARY FIGURES

THEODORE ROOSEVELT NATIONAL PARK & FORT UNION TRADING POST NATIONAL HISTORIC SITE

WESTERN BADLANDS, NORTH DAKOTA & MISSOURI RIVER, NORTH DAKOTA

The trappers were moving cautiously through the wooded bottomlands of the Grand River. It was late August 1823, and the Americans were anxious, traveling deep inside the high plains wilderness of Missouri Territory. Originally, they'd been a party of thirteen. But three days before, two men had been killed and two injured in the latest attack by a band of Arikara warriors led by Grey Eyes. Now the remaining eleven trappers were fleeing upstream from what was quickly devolving into a war between native tribes and the encroaching whites.

Their aim was the relative safety of Fort Henry, about 150 miles to the northwest near the confluence of the Yellowstone and Missouri Rivers. This log fort had been established the year before by the party's leader, former Major Andrew Henry of the Rocky Mountain Fur Company. Henry's plan was to reunite with several parties, including the remaining dozen or so trappers from a disastrous 1822 expedition, plus another seventeen from this year's expedition, who were traveling by boat up the Missouri. Together, this combined force would have a better chance riding out the winter together before seeking safer trapping grounds to the west.

Along the way, the trappers ate only as well as they could gather or hunt. Thus, Major Henry sent two experienced men about a mile ahead of the group to move discreetly while scouting for game. The hope was to limit any shooting to an absolute minimum and avoid attracting any unwanted attention from the roving Arikara.

One of the hunters, Allen, was picking his way along the riverbank when he was startled by a third figure passing through the woods nearby. Allen's apprehension soon faded to annoyance. It was only Hugh Glass. Frontier life came easily to this eccentric newcomer, a wiry forty-year-old who was a decade or two older than everyone except the major. Despite keeping to himself and rarely falling in line, Glass was respected by the party. Like the others, he'd already proven himself to be a worthy asset as both a hunter and fighter.

A War on the Plains

Back in the spring, the entire 1823 party of trappers had traveled in two boats up the Missouri River from St. Louis. By early June, they reached the Arikara Narrows, where the unruly tribe had fortified their permanent village with a palisade and trench. Expedition leader General William Ashley decided to risk going ashore to negotiate safe passage through the Arikara homelands. The tribe had been hostile toward Americans for two decades, ever since their leader, Chief Ankedoucharo, died during an 1805 visit to Washington City to meet President Jefferson. The Americans claimed illness, the Arikara murder.

General Ashley's meeting on the beach began peacefully and led to an exchange of goods. Ashley received nearly fifty horses, and the Arikara received much-needed gunpowder for their British muskets, which they had obtained through trade with the Hudson's Bay Company. But the next morning, the re-equipped Arikara ambushed the trappers' camp with a barrage of musket fire. The trappers fought back, but eleven were killed and another dozen injured, including Glass. The party was forced to abandon most of their equipment on the beach and retreat downstream to near the Cheyenne River. Ashley sent a dispatch to Fort Atkinson at Council Bluffs, Iowa, asking for reinforcements.

On August 9, Lieutenant Colonel Henry Leavenworth led a small army—about 230 U.S. infantry troops, 750 Sioux allies, and 50 trappers—to attack the Arikara village. A strong defense led to a short siege by rendering the artillery fire ineffective. The Arikara requested a peace treaty, which Leavenworth granted on terms that the trappers' horses and equipment be returned. Instead, the Arikara fled during the night, and the embarrassed army withdrew soon after. Still seeking vengeance, the remaining trappers burned the Arikara village to the ground, before fleeing west toward Fort Henry.

How Long Can He Linger?

Less than an hour after being startled by Hugh Glass, the hunter Allen received another jolt when he heard horrific screams erupting from a nearby thicket. Next came the crack of a rifle shot. Allen's first thought was an Arikara attack. As the two hunters moved toward the disturbance, the actual situation became apparent.

Moments before, Glass had emerged from thick brush and stumbled across a massive white bear with two cubs. The surprised mother grizzly, distinguished by her silver-tipped coat, had reared up on her hind legs. She slashed at Glass with claws as long as a pistol handle. The back-scrambling Glass was caught in the neck. Blood gushed, as he managed to get off a single shot at close range into the bear's furry torso.

In an instant, the grizzly was upon him, clawing and biting at flailing arms and legs. For his part, Glass fought hard. He scrambled, kicked, and slashed back with his knife. After a moment, the injured behemoth retreated near her cubs. This was the scene that Allen and his fellow hunter came upon. One of the cubs chased them back toward the river, but rifles were leveled—first from the hunters and soon the trailing men—and the trio of bears were coldly slain.

"Tore nearly all to peases," was the appraisal of Daniel Potts, reflecting later about examining the victim.

Over a dozen wounds were counted, spread across Glass's face, scalp, chest, back, shoulder, arm, hand, and thigh. The bloodied man was bandaged as best could be using strips from a spare cotton shirt. The party made camp and waited for Hugh Glass to die. But, come morning, the mangled frontiersman continued to gasp for breath. Recognizing the urgency of their perilous situation, the men used tree branches to create a crude stretcher.

Throughout that day and into the next, the trappers took turns carrying Glass through meadows of prairie grass and increasingly sparse woods. The injured man was unable to speak. But when a rescuer slipped or the stretcher was jostled, the semi-conscious victim would shudder in pain. After several days, the party reached a grove of trees with a clearwater spring. They were making terrible time. The entire party was exposed and at constant risk of attack. Glass was certainly doomed, and carrying him like this was subjecting him to untold agony.

Major Henry offered a large reward—nearly matching a full year's pay—for any two volunteers willing to wait with Glass until the end and provide him a proper burial. After a lengthy silence, a man named Fitzgerald reluctantly agreed. The second volunteer was the party's youngest member, a year north or south of eighteen. Some later called him Bridges. Others, controversially, said he was Bridger, more specifically Jim.

After the other eight trappers had left, it was just Fitzgerald and the kid in the darkening woods. They listened to the steady winds and the faint breaths of Glass. They watched for any signs of a war party. Over the coming days, the tenacious frontiersman continued to linger. Despite not speaking, he could move his eyes and occasionally his arms. When offered, he took sips of water and small pieces of food, like wild berries plucked from bushes around the spring.

Glass seemed feverish, even nightmarish. Perhaps he was having visions from his life flashing through his mind. About this bold loner, most of his fellow trappers knew very little. He had come from the east, Pennsylvania originally. Those he confided in knew a grizzly attack was only the latest in a series of tough scrapes that Glass claimed to have survived.

OUTPOSTS ON THE PLAINS

The trappers' 1823 escape route—both the lead party and the trailing twosome who deserted Glass—likely followed the Little Missouri River as it passes through the lesser-visited Theodore Roosevelt National Park. Located hundreds of miles from other national parks such as Badlands, Yellowstone, and Glacier, this 110-square-mile park stands like an outpost on the northern Great Plains.

The park is broken into three geographically separate units. Most of the 750,000 annual visitors show up from late May until early October, when they head to the South Unit for scenic drives, badlands viewpoints, and short hikes. The more remote North Unit has similar scenery and activities but with more solitude and longer hikes, including several trails that lead into park wilderness.

A Pirate and Pawnee

Less than a decade before his makeshift hospice atop leaves, Glass claimed to have been a sailor. His ship was captured in the Gulf of Mexico by pirates serving under the infamous Jean Lafitte. After about a year of forced marauding, his superiors deemed Glass a sorry fit for a buccaneer. The typical method of discharge was at the end of a rope. Instead, the captive decided to walk a plank of his own choosing. One night, the piratical crew went ashore carousing. Glass and another malcontent were left aboard the ship, which was anchored off the coast of Texas, a territory of Mexico. The two dropped over the side and swam an exhausting two miles to the southern shore of Galveston Bay.

From there they went north, across mostly treeless plains. Each carried very little: clothes, a knife, flint and steel for starting fires. They sharpened sticks into spears and subsisted by hunting the abundant game animals. Without incident, they crossed lands inhabited by tribes like the Karankawa, Tonkawa, Comanche, Kiowa, and Osage. They were deep inside the Missouri Territory of the United States. In a hilly region around the headwater streams of the Kansas River, their luck ran out.

The two men were captured by a band of Pawnee, a group which Glass said still practiced human sacrifice. This was a dubious tale. Though the practice was widely known in Mesoamerica, it was seldom seen in the North American Plains, outside of the infrequent Morning Star ceremony. Still, Glass claimed to have watched his companion be burned alive. When it was Glass's turn, he said he staved off his execution by offering a hidden possession, a pouch of highly sought vermillion, a bright red dye made from cinnabar. The Pawnee chief was pleased and declared Glass was now an adopted member of the tribe.

For several years, Glass claimed he lived as a Pawnee. During summer, he hunted buffalo and slept in a tepee. During winter, he lived in a communal lodge made of logs and earth. The Pawnee's enemies became his enemies, and he learned to fight with a tomahawk and lance. Through trade, he acquired the same rifle with which he would later land a single shot in the flank of an attacking grizzly.

During the late summer of 1822, a party of Pawnee visited St. Louis, the growing capital of Missouri Territory. They came to meet with the U.S. Superintendent of Indian Affairs William Clark. Once again, Glass jumped ship, slipping away from his adopted tribe. In January of the following year, an advertisement circulated throughout the city. It was placed by General William Ashley and Major Andrew

Henry, who sought one hundred aspiring fur trappers to ascend the Missouri River to the Rocky Mountains. In March 1823, Glass was among the brave souls who embarked.

An Unearned Reward

Now, in August, the incapacitated Glass lay in the woods several hundred miles east of the Rockies. After a few days of tending to a man who refused to die, the anxious Fitzgerald had enough. He pulled his younger partner aside and explained his position. Continuing to wait like this would mean the inevitable deaths of not just one but three. After some convincing, the kid agreed. When they collected Glass's valuables, including his knife and rifle, the muted invalid realized what was happening. When they moved him closer to the spring, he grasped at them, but his hands fell short. Then they were gone, and Hugh Glass was alone in the wilderness.

Relieved of their charge, Fitzgerald and the kid moved swiftly past the head-waters of the Grand River. After ascending some gently rising hills, they descended into the Little Missouri River valley. They followed its wooded bottomlands north, passing beneath rising badlands carved from colorful layered rocks. A shallow pass took them northwest to Fort Henry, which they reached two days after the main party. Fitzgerald reported that Glass was buried, so he and the kid received their unearned rewards.

Not long after returning, Major Henry believed a band of Blackfeet was steal-ing the trappers' horses. Seeking a safer base, in early September, he moved the fort up the Yellowstone River to the confluence of the Powder River, about 120 miles to the southwest. Later that fall, they moved again, southwest another 150 miles, to where the Little Bighorn joined the Bighorn River. In mid-November, three men went downstream on a skiff, heading for the Missouri River and points east. One of them was Fitzgerald. With him was the treasured rifle of Hugh Glass—a reminder of yet another trapper who had sadly perished in the wilderness. Or so everyone thought.

A Ghost Goes on Foot

Wind was blowing the snow into drifts around Fort Henry on the eve of 1824. The unofficial garrison at the Little Horn, now numbering a few dozen, was celebrating the arrival of yet another year despite the inhospitable environs. Outside, a gaunt man emerged from the woods and trudged toward the fort. He wore the typical garb of a trapper, leather leggings and moccasins. A cap and wool capote—a long, hooded jacket—was tied around his waist. He carried a small bundle wrapped in a blanket and clutched a new rifle. The traveler identified himself as one of the company, and the gate swung open.

When the drunken men inside saw who entered, the shouts and guffaws of celebration instantly ceased. Before them stood a ghost. A pale figure risen from a wilderness grave. The scarred and emaciated face of Hugh Glass. When the apparition spoke, the voice seemed raspy and strange. But the story the man told convinced everyone that he was, indeed, Glass, altered nearly beyond recognition by his four-month ordeal.

After being abandoned, Glass said he had deliriously drifted in and out of consciousness for nearly a week. Occasionally, he awoke and raged about his desertion. He drank palmfuls of water from the spring and plucked berries within reach. One day, he awoke next to a languid rattlesnake, with a bulge in its slender body from a recently devoured rodent. Glass lifted a nearby stone and slammed it down, crushing the venomous creature's neck. Among his few remaining possessions, Glass found a straight razor. He used it to cut up his first meal in two weeks. Since his kettle had been stolen, he ate the snake meat raw.

With renewed strength, Glass discovered he could crawl with some difficulty. The two deserters had surely continued uphill toward Fort Henry. Thus, any attempt at vengeance would have to wait. The weakened Glass would take the easier path, heading downhill along the Grand to the Missouri. His first day on the move, he dragged himself about fifty feet to the riverbank before collapsing. Reaching the nearest establishment of Fort Kiowa, 200 miles distant, seemed impossible.

After several days, Glass tried again. This time he clambered a few hundred feet. The next day he made it further, and so forth. As he progressed, his wounds bled. He cleaned the scabs with river water and bandaged them as best he could. Out of reach, his back wound festered with maggots. After what felt like a few weeks, he tested his legs and began walking. At first, he went less than a mile. Later he managed more.

For food, he called upon vital lessons learned from the Pawnee, including digging for roots with stones. Occasionally, he encountered a buffalo carcass, sometimes killed by hunters and other times by grizzlies. He pounded out marrow from the bones. Another time, he came across some wolves who were feasting on a stray buffalo calf. Glass used his razor and a piece of flint to start a grass fire. The spreading flames chased away the wolves. This landed Glass half a calf. He spent several days staying for the feast before continuing onward.

After a month alone, Glass reached the Missouri River. First, he detoured eight miles upstream to the burned remnants of the Arikara village. There he gathered vegetables from the abandoned fields and lured a roaming dog to its demise. Soon he met a party of Sioux, sworn enemies of the Arikara who similarly came to scavenge. They took pity on this mangled wanderer, treating his back wound with an astringent vegetable solution. Several Sioux took Glass by horseback to Fort Kiowa, which he reached on October 11.

General Ashley had quit the fort for St. Louis a few weeks earlier, essentially giving up on the dangerous high plains for company trapping. While the murmurs about Glass's miraculous survival began to spread, the determined man plotted his next move. He learned about a small boat, captained by Antoine Langevin, that would soon depart for Fort Henry. Despite being penniless, Glass was welcomed to re-equip on company credit. Then he joined these six men heading up the Missouri.

Only five days out, Langevin had a morbid premonition. He wrote up his will and left it with trappers at Simoneau Island. For weeks, the six-man party sailed and rowed upstream into a region devolving into guerrilla warfare. As the boat neared the Mandan villages, where the displaced Arikara now lived, the tension peaked. One of the six was French–Canadian translator Toussaint Charbonneau, former husband of Sacagawea and previously a member of the Lewis and Clark expedition. Charbonneau left one night without explanation. Next, Glass departed. He claimed he wanted to hunt his way across an overland shortcut, while the boat rounded a sweeping bend in the river.

As Glass made his way toward Fort Tilton, an outpost near the Mandan villages, he came across a roving party of Arikara. A short chase ensued, before Glass was met by a lone Mandan warrior on horseback. Seeing a chance to embarrass the Arikara, the young man scooped up the enemy of his enemy. With Glass riding double, they galloped to the fort. Glass was soon entertaining the occupants with his tale of survival. He sadly learned that Langevin's premonition came true. The Arikara had massacred all four men who had remained with the boat. So, Glass walked the remaining 200 miles through the frigid plains and sideways snows of December to reach Fort Henry.

LOOK SOUTH TO THE GLASS BLUFFS

On the Missouri River, near the Montana state line, the little-known Fort Union Trading Post National Historic Site includes a reconstruction of this important fur trading outpost that operated from 1829 to 1867. Forgotten for around a hundred years, excavations in the 1960s led to the establishment of the site. Today visitors can explore the four-sided fort and trade house on a self-guided walking tour.

Classic Hugh Glass

Inside Fort Henry, the audience of trappers had sobered up from Hugh Glass's story. The remnants of Ashley's hundred stared in disbelief at the flesh and blood trapper standing before them. The instigator of his desertion, Fitzgerald, was gone. But Major Henry pushed forward the aghast teenage accomplice to receive whatever revenge Glass sought. The squinting trapper leaned on his replacement rifle, examining the kid, who stared at the floor.

"Go, my boy," rasped Glass, after a moment. "I leave you to the punishment of your own conscience."

About six months later, Glass's confrontation with Fitzgerald went similarly. Departing Fort Henry on the last day of February 1824, Glass and four men began a roughly 1,000-mile journey to Fort Atkinson at Council Bluffs. It was classic Hugh Glass. Up the Powder River, on foot, and over to the North Platte. From there, by buffalo skin bullboat downriver atop swift spring currents.

The Arikara ambushed the five near the confluence of Laramie Creek. Glass and two others were seemingly killed, while two more white trappers got away. Yet Glass concealed himself in rocks, losing only his new rifle, not his life. So, when the two survivors reached Fort Atkinson, and they reported on the famous trapper's second demise, the news was naturally followed by the arrival of this frequently deceased man. Regarding Glass's mission of revenge, it turned out that Fitzgerald was now an enlisted man in the Sixth Regiment of the U.S. Army. He was safely in the arms of the government and beyond the reach of Glass, should he have wished to try something.

"Give me my favorite rifle," was all that Glass demanded. Then he and Fitzgerald went their separate ways.

A Frontier Celebrity

The tale of Hugh Glass and his incredible survival became the talk of the plains. A year later, the story was reported by *The Port Folio* in Philadelphia and by the *Missouri Intelligencer* in St. Louis. Over the coming decades, more retellings and articles appeared. Some sources were trappers of the era who clearly knew Glass or were present for parts of the story. Other writers referenced interviewing someone who said they knew Glass. No two stories were identical, but the basic facts were usually in agreement. Glass survived a grizzly attack and was left for dead. He crawled and walked out of a dangerous wilderness on his own.

Most authors heaped disdain upon the two deserters, especially Fitzgerald. Many years later, the kid was said to be called by the name Bridges. Only riverboat captain Joseph LaBarge suggested that the kid grew up to become famous mountain man Jim Bridger. Other observers doubted that such a solid explorer like Bridger was involved. Or they pointed out the impossible situation Fitzgerald and the kid were placed in. The two had agreed to bury a dying man within a few days, not administer an indefinite hospice in a wilderness war zone.

As time passed, people began to question Glass's story. It was all hearsay, they said. The trapper himself was the only witness, and he never even wrote about it. Was his survival embellished? Most likely yes, but to what degree was uncertain. Could the tale have been completely invented? Might it be nothing more than a frontier legend from a rough and lawless time in a young country seeking fearless heroes?

Several facts seem to support the veracity of this tale. First, that a trapper named Hugh Glass did roam the 1820s frontier is not in doubt. The second fact is that none of the other trappers present on the 1823 expedition ever challenged Hugh Glass's story as untrue. After regaining his rifle at Fort Atkinson, the destitute but triumphant survivor was rewarded with a $300 purse from soldiers who passed the hat. Glass picked up the Santa Fe Trail, making his way to Taos, New Mexico. From there, he led trapping expeditions into the red-rock country of the Eutaws, later called Utah.

Other ventures took him to the Snake River and Oregon Territory. Trapping from a canoe led him to an armed skirmish with the Shoshone, one of whom put an arrow in Glass's back. With the arrowhead lodged near his spine, Glass rode a horse 700 miles back to New Mexico where a friend cut the foreign object out with a razor. Yet again, Glass survived.

Later in the decade, Glass returned to trapping in the wilds of Missouri Territory. Though he kept mostly to himself, he was considered a frontier celebrity when spotted at mountain rendezvouses, where trappers sold pelts and acquired goods. Glass was at Bear Lake in 1827 and 1828, when his fellow independent trappers asked him to be their representative. The newly arrived American Fur Company was seeking to disrupt the mountain men's rendezvous system and establish a monopoly. The company offered higher prices to any trapper who brought all their pelts to Fort Union. Glass ferried messages between *Amfurco* and the independent trappers for several years. But unlike most of the others, Glass accepted the raise and relocated to Fort Union, near the confluence of the Yellowstone and Missouri. Across the river, he hunted bighorn sheep in hills later named the Glass Bluffs.

A third fact—in favor of Glass's legacy and against his longevity—is that this fearless frontiersman would ultimately die just like it was said that he lived. In early 1833, Glass was trapping beavers on the Yellowstone River. While walking across the frozen river, he was struck by a volley of arrows launched by a war party concealed on the opposite bank. Back at Fort Union, doubts surrounded the rumors about Glass's latest demise. Was it even possible to kill the man? However, months later, a native warrior was seized wearing some of the legendary trapper's clothing. His old foe, the Arikara, seemed to have finally gotten their nemesis. Hugh Glass and his beloved rifle were never to be seen again.

CHAPTER 21

WAS THE ST. LOUIS ARCH DESIGNED TO CONTROL THE WEATHER?

HIDDEN HISTORY

GATEWAY ARCH NATIONAL PARK

MISSISSIPPI RIVERFRONT, ST. LOUIS, MISSOURI

t was the morning of October 18, 1965, and a crowd of thousands was gathered at the St. Louis riverfront to witness a long-awaited event. After nearly three years of challenging construction, and over three decades of controversy, the world's tallest monumental arch was almost complete.

From a landing next to the Mississippi River, two shimmering legs arced into the sky. At the apex, 630 feet high, a narrow gap was held apart with hydraulic jacks. Meanwhile, a pair of construction cranes sat high atop each side. Due to an obstructed sight line, the crane operator was flying blind with only verbal instructions. During thirteen tense minutes, he slowly maneuvered the dangling keystone into the gap.

For those on the ground, and especially the workers in the air, this was a particularly apprehensive moment. Ever since the design had been proposed, many detractors insisted the Arch would never work. Some doubted the legs would meet in the middle. Even if they were joined, the critics said, the structure would soon collapse.

Yet the Gateway Arch held. In an homage to the 1869 "golden spike" of the Transcontinental Railroad, the construction team inserted a golden bolt at the top. After the truss was dismantled, the critical keystone absorbed the inward pressure of both legs. It was a principle known for thousands of years, one discovered in the ancient Middle East and perfected by the Romans. The final piece allowed the full weight of the arch to be distributed downward into the deeply sunken foundations.

A Marvel or a Hairband

Two years later, the attraction opened to the public as part of the Jefferson National Expansion Memorial. Despite the achievement, the debate surrounding the Gateway Arch lingered. For some, it was a symbol to celebrate, for others a target of ridicule.

Supporters called it a new world wonder. A rival to the Washington Monument, the Eiffel Tower, and the Great Pyramid of Giza. A modernist structure evoking the economic might of postwar America. An attraction that would boost a sagging economy and help revitalize a once-mighty city. A symbol of national aspirations and Jeffersonian ideals. A metaphorical portal to future possibilities created by a brilliant designer who influenced a nationwide aesthetic.

Opponents saw a $13-million horseshoe. A giant hairband. A massive horse-hitching post. Some residents seethed about a rigged election and government spending. Others complained that the Arch was built for tourists and that locals would rarely visit. A few blamed it for the city's downward spiral, including a troubled past involving racism and segregation. One critic suggested the design had been stolen from fascist Italy. Others dismissed the Arch as a bizarre anachronism that was predicted by a high school student during the Great Depression.

Perhaps the strangest story came many decades later. An urban legend claimed the Arch was no simple monument, but a powerful device built to control the weather. Through some unknown force, it supposedly redirected fierce storms and violent tornadoes away from the city. How had a vague idea for urban renewal become a controversial paradox? Did the Gateway Arch really have such a disturbing and possibly paranormal past?

St. Louis Municipal Parking Lot

In the mid-1930s, an influential St. Louis lawyer named Luther Ely Smith returned home with an idea. He'd just visited Vincennes, Indiana, where they were building a riverfront monument to Revolutionary War hero George Rogers Clark. Soon a towering granite monument would become that city's most prominent landmark. Eventually it would be transferred to the park service and be designated a national historical park.

As his train crossed the Mississippi River, Smith stared at the smoke-stained buildings along the waterfront and pondered some kind of monument to restore St. Louis. Since the 1904 World's Fair was held in Forest Park, what was once called the nation's Fourth City had been falling behind. Commerce was being lured to other Midwestern metropolises like Chicago. Yet pollution in St. Louis remained high due to a reliance on aging factories and fading industries powered by coal.

After increasing for over a century, the city's population was starting to decline. White residents and most construction projects were moving to the surrounding county. Left by the riverfront was an increasingly segregated Black community, and a historic but aging collection of cast iron buildings constructed during the nineteenth-century heyday. It didn't take long for the mayor and city leaders to get on board with the idea. St. Louis was considered the Gateway to the West, given the Lewis and Clark expedition had started nearby on its long journey up the Missouri River to reach the Pacific Ocean. So, a city committee was formed that proposed a riverfront monument to Thomas Jefferson and westward expansion.

The plan involved demolishing nearly forty square blocks. This included the historic riverfront business district and about 200 homes, many of them rented by African American families. Critics called it a real estate scheme disguised as a tribute. Others pointed to the steep cost, with the city paying a quarter of the cost and the federal government covering the rest.

Due to this tepid response, it seemed likely that a citywide bond vote would fail. Instead, the measure passed in a surprising landslide. When the *Post-Dispatch* newspaper launched an investigation, it found over 46,000 false ballots. Many were registered to vacant buildings and empty lots. A few suspicious districts had almost unanimously approved the project. One tiny barbershop was apparently home to nearly 400 monument enthusiasts. The election had clearly been rigged.

But this was the Great Depression, and the promise of any commerce typically won all disputes. Authorities looked the other way, and the project went forward. Due to a declaration of imminent domain, property owners were compelled to sell at hastily assessed prices. The wrecking balls arrived shortly before the 1940s. A year later, the result was a vast gravel field with just three buildings remaining. One was the Old Courthouse where an enslaved man named Dredd Scott had famously sued for his freedom.

By now, the Great Depression had ended with the start of a second world war. Monument plans were put on hold for years, and the city put the vast gravel expanse to use for the automobile age. The *Post-Dispatch* jokingly noted that the planned Jefferson National Expansion Memorial had instead become the St. Louis municipal parking lot.

A Fascist Design and a Psychic Artist

After the war, the memorial committee resumed the project with a national design competition. In response to a detailed list of requirements, 172 submissions were received. The ebullience of winning WWII combined with shifting aesthetics resulted in some pretty interesting designs.

On the modernist side, there were plenty of big, blocky structures. A massive concrete rectangle that looked like a drive-in movie screen. Seven equally spaced obelisk-like pylons, each representing historic events. A circular restaurant projecting over the river and resembling the NPS lookout towers that would later rise at Clingman's Dome (renamed Kuwohi in 2024) in the Smokies and Shark Valley in the Everglades. One famous architect, Eliel Saarinen, proposed a rectangular colonnade that looked somewhat like a four-toothed hair pin.

On the postmodern side, there were a lot of edgy and abstract sculptures. A contorted mass of steel beams that, according to the caption, symbolized the signing of the Louisiana Purchase. A stainless-steel shaft that could have been a futuristic space rocket. A huge bust of just Thomas Jefferson's head. A bizarre open-air framework of pipes and colorful panels displaying museum-like exhibits.

Spanning the middle ground between changing prewar and postwar sensibilities was entry #144. It was submitted by an up-and-coming architect named Eero Saarinen, son of Eliel. Upon inspection, several judges were struck by the proposed monumental arch.

"An abstract form peculiarly happy in its symbolism," noted one reviewer.

"Relevant, beautiful, perhaps *inspired* would be the right word," gushed another.

Eero Saarinen's arch seemed almost preordained, though a mix-up occurred when the more-established father, Eliel, was errantly informed by telegram that he was a finalist, not his son. They repeated their champagne toast when the mistake was corrected. This minor issue was soon overshadowed by a bigger controversy. When the chosen design was revealed to the public, responses ranged widely. On one side, the arch was touted as an original work of genius that would someday rival the world's greatest monuments. But to some locals, it looked like a grotesque croquet gate that might earn St. Louis a new nickname, the Wicket City.

The most damning criticism claimed the design was possibly stolen from European fascists. In the late 1930s, Italian dictator Benito Mussolini started building an enormous exposition to commemorate his new Roman Empire. Before the project was derailed by war, the goal was to blend ancient styles with modern sensibilities. On the outskirts of Rome, a demonstration grounds of fascist architecture began to rise. Plans showed cement columns and archways fronting buildings of steel and glass. There were to be wide thoroughfares passing gardens and fountains and a long man-made lake. Rising high above the entryway, there would have been a shimmering monumental arch.

The fascist design wasn't identical to Saarinen's, but it was close. They were about the same height, but Mussolini's was much wider and shaped more like a rainbow with square legs. In comparison, the one proposed for St. Louis was a narrower catenary curve with triangular legs.

In response to accusations of plagiarism, Saarinen was defiant. He admitted the designs looked similar, but it was merely a coincidence. He'd never seen nor heard of the unrealized fascist plan. While they were often associated with Roman architecture, arches were a common form that appeared endlessly in proposals. Other architects leapt to Saarinen's defense. After all, one wouldn't call a bridge builder a thief for putting a span between two towers. Eero Saarinen emerged unharmed by the complaints. He would further cement his legacy with several iconic space-age designs, including the curving tulip chair and the winglike TWA Flight Center at John F. Kennedy International Airport in New York.

During the fascist controversy, the memorial committee agreed the similarities were a non-issue. In fact, among the 172 contest submissions, several other entries had proposed variations of an arch. Back in 1915, a local architect had suggested erecting something resembling Paris's Arc de Triomphe at the St. Louis riverfront. The city was called the Gateway to the West, after all. Not the Backdoor to the East, as some arch critics were snickering. Arches were commonly associated with such portals.

Perhaps the most enigmatic premonition came from a local high school senior in 1933. In a two-page spread for the class yearbook, a talented artist named Geneva Abbott envisioned the St. Louis of the future. Her drawing showed innovative skyscrapers with tapering bases and art deco tops somewhat reminiscent of the recently completed Chrysler Building in New York. This modernized metropolis had several curving structures, and everything was framed by a towering, monumental arch with triangular legs. The prescient drawing was rediscovered in the 1960s and sent to the *St. Louis Globe Democrat*, which declared Abbot "the psychic artist."

The prophetic 1933 yearbook drawing by Geneva Abbott shows her vision for an Arch rising over St. Louis. Illustration by Geneva Abbott, 1933, Missouri Historical Society Collections/Public Domain

A Magnet for Risk

In the early 1960s, construction of the Arch began, nearly three decades after a memorial had first been proposed. It was estimated that up to thirteen workers might be killed during the project, but not a single life was lost. However, the latest Arch controversy arrived in 1964 when civil rights protesters gathered at the site. Two activists climbed the north leg ladder. Not a single Black worker or contractor had been hired. It was an early test of the recent Civil Rights Act that prohibited discrimination. Against strong resistance from white unions, only a handful of African Americans would be hired during the remainder of the project.

STEP INTO CONTROVERSY

Gateway Arch National Park is an atypical park unit that has taken a lot of flak since being redesignated in 2018. Critics point out that most NPS units designated as national parks protect vast natural landscapes filled with wildlife and outdoor recreation. Proponents of the new status typically claim that the original 1935 designation, Jefferson National Expansion Memorial, did not do justice to a beloved attraction. Some parties have suggested a change to national monument status may have been a better fit for what is now the nation's smallest national park at ninety-one acres. Skeptics say the redesignation was more about boosting tourism to the city, which declined after 9/11. That seems to be part of it, plus a desire among most states to have at least one national park.

Specific NPS designations are often a game of politics. Numerous units around the country offer landscapes and experiences similar to national parks without having that designation, including Dinosaur National Monument and Cumberland Island National Seashore. Meanwhile, there are several outlier national parks. Hot Springs National Park in Arkansas was one of the first NPS units, which today feels more like a national historical park. Dry Tortugas National Park in the Gulf of Mexico is an excellent unit to visit but has more in common with national seashores. Instead of playing the NPS name game, and judging a unit by its designation, sometimes it's better to focus on what's actually there.

Once the structure was complete, the Arch became a magnet for thrill-seekers. In the summer of 1966, a small plane flew over the city from the west. After passing above the Old Courthouse, it zoomed beneath the curving span. Inside the hollow legs, a unique cantilever elevator was being assembled. The workers startled at the echoing buzz, and the stainless-steel skin shuddered from the propeller wash. The Federal Aviation Administration had anticipated such a stunt by threatening to revoke licenses and impose hefty fines. That didn't stop another ten or so pilots from making a similar fly-through in the following years.

In the fall of 1980, a local skydiver parachuted toward the crest of the Arch. His plan was to jettison his main chute upon landing and use the reserve for a final jump to the ground. His feet touched the arcing roof, but he found no purchase on the sheer surface. A gust of wind knocked the man sideways, and he slid down the leg to his death.

A dozen years later, another daredevil arrived during early morning darkness and began climbing the Arch using suction cups. Once on top, he watched the sunrise and took photos before successfully parachuting down. Reaching the ground, he ran to a nearby car and escaped. Park authorities witnessed the event and detained two friends who were videotaping it. That, plus the fact the jumper gave several interviews to reporters, and sold photos from his endeavor, led to his later guilty plea.

An Unnatural Effect?

St. Louis rises in a region with powerful storms. It's on the edge of Tornado Alley, where cold, dry air from the northwest slams into warm, humid air from the Gulf. One result is that thunderstorms and twisters often form along a diagonal line roughly between Texas and the Great Lakes. Some are called I-44 storms, for paralleling the interstate, while others are labeled panhandle hooks.

Decades after the Arch began welcoming millions of visitors per year, an urban legend emerged. Some locals claimed that approaching storms seemed to split around the city before reforming downwind. This came to be called the *Arch effect*. Had the enigmatic architect, some wondered, designed his catenary monument to control the weather? Eero Saarinen was no longer around to respond. He had sadly died of an aggressive brain tumor in 1961, never seeing the fruition of his vision.

Some conspiracy theorists suggested the Arch might employ a supernatural technology taken from the fascists. Those overbearing invaders led by Hitler and Mussolini had sought dominion over not just humanity but nature as well. They wanted to dam the Mediterranean Sea. So, why not conquer the weather?

A QUIRKY RIDE

One way to appreciate the Arch is to consider it a quintessential attraction along nearby Route 66. Though a recent interior renovation has lessened the vibe, particularly in the underground history museum, much of the Arch feels like something torn from the 1960s. Almost like a set from a science-fiction film of the era.

Many visitors' favorite part is cramming inside a space-agey pod that zigzags up through the legs and makes an Apollo capsule feel like a 747. Atop the observation deck, you may wonder, *What am I supposed to be looking at?* Well, here are some additional highlights to check out.

Between the park grounds and the Mississippi River is the southern end of the twelve-mile Riverfront Trail, a paved bike path leading to the historic Chain of Rocks Bridge, with its iconic bend in the middle. Today it's open to only pedestrians and cyclists, and it overlooks a rare collection of whitewater rapids on this great American river. Now look west, past the Old Courthouse, which also can be toured, toward 1,300-acre Forest Park. There you'll find plenty of paths and a lake basin, built for the 1904 World's Fair, where you can paddleboard past fountains and several free attractions, including the art museum, history museum, and zoo.

Critics of the Arch effect pointed out several problems with the theory. One flaw was a type of observer bias. If you stand in one spot, while patchy thunder clouds move through the surrounding sky, most storms will probably miss you. If a resident nervously hopes that they're safe from nature's wrath, they'll watch for reasons to believe it. Due to simple chance, the worst weather will usually pass by the city without hitting it. When enough time passes between destructive storms, complacency develops and a supernatural force like the Arch effect becomes easier to accept.

Another flaw was that St. Louis has seen plenty of terrible storms, both before and after the Arch was built. This fact was driven home in 2011, when an EF4 tornado struck Lambert Airport on a northeastern corridor through the metro region. Eleven years later, a train of summer thunderstorms followed I-70 into town. The wettest day in recorded St. Louis history saw around ten inches of rainfall, which led to destructive flash flooding across the city. Standing in the storm path, safe on higher ground, was the Gateway Arch. It's not just possible but likely that another storm will strike the park grounds someday.

No evidence suggests that the Gateway Arch controls the weather. Though it is possible that another phenomenon, one that somewhat preceded the emergence of the Arch, may disrupt some weather patterns. It's called the *urban heat island effect*. Essentially, cities trap heat. Vegetation that normally has a cooling effect is cleared for development. Black asphalt streets run hot from the sun. High-rise buildings reflect light and block winds. Exhaust pipes release smog and greenhouse gases that gather overhead.

Warm air rising from cities may deflect some storms, at least the smaller ones. More study is needed to understand the phenomenon. But current theories suggest that the effect is limited when it comes to the more powerful and destructive storms that spawn tornadoes and cause flooding. Perhaps time will tell. Regardless, the Gateway Arch has become a world-famous fixture of St. Louis. A stunning piece of design and engineering. A complex symbol of a controversial past.

CHAPTER 22

WHAT IS THE FULL LENGTH OF MAMMOTH CAVE?

STRANGE DISCOVERIES

MAMMOTH CAVE NATIONAL PARK

SOUTH-CENTRAL KENTUCKY KARST REGION

P at Crowther was buzzing with excitement as she stepped outside of the airport in Louisville. The start of Memorial Day weekend made for a busy Friday night, but she and her husband were not in town for the horse races. The young couple's bags were packed with caving equipment—denim pants, jackets, boots, and helmets.

Waiting for them was Bob, a fellow member of the Cave Research Foundation (CRF). After piling into his blue station wagon, they faced their first obstacle: a line of honking cars had completely jammed the parking lot. So, Bob threw the big wagon into reverse and backed out the entrance gate. It was May 26, 1972, and there was no time to waste. The laughing passengers were expert cavers about to join an underground expedition to the most remote spot ever found inside Mammoth Cave National Park.

A hundred miles south, they pulled to a halt just after midnight in the rolling woods of Flint Ridge. The old buildings at Collins's Crystal Cave were ablaze with lights, while energetic members set up the new CRF expedition headquarters. Appropriating a common seventies' slang term, they called themselves *far-out* cavers. In their case, the meaning was literal. They probed the furthest depths, surveying a mazelike network unfolding beneath their feet.

GO UNDERGROUND

Unlike the many claustrophobic and wet passages explored by the far-out cavers, Mammoth Cave is primarily dry and known for long walking passages and vast chambers that formed over millions of years. Popular cave tours may sell out ahead of time, so online reservations using Recreation.gov are recommended. These guided cave tours range from short walks on paved paths to rugged hikes through undeveloped sections.

Several of the more rigorous excursions may appeal to national park adventurers. The toughest is the six-hour Wild Cave Tour, involving crawling through tight passages to reach remote areas. Another active option is the Violet City Lantern Tour. Using only lantern light, you leave behind the developed chambers and follow dirt paths deep inside the underground labyrinth. For three hours, you explore three miles of caverns, switchbacks, historic sites, and underground waterfalls.

Underground Everest

John Wilcox woke the team early the next morning. While Crowther cooked, Wilcox packed equipment into shoulder packs. These low-profile sling bags were ideal for the far-out cavers, who could shift them around while navigating tight passages. During breakfast, the four of them chatted about objectives. In his mid-thirties, Wilcox was the enthusiastic new director of exploration, and he had big plans for the summer.

For over two decades, CRF members had been exploring the northwestern quadrant of the expanding national park. A few miles south, the famous Mammoth Cave and its vast walk-through chambers got all the attention. But a series of lesser-known, tighter, and more challenging caves had long been theorized to connect via hidden routes in the bedrock. The first breakthrough came in 1955 when a team crossed from historic Crystal Cave into one named Unknown Cave. Five years later, they connected Salts Cave with Colossal Cave. The next year, they found a route linking Salts with Unknown.

By the early 1970s, the Flint Ridge Cave System was proven to have over sixty-five miles of traversable passageways and counting. As long as you considered *traversable* to include belly crawling through tubes filled with water up to your chin. This total mileage not only surpassed Mammoth Cave's mapped length of forty-four miles, but it was longer than the current length of Hölloch Cave in Switzerland. Flint Ridge was now the longest known cave in the world.

Yet, for decades, the biggest question was if Flint Ridge could be connected to Mammoth Cave. If so, what might be the full length of such a sprawling system? To the cavers, discovering a connection would be the spelunking equivalent of climbing Mount Everest. For outsiders, this endeavor was often hard to comprehend. Observers could watch from afar as climbers ascended a snow-capped peak. But caving happened out of sight, in dark and confined spaces where the explorers could barely turn their heads. Afterward, they emerged smeared in mud and wearing shredded clothing. Occasionally, they obtained a rare flash photograph that did little justice to their efforts.

To summit their underground Everest, a team of far-out cavers needed to enter from the Flint Ridge side. They would scramble, wade, and squirm their way through the confusing maze. Then they'd walk out of Mammoth Cave, just like the visitors on a ranger-guided trip.

Among the numerous challenges was one major topographic obstacle. The area's larger caves were mostly found beneath certain ridges within the karst landscape. Atop these ridges was Big Clifty Sandstone, a tough caprock formation that's mostly impenetrable to water except for the occasional break, or sinkhole, in the surface. For centuries, when rain fell, the runoff found its way through these sinks and continued inside the water-soluble limestone below. Convoluted stream networks gradually eroded into a roughly 350-foot-thick layer of bedrock, before emptying from outlet springs into the Green River.

Between Flint Ridge and Mammoth Cave Ridge, there was a topographic depression called Houchins Valley, where the caprock had eroded away long ago. The result was that the network of passages under Houchins Valley was deeply buried and particularly tight. Despite searching for years, no one had found a path through. Occasionally, a far-out caver might follow a conduit that tapered down to smaller than a ventilation duct. Then they carefully backed out and continued searching. Other times, the explorer might discover a lead ending in a siphon, where base-level water from the Green River filled the passage.

The furthest underground point ever reached was called Q-87, the last survey station in a crawlway tunnel blocked by rockfall. CRF maps showed this spot to be only 800 feet in a straight line from Albert's Dome inside Mammoth Cave. Six years before, an older generation of far-out cavers hit pause under the southern edge of Houchins Valley and began surveying from the more accessible passages on the Mammoth Cave side.

Then, during the spring of 1972, a prolonged drought meant the upstream dam on the Green River was releasing historically low flows. With this reduction in base-level, Wilcox saw an opportunity to finally connect the two caves. Maybe the decreased water levels would allow access to previously flooded passages that bypassed the blockage. Having young and adventurous cavers was often essential for the grueling eight hours it took to reach Q-87. Particularly helpful was someone like Pat Crowther. In addition to her slender build, she was willing to push herself inside almost any lead.

Far-Out Caving

As Wilcox unlocked the steel gate at the Austin Entrance, the team felt a cool breeze exhaling from Unknown Cave, where the air temperature was a crisp 54 degrees year-round. They donned heavy-duty kneepads made for hours of abuse. They slipped on helmets with mounted carbide lamps, igniting the burners with a loud pop.

Every trip inside was a reminder of past expeditions by numerous explorers who had slowly discovered the routes and mapped the features. The team moved swiftly through the first mile of mud and loose rocks named Pohl Avenue. They scrambled up Brucker's Breakdown, a larger example of the frequent piles created when rocks fell from the walls and ceilings.

Next came over a mile through Turner Avenue, a dry walking passage with a floor of gypsum sand. They sprayed lamplight on Old Granddad, a sparkling formation where stalactites and stalagmites had fused into a flowstone column rising floor to ceiling. Swinnerton Avenue was mostly a crouch-way for nearly half a mile, leading to a constriction called Duck Under. From here, it was just a few more miles to reach Q-87, but it would take hours. Now they went on hands and knees.

Several gravel chutes led to the Shower Shaft, essentially a drain through a rock jumble that carried storm runoff from upper channels to lower ones. Onward they crawled through standing waters in Candlelight River, before reaching the maze beneath Houchins Valley, which was mapped using letters instead of names.

To create their maps, the far-out cavers recorded compass bearings and distances by stretching a measuring tape tautly from the previous survey station to a new one. With so many kinks and rocky obstructions in the passages, sometimes the tape could be extended only a few feet at a time. Due to the narrow confines, occasionally a surveyor couldn't move their hands or head enough to see the compass reading. Then everyone had to reposition themselves until things lined up. The N Passage was dizzying enough. Then there was the Q Passage. It was only 1,305 feet long, about a third of a mile. Yet, there were so many twists that it had taken eighty-seven survey stations to map it.

One survey goal was to find new paths around blockages and challenging spots. Fortunately, today's route no longer included Agony Avenue, where, years before, cavers had to shove their bodies through a mud-filled tube. They stretched out horizontally, put their shoulders against the corner, and plowed forward by pushing with their feet. The earthy smell of the cave was inescapable. Cold mud would collect against their necks and heads. It oozed inside their ears and collars, filling their shirts like limp balloons. When the mud pile in front of them grew too large, they lunged their torsos over it and began plowing a new path. Many of the best far-out cavers had given up after one or two trips out to Q-87. Nobody ever blamed anyone for not going back.

After eight hours, the team finally crawled to where Q-87 ended at an intersecting shaft filled with breakdown. Wilcox aimed his carbide lamp at the football-sized boulders blocking the way. Curiously, these rocks weren't limestone but sandstone, which confirmed they had crossed Houchins Valley and were below the edge of Mammoth Cave Ridge. Nearly a decade ago, CRF members had tried to clear a path through the shaft. As a result, excavated boulders stretched far down the tunnel. But each time they'd tried, new rocks slipped downward with a rumble to reseal the shaft.

By now, the team was exhausted. Before reaching this turnaround point, they'd explored a few dead-end leads. In one spot, near Q-17, Crowther had followed Wilcox on a wet belly crawl to a small chamber with a tight ceiling crack. She shoved herself hands first into the crack. After passing a kink, she found she could bend her wrist but not her elbow. Crowther was stuck. Despite years of caving, she'd never been anywhere this cramped. She felt dizzy and began gasping for air.

Stop! Crowther told herself. *Relax.*

She and Wilcox yelled to each other, but Crowther's body filled the crack, which muffled their words. Slowly, she reversed each of her prior movements to wiggle back out. She plopped into the water-filled passage and sat there, shaking.

Eight hours to get in meant eight more to get out. Time to go. Luckily, the regional drought was showing no signs of abating. Terrible for water supplies, sure, but great for connecting caves. The summer of '72 might be one for the books.

SCRATCH THE SURFACE

While most of the park's modest half-million annual visitors head underground, there are eighty-two-square-miles of rugged parklands that seem almost forgotten. Up here, you'll find frontcountry and backcountry camping and hiking. Follow the trails around the visitor center to explore the surface features of the karst landscape, including sinkholes, cave entrances, and large springs where underground streams like the River Styx and Echo River burst from the bedrock.

The Mammoth Cave Railroad Bike and Hike Trail is a nine-mile gravel path that follows the former route of a tourist train that operated from 1886 to 1931. The park also has its own mountain bike trail system, with eleven miles of purpose-built singletrack rolling through the backcountry woods.

The Tight Spot

Seven weeks later, during the mid-July expedition, Wilcox and Crowther gave up on Q Passage, just like the old-timers had before them. On their way out through N Passage, the four-person team paused to rest in a small sandy-bottomed chamber at the junction with A Passage. No one had gone down there in years. CRF maps showed no leads, but Wilcox suggested they make a quick scout before leaving.

While crawling through A Passage, they squeezed beneath a particularly low ceiling later named Chest Compressor. Shortly after, they were surprised to encounter an unmapped junction. The two cavers split up. Wilcox's tunnel led to the previously mapped dead-end. Crowther, meanwhile, followed a hundred feet of virgin cave into a small room. She sprayed her carbide lamp onto a T-shaped opening in the far wall. Putting her ear to the gap, she heard loud sounds of falling water somewhere inside. This was promising. This was a going lead.

The only way to get through was by supporting herself on outstretched arms pressed down into the lower tapering portion of this T-slot. Then she kept each leg on either ledge comprising the upper bar of the T. One slip, and her body would fall into the crack and get jammed. Getting out would be tough if not impossible. After hand-walking like this for fifteen feet, she emerged from what would be named the Tight Spot. Crowther stood up in a long chamber running perpendicularly. Below her was an eight-foot tumbling waterfall, part of a river running southwest toward Mammoth Cave.

"It's very tight," said Crowther, when she rejoined Wilcox. "But we have cave!"

Pete H.

In late August, Crowther led an expedition back to the Tight Spot with plans to survey the new passageways. The team included a mix of faces. Wilcox. Richard Zopf, a bearded wisecracker with boundless energy. And a promising young caver named Tom Brucker. A few days before, the nineteen-year-old and his dad Roger had ventured underground to probe the new river downstream from the waterfall.

Now, the eager Tom showed Crowther's team the meandering way down the new river. When the ceiling rose, they walked through shallow water. When the ceiling lowered, they laid flat on the slimy river bottom, put down their elbows, and sledded on their forearms. Occasionally, their helmet-lamps illuminated the blind white fish that Mammoth Cave was famous for. A few times, Tom spotted brown fish as well. This suggested they were getting closer to the waters of the Green River.

"Hey!" shouted Tom, feeling a chill run up his spine. "An arrow!"

Carved into the mudbank were two sets of initials. "L. H. and P. H." Extending from the bar on the final H was an arrow pointing in the same downstream direction they were headed. Near the ceiling, on a limestone outcropping, there was another carving. "Pete H." The explorers searched their memories about the history of the park, trying to recall who this might be.

Kentucky Cave Wars

Mammoth Cave was first visited an estimated 5,000 years ago by ancestral Native Americans who sheltered inside the cool caverns during inclement weather. They mined the walls for gypsum and mirabilite, which they used as a digestive medicine. They left behind artifacts like cane torches, woven sandals, and shell scrapers. They carved petroglyphs and painted pictographs on cave surfaces, but nothing that resembled these English initials.

Around the late 1790s, the caves were said to be rediscovered by a frontier hunter who was chasing a bear. His name was John Houchins, and his initials didn't match. After a brief era of saltpeter extraction for gunpowder during the War of 1812, the tourists began to arrive.

In the 1830s, the enslaved guide Stephen Bishop became famous as the first daring explorer of Mammoth Cave. After using ladders to cross the Bottomless Pit, he went on to explore over ten miles of passageways. He named features like the River Styx, Fat Man's Misery, and the Snowball Room, a domed amphitheater with a ceiling encrusted with gypsum flowers. Visitors flocked from around the world to join his tours. One wealthy cave enthusiast paid for Bishop to produce a map from memory. It proved to be remarkably accurate when the cave was finally surveyed by Max Kaemper in 1908. Neither set of initials matched Bishop's, either.

Next came a bizarre era of blistering competition. Entrepreneurs searched for back entrances into Mammoth Cave so they could charge their own tour fees. Other residents discovered competing caverns on the periphery, which would later be connected by the far-out cavers. As Model Ts and early motorcars bounced along rugged dirt roads toward Mammoth Cave, highway agents—called *cappers*—would jump on the running boards and steer the tourists to newly established cash caves.

Guiding tours beneath the rocky earth was sure better than trying to farm it. One winter day in 1925, local cave explorer Floyd Collins was probing a crawlway in Sand Save, hoping to discover a business opportunity. When a boulder dislodged from the ceiling, he was pinned fifty-five feet below the surface. Rescuers repeatedly failed to extract him, and his predicament became a nationwide news frenzy. For days, reporters and onlookers gathered outside the entrance. Concerned family and friends ferried food and water inside. It was said that the heat from spectator campfires—burning outside the entrance of this inwardly breathing cave—warmed the interior. This may have caused the cave substrate to swell and destabilize. Either way, the passage surrounding the trapped Collins further collapsed. Two weeks after his entrapment, an organized party digging from the surface finally broke through the fifty feet of rock. The caver's body was cold to the touch.

Given his posthumous celebrity, Collins's corpse was put on display. The glass coffin was placed inside the entrance to Crystal Cave, near where the far-out cavers later established their headquarters. This morbid highlight was too much for a rival cave owner. He didn't think the attraction was inappropriate or anything like that. He thought it gave an unfair competitive advantage to Crystal Cave, whose cappers commandeered motor cars with promises of a macabre show.

Late one night, grave robbers stole Floyd Collins's body and dumped it in the river. Fortunately, the corpse was quickly retrieved. Floyd Collins was returned to his underground coffin. This time, the casket was covered so that the famous caver might finally rest in peace. Of course, his initials didn't match the 1970s discovery either.

But the events of the Kentucky Cave Wars—plus the destructive efforts of souvenir sellers who knocked mineral formations from the cave walls—led to a movement to protect Mammoth Cave and the surrounding landscape as a national park.

A series of land purchases and controversial declarations of imminent domain were used to assemble the park grounds during a fifteen-year period starting in 1926.

As the park grew, the superintendent encouraged new discoveries. The goal was for guides to uncover new routes for guest tours. Wait a minute—that was it. Two of those early national park guides had penetrated the deepest outskirts of Mammoth Cave. In 1938, Pete Hanson and Leo Hunt had ventured into the passages beyond where an underground boat tour floated through Echo River.

Then the Second World War spread across the globe, and the two men were shipped overseas. Hunt came back but didn't resume caving. Sadly, Hanson never made it home. The details of their discoveries were lost after World War II, until Pat Crowther and some far-out 1970s cavers went through the Tight Spot and stumbled across a piece of history.

Rumors Spread

"Pete Hanson!" shouted Crowther.

The others were stunned. The team was standing in what became known as Hanson's Lost River.

Ecstatic, they forged onward through waist-deep water, sometimes crouching with only a few feet of airspace. After a mile, it was nearly midnight. They'd exceeded their safe turnaround time. They were five and half miles from the Austin Entrance, the furthest any cavers had ever explored from that entry point.

They had no idea how much further it was to the developed passages of Mammoth Cave, and their energy was fading fast. Crowther was limping with a sore knee and hip. Wilcox's jacket was torn through at the elbows, and the exposed skin was raw. Brucker's head was spinning. Zopf, well, he was fine and bounding along as usual. Reluctantly, they made their way back toward Flint Ridge.

Up on the surface, Wilcox swore them all to secrecy. The initials in Hanson's Lost River were a major discovery, but the team hadn't made history quite yet. This operational silence worked perfectly until the next morning when Brucker opened his eyes. Two of his caving friends were standing over him.

"Guess what we found," said Brucker.

Rumors spread fast in the backwoods of Kentucky, and even faster by telephone among cavers. Now Wilcox knew the CRF needed to complete the connection before people bragged that they already had. Otherwise, it was like climbing a mountain to within sight of the summit and dismissing the final ascent as simply academic. It would be a major embarrassment if Hanson's Lost River ended in a siphon that couldn't be traversed. Covering all bases, Wilcox and Crowther donned wet suits and floated atop inner tubes through the boatable waterways inside Mammoth Cave. Nothing. Not a great sign if the outlet couldn't be found from the easier side.

Irony with Epiphanies

In mid-September, a team of six far-out cavers set out to cross the gap. This time, they carried not only the key to enter through the Austin Entrance, but the keys to exit from Mammoth Cave. With them was Cleve Pinnix, an athletic ranger who would represent the park service in the historic event.

The team's enthusiasm was palpable, and they filled the water-dripping silence with endless knee-slapping cave banter. This wasn't a cakewalk, nor was it a cake-crawl. When an enthralled Pinnix did a chimney move through Tight Tube, where you push your hands and feet outward to wedge climb through a vertical shaft, he smacked his head.

"Testing your hard hat?" ribbed Zopf.

After hours of exertion, with Pinnix coated in cake-batter mud, he emerged from the Tight Spot. Zopf was waiting with another zinger.

"You look thinner, Cleve."

Pinnix replied that his motor was burning on kneecaps, ribs, and obscenities.

The team pushed further than ever before. As they progressed single-file through Hanson's Lost River, the green water deepened. The ceiling lowered until there was less than a foot of airspace. They shivered in the icy waters, keeping their carbide lamps and airways just above the surface. Their movements kicked up waves that sloshed against the ceiling. The classic sign of a siphon. Was all the effort for nothing? Wilcox pushed forward, and slowly the ceiling lifted.

"I've got something," he shouted back. His words echoed as he emerged into a pool inside a large chamber. "It's big."

Something shiny was gleaming at the periphery of his light. It was a handrail.

"I see a tourist trail!"

"We're in Cascade Hall!" said Crowther.

Their endeavor involved an ironic twist. The first explorers to summit this underground Everest had arrived to find a visitor center on top. That didn't bother them, but something else felt irksome. Most far-out caving trips lasted eighteen to twenty-four hours. They'd been on the move for half that, and no one wanted to leave. After years of underground efforts and false leads and crushing fatigue, they belonged down here. So, they sat down and enjoyed a celebratory meal of canned food. Then they went back into Hanson's Lost River to survey the passage.

When they later expanded their maps, the CRF members would have a startling epiphany. Stephen Bishop, over a century before, had drawn a short line from Mammoth Cave representing the start of a dry passage that later became Hanson's Lost River. In the 1930s, Pete Hanson and Leo Hunt had gone a mile further down this dry tunnel. But when the Green River was dammed, and the base-level changed, it had become a river. The connecting passage would be entirely submerged once the drought ended.

The far-out cavers debated what to call their newly connected cave system. Would it be Flint–Mammoth, like they wanted, or Mammoth–Flint? The more famous name would ultimately win the argument. The moment that these six far-out cavers had passed through an almost invisible outlet into Echo River, Mammoth Cave became the longest in the world—an astounding 145 miles. With further work by the CRF, more caves and passageways would be discovered and connected to the whole. By the early 2020s, the total known length surpassed over 430 miles, with a little more being surveyed each year. The full length of Mammoth Cave is certainly higher than the current total, but no one knows by how much.

There was one final debate to resolve for the far-out cavers on that Saturday night in the summer of '72. Which exit should they take? None of them really felt like walking out of the Historic Entrance used by the ranger-guided tours, after all. They might be seen, and then the whole secret would be out. They wanted to announce their discovery in style—with a classy press conference.

Ranger Pinnix had a suggestion. Why not sneak out through the sparkling hall of the Snowball Dining Room? Everyone grinned at each other. So, this muddy but exuberant bunch in torn denim sauntered between empty tables in the strangest restaurant under the Earth. They stepped inside the elevator, bubbling with laughter. They rose through the layers of bedrock to which they owed some of the best moments of their lives. Then Mammoth Cave was quiet again, and everything went dark.

THE SOUTH

CHAPTER 23

DID AL CAPONE HAVE AN OUTPOST IN THE EVERGLADES?

HIDDEN HISTORY

EVERGLADES NATIONAL PARK & BIG CYPRESS NATIONAL PRESERVE

THE EVERGLADES, SOUTH FLORIDA

Marjory Stoneman Douglas was at her home in Miami when Hervey Allen dropped by. He was a family friend who had recently become the editor of the nonfiction book series *Rivers of America*.

For several decades, Douglas had been a beloved journalist in one of the United States' newest cities. Miami had been established in 1896, six years after she was born. Now it was the early 1940s, and she'd spent the past six months trying and failing to write her first book, a novel. So, Douglas was all ears when Allen came calling with a job offer. He wanted her to write a nonfiction book about the Miami River.

"Hervey, you can't write a book about the Miami River," blurted Douglas. "It's only about an inch long."

Still, she wanted the paid assignment, and Allen seemed open to ideas. Douglas noted that the Miami River was connected to the Everglades, and there might be a book in that. In 1915, a few years after graduating from Wellesley College in Massachusetts, she'd boarded a train heading south. Once arrived, she reunited with her father, who had started the *Miami Herald* newspaper. Slowly, the adventurous young woman began exploring the wild swamplands of the Everglades, where slow-moving waters passed through plains of saw grass between islands of hardwood forest.

By the 1920s, the Tamiami Trail was partly completed across South Florida. Douglas and friends would drive out to where it dead-ended at the Dade County line. They built fires on the asphalt and watched sunrises and the mating flights of white ibis. Near the Ten Thousand Islands, where tidal waters surged through channels between countless mangrove islands, she stared up at huge flocks of birds swooping through the sky. At Flamingo, where stilt houses rose along the edge of Florida Bay, she'd spot bald eagles, herons, and egrets.

When landscape architect Ernest F. Coe had convened a committee to advocate for the creation of a national park, he'd asked Douglas to be a member. Off the team went, exploring the region by fan boat and hot air balloon.

"All right," said Allen, that day decades later in Miami. "Write about the Everglades."

Without realizing it, this casual agreement between editor and author would set Douglas down a path that she would tread for the rest of her life. By this point, from about twenty visits, she knew the Everglades as well as any journalist, which wasn't that well yet, she freely admitted.

She knew the Everglades spread across thousands of square miles. That the birds were spectacular. That it should be a national park. That it shouldn't be destroyed. At the time, South Florida was growing rapidly. Most residents—and especially those with real estate interests—did not think highly of the Everglades. It was considered a dangerous region to be avoided. A flood-prone wetland where people went missing and decaying bodies turned up. A worthless swamp that should be drained for farm fields and housing tracts. Douglas didn't agree. Why couldn't people see this beautiful landscape for what was there? Why did they have such a bad impression to begin with? And how was she going to overcome generations of stigma and do it in less than 120,000 words?

SUBTLE SHIFTS

Stretching across 2,358 square miles, Everglades is the third-largest national park in the lower forty-eight. It sees around a million visitors per year, with most coming during the winter dry season between roughly November and April. During these milder months, the average daily high is 77 degrees Fahrenheit, and the mosquitoes are more manageable.

Most visitors take a driving tour on the thirty-eight-mile main park road starting from the Ernest F. Coe Visitor Center. Along the way, you can stop at overlooks and walk short interpretive trails, with two favorites found at Royal Palm. Keep your eyes peeled for abundant wildlife like great blue herons, roseate spoonbills, and alligators. As you progress south, watch for the subtle changes between the park's major ecosystems, including tall-grass sloughs, hardwood islands, matchstick pinelands, dwarf cypress forests, and mangrove channels near Florida Bay.

A Wild Reputation

Long before Douglas's time, the Everglades had developed a poor reputation. It is the only place in the world where both alligators and crocodiles can be found. An area so thick with mosquitoes, especially during the hot and rainy summer, that locals joked they could reach out and grab them by the handful. Traveling through these wetlands risked malaria, which was mostly eradicated by the mid-twentieth century, but would never entirely vanish from the state.

Archaeologists believe archaic humans first migrated to South Florida about 10,000 to 15,000 years ago. When Spanish conquistadors began exploring La Florida in the early sixteenth century, they encountered several powerful tribes living on the periphery of the Everglades, including the Calusa and Tequesta. They fought tenacious battles against the Spaniards, but the tribes were soon decimated by European diseases unwittingly carried from the so-called Old World to the New.

During the eighteenth century, a new group of mostly Creek Native Americans moved south into a nearly empty peninsula that was now controlled by Spain. The Creeks were fleeing from increasing conflicts with English colonies to the north. Banding together, they called themselves the Seminoles, which roughly translated as *wild runaways*.

Spanish Florida was also becoming a haven for African Americans, who often joined the Seminoles after escaping from slavery in the United States. Wealthy slave owners increasingly sent raiding parties across the border to recapture these refugees. By now, Spain's New World empire was crumbling. Seeing Florida as more trouble than it was worth, they ceded the territory to the United States in 1821.

Over a roughly forty-year period, the U.S. Army fought three wars against the Seminoles to force them from the prime coastal and farming lands and onto reservations. The Seminoles resisted this much larger force by using guerrilla tactics that relied upon their knowledge of the jungled landscape. Increasingly, the U.S. Army resorted to a strategy of *total war* by destroying Seminole homes and food supplies. By the end of the third war, only a few hundred Seminoles remained in South Florida. They retreated into the flooded wilds of the Everglades where most American settlers feared to tread.

Pathways for Crime and Storms

After the Civil War, the American Frontier pushed west during the late nineteenth century. Meanwhile, the Everglades became something of a far southeastern frontier with its own lawless ways. Ed Watson was a local hard case from North Florida. After committing some uncertain crime, possibly murder, he skipped town and went to Indian Territory in present-day Oklahoma. There, he rented farmland near Youngers Bend from Belle Starr, the famous outlaw who was an associate of Frank and Jesse James.

In 1889, a few days before her forty-first birthday, Starr left a Sunday afternoon party at a friend's house. While she was riding the river road toward home, a shotgun blast violently knocked her from the saddle. The horse bolted, and a bloodied Starr lay on the ground dying. Tracks were spotted leading to Ed Watson's cabin. One theory became that Starr had learned Watson was a wanted man in Florida.

Either way, Watson soon turned up in the Everglades, raising sugar cane and other vegetables around the Ten Thousand Islands. The area was filled with what locals called *bad actors*, but there was no community theater in these parts. Within a few years, Watson was embroiled in numerous feuds. He was a suspect in a half dozen killings, and there might have been more if he wasn't mysteriously shot to death himself.

That took care of one problem, but another hazard was poachers. By the turn of the twentieth century, bird populations in the Everglades were nearing extinction due to overhunting of plumage for ladies' hats. Widely sought were the white feathers of egrets, the pink feathers from roseate spoonbills, and the blue-gray feathers of the great heron.

In 1901, the Florida legislature outlawed the hunting and trade of wild bird plumage. But no money was allocated for enforcement. The Audubon Society sent their own wardens into the Everglades to guard rookeries during nesting season. A few years later, two of these deputies were murdered on the job. The publicity surrounding these events would lead to a national ban on the sale of wild plumage.

Poaching in the Everglades became more discreet, and now the feathers were smuggled to Cuba.

With the prohibition of alcohol in the 1920s, the trafficking of illicit goods reversed directions. Now rum runners used the dangerous swamps to move shipments of Caribbean spirits into Florida. On mangrove keys and dry hammocks—a type of wooded island rising slightly above the wetlands—moonshiners set up their stills. Illegal liquor flowed from the backwaters of the Everglades into the cities.

One trafficking route led to Miami. This urban oasis, carved from the periphery of the southeastern Everglades, was enjoying a roaring twenties. Discreet speakeasies and gambling parlors could be found from the rural swamps to downtown alleys. But the boom in commerce and construction came to a destructive end when a Category 4 storm swept through in September 1926.

The Great Miami Hurricane passed over the Everglades and inundated its headwaters, the massive but shallow Lake Okeechobee. An earthen irrigation dike burst, and the resulting flood surge killed hundreds of rural residents. Two years later, an even stronger hurricane hit the area. During both disasters, countless bodies were washed into the Everglades and never seen again.

═══ SUBTROPICAL ADVENTURES ═══

More adventurous visitors can "get back in there," by exploring lesser-visited areas. Hike or mountain bike longer trails like the seven-mile Long Pine Key Trail. Join a guided kayak trip through the River of Grass. Set up a tent or camper in a park campground. Consider biking to the observation tower on the mellow Shark Valley Loop Road, which is vehicle free except for tram tours. Take a motorboat trip through mangroves at the remote Ten Thousand Islands.

A Miami Overlord?

Around that time, in January 1928, Miami saw the arrival of an infamous new resident. Some called him Scarface due to the slash marks across his left cheek, the results of a knifing in New York City. Al Capone had grown up in Brooklyn, where he rose through the ranks of several street gangs to become a trusted enforcer for Chicago crime boss Johnny Torrio. After Torrio survived an assassination attempt by a rival gang, he went into hiding.

At the age of twenty-six, underboss Al Capone was put in charge of the entire enterprise. The Outfit made around $100 million a year from bootlegging, gambling, and prostitution. Unlike his predecessor, Capone was a flamboyant mobster. He wore brightly colored suits and ties. Instead of avoiding attention, he courted it. He gave coy interviews, reveling in the fact that police were never able to directly link him to illegal activities.

The secret to Capone's meteoric rise was a blend of clever financials and brutal violence. He employed a vast network of intermediaries such that nothing could be directly linked to the boss. No documents, no bank accounts. The titles to businesses and buildings were often in the name of law-abiding private citizens whose loyalty was secured under threat of torture or death. Plenty of the revenue that was collected by nefarious bagmen was used for public relations. Politicians, judges, and police were widely bribed, and the citizens shared in the mafia's wealth. Capone arranged charity donations, community events, under-the-table loans, and soup kitchens for the poor. Despite his underworld dealings, Capone found plenty of love in Chicago. But rival mobsters and the feds were coming for him.

"I am here for a rest, which I think I deserve," Capone said about his relocation during an interview with the *Miami Herald*. "All that I want is a fair break. I have done nothing in violation of the law in Miami and will not."

In his new city, Capone had a lawyer arrange a home purchase on his behalf on Palm Island. Then he and his family proceeded to live the lavish coastal lifestyle. They socialized with the elites at restaurants and night clubs. Held huge parties at their estate. Al was regularly seen at the racetrack, where he often shared suspiciously accurate tips about which horse might win. He took his son out on speedboat rides through Biscayne Bay.

The response from the people of Miami was mixed. The mayor, many business owners, and the workers at the establishments where Capone flung money welcomed him with open arms. Almost everyone else wanted the gangster out. Few believed he'd actually gone straight, and his occasional return trips to Chicago supported this skepticism. Yes, Capone was known to be in Florida on Saint Valentine's Day in 1929. But few doubted that he'd ordered the massacre of seven members of rival Bugs Moran's North Side Gang. The news reporters, the police, and Treasury agents led by Elliot Ness were closing in on Al Capone.

Marjory Stoneman Douglas had left the *Miami Herald* by now, but she still participated in the topic by cowriting a stage play. *Storm Warning* followed a famous gangster who meets his demise through mob justice by the local citizenry. It played at the Civic Theatre to packed houses. Capone was notorious for reading every article and book that was published about him, but he never made a showtime. He did, however, send some operatives, who sat in the back, which spiked the atmosphere on opening night.

In the end it wasn't the murders or racketeering that caught up with Capone. It was the numbers not matching his name. His home and lifestyle clearly required a hefty income. Yet he hadn't filed a return with the Bureau of Internal Revenue in years. In 1932, Capone went to federal prison for tax evasion. The sentence was eleven years hard time at the Rock—Alcatraz Island in San Francisco Bay. When the syphilis infection in his body spread to his brain, the once powerful mobster was released after seven years.

He returned to his home on Palm Island. South Florida had fallen into a crime wave during the Great Depression. Rumors had long claimed the imprisoned Capone was calling the shots. Surely, his release meant he would now rule openly as overlord of Miami. Instead, the deteriorating Capone had the mental capacities of a twelve-year-old child. For seven years, he sat by the pool before becoming bedridden with an oxygen mask. He died in early 1947, leaving behind more legends than records about his nefarious empire.

WILD DETOURS

Big Cypress National Preserve is a vast, mostly undeveloped unit with primarily unpaved roads and hard-to-reach areas. However, several highlights off Tamiami Trail are easier to explore, including the boardwalk at Kirby Storter Roadside Park. But if you really want to bring this mystery to life, and see a building foundation rumored to be associated with Al Capone, you'll want to drive or bike the partly unpaved Loop Road. Watch for the ruins of Pinecrest. Hear the sounds of wildlife. Listen for the faint echoes of bar brawls from the Gator Hook Lodge.

What Are the Everglades?

That same year, Marjory Stoneman Douglas's book on the Everglades was nearing completion. She'd spent half a decade on the project, though her biggest breakthrough happened not long after receiving the assignment. The earliest steps in her research led Douglas to the Dade County Courthouse, a towering stone building that was the tallest in Florida. There she met with an influential U.S. Geological Survey (USGS) hydrogeologist named Gerald Parker who was studying groundwater flow in South Florida.

In response to the disastrous hurricanes of the late 1920s, the U.S. Army Corps of Engineers had built two flood control structures at Lake Okeechobee. A large control levee prevented flood surges spilling out of the lake, and a drainage canal carried runoff into the Gulf. This system cut off the Everglades from its main water source, and the wetlands began to dry out. As a result, the 1930s saw a prolonged drought, which confirmed that rainfall across the region relied upon evaporation from the Everglades. As long-submerged sediments turned to powder, winds kicked up dust clouds. Then the drinking supply in Miami went bad. Saltwater was intruding into the city wells. So, Parker was called in to study the issue.

Douglas started with her main question: What exactly *are* the Everglades? Parker explained that they were not technically swamps. Those were typically slow-flowing wetlands, either fresh or saltwater, that were densely vegetated with cypress forests or mangrove shrubs. Instead, the Everglades involved a subtle flow of freshwater, both below ground through porous limestone and along the surface. Wherever this water flowed, sawgrass as tall as your head would grow. Considering her assignment, Douglas asked if the Everglades could be considered a river. Parker offered a definition.

"A river is a body of fresh water moving more in one direction than the other."

Douglas took home a vegetation map of South Florida, which she pinned to a door. She sat down and stared at the Everglades, trying to conceptualize the bigger picture. Under ideal conditions, this freshwater flowed out of Lake Okeechobee into a vast, shallow channel between two slightly elevated rises. To the east was a coastal ridge of limestone rising less than thirty feet above sea level. To the west, another ridge was composed of slightly elevated pinelands, cypress swamps, and marl prairies. In between was a sawgrass slough. It curved to the southeast and narrowed within Shark Valley before ending near Cape Sable and the Ten Thousand Islands. *Banks, channel, delta*, thought Douglas. So, she went to Parker to confirm an idea, which she later made the title of her book.

The Everglades: River of Grass became an instant classic upon release in the fall of 1947. The first edition had nearly sold out a month later, when the dedication ceremony was held for Everglades National Park. Speakers at the podium referenced and quoted from Douglas's entertaining and insightful book. It was a rebuttal to the naysayers who associated the Everglades with violence and decay and mobsters like Al Capone. It was a book that changed how people thought and talked and felt about this watery ecosystem in South Florida. Marjory Stoneman Douglas had found a way to overcome all those generations of stigma, and she'd done it with just three words.

Last Gasps of a Lost City

Old habits die hard. *River of Grass* was a powerful metaphor that shifted perceptions. But this beloved wilderness remained in a constant state of threat from competing interests. Miami was still growing. Hurricanes were striking. New canals and levees were redirecting water flow away from the Everglades.

The original national park proposal had called for protecting a much larger area, including the vast northwestern headwaters in Big Cypress Swamp. In the late 1960s, Dade County sent construction crews into the area north of the Tamiami Trail. The Miami Jetport was planned to be world's largest, with six massive runways, to accommodate a supersonic future. An expressway and monorail would bisect the Everglades and connect both coasts.

The public outcry about this latest threat to the River of Grass was swift and widespread, coming from vast swaths of the population. Native Americans, hunters, conservationists, environmentalists, and once-skeptical residents agreed with Marjory Stoneman Douglas, who had evolved into one of the region's most dedicated activists. The choice was the Everglades, and the jetport plan was abandoned. As a result of this momentum, in the 1970s, the Big Cypress National Preserve was established to purchase the land and protect over 1,000 square miles of wetlands and jungle.

Not everyone was pleased by the new plan, especially the few hearty residents who would have to move outside the new boundaries. South of Tamiami Trail, on a sandy doubletrack called the Loop Road, there was a town of a hundred or so. Pinecrest was a lawless community carved into the jungle where the unruly frontier days of the Everglades seemed alive and well—especially when considering all the murders. The roughest dive bar in all of South Florida was found here, named for a hunting tool used by poachers, the Gator Hook Lodge.

"No Guns or Knives Inside," warned an entry sign that most ignored. Out of courtesy or force, fights were usually taken to the parking lot. Another message behind the bar saw greater adherence: "In God We Trust. All Others Pay Cash."

In the dwindling days of the 1970s, as the residents of Pinecrest haggled with the government before selling, a few brave journalists made the trek to the Gator Hook Lodge to document the fading scene. Sometimes, they encountered drunks passed out on the floor at high noon. Old-timers inside talked about the good ol' days when every Saturday saw a brawl. Things were simpler back then. The women fought first, they said, and the men fought afterward.

These rough regulars talked about the Loop Road's celebrity resident, a popular fiddler named Ervin Rouse who sang "Orange Blossom Special." No one could recall how long the Gator Hook Lodge had been there, but one thing most everyone recalled was the name of a famous mobster.

"Al Capone's syndicate used to run a hotel here in Pinecrest," said Uncle Mac to Rick Gore, a *National Geographic* correspondent, in 1976. MacDonald Johnson was ninety years old, with skin as worn as an old swamp turtle. He'd come to the Big Cypress Swamp long before the national park, before the River of Grass, before even the Tamiami Trail was built. Now he sat in front of his home, a rusty school bus just off the Loop Road.

"I don't think Al himself ever came out here, though," said Uncle Mac. "I call him Al now, but when I worked for him as a waiter in Miami, it was always Mr. Capone."

Other folks told tales of Capone operating a moonshining outpost further south, on dry ground somewhere in the River of Grass. Later, this bootlegging operation would come to be associated with the legendary Lost City of the Everglades. But was there any truth to these stories, or were they just the last winking gasps from those forced to vacate these swamps? A bit of light ribbing for city reporters who came hunting for stories. Al Capone left no records behind, so one can neither confirm nor deny the claims. But does that even matter?

Perhaps the moniker *lost city* is a better fit for Pinecrest, home to the most rebellious of establishments. Where the patrons kept an eye over their shoulder for flying barstools and pool cues. Where the legend of the Loop Road is now entwined with an infamous mobster who never visited and a famous author whose spirit never left. Oh, and let's not forget about old-timers like Uncle Mac, either.

"They used to bring so-called dignitaries out here for a vacation," he continued, with a chuckle, talking about the mafia in the old days. "A man can vanish real easy takin' a walk in the swamp. And a lot of 'em did—without a trace."

CHAPTER 24

WHAT CREATED THE APPALACHIAN BALDS?

UNEXPLAINED PHENOMENA

BLUE RIDGE PARKWAY

APPALACHIAN MOUNTAINS, NORTH CAROLINA AND VIRGINIA

Once there was a massive bird that resembled a green-winged hornet, according to a Cherokee legend recorded by ethnographer James Mooney. This bird lived among the Appalachian Mountains during an ancient time when the world was filled with ferocious monsters. Children who wandered into the woods were said to be snatched and carried away into the sky. So, the tribe declared war. Yet this mythical creature always evaded them.

One day, a group of Cherokee wise men hatched a plan. Each stationed himself on the summit of a tall mountain. When one saw the bird, he yelled out, "Halloo!" When the next man saw the bird, he echoed the call. A long string of halloos followed the bird to its hiding place, on the eastern side of the Blue Ridge Mountains, near the headwaters of the Tugaloo River.

Upon arriving at the bird's cavern, the men found the entrance beyond reach. So, they prayed to the Great Spirit to bring the bird out of its den. Their wish was granted in the form of a violent thunderstorm. A bolt of lightning struck the mountain, causing the rocks of the cavern to fall away, revealing the massive creature.

After watching the courageous Cherokee slay their enemy, the Great Spirit was pleased. As a reward, he deemed that the highest mountains in their land would thereafter be bald, free of trees, so that the Cherokee could use them as lookouts.

NORTH TO SOUTH

The Blue Ridge Parkway mostly follows the crest of the Blue Ridge Mountains for 469 miles, from Shenandoah National Park in Virginia to Great Smoky Mountains National Park in North Carolina. Averaging over fifteen million annual visitors, the parkway is the busiest unit of the National Park Service. People typically go for driving tours, scenic overlooks, mountain lodges, wine tastings, and a crowded fall-colors season.

That said, the parkway is also home to excellent hiking trails and historic sites. Popular hiking areas include the rolling meadows of Doughton Park, wildflower-framed views at Craggy Gardens, and rugged formations at Humpback Rocks. Scenic waterfalls are found at Linville Falls, Crabtree Falls, and Graveyard Fields. Intriguing outdoor and indoor museums include Mabry Mill, the Blue Ridge Music Center, and the Museum of North Carolina Minerals.

Did Bartram See the Balds?

Across the southern Appalachian Mountains, dozens of mysterious bald peaks rise above the surrounding forest. They can be found from northern Georgia, across western North Carolina, and into southern Virginia. Given the prevailing conditions—including relatively low elevation, mild climate, and good drainage—one would expect these Appalachian balds to be timbered.

In fact, some bald peaks stand adjacent to tree-covered summits. The reasons for why one is bare and the other forested remains a mystery. It's not even clear when these balds first appeared. Have they been present since ancient times as some legends suggest? Other observers believe they may be a more recent phenomenon created by white settlers.

"I began to ascend again," wrote colonial naturalist William Bartram. His explorations of the Southern Appalachians happened in 1775, before widespread settlement by white Europeans. "First over swelling turfy ridges, varied with groves of stately forest trees. Then ascending again more steep grassy hill sides, rested on the top of…the highest ridge of the Cherokee mountains… This exalted peak I named mount Magnolia."

Though this famous explorer of the region makes no explicit mention of the enigmatic balds, Bartram's detailed descriptions suggest they were present during the years before the American Revolution. Bartram roughly followed old trading routes through Cherokee country, which included frequent visits to summits with magnificent and wide-open views. Other times he describes features like "natural mounds," "rock knobs," and "tufty eminences."

"The road led me over the bases of a ridge of hills," notes Bartram, about traveling near an old Cherokee village called *Sticoe* or *Stecoah*. He goes on to describe these hills as a "bold promontory dividing the fields." Though it may not be intentional, the lead adjective *bold* is derived from the Middle English word *bald*. This particular passage describes an area around the headwaters of the Tenase. Today it's called the Little Tennessee River, and several bald peaks rise in the surrounding area.

Ultimately, whether William Bartram encountered the balds seems to be inconclusive, but the signs point to these features being present before his time.

OFF PARKWAY

While road construction often leads to detours, there are other reasons to move slowly and to venture off the parkway. Continue north onto Skyline Drive, and you'll find great camping and summit hikes in Shenandoah National Park—which sees only 1.5 million annual visitors. Other detours in Virginia include stopping by Natural Bridge State Park. The mountain metro of Roanoke with its hilltop star. Two fascinating NPS units, Appomattox Court House National Historical Park and Booker T. Washington National Monument.

In North Carolina, adventures abound. Mount Mitchell State Park has the highest summit on the East Coast, at 6,684 feet. An often chilly hike leads through dense fog, slick rocks, and scraggly spruce-fir forest along the rugged spine of the Black Mountains. Nearby New River State Park offers relaxing float trips through classic Appalachian scenery. The city of Asheville has slightly more people than microbreweries. Pisgah National Forest is all about trails, both hiking and mountain biking. The Cradle of Forestry has historic walks where U.S. forestry conservation began. And continue south into Great Smoky Mountains or hop in a raft for a whitewater trip down the Nantahala River.

Stone and Metal

After the formation of the United States, new American settlers pushed into the

Appalachians. In 1799, a government-appointed surveyor named John Strother traced the Tennessee–North Carolina state line through the highlands.

"There is no shrubbage [that] grows on the tops of mountains for several miles, say five," he wrote in his diary.

Strother believed this high ridge, known as Roan Mountain, was the most "conspicuous" string of balds in the range. Today, a section of the Appalachian Trail follows this highland passage, which is still known as the longest continuous section of wide-open peaks in the Appalachians.

Early white settlers were well aware of the balds. During the warmer seasons, they herded their cattle and sheep to graze on the high-elevation grasses. This helped avoid milk sickness in the livestock, which was thought to be caused by lower-elevation plants. The practice also left the valley floors free for summer farming.

During the latter half of the nineteenth century, natural science was a burgeoning field among white Americans. Thus, some observers sought scientific explanations for these enigmatic bare spots. One theory was that recurring ice storms prevented trees from taking root. An opposing theory suggested hot and dry southeasterly winds, plus periodic lightning fires, dried them out like promontories of desert in the otherwise humid Southeast.

Around the turn of the twentieth century, logging supplanted homesteading as the primary industry. Small farmers were increasingly displaced, bought out by large timber companies. By the 1920s, over two-thirds of the area had been clear cut. In response to the concerns of residents, the federal government acquired large swaths of land for public use, including what became Cherokee National Forest and Great Smoky Mountains National Park.

During the 1930s, mountain highways were constructed, including the beginnings of the Blue Ridge Parkway. With motorists winding through the high country, the previously isolated balds became better known through tourism and recreation. This was the era of big building projects, when sweeping dams and towering skyscrapers began to rise across the country. Not surprisingly, theories about bald formation turned toward human efforts.

One theory was that the Cherokee had created the balds. The cleared areas would have been useful in several ways. As campsites. Lookouts. Lures for game animals, where marksman could take wide-open shots with bows and arrows. Critics of this hypothesis questioned if the stone tools of the time would have been strong enough to hack away the old-growth forest. So, a competing theory focused on the steel ax of the white settler.

Others suggested the balds might be the result of both cultures. Stone and then metal, plus the shared practice of woods burning. Both Native Americans and white homesteaders set periodic fires to clear the dense Southeastern underbrush. This allowed for easier passage through forests for hunters, gatherers, game animals, and grazing livestock.

BEST OF THE BALDS

If you want to experience the Appalachian balds up close, one option is the Great Balsam Mountains. This subrange of the Blue Ridge mostly falls within Pisgah National Forest, with bare summits rising high above the parkway. A common starting point is from Black Balsam Knob Road, with the Art Loeb Trail leading to a series of bald peaks offering panoramic views of rolling mountains and ridges.

A Big-Picture Theory

After the federal acquisitions throughout the Blue Ridge Mountains, forest and park managers chose to preserve the public lands in a natural state. It was found that some balds began to shrink from encroaching forest. Elsewhere, where seasonal grazing was allowed to continue, those balds usually remained intact. This provided a key clue to unraveling the mystery.

During the 1990s, advances in scientific thought and research technology encouraged experts to peer further into the past. Now longer time frames were being considered beyond the few hundred years of recorded human history. A new theory was proposed by a pair of biologists named Weigl and Knowles.

Archaeological excavations conducted nearby had revealed something big. During the last ice age, around 10,000 years ago, mammoths and mastodons roamed the southern Appalachians. These were massive herbivores—each weighing six to nine tons—that were covered in fur and had long and curving tusks. Their fellow grazers of that era included native horses, piglike tapirs, and muskox. Each of these ancient animals would eventually go extinct or die out in the region during a time when nomadic tribes started wandering into the wilderness of North America.

The new theory combined several factors unfolding over millennia. During past ice ages, glaciers formed atop the higher forested peaks in the southern mountains. When the ice receded during warmer periods, deforested summits emerged. Those that were accessible via suitable animal paths were visited by megaherbivores, leading the way for smaller grazers as well. The plodding steps and voracious appetites of mammoths and mastodons kept the trees at bay, and the balds remained covered with faster-growing shrubs and grasses. Those nearby summits that were harder to reach saw the regrowth of forests.

Eventually, humans migrated from the northwest into the southeast. Overhunting by these growing populations, combined with a changing climate, spelled doom for the mammoths, mastodons, and other ancient mammals. Though they went extinct, some grazers did survive, including the bison, elk, and deer familiar in modern times. These herbivores maintained the balds they inherited.

At some point, the Cherokee migrated into the region, most likely coming from the Great Lakes region during ancient times. Tribe members seasonally used the convenient balds for hunting, camping, and keeping watch. They seem to have incorporated the balds into legends, like those reported by ethnologist James Mooney. He spent several field seasons, from 1887 to 1890, visiting with the

Cherokee in North Carolina and Oklahoma Territory, attempting to document their culture in written form.

After the Cherokee were forcibly removed on the Trail of Tears by the U.S. government, white settlers entered the southern Appalachians. On one hand, the newcomers overhunted the wild animals that grazed on the balds. But the settlers also brought herds of grazing cattle and sheep that assumed the role of keeping the balds clear.

It was a compelling story. Perhaps the most complete theory to date. With time, further study may reveal if the mystery has been solved. In the meantime, the balds remain. They rise high above the forested ridges of the Appalachians. Atop these open summits, animals graze and hikers tread. Curious visitors can gaze out at the rolling mountains and ponder how it all came to be.

HOW DID MURDERER BRADFORD BISHOP ESCAPE?

GREAT SMOKY MOUNTAINS NATIONAL PARK

APPALACHIAN MOUNTAINS, NORTH CAROLINA–TENNESSEE STATE LINE

Forest ranger Ronald Brickhouse was in his vehicle, following smoke, as he turned off Highway 94 onto an unpaved logging road. It was around 1:00 p.m. on Tuesday, March 2, 1976, and the ranger had received a radio dispatch from a lookout at a nearby watchtower. After driving half a mile, Brickhouse found a brushfire spreading through dry grass and pine seedlings near a swamp. After ten minutes fighting flames around the edges, he radioed for help.

Then he spotted something odd. At what seemed to be the blackened origin of the blaze, there was a four-foot-deep hole that appeared recently dug. As he approached, he noticed some partly scorched carcasses. Probably wild hogs left by hunters, he assumed. Then his stomach lurched. It wasn't hogs but people. A pile of smoldering bodies.

BRAVE THE CROWDS

Great Smoky Mountains is the busiest national park in the nation, averaging over thirteen million annual visitors. That's usually more than twice the number of the next most popular park unit. One reason is the numerous surrounding metro regions. Another is the park's location at the busier end of the Blue Ridge Parkway, the most visited NPS unit in the nation. Finally, Great Smoky Mountains National Park has no entry fee, though a parking fee was recently introduced to reduce overcrowding and fund park projects.

Great Smoky Mountains's visitation peaks during October, when leaf peepers come for scenic drives and hikes through fall colors. The next most popular season is late spring through summer, when the emphasis is on waterfalls, mountain hikes, and camping. For slightly quieter times, consider visiting earlier in the spring, after school starts in mid-August but before the fall colors rush in mid-October, or later in the fall when the trees are bare.

Firefighters spent an hour extinguishing the blaze. Meanwhile police arrived, and the crime scene came into focus. An older woman in her sixties wearing a fur-trimmed coat. A younger woman in her thirties wearing jeans, a denim jacket, and tennis shoes. Three boys, each wearing pajamas and ranging from preschool-aged to a young teenager. Despite the superficial charring, it was soon determined that each person had actually died from brutal blows to the head before the fire started.

Nearby there was a singed shovel, a pitchfork, a five-gallon gas can, and tire tracks leading away. The horrific grave site sat about five miles south of Columbia, North Carolina, a small town on the Albemarle Sound that hadn't seen a murder in forty years. With little to go on, the case stagnated for about a week. But a torn price tag on the shovel, which included the letters "OCH," eventually led investigators 250 miles north to Poch Hardware in Potomac, Maryland. They posted fliers around town and waited, hoping for a lead.

Two Members Missing

In the nearby Carderock Springs neighborhood of Bethesda, an affluent suburb of Washington, DC, a concerned neighbor finally decided to call the police. For days now he'd been monitoring the seemingly empty Bishop home, a gray-shingled split-level on Lily Stone Drive. Typically, the family asked him to watch the place when they were away on vacations and ski trips. But this time they hadn't said a word. Their yellow Volkswagen Beetle was parked in the driveway, but their relatively new station wagon was gone. Something was amiss.

When a detective arrived at the home, he spotted blood spots on the front steps. The door was intact, and there was no sign of a break-in. But inside, he found a grisly scene. Dried blood was everywhere. The floors. The walls. The ceiling. One blood trail led into the den attached to the master bedroom. Another trail led up the carpeted stairs, down the hallway, and split into three paths leading into a bathroom and two bedrooms. The murderer had seemingly moved from room to room, bludgeoning the family members to death before carrying out their bodies.

"That's the Bishop family!" gasped the family babysitter, when police showed her photos of the bodies found in North Carolina.

Dental records confirmed the identification. The thirty-seven-year-old mother, Annette. A trio of boys: fourteen-year-old William, ten-year-old Brenton, and four-year-old Geoffrey. The sixty-eight-year-old woman was Lobelia, grand-mother on the father's side. Yet two family members remained unaccounted for. One was the family dog, a golden retriever named Leo. The other was the thirty-nine-year-old father, Bradford. By most accounts, he was the prototypical all-American family man. A handsome Ivy-League graduate who earned a good living as a bureaucrat with the state department. Whether dead or alive, where was Bradford Bishop?

FAVORITE TRAILS

Within the park's 816 square miles, there are many hiking trails to choose from. One favorite stop is the short but steep walk up to the park high point at 6,643 feet. Atop Kuwohi, formerly named Clingmans Dome, you'll find a sweeping modernist lookout tower.

A more strenuous day hike leads to eighty-foot Rainbow Falls in just under three miles, one way. You can continue another mile to the summit of Mount Le Conte, where only hikers can reach the highest lodge in the eastern United States. Day visitors are welcome, but reservations are required for overnight guests.

More great waterfalls can be found via short trails at Deep Creek, accessed from Bryson City. Or explore the Road to Nowhere—it was never finished and after a tunnel it dead-ends in the woods.

Who Were the Bishops?

William Bradford Bishop Jr. and his wife, Annette Kathryn née Weiss, were high school sweethearts from Southern California. As a senior at South Pasadena High, Bradford was a football hero. Annette was a junior majorette cheering him on.

They were an attractive and popular couple, and it seemed only natural they'd stay together after graduation.

In the fall of 1954, Bradford went back East to attend college at Yale. He was initially interested in studying medicine but eventually switched to a major in American studies. A year later, Annette went north to University of California, Berkeley, but left without completing a degree. After graduating in 1959, Bradford came home to marry Annette in San Clemente.

The next logical step was the U.S. Army, with Bishop enlisting later that summer. His first overseas post took them to Italy, where he worked in counterintelligence, mostly listening to radio broadcasts from the socialist republic of Yugoslavia. After four years, and an honorable discharge, Bradford and Annette moved to Florence, where he obtained a master's degree in Italian.

In late 1965, he joined the diplomatic core of the U.S. Department of State. Over the following decade, a string of foreign and domestic postings took them to Addis Ababa, the capital of Ethiopia, followed by Milan, Italy. In Los Angeles, he obtained a second master's degree in African studies. After a brief posting in Washington, DC, his final foreign post was Gaborone, Botswana, where Bradford served as deputy station chief. Along the way, he became fluent in Serbo-Croatian, Italian, Spanish, and French. The beautiful Annette was considered the perfect diplomat's wife. By day she raised their growing sons, and by night she radiantly attended the functions. Together, the Bishops were considered one of the most popular couples in the diplomatic circles.

The Bishops returned to the United States in 1974 and Bradford reluctantly accepted a desk job at State Department headquarters. He received an impressive title: assistant chief, Special Trade Activities and Commercial Treaties Division, Office of International Trade, Bureau of Economic and Business Affairs. By now, Bradford's mother was a widow who lived with the family and watched the kids. This allowed Annette to return to school after a fifteen-year break, enrolling in art classes at the nearby University of Maryland, College Park. Family life was seemingly humming right along, until that day in March 1976 when everything took a horrific turn.

FOLLOW THE FOOTSTEPS

If you want to ponder the final clues in Bradford's horrific deeds, consider these three sites. First, his car was found on the northern edge of the park in Elkmont Campground. Side note: nearby is the Cades Cove Scenic Loop. Every Wednesday from early May through late September, this eleven-mile paved loop road is vehicle free and great for cycling.

Okay, back to the murder. Next, the visitor center where Bradford's terrible trail went cold was likely Sugarlands. If he did hike away, perhaps he picked up a map here. That said, he could have started from several locations, making his way on connecting trails up to the Appalachian Trail. About seventy-two miles of this famous long-distance trail pass through the park's high country.

The theory is that Bradford went north, which would have taken him past Charlies Bunion. You can drive to the trailhead at Newfound Gap. From there, it's four rugged miles to this bedrock lookout, one way, with a total of 1,600 feet in elevation gain during an out-and-back hike. After that, please return to your vehicle as a law-abiding member of society.

A Movie-like Escape

At first, police treated Bishop as a missing person. No one who knew the family believed the friendly diplomat could do something as terrible as murder his own family. "Mr. Clean," said a colleague. An old friend called it a "preposterous notion" that Bishop was involved in the murders. According to Annette's brother, the suburban family had no connections with remote Tyrrell County where the rural grave site was found. Oh, and one other thing. Bradford Bishop may have been a spy.

Friends said he always spoke so vaguely about his work for the State Department. One neighbor, who had been a classmate at Yale, relayed an intriguing conversation. Bishop once claimed that during his army days, he "spied" on an Eastern European ski team at a meet in Italy. Was it a joke, or was there some truth to the comment? Perhaps the man was kidnapped by foreign agents, and his family was executed to implicate him? Might this be a convoluted case of international intrigue, like the recent Robert Redford film *Three Days of the Condor*? What if someone had killed Bishop and framed him?

However, upon examining the evidence taken from the crime scenes, lab techs lifted a set of fingerprints from the gas can. Additional bloodied fingerprints were found in the bathroom of the Bishop home. Both sets were a match for Bradford Bishop. The warrant was for murder. That same day, March 12, the FBI joined the multistate investigation. Photos of the wanted man appeared on television screens and in newspapers nationwide, along with identifying details. Six-foot-one. About 180 pounds. Light brown hair. An athletic man, who enjoyed jogging, swimming, and tennis at the nearby country club. He was believed to be driving a rust-colored 1974 Chevy Malibu station wagon with Maryland plates.

"The work of a demented mind," said Rufus Edmisten. The North Carolina attorney general was part of a press conference that presented Bradford Bishop as the only logical suspect. Edmisten explained that authorities now sought the public's help in capturing him.

Investigators were already well on their way to reconstructing the events. Though more details would emerge later, the basic theory was established during the first few weeks. On Monday, March 1, Bishop had been passed over for a promotion. Stewing with resentment, he'd complained to a coworker before telling his supervisor he felt ill and heading home. On the way, he stopped by several stores, where he purchased a gas can, shovel, and sledgehammer.

That night, he ambushed his wife first, in the master bedroom, while his mother was out walking the dog. When his mother returned, she became the second victim. Then he went from bedroom to bedroom, smashing the skulls of his sleeping children. He carried their bloodied bodies to the station wagon and covered them with blankets. He drove through the night. For some reason, the destination he chose was in Tyrell County, where a matching station wagon was briefly spotted. Early on the morning of March 2, he dug a grave about four feet deep before dumping the bodies and pouring gasoline. But the flames quickly spread to the surrounding foliage and the rising column of smoke forced him to depart before the sordid business was complete. Now he was on the run.

There was no evidence that Bradford Bishop was a spy, said Edmisten. But given his international pedigree, a movie-like escape did seem possible. His own passport was missing, or he could have used his position to create fake travel documents. The man might very well have arranged under-the-table passage, or even stowed away, on a ship departing from one of the nearby coastal ports. He was also a licensed amateur pilot, who learned to fly in Africa. That said, after the adrenaline wore off from his frenzied killings, he might have remorsefully committed suicide.

"He could be anywhere in the world," said Edmisten. "Or he could be down in a lagoon in eastern North Carolina."

Hidden Tensions

The tips came from far and wide. Georgia. Florida. Pennsylvania. Washington State. Even South Africa. But investigators focused on North Carolina, where a series of credible accounts arose. Between 5:00 and 7:00 p.m. on March 2, a man matching Bishop's description stopped by the Outside Sports Shop in Jacksonville, North Carolina. This small town, located near Wilmington, was roughly a two-and-a-half-hour drive southwest from the crime scene. The stop seemed to fit the profile, given Bishop was an avid outdoorsman, with interests in hiking, camping, canoeing, and fishing. The clerk, Jack Harris, rang the man up for a credit card purchase of $15.50. The signature read "Bradford Bishop Jr.," and upon later analysis, the handwriting seemed to be a match for the diplomat. The merchant copy of the receipt simply listed unspecified "sporting goods." Harris couldn't remember the exact purchase but thought it might have been for shoes.

Later, the store owner John Wheatley recalled something else. Bishop wasn't alone. With him was an attractive woman, holding the leash of a dog. According to Wheatley, she was possibly Caribbean and wore a beautiful dress.

Around 11:00 p.m. that night, about fifty miles away in Wilmington, waitress Barbara James was having trouble with an obnoxious customer. She was working the late shift at the Copper Kettle Pancake House, an all-night restaurant popular with local police. A man in his late thirties was drunk, rambling on about this and that. At one point he got into an argument with several patrons, shouting obscenities at them from several booths away.

When three plainclothes detectives came in, James discreetly informed them of the situation. The detectives sat in sight of the man, intending to arrest him for drunk driving when he left. Instead, the man quieted down, paid his bill, and inquired about the restroom. When he didn't emerge after fifteen minutes, the detectives discovered he'd slipped out through the kitchen. Upon examining photos of Bishop, all four agreed it was him. Further sightings continued around eastern North Carolina and the Outer Banks over the next ten days, but few could be confirmed.

By mid-month, new information emerged about Bishop's mental state, and further details would trickle out during the coming months and years. Since college, he'd had a history of severe depression and insomnia. In fact, he'd left Yale for a year around 1958 to seek treatment. Since then, he'd seen a string of psychiatrists and tried various remedies, including hypnosis. Some friends would later speculate that he might be manic-depressive, a condition later renamed bipolar disorder, and subject to manic episodes or psychotic breaks. At the time of his disappearance, he was taking prescription Serax, a strong anti-anxiety medication. Later studies would reveal that Serax could lead to a host of side effects, both from simply taking it or from suddenly stopping the medication.

Other friends spoke of hidden tensions within the family. A wife pushing for the desk job, so the family could have stability in the United States. A domineering mother asserting herself in the family's daily lives and dictating the son's professional development. A dwindling bank account from a family living beyond its means in a pricey neighborhood. An unstable Bishop growing increasingly resentful, all while craving the lost excitement and freedom of living in an inexpensive and stimulating foreign country. The FBI released a wanted poster suggesting Bishop was extremely dangerous and possibly suicidal.

A Trail Goes Cold

On March 12, over 250 miles east in the foothills of the Appalachians, a customer wearing a rumpled business suit allegedly entered a gun shop in Spindale, North Carolina. According to owner Thomas Gilliam, the man calmly pulled out a loaded .38-caliber pistol from a shoulder holster.

"I am a State Department employee," said the man, displaying an official ID card and asking to trade for a more powerful .357 magnum.

The owner refused, becoming upset that a loaded gun was brought inside. Not to mention, the whole story seemed suspicious. Federal agents were issued their guns. The owner explained such a trade would require a permit.

"I can get it done," said the man, explaining he didn't need a permit due to his government work.

"I don't trade guns with fucking federal agents," muttered Gilliam, and the man left. Sometime later, Gilliam said he saw photos of the wanted Bradford Bishop. Recognizing a clear resemblance, he later called police. While Bishop was known to have inherited a .38 pistol when his father died, investigators were skeptical of this witness account for two reasons. When they came to shop with scent-tracking dogs, there was no reaction. Plus, Gilliam had only come forward after the next major development was announced to the public.

About 150 miles further west, inside Great Smoky Mountains National Park, Bishop's station wagon was found on March 18. The vehicle was left in Elkmont

Campground, on the Little River, about ten miles from Gatlinburg, Tennessee. Inside were bloodied blankets, an ax, a shotgun, dog biscuits, park maps, and two capsules of Serax. The spare-tire well was filled with blood. Witnesses thought the wagon had been there for days, perhaps even a week or two. Investigators brought the scent-trained dogs, which patrolled outward from the vehicle on the trails and roadways leading through the park. The dogs only reacted once, at the nearby visitor center. But whether Bishop had stopped there on his way into the park, or on his way out, was unclear. Was the station wagon parked as a decoy, and he drove away with someone? Or did he continue on foot?

Beyond the park, there were no further sightings, and the trail went cold. In time, a prevailing theory among investigators became that Bishop took to the woods, just another experienced outdoorsman hiking with his dog. Perhaps Bishop joined the steady foot traffic of through hikers heading north on the Appalachian Trail. He'd emptied his bank account and was carrying at least $400 in cash, the equivalent of over $2,000 in the 2020s. This was more than enough to restock with backpacking food along the way. Within days, the fit Bishop would look like any other trail-weathered hiker. Within weeks, when the story had faded from the headlines, he would have been hundreds of miles away before he discreetly left the trail. Within years, he was probably living abroad, most likely in one of the European countries where he spoke the language.

Cryptic Connections

The coming years would offer only minimal developments in the case. The next credible sighting came from Stockholm in July 1978. An old friend of the Bishop family was in town. She had known them in Ethiopia during the late 1960s. She said she saw Bishop several times walking the city streets, sporting a beard.

A year later, a U.S. State Department employee from the embassy in Niger was vacationing in Sorrento, Italy. Roy Harrell stepped inside a public restroom and saw a familiar face.

"Say, aren't you Bradford Bishop?" said Harrel.

"Oh, my God, no," blurted the man, and he ran out into the pouring rain.

The next clue in the saga came in 1992, when a cryptic letter was found in the State Department file on the disgraced former employee. It was dated March 15, 1976, two weeks after the murders became a national story. It was addressed to Bradford Bishop Jr., Assistant Chief Special Trade Office, United States Department of State and written by A. Ken Bankston, a convicted bank robber imprisoned at Marion Federal Penitentiary in Illinois. The contents indicated it was the sixth letter from Bankston, on a topic of a secretive nature. The first paragraph was hard to interpret, other than making references to a trio of people, including the "Attorney General in Mexico." The second paragraph was more revealing.

"Now in Answer to your question," wrote Bankston. "Yes I am most sure she is in the North Carolina State penitentiary. I do not know why Sonny would tell you something that Could very easily be proved. When I wrote you in February, letter #5 I explained that she was there and that David Paul Allen knew this 'Sonny' in Atlanta. I am sure he is a Capable person and that he knows all about Creswell. In fact David said you Could walk to phelps lake from Creswell. I think its about five (5) miles. I really don't see what this has to do with me Mr. Bishop. I was only interested in Mexico and/or Central America as you know. I suggest you and David get together on this as he is well known in that area.

"Mr. Bishop I will not write you again until I transfer to North Dakota. I am really glad of this as I am fed up with the feds. Ha. Ha."

Creswell is a town about ten miles west of the shallow grave site where the Bishop family bodies were found. Phelps Lake is five miles southwest of Creswell. And Tyrell Prison is a North Carolina state work farm about nine miles north of the grave site.

Otherwise, the meaning of the letter was unclear. Being in prison, did Bankston miss the news of the murders and send his letter without realizing Bishop was on the run? Was it just a ruse, suggesting Bankston had inside information, designed to score a reduced sentence? If so, would he have had access to the geographic details needed to fabricate the letter? Or was this a real correspondence, a letter written genuinely, and perhaps sent for some nefarious reason?

And who might this woman in the state prison be? Following such a hypothetical, after being released from incarceration at the work farm, did she briefly stay in Creswell before walking the five miles to Phelps Lake for a discreet rendezvous? After murdering his family, did Bradford travel to Tyrell County to dump their bodies *and* pick up this woman—perhaps the same one allegedly seen by the owner of the outdoor store in Jacksonville, North Carolina?

A Final Surprise

In 2014, the FBI named Bradford Bishop one of its ten most wanted fugitives, and he remained on the list for about four years. A series of age-progressed images showed what the man might look like in his old age. By now the theory was that Bradford Bishop could very well be living in plain sight in the United States.

The most recent development in the saga came in 2021. A woman in her early sixties, who was adopted as a child, stepped forward claiming she was the daughter of the fugitive Bradford Bishop. She had taken a DNA test and performed genealogical research with several distant relatives. When Kathy Gilchrist sent her DNA profile to the special agent now in charge of the investigation, the reply was in the affirmative. The FBI lab conclusively determined her to be the wanted man's biological child.

Following events backward in time, Gilchrist had been born in 1958 in Massachusetts, the same year that Bishop took his one-year psychiatric leave from Yale, located in the adjacent state of Connecticut. Perhaps there were other unknown children out there, some pondered, fathered by a disturbed and haunting figure. A man who brutally murdered his seemingly perfect family and left behind a trail of frenzied and clumsy clues that abruptly ended in the wilds of Great Smoky Mountains National Park. Beyond there, Bradford Bishop somehow got away.

CHAPTER 26

WHAT HAPPENED TO THE LOST COLONY OF ROANOKE?

BAFFLING DISAPPEARANCES

FORT RALEIGH NATIONAL HISTORIC SITE

OUTER BANKS, NORTH CAROLINA

Smoke was rising from the forested north end of Roanoke Island when John White came ashore at daybreak, not far from the settlement. It was his granddaughter Virginia Dare's third birthday, August 18, 1590. White hoped to find her along with over a hundred men, women, and children. The first English colony in the New World. Three years before, these beleaguered colonists had petitioned a reluctant Governor White to return to England for help. Since that time, he'd been delayed by naval wars, raiding pirates, and disastrous storms.

Just yesterday, one boat had sunk, and seven sailors drowned in high seas while trying to row to the island. Now, White and his remaining party of eighteen men followed the smoke but found only a small wildfire amid grasses and trees. Continuing along the coast, they spotted fresh prints from bare feet in the sand. Perhaps they'd been made by local tribesmen, yet the party saw no one. Approaching the townsite, they inspected three letters carved on a tree: "C R O."

Since White departed, the colonists had erected a fortified palisade of tree trunks. Inside, the search party found the log cabins dismantled and the village overgrown by weeds. Most valuables were gone, except for heavy items like bars of iron and lead from the blacksmith forge. There were no signs of attack, although five buried chests had been unearthed. Three belonged to White, who found his possessions pilfered and destroyed. Some men went to search for the colonists' boats but found nothing. The Roanoke Colony had simply vanished. The only remaining clue was a single word carved on a palisade trunk: "CROATOAN."

═══ FIND THE FORT ═══

Located near the northern tip of Roanoke Island, Fort Raleigh National Historic Site is a small NPS unit that preserves the site of the Roanoke Colony, the first English settlement in what became the United States. There are museum exhibits and an introductory movie at the visitor center. An outdoor theater shows the long-running symphonic drama *The Lost Colony*.

A short nature trail winds through the colony site, which includes a star-shaped earthen fortification, reconstructed to resemble one built by the English in the 1580s.

A second trail relates to events that happened centuries later. During the U.S. Civil War, the Union-occupied island became home to formerly enslaved African Americans. The Freedom Trail leads just over a mile to the site of the 1860s Freedmen's Colony at the edge of Albemarle Sound.

An Ominous Start?

Six years before, in 1584, Queen Elizabeth of England chartered Walter Raleigh to establish an English colony on the North American coast, a base from which to disrupt Spanish dominance and shipping in the New World. In July, a reconnaissance expedition of two ships sighted land off Cape Fear and explored northward along the Outer Banks. After landing at Roanoke Island, they were impressed by its prospects and made friendly contact with several tribes of local Algonquians. The explorers returned to England with embellished tales of riches and two native men, Wanchese of the Roanoacs and Manteo of the Croatoans.

An engraving created by artists Sheppard and Linton in 1876 depicts John White's 1590 party discovering the word "Croatoan" carved into a tree at the abandoned colony site on Roanoke Island. *The Lost Colony*, design by William Ludwell Sheppard, engraving by William James Linton, A Popular History of the United States/Public Domain

The following year, a military expedition of seven ships with 600 sailors and soldiers set sail. One ship sank while crossing the Atlantic, but the remaining six reached Roanoke in late June. Among the men were Manteo, Wanchese, and John White. An artist and mapmaker, White made detailed watercolor drawings of local tribespeople, animals, and landscapes. Wanchese immediately fled across the sound to his people, but Manteo remained with the expedition as a translator.

Because the waters in the sound around Roanoke Island were so shallow, the large ships had to anchor off the Atlantic Coast, exposing them to weather and heavy seas. When the cargo ship was damaged, most of the colony's food provisions were ruined by saltwater. As a result, the majority of the expedition returned to England to resupply, while one hundred men stayed on the island in temporary shelters. These remaining colonists spent the following months searching the region for a new location with a better harbor.

Growing and gathering food proved to be harder than expected, and soon the colonists were relying on local Algonquians to survive. Meanwhile, the natives were contracting diseases, like smallpox, brought unwittingly by the European visitors. Relations deteriorated into the spring of 1586, when the Secotan chief from across the sound plotted to starve out and remove the colonists. Learning of the plot, English soldiers attacked and killed the chief. A few days later, by chance, an English fleet passed through led by Sir Francis Drake, who agreed to evacuate the men back to England. The following month, the planned relief ships arrived from England. Finding the settlement deserted, they left a small garrison of fifteen men to maintain their claim on the island.

Peril or Peace?

The following year, Sir Walter Raleigh—recently knighted by the queen for his efforts to secure England's place in the New World—turned to John White to re-establish an English colony. This time it would be a smaller affair with farmers and families, including White's pregnant daughter and her husband. A new location was selected in Chesapeake Bay. In late July 1587 three ships stopped at Roanoke Island to retrieve the garrison. They found only an overgrown settlement and some human bones. Even worse, the captain of the returning fleet refused to take the colonists any further, citing the late time of year and the need to repair the damaged ships. Forced to stay, the colonists began rebuilding the village.

Soon after arrival, a colonist was out catching crabs when he was ambushed and killed by arrows. Led by Manteo, twenty men from the colony traveled south to Croatoan Island to seek peaceful relations. Meeting with Manteo's mother and other leaders of the Croatoan tribe, their offer was accepted, provided the colonists agreed not to take from the island tribe's limited corn. The Croatoans explained the Secotan were responsible for the recent attacks, retaliation for the previous group killing their chief. It was they who had attacked the English garrison the previous year, killing several. The survivors had escaped by boat but were never seen again. It was also the Secotan who recently killed the lone colonist. The Croatoans agreed to mediate peace, saying they would bring the Secotans' reply within one week.

When no word came, White and twenty-five men were guided by Manteo across the sound to the Secotan village. The English sought their revenge by attacking at dawn, surprising some tribespeople around a fire. After injuring several, the attack was halted upon a disturbing discovery. The tribespeople were Croatoans who had come to scavenge from a Secotan village that had been abandoned before the anticipated reprisal by the English.

While Manteo once again tried to smooth relations, the colonists grew increasingly fearful about their perilous situation. Was it too late for peace? A few days later, White's granddaughter was born, christened Virginia for being the first English child born in the new territory. Soon afterward, the colonists came to White. They asked him to return to England with the ships, now repaired and ready to depart. The governor initially refused but eventually relented due to the need for additional supplies. Before White departed, the colonists expressed their intention to relocate fifty miles to the northwest, up Albemarle Sound. To inform White of their whereabouts upon his return, the colonists would carve their new location into trees on Roanoke Island. If the colony was under distress, they would add a Christian cross pattée.

When White sailed, he intended to return the following summer. But a series of unfortunate events repeatedly impeded his return. Upon arrival to England, reports told of a Spanish armada preparing to attack England. To aid the nation's defense, Queen Elizabeth forbade any ships from leaving during 1588. Still, White managed to arrange an exception for two small ships unfit for combat. However, while en route they were attacked by pirates and the supplies were looted. After England defeated the Spanish Armada, the shipping ban continued as Queen Elizabeth directed a counter armada to attack Spain in 1589. Thus, it wasn't until 1590 when Sir Raleigh arranged for White to join a privateering convoy that would dispatch two ships north from the Caribbean to visit the colony.

ACROSS THE SOUND

Within sight of Fort Raleigh, on nearby Bodie Island, is the Wright Brothers National Memorial. This small NPS unit, located in the Kill Devil Hills just south of Kitty Hawk, preserves the site of the brother's historic first plane flight in 1903. Outside the museum, there's a replica hangar and walkways that follow the flight paths and lead to a large hilltop monument.

Better Left Lost?

After months of participating in violent raids on Spanish vessels, an anxious White finally reached Roanoke Island in late August 1590. Upon inspecting the two carvings, one written as "C R O" and the other "CROATOAN," he noted the lack of distress symbol. This suggested the colonists had peacefully relocated to the friendly island to the south, where Manteo had been born. White's party returned in their boats to the two ships. Though they had not seen anyone—neither Croatoans nor colonists—upon sailing past the island the previous week, they had observed rising smoke. They agreed to head south the next day to search Croatoan Island.

That night, a nasty storm blew in. The anchor cable snapped, and the ship was blown to sea without its freshwater cask, which had been left ashore. The captain decided to head for the Caribbean to resupply. From there, White could return for the colonists the next year. But more storms bore down on the ship, and howling winds blew the ship northeast until the only safe harbor that remained was England. Once again White had failed, and he never tried again.

"To the merciful help of the Almighty," White wrote about the lost colonists in 1593, "whom I most humbly beseech to helpe and comfort them, according to his most holy will and their good desire, I take my leave."

TOWN AND BEACH

Further bring this mystery to life with two additional stops. First, located in the nearby town of Manteo, the Roanoke Island Festival Park is an indoor-outdoor museum with a trio of historical recreations: an Algonquin coastal village, several buildings from the English colony, and a seaworthy English merchant ship from the 1580s expedition.

Extending south of Roanoke Island for seventy miles along the Outer Banks from Bodie Island to Ocracoke Island is Cape Hatteras National Seashore. This park unit preserves Hatteras Island, previously known as Croatoan Island, the possible last location of the lost colony. There are lighthouses to visit, a few trails for hiking, and miles of undeveloped beach to explore while pondering the mystery.

In subsequent years, Sir Walter Raleigh saw a benefit in allowing the colony to remain lost. As long as their fate was in doubt, his claim to Virginia was valid. In 1595, he set sail himself, claiming to search for the colonists. But the real objective was seeking El Dorado, the legendary lost city of gold. On the return voyage, they

---

sailed past the Outer Banks but didn't even stop. Seven years later, Raleigh mounted another alleged recovery voyage. This time the real objective was harvesting sassafras south of the Outer Banks. Once again, no search was made of Croatoan, later renamed Hatteras Island.

More attempts to locate the colonists were made during the early seventeenth century, including investigations launched from the new colony of Jamestown, located to the north. All efforts failed for various reasons. Rumors of the colonists' fate ranged widely. Some said they lived peaceably among local tribes for decades. Others told tales of a European-style village hidden in the pine forests of the mainland, where mixed families of Algonquians and English wore elaborate clothing and lived in walled houses. Another version claimed that after the colonists relocated, possibly to Chesapeake Bay, they were massacred by a suspicious tribe. Yet for years to come, visitors to the area would report encounters with tribespeople, and tales of their ancestors, who had light skin and gray eyes.

CHAPTER 27

WHO WAS NED SIMMONS?

HIDDEN HISTORY

CUMBERLAND ISLAND NATIONAL SEASHORE

ATLANTIC SEA ISLANDS, GEORGIA

A full moon was rising into the night sky when sixty-six enslaved men, women, and children slipped away from a plantation on the St. Johns River in northern Florida. After boarding a flat-bottomed barge, they sank oars and poles into tannic blackwater. For hours, they followed the tides through inland channels winding between cordgrass. Moss-draped cypress trees cast ominous shadows in the milky light.

It was February 23, 1815, and the Florida refugees' destination was Cumberland Island, thirty miles north, just off the coast of Georgia. Six weeks before, a British Royal Navy fleet had landed about 1,500 troops on this long and narrow barrier island. The War of 1812 was in its third year, and the British hoped to incite fears among white Americans of a slave insurrection along the Southeast coast. During raids on mainland towns and plantations, the British pinned to trees a proclamation:

"That all those who may be disposed to emigrate from the United States, will with their families, be received on Board his Majesty's Ships... they will have their choice, of either entering into His Majesty's Sea or Land Forces, or being sent as Free Settlers to the British possessions in North America or the West Indies..."

For weeks, enslaved people across the low country fled to British patrols. Others rowed boats or paddled canoes. Those who reached the southern end of Cumberland Island discovered a bustling winter fort with the Union Jack flag flying overhead. British Admiral George Cockburn had installed his headquarters in the four-story Dungeness mansion, which was the tallest landmark for miles.

When the Florida refugees arrived at Cumberland Island early the next morning, they went ashore at a hastily constructed wharf. They may have been amazed to see that over half of the British troops were Black. Some were recently freed African Americans who had joined the British Colonial Marines the previous year during the Chesapeake Bay campaign. Others were Caribbean members of the West Indian regiments, originally purchased as slaves by the British government but eventually freed after their military service.

Many of these Black troops had already fought dozens of skirmishes and battles against U.S. forces. They had joined the British attack on Washington City, which included the burning of the Presidential Mansion and Capitol Building. They'd also been repelled at Baltimore, where a combined force of white Americans, free African Americans, and enslaved Black people had defended the city. This victory was later immortalized by Francis Scott Key in "The Star-Spangled Banner."

Like the majority of escapees who reached Cumberland, most of the Florida refugees opted for relocation to a British colony. They were transported to nearby ships to await evacuation. Those who chose to join the Colonial Marines remained on the island to train with fellow Black recruits.

One recently freed recruit was Ned Simmons. Limited written records were made during the brief British occupation of Cumberland Island. Even fewer such documents survived. What little is known about this mysterious man and other escapees comes from plantation slave rolls, British military records, scant news articles, petitions, letters, and diary entries. Over the decades, a faint picture emerged about this individual who lived a remarkable and tragic life on Cumberland Island long ago.

A Fleeting First Chance

Ned Simmons was born into slavery around 1763, probably in the low country of South Carolina. He was acquired early in his life by future Revolutionary War General Nathanael Greene. It's quite possible that Simmons served alongside General Greene while fighting against the British. In 1791, Simmons helped escort George Washington through cheering crowds in Savannah, as part of the first president's celebratory tour of the southern states.

During those early years of a new republic, many enslaved African Americans believed freedom was on the horizon. To encourage participation in the revolution, white slaveholders had promised emancipation in exchange for military service. The northern states, with their industrial-focused cities, had abolished slavery by the turn of the nineteenth century. But the southern states, with economies focused on slave plantations, refused to do the same.

Around the turn of the nineteenth century, Simmons was sent to Cumberland Island. He became a carpenter for Louisa Greene Shaw, inheritor of the Dungeness estate and the largest slaveholder on the island. When the British arrived in 1815, all 150 of Shaw's slaves chose freedom with the British. About half were taken aboard ships to await embarkation. The rest opted to assist at the fort, or they joined the Colonial Marines. Simmons was among the first to volunteer, and he received a musket and an older 1808 redcoat uniform.

The only person surprised by the sudden abandonment was the slave owner herself. She requested that the former slaves, including Simmons, line up on shore so she could address them.

"She gave them a long talk," wrote a family friend later in life. "Told them how kind they had been treated by all the family. All this had no effect."

On March 6, two American officials arrived on the island as representatives of the Cumberland plantation owners. They presented Admiral Cockburn with a recent issue of the *National Intelligencer*, a Washington City newspaper. After three years of bloody battles, burned cities, and massacres by both sides, the war had essentially ended in a draw. The newspaper included the text from the ratified Treaty of Ghent, stating that all territory and property taken during the war, including slaves, must be restored without delay.

When the representatives protested about Black people remaining aboard British ships, Admiral Cockburn became angry. British attitudes had been slowly turning against slavery in recent years. Cockburn believed those already freed should remain subjects of the growing British empire. Attempting to stall, Cockburn declared that a newspaper article carried no authority in the matter. He demanded he be provided with a certified transcript. The admiral said he must request instructions from his superior, and the representatives returned to the mainland to await his reply.

The following day, winds and rain descended on the island. After closely reviewing the treaty, Cockburn presented his plan to the evacuating fleet commander. When the weather lifted, all but a few ships were gone. They had sailed under cover of fog, carrying away hundreds of freed people.

When the American representatives returned, they were not pleased with Cockburn's narrow reading of the treaty. Only confiscated property that remained on Cumberland Island as of the ratification date, February 17, 1815, would be returned. All Black people who had already departed would remain free. This included about 1,500 from Cumberland and 2,500 from other theaters of the war. They were already on their way to Trinidad and Nova Scotia.

However, Cockburn's interpretation carried some sad consequences. Eighty-one Dungeness slaves, who had been among the first to join the British, would be restored to Louisa Greene Shaw. Ned Simmons, who had known only two months of freedom after roughly fifty years in bondage, would be left behind. As British soldiers stripped away his musket and uniform, a distraught Simmons was said to hold tight, according to family stories later told to a historian. Afterward, all that Simmons clutched was a single metal button torn from the overcoat.

A NEARLY EMPTY ISLAND

Some of the least-known units in the National Park System end up being some of the best. Such is the case with Cumberland Island National Seashore, which sees less than 100,000 visitors per year. Here you'll find forests of twisty live oak, pathways lined by saw palmettos, tidal wetlands, and eighteen miles of undeveloped beach on the Atlantic Ocean.

The reason it's so empty? There's no bridge leading to one of the largest barrier islands in the Southeast. You have to take the small passenger ferry from the colonial town of St. Marys or a private charter. The island is mostly free of vehicles, though there are occasional guided van tours. Otherwise, most visitors hike or backpack on the sandy trails and roads, the latter of which you can ride on suitable bikes. Camping is possible at several sites.

The southern end of the island is where you'll find historic sites like the Dungeness Ruins. The mansion once belonged to the Carnegie family before they sold most of the island to the park service in the 1970s. Near the island's midpoint is the preserved Plum Orchard, where you can explore the grounds and tour a plantation home. The northern half of the island is a coastal wilderness of tangled jungle where few will ever tread.

An Artifact Found

After the War of 1812, slavery across the South became more entrenched. The escape of so many to the British increased suspicions and resentment among southern slaveholders toward all African Americans, both enslaved and free. State legislatures passed harsh laws to prevent individual slave holders from being able to free their slaves at all. As the nineteenth century progressed, the expanding United States increasingly split into two camps: those who were for continuing slavery and those against.

When the Civil War broke out in 1861, Ned Simmons was nearly a hundred years old and still living on Cumberland Island. Word of the Emancipation Proclamation arrived in 1863. Simmons joined a sixty-year-old woman named Lucinda Dorrell, who may have been his daughter, and her seventy-three-year-old husband, Jack. Together, the three of them used a rowboat to cross the St. Marys River to reach Union-occupied Fernandina. When they crossed the Union lines, a soldier noted their arrival in a logbook.

Simmons stayed in a house with some missionaries who helped him learn to read. This is where an unnamed Union correspondent met the man, asking him, "Why learn now, at the end of your life?"

"As the tree falls, so it shall lay," answered Simmons, offering a paraphrase from *Ecclesiastes*, which he perhaps had learned during makeshift church services held amid the salt-pruned oak forests of Cumberland Island.

The unnamed reporter described their 1863 visit in a brief article later collected in a book titled *The Civil War in Song and Story*, one of the few glimpses of a mysterious life spanning a century.

About Ned Simmons, only a few things are certain. We know that he lived enslaved on Cumberland Island. That he escaped from slavery twice. He fought with the Patriots against the British during the American Revolution. He served with the British against the Americans in the War of 1812. A few weeks after becoming a free man for the second time, we know that Ned Simmons passed away.

More than a century after Simmons's death, in 1969, two archaeologists excavated the ruins of a slave cabin on Cumberland Island. After careful consideration, a local researcher named Mary Bullard connected the dots between scant sources, names, and dates. She theorized that this cabin may have once been the home of Ned Simmons. Among the artifacts unearthed was a single metal button from an 1808 military uniform.

CHAPTER 28

DID SOLDIERS' WOUNDS GLOW AFTER A CIVIL WAR BATTLE?

UNEXPLAINED PHENOMENA

SHILOH NATIONAL MILITARY PARK

PITTSBURG LANDING, EASTERN TENNESSEE

After the bloody Battle of Shiloh ended in a draw, Union General Ulysses S. Grant rode through on horseback to survey the aftermath. Reaching one open field, where Confederate soldiers had made repeated charges, he paused. It was so covered with the dead, he later remarked, that one could walk across the clearing, stepping on bodies "without a foot touching the ground."

The battle had begun on the morning of April 6, 1862, when Confederates launched a sneak attack on the encamped Union Army, not far from the Tennessee River. Soon, a ferocious firefight was unfolding amid farm fields and oak woodlands. On each side, about 1,700 soldiers were killed and over 8,000 wounded. The battle was the first major engagement of the Civil War, and it saw more casualties than in all prior U.S. wars combined. The conflict would drag on for four disastrous years, far longer than anyone expected.

Dead soldier's uniforms—blue for the Yankees and gray for the Rebels— were riddled with holes and stained with blood. Many bodies were slumped forward, face down in the mud from recent rains. These soldiers had expired while trying to crawl away from the onslaught of minié balls, artillery shells, and cannon fire. Behind the thinnest of saplings, soldiers' bodies lay where they had hugged the ground desperate for cover, often sprinkled with leaves and twigs shot from the trees above. In other places, the dead were piled in contorted positions, arms outstretched or erect, with rigor mortis preserving the final moments when they fell.

U.S. MEMORIALS

Throughout the country, the park service manages numerous units related to military sites, battlefields, and war memorials. While some units reflect conflicts that happened overseas, like World War II, most units preserve battlefields on U.S. soil, primarily from the American Revolution and Civil War. Overall, the most visited of these units, by far, are the war memorials on the National Mall in Washington, DC.

A Glimmer in the Darkness?

For the thousands of wounded who were unable to stagger off the battlefield during the first day, help would not come quickly. After the regrouping, Union lines held, the Confederates withdrew, and the gunfire ceased. Yet the injured continued to writhe in pain. They lay in pooling blood that gave off a musky odor. With night-fall came dropping temperatures and a return of the rain. Many of the wounded soldiers found themselves shivering in growing puddles of water.

In the dark, as cries for help filled the night, it was later said that some of the soldiers' wounds began to glow. A faint blue–green iridescence supposedly formed where flesh had been torn open by flying missiles or thrusting bayonets.

Into the second day, medics labored to carry the wounded soldiers away. Once they reached the hospital tents, it was said that those whose wounds had glowed saw a higher chance of survival and recovery than those whose wounds didn't glow. As a result, the bizarre phenomenon became known as the *angel's glow*, which some nineteenth-century observers attributed to divine intervention.

For years, the legend of the life-saving angel's glow persisted. Long after the Civil War was won for the Union on April 9, 1865, when General Robert E. Lee surrendered to General Grant at Appomattox Court House in Virginia. Long after Congress established the Shiloh National Military Park in 1894, which was trans-ferred to the National Park Service roughly forty years later.

Many people doubted that the angel's glow existed at all. Even as the story was retold, it was mostly dismissed as a haunting legend, perhaps something misinter-preted by the delirious soldiers who survived those harrowing nights in the woods. Or maybe the glow was just a dim reflection of a crescent moon, shining through patchy clouds, mixing with fog and lingering smoke?

Mysteriously, no contemporaneous accounts have been found that describe the angel's glow. Grant didn't describe it in his memoir, nor was it mentioned in any accounts by soldiers or doctors present. Perhaps it was an invented tale that offered a literal bright spot to an otherwise dark time in American history. Was such a glowing wound even scientifically possible?

A Realistic Hypothesis

Roughly one hundred and forty years after the Battle of Shiloh, in 2001, a seventeen-year-old named Bill Martin visited the national military park. After learning about the legend of the angel's glow, he had a question for his mom, a microbiologist with the U.S. Department of Agriculture. Could the bioluminescent bacteria that she studied be the cause? She suggested he do a science experiment to find out.

TYPICAL VISIT

Shiloh follows the typical layout for most NPS military parks and battlefields. The focus at the fifteen-square-mile park is a self-guided driving tour. Along this thirteen-mile park road, there are twenty-two stops at significant battle locations and monuments. A national cemetery is located on site. The visitor center includes an extensive museum where you can learn more about the battle's role in the larger Civil War.

Shiloh averages under 400,000 visitors per year. This is more than many NPS military sites, but less than the most famous Civil War sites, like Gettysburg National Military Park in Pennsylvania or Chickamauga & Chattanooga National Military Park on Lookout Mountain in Tennessee, which hover around a million annual visitors.

Bill and his friend Jonathan Curtis conducted research into the bacteria, *Photorhabdus luminescens*, and the environmental conditions during the battle. This type of bacteria lives in parasitic worms called *nematodes*, which may have been present in the mud at Shiloh where the wounded soldiers lay through the night. Following their typical process, the nematodes would have regurgitated the bioluminescent bacteria into the wounds, which caused them to glow.

The climate during early April in this part of Tennessee meant the nighttime temperatures were probably cool enough to support the luminescent bacteria. In turn, this would have killed more dangerous bacteria that cause infections and gangrene. One catch was that the human body is too warm for the luminescent bacteria to survive. But if the wet soldiers became hypothermic, that might have lowered their body temperatures enough for the bacteria to multiply. Thus, the soldiers with glowing wounds might have been less prone to infection than the others. When the soldiers warmed up in the hospital tent, the luminescent bacteria would have died.

The two students submitted their findings to an international science fair competition held in San Jose, California. They won first prize. While the mystery wasn't solved and the legend remained unverified, the students' project was certainly impressive. They had demonstrated that the legend was scientifically possible. And whether it happened or not, there was at least a chance that the angel's glow was real.

PARK-LIKE PLACES

Like other NPS units, military parks typically have opportunities for outdoor recreation. At Shiloh, there's a 1.1-mile interpretive trail through the Shiloh Indian Mounds village. In addition, locals and visitors will often walk, run, or ride bikes on the park road.

CHAPTER 29

IRON IN THE MUD?

HIDDEN HISTORY

VICKSBURG NATIONAL MILITARY PARK

YAZOO RIVER, VICKSBURG, MISSISSIPPI

M y God, stop the boat!" said the searcher.

Edwin Bearss and two friends were in a small motorboat on the muddy Yazoo River. It was November 1956, and they were sixteen miles upstream of Vicksburg. They were watching a pocket compass, and the needle was making wild 180-degree swings. Could this be it? The wreckage of the USS *Cairo*?

Bearss was an NPS historian at Vicksburg National Military Park, which preserved the battlefield from a critical Civil War siege in 1863. At the time, Vicksburg was a fortified Confederate city, perched on a bluff overlooking the confluence of the Yazoo and Mississippi Rivers. After an eight-month campaign, the Union would prevail, gaining control of the vital waterway.

But before the campaign began, the shallow-draft *Cairo* was sweeping mines in the Yazoo River. It was one of seven City-class ironclads used by the Union to patrol the basin. With 2.5 inches of iron-plate armor, these 175-foot gunboats would prove to be revolutionary, bridging the transition from plank warships to steel battleships. Yet the wooden hulled ironclads were far from unsinkable.

Upon coming around a bend, the *Cairo* was rocked by an explosion. Wired mines had been triggered by rebels hiding on shore. The blast tore a hole in the ship's bow, and water poured through the breach. In the wheelhouse, the pilot swung the listing ironclad into the riverbank. Fortunately, every crewman managed to escape onto shore before the 500-ton ship drifted away with the current. Slowly it sank beneath the murky waters.

After the war, there was occasional talk about raising the *Cairo* from its muddy tomb. The location was generally known. But as the years crept by, and the survivors passed away, the ship was forgotten and the site lost. Some records said it was near the right bank, others said the left. One report put it upstream from Snyder's Bluff. Local farmers claimed it was closer to the piers of the old bridge. At low water, sunken wreckage sometimes did emerge there, but this turned out to be Confederate defensive rafts. People periodically searched for the *Cairo* and always came up empty.

A photograph showing the USS *Cairo* ironclad during the Civil War era. U.S. gunboat *Cairo* - Mississippi River Fleet, between 1861 and 1865, Library of Congress.

A Relic Revealed?

With the centennial of the *Cairo*'s sinking approaching, Bearss decided to settle the matter. He and his friends studied old maps, accounts, and reports. They waited for a low-water day in 1956 and motored to the likeliest spot. When the compass needle started bouncing, they traversed back and forth to confirm the finding. There was something big down there, hidden beneath the muddy waters. It was clearly magnetic. After blazing a nearby tree, they motored downstream at top speed.

BATTLEFIELD AND BOAT

Just like the Civil War siege it commemorates, Vicksburg National Military Park encircles much of this Mississippi River town. Park highlights include a self-guided driving tour along the sixteen-mile park road. There's also a twelve-mile hiking trail that winds through the hilly battlefield. The most unique aspect of this NPS military unit is stepping aboard the restored ironclad at the fascinating USS *Cairo* Museum. Perched on a high bluff nearby, downtown Vicksburg retains many historic buildings and sites worth exploring.

Later, they returned to the river with a twenty-foot iron bar. At first, the probe went down fifteen feet and touched clay. A few feet upstream, it struck something solid about six feet down. Sure felt like iron hitting iron. Over the next few weekends, they devised a system to stabilize their boat in the steady current. They dropped an anchor in the channel and ran a rope to a man on shore. Moving the probe a few inches at a time, they recorded the depth and feel upon striking the sunken object.

A resulting dot diagram gradually revealed the dimensions. A long flat top of wood. Sloping iron sides. Toward the front, an armored pilot house. It was clearly an ironside. Over the coming years, divers began exploring the wreck. Artifacts were retrieved, including the mounted guns, which were found to still be loaded. Then, in the mid-1960s, a complex retrieval operation used barges and cables to raise the *Cairo* in three pieces.

After over a decade of restoration and preparation, the reassembled USS *Cairo* was put on display at the Vicksburg National Military Park. A new redbrick museum was built next to a vast canopy, where visitors could board the Civil War gunship. While four sunken ironclads have been raised from the depths, the *Cairo* remains the most intact. A mix of waterworn timbers and reconstructed segments, still clad in its original plates of armor. A piece of living history preserved by the same dense muds that long concealed it. After being lost for a century, the *Cairo* had been found. A haunting relic from a troubled time.

CHAPTER 30

IS A 1980s TREASURE BURIED NEAR THE OLDEST STONE FORTRESS IN THE UNITED STATES?

CASTILLO DE SAN MARCOS NATIONAL MONUMENT

MATANZAS RIVER, SAINT AUGUSTINE, FLORIDA

t's an adventure," explained Byron Preiss. "The stones that are worth the most will be the hardest to find."

It was the fall of 1982, and the twenty-nine-year-old publishing phenom was giving promotional interviews to newspapers around the country. His latest endeavor was titled *The Secret: A Treasure Hunt*, a puzzle book containing surreal illustrations and cryptic verses. By deciphering clues, readers could reveal directions to twelve so-called treasure "casques" around the country. Inside each one was a key that could be exchanged for a gemstone valued around a thousand dollars. The casques were said to be buried in parks, no deeper than three feet. Preiss figured the first would be found within a month.

"You can imagine what airport security people say to a man trying to carry a six-foot shovel onto a plane," joked Preiss. "I tried to convince them I was on a horticultural expedition."

Starting the year before, Preiss spent nine months traveling the country to bury the casques. He disguised himself to resemble a groundskeeper and discreetly began to dig. Occasionally, dogs barked at him or park-goers watched him suspiciously. One time, the police were called, and Preiss hid in the bushes when the patrol car arrived.

"This book has ruined me at cocktail parties," he said. "If anyone asks me if I've ever been to a certain city, I always have to say yes... I can't let anyone rule out any possible location."

A Tepid Response

Early reviews of *The Secret* were mixed. In addition to the puzzling illustrations and verses, the 224-page book relayed a whimsical mythology. Some critics praised the creativity and humor, while others said it was less fantasy than farce. Early chapters told of the Fair People—fairies, goblins, leprechauns, and other creatures—who immigrated from the Old World to the New before the age of humans. Twelve of these arriving nations brought their treasured jewels, which they left for later people to find in hopes they would live harmoniously with nature. Hidden within those earliest chapters were clues to unraveling the secret locations.

The remaining 200 pages were satirical fairy tales that turned out to be disconnected from the treasure hunt. The two coauthors and Preiss had all been affiliated at various times with *National Lampoon* magazine, and this showed in the playful characters. There were *Tupperwerewolves* and spirits like *Elf S. Presley*, who accompanies showbiz folks on the road. A *Philharmonic orc*, who provided "food stamps for the upper class" in the form of public grants for the arts. Eighties' book critics particularly chuckled at the *Maître D'eamon*, who haunted gourmands with tables by the kitchen. Some said the book was hilarious. Others called it a silly spoof.

Despite the early attention, *The Secret* did not cause a nationwide frenzy as hoped—unlike what had happened to the puzzle book it sought to emulate, *Masquerade*, which had become the talk of Britain several years before. Preiss's puzzles proved much harder to unravel than anticipated. Months passed without a single casque being unearthed. While hundreds of readers did write Preiss, claiming to have located a site, none were close.

"The [casques] will stay in the ground until someone digs them up," he told a reporter. "If I should die, get hit by a truck or something, one person has been instructed to open the directions to the remaining treasures. They are locked away in a bank vault."

AN IMPORTANT DISCLAIMER

Before you hop on a plane with a shovel, like Preiss, and show up in sunny St. Augustine, please recognize a few important facts. Much has changed since the 1980s, and that six-foot shovel is not on the TSA list of approved carry-on items. Many enthusiasts are searching for the remaining casques, so don't don sunglasses and a fake mustache and think you can waltz into a public or private park and secretly dig unnoticed. The only legal way to approach solving this mystery is to contact the relevant property managers and ask permission. To do otherwise courts serious consequences, including citation or arrest for vandalism and trespassing. Also, to reduce the potential for conflict, Preiss made it clear that no casque is buried in a dangerous location or a forbidden area closed to the public. For some, just contemplating the mystery and visiting these remarkable sites will be enough.

One Puzzle Is Solved

A year later, during the summer of 1983, three high school friends in Chicago made a breakthrough. Following the clues, the teenage boys matched the fifth illustration and twelfth verse to the Windy City. The image depicted a Gaelic hobgoblin. Atop its head was a bizarre castle with a series of intriguing shapes. One projection resembled the downtown water tower, with the addition of windmill blades. Other shapes matched city sculptures. So, next they turned to the verse.

The friends deciphered "Where M and B are set in stone" as a reference to two statues depicting figures on horseback—man and beast. They identified the *Bowman* and the *Spearman*, flanking Congress Parkway at the entrance to Grant Park. This matched the illustration, in which a silhouette of the Bowman could be seen projecting from the castle.

"And to Congress, R is known" referred to the railroad that ran behind the statues. From there, they could see the statue of a seated Abraham Lincoln just inside the park. "L sits and left / Beyond his shoulder" led them to a rectangular park space bordered by lines of trees. "The end of ten by thirteen" didn't match up, but there was a "fence and fixture" of the same shape depicted on the illustrated castle.

The friends could hear "the sounds / of rumble"—the trains. Regarding "brush and music / hush," the answers seemed to lie across the street. The Art Institute of Chicago, with its *Fountain of the Great Lakes* statue partially depicted in the illustration. Plus, a band shell sat near the corner of Jackson and Columbus.

Back in February, the boys had started digging but turned up nothing. One of them sent a letter to Preiss, inquiring if they were close or if the treasure had already been found. Months passed with no reply, so, in July, they called his office in New York. The assistant who answered claimed that there was no treasure in Chicago. The friends still felt convinced. The next day they tried again and asked to speak directly with Preiss.

"You have the answer," said Preiss. "I don't see why you can't find the right spot."

The friends returned to the park and continued to dig until the area was pockmarked by holes. The problem lay in the line, "the end of ten by thirteen." Preiss had used two intersecting rows of trees as a landmark. In less than two years, several had been removed. During a final call, the boys begged for help. Preiss mailed them a snapshot he'd taken of his burial site. In August, they dug a three-foot hole at the corresponding spot. They were about to give up, when the casque tumbled from the crater wall. The first treasure had been found.

A New Hunt Begins

Years passed, then decades, without a second casque being found. Preiss moved on to other projects. *The Secret* was mostly forgotten beyond the few diehards with fraying copies. With the revolutionary rise of the internet came a way for old and new enthusiasts to gather. Now internet discussion boards and websites rekindled interest in the hunt. As searchers shared their research and theories, a consensus emerged. Illustrations were paired with verses and gemstones. Other clues were gleaned from the early mythology chapters.

Suspected locations were identified for the remaining casques, with varying levels of confidence and precision. New York City, possibly near the harbor. Milwaukee's was most likely inside Lake Park. San Francisco, seemingly at Golden Gate Park. Another location might be in the Outer Banks, as the third illustration depicts an outline of Roanoke Island. Further clues in the corresponding eleventh verse potentially led to Fort Raleigh National Historic Site.

In the late 1990s, a determined lawyer named Brian Zinn found his fifteen-year-old copy of *The Secret* in a box. Resuming his search, he focused on the fourth illustration. Some help from an online forum pointed him to the Greek Cultural Garden in Cleveland. "Socrates, Pindar, Apelles," read the fourth verse. The names appeared on a stone wall built to resemble the Parthenon in Athens. Clues led behind the wall, and the lawyer shoveled a dirt bed until he struck something. The plexiglass box had shattered. The ceramic casque was covered with clay and missing its top. Still inside was the key. More than twenty years after burial, the second treasure had been found.

PRESENT MEETS PAST

In addition to exploring historic St. Augustine, a highlight for many is exploring Castillo de San Marcos National Monument. By day, visitors often wander the grounds and admire the impressive fortress. Next, step back in time by crossing the drawbridge and passing through the sally port. From the courtyard, you can access several interior chambers with exhibits and climb the stairs to the gun deck. At night, people sit along the sea wall as the city lights splash across the water.

Heading north leads to the Fountain of Youth Archaeological Park, which has a recreation of what the town of Seloy may have looked like. Some enthusiasts of *The Secret* have made a strong case for this location closely matching the clues, but others are less convinced that Preiss would have snuck inside a gated park and buried the casque on private property.

Further north is Fort Mose Historic State Park, located on the banks of a tidal wetland. The park preserves the site of the first legally sanctioned settlement of free African Americans, established in 1738, in what became the United States. A reconstruction of the fort is scheduled for completion during 2025.

About fifteen miles south of the Castillo, Fort Matanzas National Monument preserves the Spanish watchtower that guarded the southern approach to St. Augustine. This intact coquina structure rises from an island in the Matanzas River and is reached by short ride on an NPS ferry.

"He was very similar to 'the absent-minded professor,'" Zinn later posted on a message board about Byron Preiss. It took the publisher about a year to find the key to the bank vault. Then Zinn traveled to New York City to retrieve his prize. He waited outside, while Preiss sifted through the safe deposit box for the first time since the Chicago discovery. He mentioned that the solutions to all twelve puzzles should have been inside but discovered they were missing. Instead, he came across $25,000 in savings bonds that he'd forgotten about. When he emerged, he held a blue gem wrapped in tissue paper. Instead of the aquamarine linked to the image and verse, neither of them noticed that Preiss accidentally handed Zinn a sapphire.

Sad End to the Hints

Later that summer, there was some sad news. At the age of fifty-two, Byron Preiss died in a car accident in East Hampton, New York. He was survived by his wife and two daughters. The online treasure hunting community that had sprung up around *The Secret* was shocked. They posted tributes to Preiss and described messages exchanged with him over the years that offered further hints. A user mentioned an email thread that seemed to be one of Preiss's final replies about the hunt.

"There is a treasure in Houston," wrote Preiss. "After twenty-two years, all I can say is l—"

The rest of the message was truncated. Preiss had clicked send before completing the sentence. Many thought the Houston casque was in Herman Park. Other proposed locations included New Orleans, Montreal, and White Point Garden in Charleston, South Carolina. With time, word came that the gems would still be awarded to those who found the casques. However, Preiss's solutions were never found. There would be no further clues. The searchers were on their own now.

Fourteen years later, a third treasure was found in Boston. Jason Krupat was a game designer and a newly obsessed fan of *The Secret,* which he learned about from an episode of *Expedition Unknown* on the Discovery Channel. While out on a jog in July 2019, he panicked while passing Langone Park, his theorized location. Construction crews were tearing up the baseball fields. This was near the beach that Paul Revere departed from on April 18, 1775, after seeing two lanterns hanging in the window of a nearby church tower. "Eighteenth day / Twelfth hour / Lit by lamplight" read one part of verse three, while the eleventh image matched some nearby landmarks. "Feel at home." When Krupat relayed his theory to the construction managers, they thought he was crazy. Then their excavator unearthed a casque beneath home plate.

The last of the twelve treasures was linked to St. Augustine in Northeastern Florida. Clues seemed to match the sixth image and ninth verse with what was commonly called the oldest city in the continental United States. More specifically, searchers identified several potential spots around the vicinity of the nation's oldest masonry fortress, Castillo de San Marcos. Like most of Preiss's puzzles, unraveling the secret seemed to involve understanding the search area's history.

Clues from the Past

In 1513, Spanish conquistador Juan Ponce de León led three ships north from Puerto Rico to search for the rumored islands of Beniny, later known as Bimini. After sailing through a disorienting storm for two days, they sighted what they believed to be a large island. It was early April, so they named it *La Florida*, due to the lush landscape and the Easter festival of flowers. Before going ashore, an approximate landing latitude was recorded in the ship's log as 30°, 8', a spot just north of present-day St. Augustine. After the explorer died eight years later, a legend would evolve that he was searching for the mythical Fountain of Youth.

But first, from St. Augustine, Ponce de León's 1513 expedition sailed south along the coast, encountering a powerful current. Despite the strong wind at their backs, the current pushed the boats northward. They had encountered the Gulf Stream, a warmwater ocean current flowing from the Caribbean along the east coast of North America and turning east across the Atlantic to Europe. This would become a vital trade route for the Spanish treasure fleet, which carried plundered silver, gold, and other valuables from the New World to the Old.

About fifty years later, the French explored the northeast coast of La Florida. Near the outlet of the St. Johns River, they established Fort Caroline. The Spanish king responded by dispatching conquistador Pedro Menendez to establish a rival colony to protect the trade route and expand the empire. Land was sighted on August 18, 1565, the day of St. Augustine. A Spanish fort was soon erected near the Timucua town of Seloy.

The French attempted a first strike, sending ships with soldiers south. Instead, they encountered a rough storm and shipwrecked south of St. Augustine. This provided an opportunity. Menendez marched 500 Spanish soldiers overland to Fort Caroline and launched a surprise attack at dawn. While some of the 250 colonists escaped, all but sixty women and children were slaughtered. The Spanish next went south and surrounded the camps of the shipwrecked survivors. Over one hundred soldiers were convinced to surrender in hopes of fair treatment. Instead, Menendez had the captives executed. When another 150 shipwreck survivors appeared, they were executed as well. Henceforth, the inlet was named Matanzas, the Spanish word for *massacres*.

The next combatants were the English, and they destroyed St. Augustine twice in eighty years. After the Spanish were blamed for the mysterious disappearance of the Roanoke Colony, Sir Francis Drake burned the wooden fort to the ground. Then in 1668, privateer Robert Searles plundered the townsite. As a result, the Spanish began to build Castillo de San Marcos, a four-bastion star fort made of solid coquina. Similar to limestone, this sedimentary rock is a jumble of shell and coral fragments, naturally cemented together in sea water by calcite mineralization. The fort was completed in 1695, after twenty-three years of construction.

Castillo De San Marcos as seen from the air in 1965. Jack E. Boucher for Historic American Buildings Survey. Castillo de San Marcos, 1 Castillo Drive, Saint Augustine, St. Johns County, FL, Jack E Boucher, Historic American Buildings Survey, Heritage Documentation Programs, Library of Congress/Public Domain

THRILL OF THE CHASE

In 2010, an eccentric New Mexico art dealer spawned a famous treasure hunt when he self-published a memoir titled *The Thrill of the Chase*. Author Forrest Fenn wrote that he'd hidden a chest filled with over $1 million in gold and jewels on public land in the Rocky Mountains, somewhere north of his home in Santa Fe. To find the location, Fenn explained that seekers needed to decipher a poem containing nine clues, plus stories in the book offered further hints. His hope was that the chase would inspire more people to get outside and develop an appreciation for wild places.

Treasure seekers were soon combing a vast search area in the Rocky Mountains north of Santa Fe. The hunt became increasingly controversial, as thousands of frenzied searchers joined the fray and their behavior grew increasingly reckless. At least five people died while searching, plus others were arrested for trespassing on private property or digging illegally in public parklands. As the 2010s came to a close, Fenn was repeatedly pressured by authorities to end the search and retrieve the treasure. Fenn refused, saying this would be unfair to the vast majority of law-abiding searchers who had invested years of their lives in the chase.

In the summer of 2020, a treasure hunter named Jack Stuef scraped fallen twigs and dirt away from a remote spot next to a river inside Yellowstone National Park in Wyoming. After a decade-long hunt, and only months before Forrest Fenn died at the age of ninety, the chase was over. The treasure was found.

Castillo de San Marcos was tested twice by the English. The governor of the Carolina colony attacked in 1702 as part of Queen Anne's War. The governor of the Georgia colony did likewise in 1740, as part of the War of Jenkins' Ear. Both times, the fort's coquina walls simply swallowed the fired cannonballs, and the occupants outlasted the sieges. Afterward, the Spanish constructed a coquina outpost to guard the southern inlet of the river, a two-story watch tower now called Fort Matanzas. Another defensive fortification was built north of St. Augustine. The Spanish directed arriving Black refugees, who were escaping from slavery in the United States, to join their militia and occupy this townsite, named Fort Mose.

However, protecting such a vast New World empire was increasingly costing Spain more than they could afford. After three centuries of Spanish domination, Florida was ceded to the United States in exchange for a border agreement in the Southwest. Castillo de San Marcos came under control of the U.S. military, which used it in various ways, including as a prison for Native Americans during wars with the Seminoles. In the 1930s, the fortress was transferred to the National Park Service for preservation as a historic monument.

Deciphering the Verses

"The first chapter / Written in water" begins the ninth verse of *The Secret*, which is typically linked to St. Augustine. Perhaps this is a reference to Florida's original governing document, the Spanish Constitution of Cádiz. The Plaza de la Constitución commemorates the event, located in the old town near a statue of Ponce de León. This first constitution was only in effect for a few years, from 1812 to 1815 and again from 1820 to 1821. One could say it was never set in stone but writ in water.

Look now to the sixth image, which depicts a rocky promontory rising near a body of water. Standing on this precipice is a horseback rider wearing a costume and classic morion helmet associated with conquistadors. Atop a planted staff, a colorful banner flaps in the wind, making a shape resembling the course of the Matanzas River. Embedded in the flag is a symbol with four sharp corners. It matches the outline of Castillo de San Marcos's bastions, covered by a circle with a small square in the center.

Turn the image sideways, and the rocky promontory somewhat resembles the rounded northern end of Anastasia Island. The straight staff could be the Bridge of Lions, found south of the monument. Furthermore, in places, the rocky promontory somewhat resembles the jumbled matrix of coquina. Other spots resemble the Castillo's walls of fitted coquina blocks. And several triangular protrusions on one side of the promontory resemble the sea wall surrounding the fortress.

Turn the image back, and glance at the bottom right corner. Rising from the water is a rocky outcrop and a tall palm tree. This recalls the original state seal of Florida, adopted in 1868. It was criticized for depicting mountains in a region that has none and replaced in 1985. However, in the image from *The Secret*, the outcrop bears a striking resemblance to the sloping stone bastions at Castillo de San Marcos, especially when considering that the surrounding moat held water until 1996, when it was drained.

Return to the verse. "Shell, limestone, silver, salt." Two components of coquina? A precious metal carried by the Spanish treasure fleet? The brackish water of the inlet? "Near men / With wind rose." A reference to a type of compass rose, used on early nautical charts by Spanish explorers?

"Behind bending branches" might first refer to the twisty southern live oak found along the coast. Even more oaks were present on the Castillo grounds during the 1980s before more recent storms uprooted trees. "And a green picket fence" is harder to place. Along with other clues, it has pointed some searchers nearly one mile north to the Fountain of Youth Archaeological Park, believed to be close to where Ponce de León landed in 1513. The park is a privately owned and ticketed attraction, but one that does have a green picket fence. Returning to the Castillo, the closest match is a recreation of the Old Town Wall. First erected in the early 1700s, it's also called the Cubo Line. Originally, it was a palisade, essentially a fence, which was later improved to a defensive wall of vertical palm logs. In the 1960s, the park service recreated the latter wall and originally planted green grass across its narrow top.

"At the base of a tall tree" was likely a reference to a towering palm, and one that may have been lost to a hurricane during the intervening four decades. "You can still hear the honking" could come from irritated drivers on San Marco Avenue, the busy thoroughfare bordering the monument. Or maybe it's a reference to birds. Geese certainly honk and can be found on the fort grounds at times. Roseate spoonbills, which match a mythology clue of "pink, long-legged birds," may be found wading in nearby wetlands. They don't exactly honk, but they sometimes make a guttural grunting. "Stars move by day" could be a reference to the American flag, which in the 1980s flew atop the Castillo next to New Spain's Cross of Burgundy.

"Sails pass by night / Even in darkness" perhaps refers to boats in the harbor, aided at night by the St. Augustine lighthouse. "Like moonlight in teardrops" is a puzzler but may refer to the poem "Moonlight in Old St. Augustine." "Over the tall grass" could be the fort green, the grassy sloping hill leading up to the first defensive wall. "Years pass, rain falls" could refer to a feature on the Castillo's outer walls. Small spouts in the parapet walls drain the fort's gun deck during rainstorms. Beneath each of these is a water stain, a rough triangle of weathering and moss, which almost resembles a teardrop. A final clue may be found in the first letter in each of the final five lines of the verse, above. Together they spell out the Spanish name for the Timucua town of Seloy.

So, where is the casque? It could be on the grounds of the Castillo de San Marco. Or it may be buried at the Fountain of Youth Archeological Park or in another green space like the Plaza de la Constitución. Though numerous observers believe the clues point to St. Augustine, it may not be here at all. There could be other Florida cities, with a conquistador history, where the clues can be made to match.

It has been over four decades since Byron Preiss would have traveled to the oldest city in the United States. And this is a coastal location that's prone to regular floods and hurricanes, so it's entirely possible the casque was destroyed. We may simply never know. What was once just a treasure hunt has become a series of lingering mysteries. Three have been solved. Nine casques remain. One of them may or may not be here. This is the legacy of the *The Secret*. Maybe you will be the one to solve the mystery...

NORTHEAST

CHAPTER 31

WHO CARVED THE *MONA LISA* OF THE MOUNTAINS?

STRANGE DISCOVERIES

NEW RIVER GORGE NATIONAL PARK AND PRESERVE

APPALACHIAN MOUNTAINS, WEST VIRGINIA

Gene Kistler was picking his way through the forest along the rim of the gorge. The path was rough and slippery, filled with roots and moss-covered rocks. Far below, the New River turned white where it tumbled through rocky riffles. Just upstream was the famous New River Gorge Bridge, with its slender steel beams and iconic arch. Upon completion in 1977, for a period it was the highest and longest of its kind in the world.

Now it was the mid-1980s. Kistler was a rock climber following a faint approach trail to a popular climbing area called Ambassador Buttress. He wasn't far from Fayette Station Road when his eye caught something odd. A mossy boulder, resting on the hillside, was somehow looking at him.

An oval face was carved into soapstone, a soft metamorphic rock composed of talc and schist. It had a triangular nose, a sharp brow, and penetrating eyes. Given the flat lips, Kistler couldn't tell if the face was sad or happy.

AN ADVENTUROUS GORGE

Redesignated in 2020, the New River Gorge National Park & Preserve offers some unique experiences for an NPS unit. For many of the park's roughly 1.5 million annual visitors, the emphasis is on river activities like whitewater rafting and fishing or rock climbing on the canyon's cliffs. That said, several stunning hiking trails can be found along the rim of the gorge. The most popular is the Endless Wall Trail, near the Canyon Rim Visitor Center, which offers iconic views of the inner gorge. For a less-crowded option, head south for similar views at the Grandview Rim Trail. For a mellower walk, check out the railroad ghost town of Thurmond. But know that the unit's 114 square miles mostly parallel the precipitous river corridor, which means you often have to drive a long way out and around to reach other parts of the park.

"Like the *Mona Lisa*," he would later say.

Back in the late 1970s, the park service had designated the area as a national river. As more people came, some wanted to visit the stone face. In the nearby town of Fayetteville, just across the gorge, Gene and his wife Mara opened a rock-climbing shop. They offered directions to this piece of folk art. Gene considered it a benevolent spirit of the forest. Many people would ask, "Who carved the mysterious face?"

Gene's theory was a coal miner by the name of Johnson. He lived nearby during the 1950s, and the foundations of his home can still be seen beneath ferns further down the trail. Johnson had placed bricks and stones along the rough path. He also carved his last name into a rock that serves as a step across a steep creek tumbling into the gorge. When coal mining declined throughout the area, the man likely had some time on his hands. But why he carved this calm face into stone, and who it might be, remains unknown.

GRAND CANYON OF THE EAST?

Numerous gorges are touted as the grandest in the East, including the Genesee River Gorge in New York, Pine Creek Gorge in Pennsylvania, Linville Gorge in North Carolina, and Tallulah Gorge in Georgia. But one argument in favor of the New River Gorge's claim is that, just like the real-deal Grand Canyon in Arizona, both parks have whitewater rafting trips available from spring through fall.

Unlike rafting the Grand Canyon, which mostly requires multi-day trips, there are several options for guided day trips on the New. One summer favorite is the Lower New River Gorge, with trips running for either eight or twelve miles through class III–IV rapids in the heart of the park. Meanwhile, easier class II–III sections can be found upstream. Nearby, during September and October, the Gauley River offers several rowdy rafting trips ranging from class III and IV to big-water class V.

LOOK BEFORE YOU LEAP

The park is most famous for Bridge Day, the third Saturday in October, when pedestrians are allowed to walk across the New River Gorge Bridge—and when brave BASE jumpers are allowed to leap from its heights into the gorge below.

SEE THE FACE?

The land status surrounding the stone face is tricky. Some say it's private property, while others claim the approach trail has long been established as a public right-of-way. One option might be for NPS to acquire the parcel and preserve the face as a historic site. If you're considering searching for the stoneface, stop by the Kistlers' old shop, Water Stone Outdoors in Fayetteville, West Virginia. It's under new ownership, but someone should be able to provide an update.

CHAPTER 32

THE SECOND-OLDEST RIVER IN THE WORLD—AND THE "NORTHIEST"?

HIDDEN HISTORY

NEW RIVER GORGE NATIONAL PARK AND PRESERVE

APPALACHIAN MOUNTAINS, WEST VIRGINIA

Spend time around the New River, and you'll come across several minor mysteries to ponder. To start, the reason it was named the New is unclear. In the 1650s, an early English explorer named it the Wood River after himself. A century later, it was being called the New for uncertain reasons. Some said it came from a Native American name meaning *new water*. Others said a man with the surname New operated a ferry on the river. Another version claimed a road surveyor in the 1760s was using a map that didn't show the gorge, so he added it as a New River.

Perhaps the most fascinating legend is that the New is the oldest river in

North America and the second-oldest river in the world after the Nile in Egypt. But is there any truth to this? Part of the reasoning behind the claim is that the New is one of the few rivers cutting directly through the ridges and rises of the Appalachian Mountains. Two other rivers that do this are the Susquehanna River in Pennsylvania and the French Broad River in North Carolina, which are also theorized to be remarkably old.

On the New River, some rocks exposed inside the gorge are estimated to have formed around 320 million years ago. At some point during the following sixty million years, the Appalachian Mountains began to rise due to uplift from the collision of the African and North American continents. The theory became that the New River formed sometime in that window, between about 320 and 260 million years ago, maintaining its course by eroding into the mountains as they rose up around it. However, the origin of today's mountains is a matter of debate, and they may have risen much later. Thus, the New River could have formed around sixty-five million years ago or even more recently.

So, how does that compare to the Nile? Well, current theories point to a much younger age for Africa's famous river, only about thirty million years old. Meanwhile, there are other rivers that are believed to be much older than the New. The ephemeral Finke River, in the deserts of Central Australia, is now theorized to be the world's oldest. Reason being the meanders of the Finke cut deeply into bedrock that is estimated to have been uplifted about 400 to 300 million years ago. More research is clearly needed, and theories will likely continue to evolve.

In the meantime, it's been known for some time that the New is a special river that's likely quite old. But the real reason behind the claim that it's the second-oldest river in the world actually comes from politicians seeking to protect it. Back in the 1970s, various sections of the 360-mile river were endangered by proposed dam projects. Both regional politicians and many among the general public were generally against the dams and in favor of preserving the river for its natural and recreational values. The opposition to damming the New coalesced around the argument that the river is one of the most beautiful and oldest in the world.

With time, the claim about the New being among the oldest rivers slowly strengthened with the dropping of all but one qualification, the secondary status to the oft-romanticized Nile. This choice of comparison wasn't based on scientific theory. It had more to do with the Nile being associated with one of the oldest civilizations, which built the pyramids of Ancient Egypt.

After the New River Gorge became a unit of the National Park Service, and tourists began arriving for outdoor adventures, this modern myth proved to be a perfect promotional tool. *The biggest whitewater on the oldest river.* Even though the veracity of the claim is suspect, the fact that visitors return every year confirms that New River Gorge was definitely worth protecting.

MELLOW HEADWATERS

If you're looking for a flatwater paddling experience on the New River, instead of whitewater, then consider heading upstream. Due to some atypical topography seen in parts of the Appalachians, one could call the New an inverted river. Many whitewater rivers are steepest in their mountain headwaters, and the gradient becomes mellower as the river reaches lower elevations.

However, the lower reaches of the New have more rapids, with the whitewater becoming increasingly rowdy while progressing through the gorge. Meanwhile, the mountain headwaters of the New River can be quite calm and more typical of a float stream meandering through valleys. One of the best places to explore these mellow upper sections is at New River State Park in North Carolina.

The New Is the "Northiest" River?

Spend even more time around the New River and you'll hear even more strange "facts." Some echo the oldest saying, discussed in this chapter, by claiming the New is one of only two rivers in the world that flow north, the other being the Nile in Egypt. Other times, this "northiest" statement is qualified as the New being one of a very few rivers in North America that flows north. Yet neither of these claims is accurate.

In the United States alone, plenty of rivers flow north for either the majority or entirety of their length. The Deschutes River in Oregon. The Bighorn in Wyoming. The St. Johns River in Florida. The Niagara River in New York. The list goes on. The reason for this misconception may be that, when we look at a map, we tend to think of north as "up" and south as "down." But in the real world, water flows downhill in all directions, and most runoff eventually finds its way to the sea.

A few quirks of U.S. geography may reinforce the misconception. Due to an inwardly tapering coastline, the lower forty-eight is often surrounded by water to the southwest, south, and southeast. Thus, many inland rivers end up flowing in those directions. But *up* in Canada, which is surrounded by water to the north, numerous rivers flow in that direction on their way toward the Arctic Ocean.

CHAPTER 33

DID POCAHONTAS SAVE JOHN SMITH'S LIFE?

LEGENDARY FIGURES

COLONIAL NATIONAL HISTORICAL PARK

JAMESTOWN, TIDEWATER REGION, VIRGINIA

L et us play, and dance, and sing," recited the bejeweled performer. She entered the scene accompanied by a half dozen dancers, each wearing colorful gowns and masks with feather head plumes. "Let us now turn every sort, o' the pleasures of spring, to the graces of a court."

The jovial performers commenced to twirl around an intricate stage with shifting sets—artistic renditions of clouds, stars, and flames—moved by concealed stagehands. Thus began *The Vision of Delight,* a masque held in the ornate Banqueting House at Whitehall Palace in London for the pleasure of King James and Queen Anne. Surrounding the monarchs, the smoky hall was filled with loud courtiers who feasted and talked and laughed along with the pageantry.

It was January 5, the twelfth and final night of the Christmas celebration, in the year 1617. Among the audience was a most honored guest from across the sea. She wore the finely embroidered dress, petticoat, and lace collar of an English lady. Yet her facial features resembled those of the native peoples found in the New World.

An engraved portrait was currently circulating around England to commemorate the famous visit. The caption described the woman as "Matoaka, also known as Rebecca, daughter of the most powerful prince of the Powhatan Empire of Virginia." The first name was from her childhood. The Christian name was from her baptism and conversion several years before. With time, she would come to be known by a nickname given during her youth for her curious and playful nature: Pocahontas.

The famous engraving depicting Pocahontas during her visit to England in 1616 made by Simon van de Passe. Simon van de Passe, *Pocahontas*, 1616, National Portrait Gallery, London/Public Domain

Truth to a Legend?

Six months before, Pocahontas and her party had disembarked in Plymouth, England, after a long sea voyage. Her husband was an Englishman named John Rolfe, the Virginia Company's most successful farmer. He had cultivated the colony's first cash crop, a successful strain of sweet tobacco for export to England. With them was their son, Thomas, only a year and a half old. The visit was more about business than diplomacy. New investors and colonists were desperately needed across the Atlantic.

Most noticeably, the Rolfe family was accompanied by a dozen members of the Powhatan nation, including men, women, and children in their traditional dress. One was an elder named Tomocomo, who wore facial paint and shaved one side of his hair while weaving the other side into a long braid. Pocahontas's father, whom the English called Chief Powhatan, had asked Tomocomo to count the number of people in England. The trusted adviser began by making notches on a stick but quickly gave up after realizing it must be millions.

The delegation traveled by horse-drawn coach, taking a week to reach London. During that time, an old friend of Pocahontas's, John Smith, wrote a letter of introduction to the queen. As a soldier and explorer, Smith had been one of the earliest leaders at the struggling Jamestown settlement. During the first winter, with colonists dying of starvation and disease, he led an expedition upriver to secure corn from tribal villages.

When a Powhatan hunting party attacked, two of Smith's companions were killed, and he was taken prisoner. Held for several weeks, he was spared after becoming the first Englishman to meet Chief Powhatan and his beloved daughter. For Jamestown, the twelve-year-old Pocahontas would become a godsend, an emissary bearing peace and much-needed food.

In his 1617 letter, Smith humbly beseeched the queen to grant Pocahontas all the dignities of visiting royalty. As a testament to her worth, he shared the true nature of their relationship. It was a new story previously unmentioned in his publications about the colony. This account, with future elaboration, would become an American legend.

Nine years before, Smith claimed, he was brought before Chief Powhatan during a grand feast. Two large stones were placed on the ground, near an open fire. Members of the crowd suddenly grabbed Smith and set his head upon the stones. They raised their clubs to strike. At the very moment of his execution, Pocahontas intervened. Rushing forward, she knelt beside the captive foreigner and laid her own head upon his, daring the mob to bludgeon a child as well. Chief Powhatan was so moved by the gesture that it supposedly ushered in a welcome era of peace.

It was a memorable and moving story, one that seemingly soothed the growing hostilities between English colonists and Native Americans. Yet, why had it taken so long to be told? Convenient, some said. Almost too convenient. Was there any truth to the legend?

Few accounts from colonists have survived over the centuries. Those that have been discovered shed light on the horrific early years for the Virginia Company and the gracious actions of Pocahontas. One such account was written contemporaneously by John Smith, *A True Relation of Such Occurrences of Noate as Hath Happened in Virginia,* published in 1608. Another publication that year was *A Discourse of Virginia* by Captain Wingfield. In 1612, an English minister named William Symonds collected narratives from several colonists into *The Proceedings of the English Colonie in Virginia.*

About sixteen years after the events took place, Captain Smith expanded on the Jamestown story. Published in 1624, *The Generall Historie of Virginia, New-England, and the Summer Isles* offered Smith's first account of his capture by Chief Powhatan and rescue by Pocahontas. Smith shared the letter he claimed to have sent to the queen seven years before, and he described a tense reunion with Pocahontas in England during 1618. This book would become a critical source for the early history of Jamestown.

Once out in the world, the story of the young savior Pocahontas would take on a life of its own. When combined with the limited firsthand accounts, colonist letters, and retold narratives, these earliest sources would give rise to both the legend and the controversy. What really happened during those early years at Jamestown?

Stories Diverge

On April 26, 1607, three English ships carrying over a hundred men and boys dropped anchors off Cape Henry near the mouth of Chesapeake Bay. During four months at sea, they had battled storms and sea sickness. They had followed roundabout currents across the Atlantic, with stops in Spain, the Canary Islands, and Puerto Rico. Finally, the first colonists of the Virginia Company had reached the New World.

When a scouting party went ashore, they were swiftly driven back by a volley of arrows from a charging war party. Over the past century, Native American coastal tribes had learned to associate the arrival of European sailing ships with conflict and death. For three weeks, the colonists cautiously searched the region for a suitable townsite. Recurring skirmishes with local tribes and a fear of Spanish attack led the colony president, Captain Wingfield, to select an uninhabited peninsula on the James River. Located fifty miles inland, the spot was highly defensible but a poor choice for a settlement.

Jamestown arose on a small swath of dry land between the river and the woods. Otherwise, the peninsula was mostly swampy wetlands, which issued oppressive clouds of mosquitoes. Due to the reach of the tides, the James River was brackish and unsuitable for drinking water. The soil was sandy and not ideal for crops.

Making matters worse was the timing. Unwittingly, the settlers arrived during a major drought. Plus, it was too late in the season to make much headway toward clearing farmland and planting enough crops. When Captain Newport and the two larger ships set sail for England, the colonists were left with a meager supply of rations, mostly grain-meal. Within months, about a third of them would be dead.

In search of food, John Smith began making his forays into the surrounding region, often by boat. The first expedition took Smith up the James River, to where huge cascades blocked the channel. This would become the future site of Richmond. That winter, he was exploring a tributary named the Chickahominy River, when his party was attacked. After two fellow colonists were killed, the explorer was captured and brought before Chief Powhatan.

PATHS TO THE PAST

Colonial National Historical Park preserves several sites spanning the midsection of the Virginia Peninsula, which extends east of Richmond into Chesapeake Bay. The scenic Colonial Parkway runs for twenty-three miles through wetlands and forests while connecting the popular historic triangle of Jamestown, Williamsburg, and Yorktown.

Historic Jamestowne is a waterfront archaeological park and memorial comanaged by the National Park Service and Preservation Virginia. Highlights include preserved ruins, recreated structures, and restored buildings, like the brick Jamestown Church. The Voorhees Archaearium is an on-site archaeology museum with excavated artifacts and exhibits about the colony.

Starting near the visitor center, a five-mile Island Drive loops through the swamps and woods of Jamestown Island, with several interpretive stops and short walks. Just outside the NPS unit, Jamestown Settlement is a state-managed living history museum, with a recreated townsite and actors in period dress.

Found inland, Colonial Williamsburg is a vast living history museum set in the historic district of the small city. Operated by a private foundation, hundreds of buildings from the seventeenth through nineteenth centuries have been restored or recreated, with costumed reenactors running tourist shops and providing demonstrations.

Yorktown Battlefield is found at the eastern end of the parkway next to the York River. This NPS unit preserves sites from the 1781 Siege of Yorktown, where George Washington and the Continental Army secured a decisive victory against the British during the American Revolution. In addition to a small museum, a driving loop leads through the battlefield. Nearby, the state-managed American Revolution Museum combines indoor and outdoor history exhibits.

Here, the story diverges into two versions of events. Smith's 1608 version describes Chief Powhatan inquiring why the English had come and requesting that Smith relocate the colony from Jamestown to near Powhatan's village. Replying carefully, Smith claimed a Spanish attack had driven the English off course. The captain made no mention of their plans to establish a permanent colony at Jamestown. He agreed to move as requested, though he had no intention to do so. Smith's deference pleased Powhatan, who soon had his men escort Smith home. There was no mention of Pocahontas saving the Englishman from certain death. That said, Smith did make curious references to ceremonies with wild howling and violent gestures.

"So fat they fed mee, I much doubted they intended to have sacrificed mee," he wrote about these ceremonies, which is the closest reference to the near execution he described in 1617 and 1624.

A Friendship Begins

Upon returning to Jamestown in early January 1608, Smith found that less than forty colonists remained alive. Fortunately, Captain Newport soon arrived in the first of several supply ships sent during those early years. Sometimes these so-called relief missions brought more problems than provisions—in this case, another hundred male settlers to feed. After a careless fire burned the first fort to the ground, the survivors huddled in the ruins as the James River froze over. Only half of them would survive the winter.

With the thaw of spring came the arrival of a new face. Smith's 1608 account, plus others that followed, describes Pocahontas arriving to Jamestown after being sent by her father. She brought venison and bread in exchange for the release of several tribesmen being held as prisoners by the English. She was only twelve years old and spent time cartwheeling with the boys. The English released the prisoners, and Pocahontas's spirited presence and food deliveries became a welcome sight at the fort.

Several other stories about young Pocahontas came down from various accounts. One concerns a tribal performance given for the English, first described by Symonds in 1612. It came to be called a *Virginia Maske*. Thirty young women emerged from the forest, wearing only leaves, colorful body paint, and stag horns on their heads. Their leader was further adorned with an otter-skin skirt and a quiver of arrows on her back. Clutching a bow and arrow in her hands, she led the group in an hour-long performance with singing and dancing. In 1624, Smith added a name. The leader, he said, was Pocahontas.

During the summer of 1608, Smith resumed exploring the regional water-ways. Sailing and rowing a small boat, a crew of a dozen traveled thousands of miles during two expeditions. During the first, they followed the Potomac River upstream to the present-day location of Washington, DC. During the second, they reached the northern ends of Chesapeake Bay.

Upon his return to Jamestown, Smith created the first detailed map of Virginia, which would be used by Europeans for decades. In the front matter, Smith men-tioned Pocahontas in a sample of her people's language. The translation described an exchange of gifts. She brought two small baskets, and Smith gave her white beads for a necklace.

All sources show that Pocahontas and John Smith held a fondness for one another. The captain was eventually elected leader of the colony, partly due to his successful dealings with the Native Americans. Later observers would speculate about, and sometimes invent, a romantic relationship between the late-twenties Smith and the pre-teen Pocahontas. However, the historical record remains silent on the matter.

The penultimate meeting between the two was relayed by Symonds in 1612. It began with a contentious negotiation between Chief Powhatan and Smith over weapons and food. The English became suspicious, though the relations remained cordial enough. With their boat beached due to low water, they waited until mid-night when the returning tide allowed them to depart. Smith expanded on this nighttime scene in 1624. While the English party waited near their boat, Pocahontas crept from the dark woods. Though such a betrayal might warrant her death, she explained that her father was preparing an ambush. Smith greatly appreciated the warning, which prompted them to flee.

In the fall of 1609, Smith was sleeping in his canoe when a mysterious spark ignited his gunpowder pouch. The explosion tore the flesh from his thigh and ignited his clothes. To put out the flames, Smith flung himself into the water. He nearly drowned from the shock. The wounds were so severe that he was put aboard a ship to return to England. Few believed Smith would survive, and Pocahontas was told that he died.

By Force or by Choice

Conflicts between the Jamestown colonists and the local tribes only worsened once Smith was gone. Chief Powhatan forbade Pocahontas from visiting Jamestown. Without her gifts of food, the colony suffered its worst winter yet. By now, their numbers had grown to several hundred. Of these, only sixty survived the Starving Time to see the next spring. New waves of settlers and reinforcements continued to arrive, and the colony took an increasingly militant approach. The Virginia Company established settlements throughout the Tidewater region. During the first Anglo–Powhatan War, both sides murderously sacked each other's villages.

In December 1612, an English captain lured Pocahontas aboard a ship and confined her in the fort at Jamestown. The ransom demand was a cease-fire and exchange of prisoners. This prolonged stalemate lasted for several years. Though minor hostilities continued, the era became known as the Peace of Pocahontas. During her time in captivity, whether by force or choice, she embraced the English ways. She adopted their clothing, learned their language, and embraced Christianity.

Pocahontas met the entrepreneurial John Rolfe, who was enjoying a notable success. He had cultivated a new strain of sweet tobacco to compete against the Spanish monopoly. Now, the colony had a prayer for profitability, but new inflows of capital and settlers were needed to leverage this enterprise. After Pocahontas and Rolfe were married, with blessings from both sides, their son was born. In this interracial family, the Virginia Company saw an opportunity, the perfect ambassadors to promote New World opportunities.

A Tense Moment of Truth

The family spent nine months in England, during which Pocahontas would receive an audience with the queen and the bishop of London, among other officials. She and Tomocomo would meet the king at the Twelfth Night masque. They almost didn't grasp the significance, since their guide to English culture, John Rolfe, was not invited. His was a scandalous situation among the aristocracy, given he was a commoner who had married an Indian princess.

Pocahontas appeared to be astonished by what she saw. In Virginia, the thatched log homes were small. The meadows and swamps were empty save for the chirping birds and other animals. The old-growth forests rose high overhead. In London, the trees were small. The squares were noisy and filled with people and horses. Stone buildings rose high overhead.

Those who observed her believed Pocahontas was thrilled by the so-called Old World, which seemed far more modernized than her own. But the air did not agree with her, filled with smoky fumes. Some of her companions were similarly coughing and taking ill. So, Rolfe moved the family outside the city to Brentford in Middlesex.

That's where they were living when John Smith finally came to a social gathering. When he greeted his old friend, Pocahontas seemed upset. She turned away and covered her face, before stepping out from the party for several hours. The captain was surprised. He had expected the princess to be happy about their reunion. When Pocahontas returned, Smith wrote that he received some terse words, including a reminder of all that she had done for him.

"You did promise Powhatan," said Pocahontas. "What was yours should be his, and he the like to you. You called him father, being in his land a stranger. And, by the same reason, so must I do you."

Smith replied that he dared not accept this customary title of respect from the daughter of a king. Pocahontas, with a composed expression, continued.

"Were you not afraid to come into my father's country, and caused fear in him and all his people, but me, and fear you here I should call you father? I tell you then, I will, and you shall call me child, and so I will be for ever and ever your countryman. They did tell us always you were dead, and I knew no other till I came to Plymouth."

Pocahontas explained that Chief Powhatan had commanded Tomocomo to learn the truth about John Smith's demise, despite what was reported by the colonists eight years before. "Because your countrymen will lie much."

Centuries later, historians would still puzzle over the meaning of this alleged encounter. It was one of the very few times that words attributed to Pocahontas would be directly recorded. Many believed that Smith was prone to exaggerate in his writings, especially concerning his numerous brave deeds. Yet, here was a raw moment that rang true. As a child, Pocahontas had gone to exceptional lengths to help John Smith and the English. Now she was an early-twenties woman who seemingly felt taken for granted by her oldest friend among them.

But how this exchange reflected upon the legend was unclear. Had Pocahontas saved Smith's life? Returning to the moment of his execution, some scholars claimed the captain may have misinterpreted a choreographed ceremony. Perhaps Powhatan sought to obtain Smith's allegiance by having Pocahontas symbolically save him. Or maybe everything happened as reported, including Pocahontas's nighttime warning. Perhaps Smith withheld these stories to protect the girl from any repercussions for aiding the other side. Then again, upon seeing Pocahontas in England and discovering she felt her vital efforts went unappreciated, might Smith have decided to rectify his oversight? His story would not just elevate her role in history but secure a legacy. Though, this would not happen during her lifetime.

A Troubling End

Pocahontas so enjoyed England that she was not yet ready to leave the Old World. But her husband had business obligations in the New World to the Virginia Company. That March, the party boarded a ship bound for the west. While sailing down the Thames River, Pocahontas's respiratory problems took a turn for the worse. The family went ashore in Gravesend, as her breathing became increasingly strained. The condition was later theorized to be tuberculosis or pneumonia from a

European disease for which she had no immunity. Their two-year-old son Thomas was also ill. He would fortunately survive. His mother was not as lucky. A grief-stricken Rolfe was convinced to leave his son behind to recuperate with an English lord, while the rest of the party resumed the voyage.

After Pocahontas was buried at St. George's Church in Gravesend, the lives of many in Virginia unraveled. Tomocomo would rage about the improprieties of the English. To meet the demand for labor in the colony, slave ships would start bringing enslaved Africans to work the expanding tobacco fields. Chief Powhatan, grief-stricken at the loss of his daughter, would die within a year of learning the news. His aggressive younger brother, Opechancanough, would assume leadership of the Tidewater region.

In 1622, Opechancanough shattered the Peace of Pocahontas with a surprise attack. Over 300 people, a quarter of the Virginia Colony, were massacred. John Rolfe was among those who died around that time, though the exact cause is unknown. The father never reunited with his son. As an adult, Thomas returned to the colony of his birth. Perhaps his mother would have been pleased, given the words John Rolfe reported she had spoken on her deathbed in 1617.

"All must die," Pocahontas had said. "'Tis enough that the child liveth."

CHAPTER 34

WHO WAS INVOLVED IN THE CONSPIRACY TO ASSASSINATE ABRAHAM LINCOLN?

INFAMOUS CRIMES

FORD'S THEATRE NATIONAL HISTORIC SITE

TENTH STREET, WASHINGTON, DC

A bright sun shone directly overhead as soldiers and spectators gathered in the courtyard of the Washington Arsenal. Those lucky enough to be allowed inside, just over a thousand people, waited anxiously amid heavy air and stifling heat for the arrival of the condemned. Observant reporters milled around, jotting notes about the fervent mood. On a nearby platform, a photographer adjusted his plate camera.

Beyond the high brick walls, the dusty streets of Washington, DC, were in chaos with crowds pressing toward the fort, hoping for a glimpse of the morbid event. It was July 7, 1865, execution day for the murderous conspirators in the assassination of the nation's greatest president, Abraham Lincoln.

Inside the courtyard, a large wooden gallows had been erected, wide enough to hang all four convicted criminals at once. The scaffold stood about twelve feet high, roughly the same height from which the assassin himself, John Wilkes Booth, had leapt from the box to the stage of Ford's Theatre. Soon his compatriots would join their leader in the sweet agony of retribution. In the grass nearby, four pinewood coffins rested next to four freshly dug graves.

At a quarter past one, the presiding general escorted the death procession through the yard. The first prisoner was Mary Surratt, wearing all black—dress, bonnet, and veil. The Confederate sympathizer. The boardinghouse owner. The keeper of the nest that hatched the egg, according to the recently sworn-in President Andrew Johnson, who had ignored all requests for clemency. In her midforties, Surratt was far older than the other three, yet she alone refused to acknowledge her guilt. Soon she would become the first woman ever executed by the U.S. federal government. Her limp frame was practically carried up the steps by soldiers and priests and deposited on the chair beneath her noose.

Next came none other than Lewis Powell. The Confederate agent. The expressionless villain. The most brutish assailant of the bunch. Thankfully, his bloodied victim, Secretary of State William Seward, had survived. Yet what of the public servant's family? A stricken wife lay dead of a heart attack brought on by the stress. A daughter in shock. One son with a broken skull, the other viciously stabbed. The coldly handsome Powell was the youngest conspirator, just twenty-one years. For his burial garb, he wore the borrowed undershirt and trousers of a Union soldier.

Behind came the last two. David Herold, the Confederate courier. Age twenty-three, he was mocked as Booth's loyal dog and hapless guide through the swampy wastelands. Finally, George Atzerodt, the cowardly deserter. A drunken wretch and imbecile of thirty years who couldn't muster the courage to approach his assigned target, the vice president. Despite their sloppy appearance, at least the last two doomed men wore fearful expressions of sorrow and proper suits to their final appointment. Once all four were seated, the priests blessed them and read statements from each of the condemned. The general relayed the execution warrant.

"Mrs. Surratt is innocent," declared Lewis Powell as tears came to his eyes. "She doesn't deserve to die with the rest of us."

"May we all meet in the other world," said Atzerodt in his thick German accent. "God take me now."

The four prisoners were put to their feet and urged forward. Shoes and hats removed. Arms and legs bound with white cloths. Ropes placed around their necks. Heads covered with white hoods.

"Don't let me fall," said Mary Surratt, as she became dizzy.

The hinged ledge dropped, and the four conspirators plummeted. Surratt and Atzerodt seemed to die instantly. Powell convulsed wildly, his knees flying upward, for two minutes. Herold took the longest, slowly struggling against the noose for five minutes before his breathing ceased. The lifeless bodies were left hanging for a half hour before being cut down.

Justice had been swift, less than three months from crimes to convictions. Yet the punishments did little to end the debates that would haunt the nation for decades. Had the correct four been executed? Was Mary Surratt perhaps innocent and a victim of association, as Lewis Powell proclaimed? Then there was her son, the known Confederate spy, John Surratt. In the months and years following the assassination, he successfully evaded capture, seeming to have left his mother to die upon the scaffold in his place.

And was the justice meted out by the military tribunal actually fair or more focused on speed? A quick fix for a fuming public? After all, four other defendants had been convicted but given lesser sentences. The day after the executions, those four were en route to a remote island prison. Meanwhile, two perhaps equally guilty accomplices went entirely free in exchange for their testimony. But was their account honestly recalled or perhaps coached to obtain a desired outcome?

Worst of all, some believed John Wilkes Booth didn't really die at the hands of pursuing Union soldiers. The body brought back to Washington may have been a lookalike. The capture may have been staged by an embarrassed military after they allowed the bold assassin to murder with impunity and then slip through their fingers and flee the reunified nation.

Finally, perhaps the biggest question of all: How far did this conspiracy reach? To the ranks of the Confederate Secret Service—or even higher? One witness would claim that, upon learning that only Lincoln perished and the other two survived, the disgraced Confederate president complained the job should have been done better. Did Jefferson Davis order the assassinations?

In due course, much would be revealed, though time would always come easier than answers.

SCENE OF THE CRIME

Ford's Theatre National Historic Site preserves the building where Lincoln was assassinated. Visitors can take a self-guided walking tour through the restored interior. Timed-entry tickets are required, and reservations are recommended. The tour typically starts in a basement museum focusing on events and artifacts related to the assassination. These include the Derringer pistol Booth used in the murder and other pieces of evidence from the trial against the conspirators.

The Presidential Box has been recreated to resemble how it looked in 1865, though the interior is closed to prevent damage. Visitors can peer inside through a glass partition and view the decorated exterior from the nearby balcony and the house floor below. Ford's Theatre remains in operation and tickets are available throughout the year for various stage plays. The NPS unit continues across H Street at the Peterson House, which preserves the boardinghouse where Lincoln was carried and died the next morning.

A Syndicate Forms

It was the night of April 11, 1865, and all of Washington, DC, was aglow. Every gas and oil lamp seemed to be lit. Candles flickered in windows. Lanterns hung from ropes, and limelights cast bright spots across buildings. Bonfires flickered in the streets, while fireworks burst in the misty sky. A grand illumination, as it was called. A celebration. General Robert E. Lee had surrendered at Appomattox Court House. Jefferson Davis had fled. The tenacious Confederacy had fallen after four years of terrible war.

The White House was brilliantly lit for the occasion, casting a yellow glow across an immense crowd. They'd gathered on the North Lawn to hear Lincoln's speech. He now stood at the open second-floor window.

"We meet this evening, not in sorrow, but in gladness of heart," began the president.

He spoke briefly of the fall of Richmond, capital of the Confederacy, and the honor of General Ulysses S. Grant and his brave soldiers. Much of the speech was focused on the importance of reconstruction and welcoming the secessionist population back into the Union. For the first time, the author of the Emancipation Proclamation publicly expressed his belief that formerly enslaved freedmen be given the right to vote.

"That will be the last speech he will ever make," seethed a voice in the crowd.

It was John Wilkes Booth, who raged to his associate, Lewis Powell, about the prospect of Black citizenship. Booth was a well-dressed young man of twenty-six and a prominent and wealthy actor from a famous theatrical family. Known for energetic and athletic performances, he'd once been called the most handsome man in the nation. Both friends were Confederate sympathizers who believed that African slavery was a divine right of white Americans. Back in 1859, when the federal government executed the militant abolitionist John Brown, for his raid on the federal armory at Harpers Ferry, an enthralled Booth had snuck in to watch.

Over the last year, as the South's defeats mounted, Booth increasingly regretted not taking up arms for the cause. In October 1864, he traveled to Montreal. The

Canadian city was a hub for so many Confederate intelligence agents that it was called "Little Richmond." The particulars of this trip never came to light, but some claimed Booth met with agents and discussed a plot to kidnap President Lincoln and hold him for ransom in exchange for the release of captured Confederates. Booth sought rural contacts in southern Maryland, a swampy region filled with sympathizers, who could help him plan the operation and escape route.

Not long after Lincoln's reelection, Booth met with a country doctor named Samuel Mudd in southern Maryland. In turn, Mudd came to Washington, DC, and introduced Booth to John Surratt, a Confederate spy and courier. Until recently, John's mother Mary had operated a tavern fifteen miles southeast of the Capitol in Surrattsville, a common meeting place for sympathizers and agents. In October, for uncertain reasons, Mary had relocated to a DC townhouse on H Street that she'd inherited a few years before when her husband died.

One of the first renters at Mary Surratt's boardinghouse was Louis J. Weichmann, who'd been friends with her son since college near Baltimore. Other associates of John's regularly visited the Surratt boardinghouse. One was David Herold, a pharmacist's assistant, who knew John Surratt from military academy when they were teenagers. Another was George Atzerodt, a German-born repairman who immigrated as a child to a Maryland river town and later helped agents like John Surratt cross the Potomac River.

Into the boardinghouse fray arrived the charismatic Booth. His performances earned him a yearly income over $20,000, worth nearly three-quarters of a million dollars in the 2020s. Thus, the actor had not only the motivation but the money to attempt something decisive. Booth brought his own sympathizing associates, including childhood friends Michael O'Laughlen and Samuel Arnold. With each day, the Confederate cause seemed increasingly lost, and these radicalized compatriots grew more desperate. Something had to be done to turn the tide, and so the plan to kidnap Lincoln moved swiftly ahead.

The last to join the conspirators quickly became one of the most important. John Surratt met Lewis Powell in Baltimore when Surratt came to obtain a boat so they could transport the captured president across the Potomac. At age seventeen, Powell had lied that he was old enough to join the Florida infantry. During several years of war, he'd become a battle-hardened killer who saw fierce combat from the Peninsula to Fredericksburg and Gettysburg. Captured by the Union, he became romantically involved with his nurse, who helped him escape. Rejoining the cause, he shifted to bushwhacking raids with Mosby's Rangers. Nicknamed Lewis the Terrible, it was said he had used a slain enemy's skull for an ash tray. With the war slipping away, he deserted the front lines for smoky back rooms as a clandestine agent.

Powell took an instant liking to Booth and his nefarious scheme. Accepting an offer of funding, he made his way to DC in the early months of 1865 to plot with the others at Mary Surratt's boardinghouse.

A Change in Plans

On Friday morning, April 14, 1865, John Wilkes Booth stopped by Ford's Theatre to pick up his mail. In the ornate lobby, Booth learned from Ford's brother that Lincoln and his wife would be in attendance that night. The performance was *Our American Cousin*, a raucous comedy about an uncultured American meeting his aristocratic relatives in England. A perfect fit for the jubilant postwar atmosphere permeating the Capitol. Immediately, the fuming Booth recognized an opportunity. Not to kidnap but to kill.

The rest of the day was a flurry of preparations. Booth visited the boardinghouse several times, at one point asking Mary Surratt to deliver a package containing binoculars to her rented tavern in Surrattsville. Weichmann drove the wagon, as he'd done before in his efforts to help Booth and Surratt. Once arrived, she allegedly told the tenant, John Lloyd, to get ready the carbine rifles and ammunition previously hidden there. They'd be needed that night. Later, the testimony of these two compatriots would doom the boardinghouse owner to death.

At some point, Booth delivered a sealed letter to his friend, a fellow actor, asking that it be delivered to the *National Intelligencer* newspaper the next day. At another point, Booth stopped by the Kirkwood House, where the vice president resided when in town. Booth scrawled a curious note, with unclear intentions. Perhaps it was to ascertain Johnson's whereabouts or maybe a hasty attempt to implicate him?

"Don't wish to disturb you. Are you at home? J. Wilkes Booth"

Later in the day, Booth returned to Ford's Theatre. He sought out carpenter Edmund Spangler, who had finished readying the president's box. The older Spangler was a longtime family friend of Booth's who shared his Confederate sympathies. Perhaps now was when Booth hid a music stand bar just inside the private entryway, which he'd later use to barricade the outer door. Either way, the actor invited Spangler and his fellow stagehands for an afternoon drink at the adjacent Star Saloon. There, he explained he'd be returning for the evening performance.

Booth's final task was to inform his conspirators of the murderous new plan. At 8:45 p.m., he gathered with three of them at the Herndon House, where Powell stayed, a block from Ford's Theatre. The war was over, Booth argued, so there was nothing left to ransom for. All that remained was cutting off the Union's head in one fell swoop. Lincoln, the president. Johnson, his second. Seward, the secretary of state. In the chaotic aftermath, the South might rise again.

Booth explained that he'd laid the trap throughout the day and would use his influence at Ford's Theatre to gain entry. He might also strike down General Grant, who was said to be accompanying the first couple. At Booth's request, earlier that day, Atzerodt had booked the room directly above Johnson's at the Kirkwood House. Now the reason was laid bare. Meanwhile, Herold knew well the city and region, so he would guide Powell to the home of Seward, who was in bed recovering from a carriage accident. Powell would gain entry by presenting a bottle of medicine and saying the doctor had given special instructions for him alone to administer it. Then each would flee into the South, where they expected protection from the common folk.

Powell seemed enthused. Herold nervous but in agreement. Atzerodt briefly resisted the violent demand but acquiesced to Booth's insistence. There was clearly no time for debate. All had to make haste with little over an hour before the appointed time.

═ MONUMENTS, MUSEUMS, MEMORIALS ═

Further National Park Service sites can be found around Washington, DC, related to the events and figures from this mystery. The most famous is the Lincoln Memorial, a neoclassic temple housing a massive marble statue of the fallen president. It's found on the west end of the National Mall, which is managed by NPS and known for many popular monuments and museums worth visiting.

The Civil War Defenses of Washington are a series of NPS sites related to the Union Army's defensive fortifications surrounding the capital city during the war. The most famous is Fort Stevens, which was attacked and successfully defended in 1864. Today it has been partially reconstructed in northwest DC. Outside the city, there are several sites related to Booth's escape, including the Surratt House Museum in Clinton, Maryland, and the Mudd House Museum in Waldorf, Maryland.

A Conspiracy Unfolds

With the shortest distance to travel, Booth gathered courage at the Star Saloon with whiskey and water. Perhaps he took note that Lincoln's lone bodyguard for the evening was also in the tavern. He had left his post during intermission and never returned. Around ten minutes after ten, Booth mounted the stairs inside Ford's Theatre and emerged at the rear of the second-floor balcony. Several audience members noticed as he briefly stood on the periphery, watching the play. Eventually, he walked softly around to the outer door of the box, where Lincoln's valet sat. After presenting his calling card, the famous actor was waved inside.

Within the short hallway, Booth barred the outer door as planned. He withdrew his .44-caliber Deringer, loaded with a single shot, and cocked the hammer. He knew the play by heart and waited for the lead actor to blurt his signature response to an English lady who calls him uncivil.

"Don't know the manners of good society, eh?" said Harry Hawk. "Well, I guess I know enough to turn you inside out, old gal. You sockdolagizing old man-trap!"

When the audience erupted in laughter, Booth pushed open the inner door and stepped forward. The president was seated in a cushioned rocking chair, laughing along. The pistol was leveled at the back of Lincoln's head.

A sharp report of a gunshot echoed through the theater. The audience startled, though most assumed it was part of the act. Not so inside the box. Major Henry Rathbone and his fiancée had accepted the invitation after General Grant canceled. Now Mary Lincoln and Clara Harris screamed as they realized what had happened.

Through the smoke, Rathbone saw a man standing behind the slumped president. The major sprang from his seat and seized the shooter. Booth wrested free and drew his eight-inch dagger, thrusting the blade forward. Rathbone deflected it with his upper arm, earning himself a vicious gash. Suddenly, blood was everywhere.

Booth dashed for the front of the box, and Rathbone's grasping hands caught only clothing.

In an instant, Booth vaulted the railing and leapt from the twelve-foot height. As he fell, the riding spur on his boot caught a U.S. Treasury flag that decorated the exterior of the box. Booth landed awkwardly and stumbled but quickly righted himself.

"*Sic semper tyrannis!*" Booth shouted, brandishing his bloody dagger. "The South is avenged."

The audience was in shock. Some people recognized the famous actor as he ran off stage and out a back door. Others immediately understood Booth's Latin words, the Virginia state motto, "Thus always to tyrants."

Two military doctors were in attendance. One rushed to the barred door, which Rathbone soon opened. Another doctor was lifted by the crowd to the railing. Lincoln was alive, but barely breathing. A quick examination identified a bullet hole with little blood in the back of the skull. The wound was deemed mortal. The doctors organized a party to carry Lincoln from the theater into the street. Outside, the postwar celebratory mood had already evaporated, replaced by a pensive silence. Word had spread quickly through the streets. The party carried the fallen president over to the Peterson House. Inside a rear bedroom, Lincoln was placed diagonally so his tall frame might fit the bed.

All through the night, the president lingered. His grief-stricken wife and eldest son were often at his bedside. The president's physician, the surgeon general, and the two responding doctors took shifts attending him. The highest members of the U.S. government descended on the home. Upon entering the room to pay their respects, they often fell into deep, inconsolable sobbing. Abraham Lincoln breathed his last at twenty-two minutes after seven in the morning.

During the night, Secretary of War Edwin Stanton had occupied the front drawing room, from where he directed the pursuit of Booth and his accomplices. A coordinated conspiracy was unraveling before his eyes, and the full might of the military would respond in kind. Upon learning that Lincoln had expired, some said Stanton offered a powerful epitaph:

"He now belongs to the ages."

A Hero or a Madman

From Ford's Theatre, Booth rode his horse south. At the Navy Yard Bridge, he was stopped by a Union soldier. Martial law remained in effect, and civilians were forbidden to cross after 9:00 p.m. The convincing actor talked his way past the sentry. Less than an hour later, David Herold was also allowed to cross. The two conspirators soon reunited in Maryland and rode to the Surratt Tavern. The tenant John Lloyd later gave testimony about their visit, saying they collected a carbine rifle and field glasses. Booth remained on his horse, drinking whiskey, when he shared the news. He was pretty certain they had assassinated Lincoln.

Around 4:00 a.m., the conspirators reached Dr. Samuel Mudd's home, where

Booth sought medical treatment. His fibula, the smaller bone in the lower leg, had been broken, supposedly from landing on the stage. Mudd set the bone and splinted it, providing a custom boot and crutches. Booth paid the doctor. It's unclear how much the men told Mudd and when he learned the kidnapping plot had turned to assassination. Booth and Herold stayed and slept for some hours, likely leaving after dark on Saturday evening. Mudd kept quiet until Sunday when he asked his cousin to alert the authorities. During his first two interviews, Mudd repeatedly misled investigators about his relationship with Booth. This, along with witness testimony about his involvement with John Surratt, later led to his conviction and life sentence.

Over the following week, a series of local sympathizers and Confederate agents helped Booth and Herold move south toward the Potomac. Sometimes the fugitives claimed to be Confederate soldiers. Occasionally, they admitted their true identities. Near the river, they spent several days hiding in a pine thicket inside Zekiah Swamp. On the night of the twentieth, they retrieved a hidden boat and tried to cross the foggy Potomac. After veering off course, they landed upstream in Maryland. The following night, they finally succeeded in crossing the river. Then they hid at farms as they progressed further into Virginia.

By now, the largest manhunt in U.S. history was underway. In addition to federal troops, private citizens took to the search spurred by vengeance and rewards, including an unprecedented $100,000 for Booth. Newspapers, passed to the assassin throughout his escape, reported massive crowds of mourners descending on Washington, DC, to view the embalmed Lincoln in his casket. A funeral train was being prepared to embark on a 1,700-mile procession across the grieving nation.

Instead of being hailed as a hero, like Booth had expected, he was labeled a madman and a monster. He believed that the cunning manifesto he'd authored would absolve him. Therefore, he reasoned, the newspapers were refusing to print it out of spite. In reality, when Booth's friend had opened the letter and read its contents, he had fearfully burned it.

Even prominent citizens across the South were publicly expressing sorrow.

Yes, Lincoln had been their sworn enemy, but the horror of the attacks was beyond the pale. The shame of losing the war was now augmented by a fear of northern retribution. Many of the same newspapers that once pilloried Lincoln now offered condolences and conciliation.

Adding to the insults, four of Booth's coconspirators had already been arrested. During a nighttime search of the H Street boardinghouse, far more was discovered than evidence of sympathizing. Federal agents were inside the house when the bell rang. The agents answered the door to find on the step a suspicious man with a pickax. He claimed he was an itinerant ditch digger hired by Mary Surratt, but the situation suggested otherwise. The hour was late. The man strangely wore his own torn shirt sleeve as a stocking cap disguise. His hands were uncalloused and his boots expensive.

It was Lewis Powell. After stabbing Seward, he had hid for three days on the outskirts of the unfamiliar city. The federal agents called Mary Surratt into the brightly lit hallway. From less than three paces, the boardinghouse owner repeatedly swore she'd never met the man before.

Both were taken into custody. When Powell later declared the woman's innocence from the scaffold, some felt he sought to atone for his foolish return that implicated her. A few days later, Atzerodt was captured. Despite fleeing from the Kirkwood House as a failed assassin, the hapless accomplice had left behind a trail of evidence. A loaded revolver under the pillow, plus a large bowie knife, a map of Virginia, and a bank book belonging to J. W. Booth.

"The country is not what it was," ranted Booth in his diary during the flight. "This forced union is not what I have loved. I care not for what becomes of me. I have no desire to out-live my country."

Prophetic Words

Acting on tips from a series of witnesses, around 2:00 a.m. on April 26, a detachment of New York cavalry soldiers surrounded the Garrett family's tobacco barn near Port Royal, Virginia. Their orders were to take the assassin alive. Peering through the gaps between planks, the soldiers spotted a man pacing inside. Another seemed to be standing in shadows. Eventually, an officer issued a demand to surrender. Booth retorted that he had but one working leg. Instead, the soldiers should withdraw, so that he and the captain could fight an honorable duel. When this request was twice refused, Booth responded in his theatrical voice.

"Well, my brave boys, prepare a stretcher for me!"

David Herold soon surrendered and came out, naïvely believing he'd done little wrong and would be freed. Booth lingered inside, supported by a crutch. The commanding officer's decision was to burn the barn. As the flames rapidly spread, Booth dropped his crutch and moved frantically about. He tried but failed to stomp out the fire. Still holding the rifle, he moved toward the door. The crack of a pistol was followed by Booth collapsing. Believing the assassin was turning to fight, a soldier had fired a single shot, which struck him in the neck. A dying Booth was carried to the nearby farmhouse, where he was laid atop a straw mattress on the porch.

"Tell mother I die for my country," he said at one point.

Like the president he had slain, Booth lingered for hours. The bullet had impacted his spinal cord, and he was paralyzed. After three hours, his breaths became increasingly labored. He asked for his hands to be raised in front of his face, so that he could see what he couldn't feel. Then John Wilkes Booth muttered his final words: "Useless, useless."

Lingering Doubts

The assassin's corpse was taken by wagon and boat up the Potomac to the docked ironclad USS *Montauk* in Washington City. Before the autopsy, an inquest was held to confirm the identity. At least ten individuals who could recognize the famous actor during his life agreed it was Booth. These included a doctor who had removed a tumor from his neck in 1863. When the wound didn't heal properly, it left a nasty scar. Like a morbid premonition, Booth had repeatedly lied to friends that it was from an old bullet wound. Other examiners included a dentist who recognized two fillings in Booth's teeth. A clerk at the National Hotel, where Booth frequently stayed, recognized the neck scar, his vest, and a small tattoo near the wrist. Just three letters: J.W.B.

The body was in poor condition. The skin was yellowed and freckling from decomposition. The hair was matted and the face gaunt from weight loss during twelve days on the run. Booth had made some minor efforts to conceal himself, including trimming his hair and mustache and starting a beard. Each of the ten examiners agreed the mangled corpse was John Wilkes Booth. Still, doubts would linger and even grow for generations, especially after a single postmortem photograph—both the plate and print—vanished without a trace.

The military tribunal commenced only a few weeks later. An onslaught of 371 witnesses filed into the smoky courtroom at the Washington Arsenal. Their testimony began just three days after the defendants were offered legal counsel, which almost guaranteed the result. The prosecutors had two objectives: prove the guilt of Booth's compatriots and link the conspiracy to the Confederate government and its leader, the recently captured Jefferson Davis. Despite the questionable practices of the court, and with the exception of Mary Surratt, many contemporaries felt the evidence was overwhelming against those conspirators who were sentenced to death.

The day after the executions, the remaining four were sent to an island prison in the Gulf of Mexico. Fort Jefferson in the Dry Tortugas off the southern tip of Florida. Edmund Spangler was the only defendant found not guilty of conspiracy. He had clearly helped Booth at Ford's Theatre, though he seemed unaware of the assassin's intentions. One audience member testified that, after the shooting, Spangler let Booth run right past him. Most observers believed Spangler innocent. Some joked he got six years hard labor for holding a horse.

The other three received life sentences. Two years after their arrival at Garden Key, there was an outbreak of yellow fever. Michael O'Laughlen died from the disease, as did the prison doctor. Samuel Mudd took over the job. For his efforts during the crisis, he won the admiration of the fort's soldiers. They petitioned for a pardon from President Johnson, who granted one for all three in 1869.

Conspirator John Surratt remained at large for several years after his mother was executed. Using various aliases and disguises, he fled from Canada to Europe and Egypt, where he was caught by U.S. officials and extradited home. The Supreme Court had since ruled that a military tribunal was unconstitutional when civilian courts were operating. So, the former rebel agent was finally tried in a Maryland court for his role in the murder plot. The nation's mood had calmed since those frenzied and fearful days in the spring of 1865. The result was a split jury, and John Surratt went free.

A SUBTROPICAL FORT

Today, the prison where the four inmates were sent is located in Dry Tortugas National Park, which protects a chain of coral islands west of the Florida Keys. Built in the 1860s to protect U.S. shipping routes, Fort Jefferson is a massive redbrick fortress rising three stories above the translucent waters of the Gulf of Mexico. Only about 75,000 people visit the park each year due to limited space on the daily ferry from Key West. Tickets often sell out months ahead, though charter boats and float planes are also available. Once on the island, visitors can explore the hexagonal fort, wander the empty beaches, and snorkel along the defensive walls.

An Incomplete Job

During the 1865 military tribunal, both prosecutors and their witnesses made many damning claims about the role of the Confederate government and their nefarious secret agents. The secessionist president, Jefferson Davis, had finally been captured. Now they sought to link him to Lincoln's murder. However, little to no evidence emerged. The most damaging witnesses turned out to have lied, either to curry favors or punish the opposing side.

A network of around eleven conspirators had been exposed. The assassin, the fugitive, seven convicts, and two lucky witnesses who were granted immunity. However, repeated clues and red herrings suggested to many there was wider involvement beyond those already identified. A scrap of testimony. A line in a confession. A rediscovered document or letter.

Regarding Jefferson Davis, the evidence was limited to rumors and hearsay. Lewis Bates, a North Carolina railroad superintendent, testified he was present in Charlotte when Davis received a general's telegram with news of Lincoln's assassination. According to Bates, Davis read the telegram aloud and then said something to this effect: "If it were to be done, it were better that it were well done."

Some observers have suggested this is a rough paraphrase of a Shakespeare line, spoken by Macbeth, when he's debating whether to murder King Duncan of Scotland. "If it were done when 'tis done, then 'twere well / It were done quickly." But if so, did these words come from Davis or did Bates invent them? A few days later, in Charlotte, Bates claimed to overhear a conversation between Davis and one of his generals, who believed Lincoln's murder would be unfortunate for the people of the South.

"Well, General, I don't know," is how Davis responded, according to Bates. The former president reiterated his original response and added, "If the same were done to Andy Johnson, the beast, and to Secretary Stanton, the job would then be complete."

A Spy or a Cipher?

More loose ends would follow. In a rambling confession recorded by a detective, George Atzerodt claimed that Booth was racing to assassinate Lincoln before a rival group succeeded. Supposedly, agents in New York were planning to bomb the Executive Mansion.

Atzerodt went on to describe a mysterious confederate spy named Kate

Thompson or Kate Brown, who went by several names and knew all about the affair. He described her as an attractive young woman of twenty with black hair and eyes. Weichmann's testimony revealed that Mrs. Surratt had called her Slater. A blockade runner and dispatch courier from North Carolina who traveled from Washington to Richmond to Canada. She spoke French, which she used to conceal herself, along with a black veil. Investigators tried to discover who she was but failed. She left Washington sometime before the assassination and was never seen again. Some called her the Veiled Lady, though her name was said to be Sarah Slater.

When it came to John Wilkes Booth, that the assassin died seemed certain. But he took several mysteries to the grave surrounding two personal effects. Before he expired at the Garretts' farm, numerous items were collected. His rifle and revolver. Two daggers and a compass. Of particular note was an appointment book, used as a diary. Booth had written five pages of entries during his twelve-day escape. The diary was never admitted into evidence during the trial. It went missing for several years, before turning up in 1867 in a file at the War Department. By now, at least eighteen pages immediately preceding Booth's escape entries had been cut out. What might those pages have revealed and who removed them? Some posit the diary contained a confession listing the true nature of the conspiracy, although the pages may have simply been used by Booth for notepaper.

A final enigmatic item was found during a search of Booth's room at the National Hotel. Among his papers was a cipher table, also called a Vigenère square. During the trial, prosecutors called it a Confederate cipher, claiming it matched a method used by Richmond officials to communicate with rebel spies. An opposing view points out that this was a simple encryption method commonly used at the time, even by children.

It was a single page, written in Booth's own hand. A grid of alphabetic letters used to encode and decode secret messages. Perhaps it was a spy's sheet? Or perhaps it was a final piece of theatrics left behind by a troubled thespian, a self-declared spy who believed himself to be the savior of the republic from a horrible tyrant.

And perhaps those endless claims of a top-down conspiracy were more about those who lived than about justice for a president who died. Booth and his accomplices were bold, yes. But otherwise, they were a sloppy and impulsive clutch of assassins. Many great men, stoic soldiers, and government officials were not just enraged but embarrassed and looking to save face. The truth about whether Booth and his boys were egged on by Jefferson Davis's agents will likely remain in the shadows.

Few facts remain. Abraham Lincoln, the nation's celebrated savior, was struck dead by the bullet of a ruthless assassin. John Wilkes Booth's name will forever live in infamy—not as a spy, but as a murderous brute who threw away a life and a career and the love of the people. So useless. Useless.

An artistic depiction of the assassination of President Lincoln by J. Wilkes Booth, based upon a work by T. M. McAllister, that was made during the decade after the event. Lincoln assassination slide, 1900, unattributed/Public Domain

CHAPTER 35

COULD A KAYAKER SURVIVE NIAGARA FALLS?

BAFFLING DISAPPEARANCES

NIAGARA FALLS NATIONAL HERITAGE AREA

WESTERN NEW YORK, UNITED STATES–CANADA BORDER

Sightseers on shore gasped when they spotted a kayaker in the rapids upstream. They were watching from the railing of the pedestrian walkway on the Canadian side of Niagara Falls. Named for its semicircular shape, Horseshoe Falls was essentially an amphitheater of rushing waters plunging 180 feet into a misting whirlpool below. Now a lone paddler, in a long red kayak, was threading his way atop a jet of swift current toward the center of the brink.

As onlookers gathered, shouting and pointing, the kayaker lifted his yellow-bladed paddle over his head and twirled it like a lasso. It was Tuesday, June 5, 1990, and the daredevil was Jesse Sharp from Tennessee. Approaching the drop, he made several paddle strokes to stay straight. The bow of his boat dipped as he reached the brink. The stern briefly lifted out of the water and reflected the glare of the sun.

After over a decade of dreaming about this moment, Sharp was suddenly falling over the edge of Niagara Falls. His boat went nearly vertical and sank into the churning curtain of whitewater, leaving only his head and torso visible. Then his body disappeared, followed by his paddle blade. A few glimpses of color tumbled into the maelstrom and vanished. For several minutes, onlookers scanned the boils and froth in the pool below, but nothing surfaced. Jesse Sharp was gone.

WATERFALLS AND MORE

Niagara Falls is famous for three waterfalls on the international border of the United States and Canada. The largest is the iconic Horseshoe Falls, mostly located in Ontario, on the eastern Canadian side. Here, 90 percent of the Niagara River plunges over a U-shaped drop, falling 180 feet into a tumult of rising mist.

American Falls and its smaller neighbor, Bridal Veil Falls, are found in New York state, on the western U.S. side. These two falls, each about a hundred feet in height, together carry about 10 percent of the Niagara River's flow, before landing on a boulder slope next to the main channel.

Most visitors focus on viewing opportunities. Paths and platforms are found throughout the area. Tour boats ply the waters below. Tunnels lead behind the falls. The Skylon Tower and SkyWheel rise above. While much of Niagara Falls has a city and theme park vibe, a series of outdoor and historical highlights may appeal to national park travelers.

A Plan to Succeed

Eleven years before, Sharp had strapped his kayak to the roof of his car and drove to upstate New York. After three seasons of paddling increasingly challenging rapids around the Southeast, the eighteen-year-old was considering something much bigger. He stopped by the United Press International office in downtown Buffalo to see if they might want to cover the endeavor. There he met photographer Eric Demme and reporter Tom Campbell.

"What makes you think you can go over Niagara Falls in a kayak?" asked the skeptical Demme.

The young man explained that if he built up enough speed before going over the lip, he could propel his kayak outward from the falling water and avoid being crushed at the bottom. The two older men convinced him to sleep on it. Then they contacted his folks in Nashville, who came the next day and brought him home. While Sharp may have walked away that time, he never gave up on the idea.

A recent graduate of Hillsboro High, Sharp went on to attend the University of Tennessee. Afterward, he joined the U.S. Army and was stationed with an infantry unit in Louisiana and South Korea. In 1989, he was discharged and went back to his home state. He spent the following two summers living in a tent next to the Ocoee River, known for its tumbling class III and IV rapids. With the Ocoee as his base, Sharp began extensively training for, and talking about, his plan to run Niagara Falls.

Technically, Sharp wasn't actually a kayaker but a white-water canoer. For the attempt, his boat would be a state-of-the-art Perception Gyra Max. Just under thirteen feet long, this plastic decked canoe was nearly identical to a kayak, but it was paddled while kneeling using a single-bladed paddle, not a double. In this boat, called a C-1, Sharp ran laps not only at the Ocoee but on increasingly steep rivers and creeks throughout the Appalachians. According to other whitewater boaters, Jesse launched himself off waterfalls that were thirty, forty, even sixty feet in height. However, none of these practice hucks could rival the 180 feet of Horseshoe Falls, about eighty feet taller than the highest drop ever kayaked at the time.

A DIFFERENT TYPE OF PARK

Designated by Congress in 2008, the Niagara Falls National Heritage Area is a collection of natural, historical, cultural, and recreational sites mostly following the river corridor for a dozen miles from Niagara Falls to Old Fort Niagara. Unlike national parks and other NPS units, over sixty National Heritage Areas in the United States are not composed of federally owned and managed lands. Instead, NPS assumes an advisory role to help state and local entities manage the typically disconnected sites found throughout a wider region.

Where Might He Land?

By mid-1990, Sharp decided he was ready. With three whitewater friends, he arrived in the city of Niagara Falls, Ontario, on Monday, June 5. As the four boaters walked toward Horseshoe Falls, a plume of mist rose high into the air. From different vantage points along the pedestrian walkway, Sharp scouted out the line he would take down the river and over the edge.

From a whitewater paddler's perspective, a waterfall could be broken down into a few different features. The entry above the drop. The lip, where the flow began to plummet. And the curtain of falling water. Along the lip of the falls, there were occasional promontories in the underlying bedrock. These created jets of turbulent water that protruded from the rest of the curtain. At the bottom of the falls, these various sheets and jets thunderously recirculated in piles of churning water. This recirculation zone was a dangerous spot in any powerful rapid because it could trap a paddler, turbulently spinning them underwater for lengthy periods of time.

Based on lessons learned in the Southeast, Sharp's plan was to launch off one such promontory, about a third of the way around the falls from the Canadian walkway. Hopefully, he would catch one of these jets as well. The combined momentum would ideally land him on the downstream side of the recirculating piles, and he would be flushed away from the curtain. After rolling up, he would paddle downriver for four miles through the class V+ rapids of the Niagara Gorge, including the circular Whirlpool Basin, with its swirling currents.

The rest of the day was logistics. With his friends, Sharp shuttled his car to the take-out in Lewiston, New York, leaving his wallet and keys inside. Returning to the Canadian side, he waited until after dark. Then he hid his kayak and gear under a tarp by the river. He even made dinner reservations for Tuesday night, to celebrate a world record as the first person to kayak over Niagara Falls.

Should Sharp make it, he would certainly become famous, though he wouldn't be the first person known to survive purposefully going over the falls. That distinction went to Annie Edson Taylor, a sixty-three-year-old schoolteacher from Michigan who sought celebrity to pay for her retirement. In 1901, she survived inside a wooden barrel, emerging below the falls with minor bleeding from a three-inch head wound.

"I would rather face a cannon, knowing that I would be blown to pieces, than go over the falls again," she woozily told a reporter.

Copycats in similar barrels soon followed. Some succeeded while others failed. The year before Sharp's 1990 attempt, a pair had gone over in a two-man reinforced steel barrel. Their dubious reason, they claimed, was to discourage kids from doing drugs. They became the eighth and ninth people known to survive the falls. A few months later, the Canadian government tried to discourage further attempts by raising the fine for going over the falls from $500 to $10,000.

Despite the occasional survivor, most people who went over the falls were killed by drowning or blunt-force trauma. Some were swept over accidentally after falling into the river from boats or shore. Others leapt purposefully, seeking suicide or thrills. Should Sharp fail, he would join thousands of other victims, with an average of roughly three dozen fatalities per year.

═══ **HERITAGE MEETS ADVENTURE** ═══

Within the National Heritage Area, a series of historic state parks offer walking paths and hiking trails around the falls and through the infamous Niagara Gorge, with its powerful rapids like the Niagara Whirlpool and Devil's Hole. Where the Niagara River empties into Lake Ontario, Old Fort Niagara was built in 1726 to protect the overseas territory of New France. The so-called French Castle is the two-story centerpiece of Fort Niagara State Park, while a series of paths lead beyond the defensive walls through the surrounding grounds.

A Few Signs Emerge

Shortly after 1:00 p.m., Jesse Sharp pushed off into the Niagara River. He was bare-chested, purposefully forgoing his life jacket. He hoped this might allow him to sink below the recirculating piles and be swept downstream by fast currents that typically lurk below waterfalls. Sharp also left behind his helmet, figuring it wouldn't help much anyway. Plus, it would obscure his face in the photos and videotape that his friends were shooting from shore.

Sharp deftly navigated through ledge rapids. He passed around a series of low diversion dikes designed to funnel water toward the main attraction—the dramatic center of Horseshoe Falls. Sharp passed a small island where the wreckage of a steel scow had become lodged in rocks during 1918. When the paddler was a half mile from the edge, authorities spotted him from shore.

Operators at the International Control Dam, located a mile upstream, quickly lowered the water being released. But this had little if any effect. Sharp had already passed most exposed river rocks, and he was zooming at five miles per hour through a swift channel of deeper water. After twirling his paddle over his head,

Sharp made a series of strong strokes to keep his line straight and build speed. Then he went over.

"He didn't shoot out at all," said Staff Sergeant Fred Hollidge of the Niagara Parks Police. "He just dropped like a ton of bricks."

The spectators were shocked. They watched and waited for any sign, good or bad. Slowly, the crowds of incredulous onlookers dispersed. Far fewer were watching after ten minutes, when Sharp's paddle floated to the surface. The yellow blade and blue shaft were intact. About an hour later, his red C-1 surfaced near the dock for the *Maid of the Mist* sightseeing boat.

The Niagara Parks Police inspected the boat. Despite the ride, it showed minimal damage other than some scuffs and small dents. The spare paddle was still lashed to the deck. A plastic flotation bag was found inside. Even Sharp's blue neoprene spray skirt was still loosely attached, connected to the cockpit rim using small strings and screws—a makeshift rig designed to reinforce the skirt from implosion upon impact. All signs pointed to Sharp being wrenched from the boat underwater. Authorities claimed the body might not surface for weeks.

═══════ SEE THE SPOT ═══════

If you want to see where Jesse Sharp plunged over Niagara Falls, grab your passport and head to the Canadian side. The paved pedestrian path and platforms between the river and Niagara Parkway offer the best views. This is where the infamous series of photographs were taken that document Sharp's attempt.

A Fearless Return?

Within a few years, daredevils resumed their efforts at Niagara Falls. Most of them went over in barrels, but occasionally someone tried something different. In 1995, a thirty-nine-year-old aspiring stuntman from Southern California rode toward the brink on a jet ski bearing the words SAVE THE HOMELESS. On his back was a parachute. Some claimed it had been customized with a rocket designed to propel the thrill-seeker safely away from the falls before the chute opened and carried him to safety. As the jet ski dropped away beneath him, Robert Overacker jumped. He flew forward with his arms and legs spread. His parachute failed, and his lifeless body was pulled from the waters by crew members aboard the *Maid of the Mist*.

Jesse Sharp's body, however, was never seen again. The impact alone might have killed him or at least knocked him unconscious. Perhaps his head was slammed against the front or back deck of the boat. Even with a helmet, the chances of survival seemed slim. If Sharp did stay conscious upon landing, next came the underwater maelstrom. His paddle was seemingly held for ten minutes. A recirculating person would drown much quicker. The vast majority of observers believed that he had died.

Yet among some whitewater boaters around the Southeast, it was rumored that Sharp had survived. One might see his name spray-painted on an outhouse or overpass. They might hear stories about kayakers who claimed to have been scouting on shore when a solitary paddler passed through a rapid, twirling his paddle before disappearing out of sight. Or raft guides on famous rivers, like the Zambezi in Africa, might claim they saw an object swept over 350-foot Victoria Falls. They would initially assume it was a log or a croc, only to realize afterward it was a fearless C-boater.

Over the following decades, the sport of extreme kayaking progressed. Taller and taller waterfalls were successfully run, eventually surpassing the height of Horseshoe Falls. In 2009, professional kayaker Tyler Bradt set a world record by hucking off 189-foot Palouse Falls in Washington. No one since Sharp has tried paddling over the dangerously retentive Niagara Falls, though some have considered it before walking away. In the meantime, around the Southeast, affixed to rusty vehicles with old-school kayaks on the roof, one might spot the occasional faded bumper sticker offering a different version of events: JESSE LIVES.

CASE FILES & SOURCES

A Note from the Author

This book presents dramatized but true shortform stories about mysteries that are closely related to units of the National Park Service. As a result, *Mysteries of the National Parks* is a work of narrative nonfiction that is based on verifiable facts, and it is not a scholarly work of history. My primary goal is to bring these mysteries to life *on the page*. Each chapter touches on a secondary objective by suggesting ways to further bring the mystery to life *on the ground* by visiting the corresponding sites and parks.

To faithfully dramatize these historical events into shortform stories, I have called upon a wide variety of source materials. Primary sources include contemporaneous newspaper articles, official reports, trial transcripts, diary entries, witness accounts, photographs, drawings, videos, maps, and more. Secondary sources include peer-reviewed journal articles, scholarly books, academic studies, opinion pieces, and more. A third source of material and insight comes from my own experiences visiting many of the national park units and settings featured in this book.

The sources used for each story are listed in this section by chapter. It's important to note that reconstructing the mysteries involved several challenges. There are often major gaps in historical records, particularly in stories about hidden histories. While each mystery is rooted in fact, evolving myths have often become the dominant version of events, and this is particularly true for legendary figures.

With all mysteries, but especially baffling disappearances and infamous crimes, the source materials can include conflicting witness accounts and questions about reliability. There are mysteries in which contemporary and later observers have speculated that witnesses or authors may be outright lying or partly exaggerating to advance their own agendas. In the case of unexplained phenomena and other chapters, the mysteries can be concealed within dense scientific papers and academic debates.

When possible, I have tried to point out these information gaps, theories, debates, and controversies about fact versus fiction within the stories. However, I also had to temper a desire to exhaustively catalog all relevant information with condensing the materials into stories of suitable length. While writing this book, there were times when my entire office looked like a detective's bulletin board. Scattered papers and books were filled with notes about obscure clues and meandering arrows pointing to fuzzy images. But to produce stories of several thousand words per mystery, I often had to cut or summarize important developments and major events.

To share how the mysteries were dramatized into shortform stories, I have included a short essay about each chapter—a case file. These case files discuss how sources were used, including where quoted dialogue was found, how details were obtained, and how facts were verified. Within the stories, I have tried to keep authorial intrusion and my own theories to a minimum. In the case files, I occasionally elaborate upon my reasoning and further theories behind the mysteries. Essentially, the case files provide a behind-the-scenes glimpse into my efforts to reconstruct the mysteries of the national parks. I hope readers have as much fun learning about these mysteries from their favorite parks as I have had unraveling them.

CASE FILE #1

Did Kenneth Arnold Spot the First Flying Saucer?

When I was growing up, my mom and I loved to watch *The X Files* on TV. The stories were set across the country and world, but the first five seasons were mostly filmed in British Columbia, and sometimes amid rugged outdoor settings. It was this moody mix of mystery and oddity, puzzling adventures in wild landscapes, and science crossed with futuristic invention, that I wanted to create in this book. But with one major difference: the reconstructed stories in *Mysteries of the National Parks* dramatize historical events and scientific discoveries instead of transforming fact into fiction.

The opening scenes depicting Kenneth Arnold's sighting, and subsequent scenes dramatizing his experiences, come mostly from his 1952 book coauthored with Raymond Palmer, plus many statements Arnold made that were published in news articles during the days following the events. Later interviews were also essential, particularly with radioman Ed Murrow (1950).

Maps of the regions related to the sightings were examined, and photos and imagery were also useful, especially those found in the Project Blue Book file on Arnold's sighting, declassified around 1963. This includes drawings by Arnold, hired artists, and investigators that depict the objects he saw near Mount Rainier.

In addition to those primary sources, the words of Bill Bequette were closely studied, including his short AP dispatch and longer article (both June 26, 1947), which provide the direct quotes in my reconstructed story. Also helpful were Bequette's 1988 interview with LaGrange (published 1998), and retrospectives by Denson (1997) and Wright (2017), the latter of which includes an interview with Arnold's daughter.

Descriptions of the spreading worldwide phenomenon come from surveying 1947 news articles, especially those in the *New York Times.* The quote of Byron Savage comes from an AP article printed in the *Seattle Times* (June 26, 1947). Some of the more humorous encounters, including the Chicago circular saw, come from Schumach (July 8, 1947).

Scenes from the Flight 105 sighting and the experiences of Emil "Big Smithy" Smith come from numerous sources, including Heil (1947), Eustace's army report (1947), Ladd's FBI report, and Arnold (1952). The latter book provides the dialogue attributed to Big Smithy and the flight attendant, with the coauthors implying it is a narration of the pilot's account. As the story takes increasingly bizarre turns, the four sources listed here provide the majority of source material.

The *Tacoma Times* article, alleging a conspiracy to down the B-25, is reprinted in Arnold (1952) and other sources. The summary and analysis of the Roswell incident comes from numerous sources, including Schumach (July 9, 1947), Denson (1997), and Bloecher (1967). The latter article also informs the conclusion in the chapter, along with details from my examination of many individual incident reports from Project Blue Book, including "Mt. Rainier, Washington, 24 June, 1947," and "Boise, Idaho, 4 July 1947," plus the summary and conclusions document (1966).

Regarding Fred Crisman, well, I went down the rabbit hole. Some theorists claim he's the point man for numerous conspiracies in American history. Not only did Crisman allege that the Maury Island incident was a military cover-up, but the dude claimed he battled supernatural cave dwellers in Burma during World War II. Later, his name was linked to the assassination of President John F. Kennedy. With diminishing public confidence in the limited 1963 conclusions of the Warren Commission, Congress ordered a follow-up investigation in 1976. On page ninety-one of their second report is a discussion of a now-infamous figure (with minor typo): Fred Lee Chrisman.

After examining these vast swaths of source materials, I concur with other skeptics who believe the key to unraveling much of the mystery surrounding the 1947 UFO craze lies in understanding world events and public attitudes of the era. The most destructive and violent war in human history had ended just two years before, with the catastrophic detonations of two atomic bombs. Already the next war was on the horizon with the world's other victorious superpower and the West's ideological adversary, the Soviet Union. For now, it was being called a cold war, but many Americans feared it would turn hot with nuclear weapons being directed at the U.S. mainland. Classified aircraft, missiles, rockets, and balloons were being tested in the skies, and they sometimes veered off course and crashed. With everyone anxiously watching the skies for clues to the future, and signs of attack, conditions were primed for a mass panic. The results would linger for decades.

Yet not all sightings can be explained. The situation continues to this day, amplified by recent admissions by the U.S. military during congressional inquiries. Whether witnesses are spotting experimental spy drones or grainy videos are capturing unknown atmospheric phenomena, a mystery in our skies lingers. To paraphrase *The X Files*, something is out there.

Sources

Arnold, Kenneth, and Raymond Palmer. *The Coming of the Saucers*. Originally published 1952. Reprinted online by Global Grey eBooks, 2018. www.globalgreyebooks.com/coming-of-the-saucers-ebook.html.

Associated Press. "Boise Flyer Backed by Observers." *Seattle Times*, June 26, 1947.

Associated Press. "Military Planes Hunt Sky Discs with Cameras in Vain on Coast." July 6, 1947.

Bequette, Bill. "Boise Flyer Maintains He Saw 'Em." *East Oregonian*, June 26, 1947.

Bequette, Bill, credited as Associated Press. "Supersonic Flying Saucers Sighted by Idaho Pilot." *Chicago Sun*, June 26, 1947.

Bloecher, Ted. "Report on the Wave of 1947." Originally published 1967. Updated by National Investigations Committee on Aerial Phenomena. Accessed July 3, 2022. http://kirkmcd.princeton.edu/JEMcDonald/bloecher_67.pdf.

Denson, Bryan, and Jim Long. "Fifty Years of UFO, the Truth Is Still Out There." *Oregonian*, June 22, 1997. www.oregonlive.com/history/2015/05/1997_story_fifty_years_of_ufo.html.

Eustace, Hal L. Report on "Flying Saucer" Reports in Pacific Northwest for 732nd Base Unit, 102nd AACS Squadron, U.S. Army Air Corps, Tacoma, Washington, 26 July 1947.

"'Flying Discs' Fail to Stir Air Forces." *New York Times*, July 3, 1947.

Garber, Megan. "The Man Who Introduced the World to Flying Saucers." *Atlantic*, June 15, 2014. www.theatlantic.com/technology/archive/2014/06/the-man-who-introduced-the-world-to-flying-saucers/372732.

Godlewski, Meg. "A Commando Entombed on Mount Rainier." *Flying* magazine, December 10, 2021. www.flyingmag.com/a-commando-entombed-on-mount-rainier.

Heil, Henry. "'Flying Discs' Called Real by Two Air Veterans." *Chicago Times*, July 7, 1947.

Lacitis, Erik. "First Man to See 'Flying Saucers' Tells It Right." *Seattle Times*, June 25, 1977.

Lacitis, Erik. "'Flying Saucers' Became a Thing 70 Years Ago Saturday with Sighting Near Mount Rainier." *Seattle Times*, June 24, 2017. www.seattletimes.com/seattle-news/northwest/flying-saucers-became-a-thing-70-years-ago-saturday-with-sighting-near-mount-rainier/.

Ladd, D. M. Report to the Director on "Flying Discs." Federal Bureau of Investigation. August 14, 1947.

Lagrange, Pierre. "A Moment in History: An Interview with Bill Bequette." *International UFO Reporter*, Winter 1998.

Lagrange, Pierre. "'It Seems Impossible, But There It Is.'" *Phenomenon: From Flying Saucers to UFOs— Forty Years of Facts and Research.* Edited by John Spencer and Hilary Evans. Macdonald & Co., 1988. 26–45.

Lee, Russell. "1947: Year of the Flying Saucer." National Air and Space Museum. June 24, 2022. https://airandspace.si.edu/stories/editorial/1947-year-flying-saucer.

Murrow, Edward R. "Transcript of Ed Murrow-Kenneth Arnold Telephone Conversation." Transcribed by Project 1947. Accessed June 26, 2022. www.project1947.com/fig/kamurrow.htm.

New York Times. "Those Flying Saucers." July 6, 1947. https://www.nytimes.com/1947/07/06/archives /those-flying-saucers.html.

Schumach, Murray. "'Disk' Near Bomb Test Site Is Just a Weather Balloon." *New York Times*, July 9, 1947. www.nytimes.com/1947/07/09/archives/-disk-near-bomb-test-site-is-just-a-weather -balloon-warrant-officer.html.

Schumach, Murray. "'Disks' Soar over New York, Now Seen Aloft in All Colors." *New York Times*, July 8, 1947.

Select Comm. on Assassinations. "Final Report of the Select Committee on Assassinations." United States House of Representatives Report No. 95–1828, pt. 2. January 2, 1979. https://ia800903.us .archive.org/9/items/reportofselectco1979unit/reportofselectco1979unit.pdf.

"Supersonic Plane Seen in Few Years." *New York Times*, November 16, 1947. www.nytimes.com/1947 /11/16/archives/supersonic-plane-seen-in-few-years-new-skyrocket-completed-for-navy.html.

U.S. Air Force. "Project Blue Book." February 1, 1966.

Wright, Phil. "The Sighting." *East Oregonian*, June 16, 2017. www.eastoregonian.com/news/local/the -sighting/article_1dc33f61–868d-5c36-b159–87c8465fb662.html.

CASE FILE #2

Who Was the Stagecoach Robber Who Posed for a Photograph?

Along with NPS units like Point Reyes National Seashore, Muir Woods National Monument, and Fort Point National Historic Site, Yosemite was the first major national park I visited as a young boy. Over the years, I've returned maybe two dozen times. I've climbed Half Dome in moonlight, guided several park trips, explored the winter backcountry, paddled area rivers, and hiked and backpacked throughout the wilderness. Thus, I knew I wanted to include a mystery from one of my favorite parks.

However, many mysteries about Yosemite relate to missing person cases. Tragic and ominous, yes, but lacking the drama and intrigue sought for this book. So, I focused on this bizarre unsolved crime, which I first encountered in Patterson (1985) during research for my book *Discovering the Outlaw Trail.*

To reconstruct this story, I mostly relied upon the three cited newspaper articles from the *Fresno Morning Republican,* based upon interviews with Anton Veith and other witnesses in 1905, which provide all quoted dialogue. The discovery of the makeshift horsehoof shoe and its placement in the Yosemite Museum comes from Johnston (2005). It's possible I visited the museum when I was young and saw this artifact but wasn't paying close attention.

Historical context, particularly helpful in the story's conclusion, came from Moody (1998) and *Madera Tribune* (accessed 2023). I looked closely at historic and contemporary maps to understand the old stage route.

That leaves the robbery photo, itself, which I have looked at for years now. I believe that it's genuine. My reasoning is that it's unlike any of the fakes from that time period. You can barely see the robber and tell precisely what's happening. If it were a fabrication, this would be a lot of work and expense—involving at least two and as many as eleven conspirators, whose travel plans were waylaid—to produce a sloppy image that was unlikely to sell for much profit. There's no record of anyone at the time questioning the story, nor has there been since.

Some things are just too goofy to be doubted. I mean, he put a glove on the barrel of his gun and walked into the woods on horsehoof shoes. Dude's definitely not a hero. But he's close.

Sources

"Gentleman Robber." *Fresno Morning Republican*, August 20, 1905.

Johnston, Hank. "The Man Who 'Kodaked' the Yosemite Road Agent." *Yosemite: A Journal for the Members of the Yosemite Association* 67, no. 2 (Spring 2005). https://www.yosemite.ca.us/library /yosemite/67–2.pdf.

Madera County Historical Society. "Robbers Posed Threat to Stagecoach Passengers." *Madera Tribune*. Accessed April 5, 2023. www.maderatribune.com/single-post/robbers-posed-threat-to -stagecoach-passengers.

Moody, Ralph. *Stagecoach West*. Bison Books, 1998.

"No Word of Bandit." *Fresno Morning Republican*, August 18, 1905.

Patterson, Richard. *Historical Atlas of the Outlaw West*. Johnson Books, 1985.

"Remarkable Photographic Snap of the Yosemite Stage Robbery." *Fresno Morning Republican*, August 20, 1905.

CASE FILE #3 ═══════════════════════════════

An Old or Young Valley? A Haunted Park Lodge?

During my lengthy search for Yosemite mysteries, I turned up smaller items that I wanted to include but they didn't have enough material to sustain longer stories. This and similar discoveries led to some shorter chapters throughout the book.

A Valley of Mystery: I'd learned a little about the geologic history of Yosemite during visits and my geology degree at University of California, Davis. I supplemented this base knowledge with a survey of current theories, which led me to a University of California, Berkeley press release (2022) summarizing the research later published in the GSA Bulletin by Cuffey (2023).

A Haunted Park Lodge: I'm lucky to have stayed at the Ahwahnee when I was young, and I've stopped by since, which was helpful in describing this mystery. Key details came from a very astute NPS archives intern (2023), plus "Chapter 7: Myths and Legends" in Clark (1904) and "The Legend of Po-ho-no," in Taylor (1926).

Sources

Archives Intern (GW). "Yosemite: The Weird and the Wonderful." National Park Service, March 20, 2023. www.nps.gov/yose/blogs/yosemite-the-weird-and-the-wonderful.htm.

Clark, Galen. *Indians of the Yosemite Valley and Vicinity.* H.S. Crocker Company, Inc., 1904.

Cuffey, K. M., A. Tripathy-Lang, M. Fox, G. M. Stock, and D. L. Shuster. "Late Cenozoic Deepening of Yosemite Valley, USA." *GSA Bulletin* 135, no. 5/6 (May/June 2023): 1547–1565.

Repanshek, Kurt. "Nation's First Park Ranger Hears Crying Ghost." National Parks Traveler, October 29, 2008. www.nationalparkstraveler.org/2008/10/nation-s-first-park-ranger-hears-crying-ghost.

Taylor, Katherin Ames. *Lights and Shadows of Yosemite.* San Francisco: H.S. Crocker Company, Inc., 1926.

University of California Berkeley. "How Old Is California's Yosemite Valley?" ScienceDaily, October 20, 2022. www.sciencedaily.com/releases/2022/10/221020130237.htm.

CASE FILE #4 ═══════════════════════════════

Are Bodies Buried inside Hoover Dam?

This chapter focuses on a popular legend told around the country, including out West among river runners and outdoorsy folks. Among that group, the myth about bodies buried inside Hoover Dam often seems part of larger derision toward controversial dam projects. Meanwhile, other citizens who seem more supportive of large dams tend to talk about the fatalities with a tinge of awe at the scope of the monumental project.

I have mixed feelings about these massive dams. They are certainly impressive in terms of engineering, and our society is currently dependent upon their ability to store water—though a century of fluctuating climate and storage levels has shown how temperamental our reservoirs really are. Plus, big dams have caused some major problems, including damaging ecosystems and flirting with catastrophes. The possibility of a major dam collapsing during our lifetimes is probably much higher than most people realize. One recent close call was a near-collapse of Oroville Dam in the Northern California foothills in 2017. Someday, the rain may not stop in time. If so, we will witness some horrific repercussions.

While the legend in this story is easily and frequently debunked, I was curious about the origin behind it and why it endures. To understand the lingering myth, I examined a range of contemporary articles, including Veronese (2012), Robison (2013), Kudiali (2015), and more. The opening scene and quoted dialogue come from FDR's speech (1935), plus an examination of historical photos taken that day. The various controversies surrounding Hoover Dam come from a broad survey of sources, including Stevens (1988), Hiltzik (2010) and Reisner (1993). The latter source plus Latham (1998) are used to discuss the Glen Canyon Dam incident in 1983 and to imagine what a hypothetical overtopping might look like.

To dramatize the project construction—including accidents, injuries, and fatalities—I consulted the Bureau of Reclamation fatality records and books like Hiltzik (2010) and Stevens (1988). I also watched the numerous documentaries about the project including the Interior Department's propaganda film (1955) and the PBS American Experience documentary (1999), which has an excellent series of companion clips, articles, and historical photos. Many descriptions of the various locations in the chapter come from my own explorations of the rivers, canyons, and deserts across the West. I have visited Glen Canyon Dam, Lake Powell, Hoover Dam, and Lake Mead. Many outdoor enthusiasts choose to skip these places. I suggest visiting them at least once to see what they're like.

Sources

Bureau of Reclamation. "Hoover Dam." Last updated July 13, 2022. www.usbr.gov/lc/hooverdam /history/articles/articlesmain.html.

Bureau of Reclamation. "Hoover Dam: The Story of Hoover Dam—Essays." Last updated March 12, 2015. www.usbr.gov/lc/hooverdam/history/essays/fatal.html.

Hiltzik, Michael. *Colossus: Hoover Dam and the Making of the American Century.* Free Press, 2010.

Kudiali, Chris. "Knowing Vegas: Are There Really Bodies in the Cement of Hoover Dam?" *Las Vegas Review-Journal,* October 8, 2015. www.reviewjournal.com/uncategorized/knowing-vegas-are -there-really-bodies-in-the-cement-of-hoover-dam.

Latham, Stephen E. "Dam Failure Inundation Study." U.S. Department of the Interior, Bureau of Reclamation. July 1998. www.riversimulator.org/Resources/USBR/GCDDamFailure.pdf.

Public Broadcast Service: American Experience. *Hoover Dam*. Aired January 18, 1999, on PBS. www
.pbs.org/wgbh/americanexperience/films/hoover.

Reisner, Marc. *Cadillac Desert: The American West and Its Disappearing Water*. Penguin Books, 1993.

Robison, Mark. "Fact Checker: A Look at Nevada Myths." *Reno Gazette Journal*, October 26, 2013.
www.rgj.com/story/news/2015/06/02/fact-checker-a-look-at-nevada-myths-hoover-dam
-deaths-union-gold-501-jeans-origin/28325399.

Roosevelt, Franklin D. "Address at the Dedication of Boulder Dam." American Presidency Project.
September 10, 1935. www.presidency.ucsb.edu/documents/address-the-dedication-boulder-dam.

Stevens, Joseph F. *Hoover Dam: An American Adventure*. University of Oklahoma Press, 1988.

U.S. Department of the Interior. *The Story of Hoover Dam*. 1955. Film, 31 min.

Veronese, Keith. "Who Is Buried in the Hoover Dam?" *Gizmodo*. March 16, 2012. https://gizmodo
.com/who-is-buried-in-the-hoover-dam-5893183.

CASE FILE #5

Why Are Coast Redwoods So Tall and Giant Sequoias So Big?

I'm lucky to have visited the big trees for so long, I can't even remember when and where I initially saw them. The first was probably an old-growth redwood at Muir Woods when I was very young. My first giant sequoia was probably in the Merced Grove near Yosemite Valley. I knew that they were native to our wider region, that they were the tallest and biggest in the world, and that I liked them. Beyond that, I mostly took them for granted. Their massive trunks rose high above, we walked beneath, and that was that.

As the years passed, and I moved away and explored other forests, I began to wonder more about these unique big trees. I haven't visited all the many iconic trees that John Muir did during his national and world travels, but I've been able to see a few famous specimens. The ancient bristlecone pine groves in the Basin and Range Province. The world's stoutest tree, a Montezuma cypress named Arbol del Tule, in Oaxaca, Mexico. Towering tulip poplars in the Smokies and loblolly pines at Congaree National Park. Massive bald cypress along the blackwater rivers of the Southeast. Thus, unraveling the mystery behind the coast redwoods and giant sequoias seemed to be a perfect chapter for this book.

The opening scenes depicting John Muir's 1875 expedition to document the giant sequoias come mostly from his book *Our National Parks* (1901), especially "Chapter 9: The Sequoia and General Grant National Parks." Muir provides the quoted dialogue attributed to Hale Tharp and the shepherd. Details about Muir's arboreal expeditions around the world are culled from various compilations of his extensive travels.

The descriptions of human history related to the redwoods come primarily from

Johnstone (2001). Details about the logging era come from a broad survey of secondary sources, including those listed in the final paragraph in this section. The scenes depicting the Discovery Tree come primarily from *Hutchings' California* magazine (1859), Hickman (2013), and Muir (1901), with the latter source providing the quote attributed to the author (a reaction that is often misquoted today). The summary of redwoods conservation history comes from Schrepfer (1980) and other sources.

Descriptions of the fossil record, the geologic history of redwood ancestors, their shrinking range, and the discovery of the dawn redwoods come from Harvey (1985), Ma (2003), Libby (2016), and other sources. Details about redwood biology, distribution, and genetic complexity—including fairy rings, albino ghosts, and the Redwood Genome Project—come from numerous sources, including Douhovnikoff (2007), Fimrite (2019), California Curated (2021), Frost (2021), Kerlin (2022), and Save the Redwoods League (accessed 2024).

Sources

California Curated. "Why Are California's Redwoods and Sequoias So Big and Tall?" March 4, 2021. https://californiacurated.com/2021/03/04/why-are-californias-redwoods-and-sequoias-so-big/.

Douhovnikoff, Vladimir, and Richard S. Dodd. "Clonal Spread in Second Growth Stands of Coast Redwood, Sequoia Sempervirens." USDA Forest Service General Technical Report PSW-GTR-194, 2007. https://research.fs.usda.gov/treesearch/28246.

Fimrite, Peter. "California Scientists Unravel Genetic Mysteries of World's Tallest Trees." *San Francisco Chronicle*, April 23, 2019. www.sfchronicle.com/science/article/California-scientists -unravel-genetic-mysteries-13786816.php.

Frost, Garrison. "Explaining the Mystery Behind Fairy Rings in the Redwoods." Save the Redwoods League. July 30, 2021. www.savetheredwoods.org/blog/explaining-the-mystery-behind-fairy -rings-in-the-redwoods.

Harvey, H. Thomas. "Evolution and History of Giant Sequoia." *Proceedings of the Workshop on Management of Giant Sequoia*, May 24–25, 1985. www.fs.usda.gov/research/treesearch/27502.

Hickman, Leo. "How a Giant Tree's Death Sparked the Conservation Movement 160 Years Ago." *Guardian*, June 27, 2013. www.theguardian.com/environment/blog/2013/jun/27/giant-tree-death -conservation-movement.

James, Harlean. *Romance of the National Parks*. Macmillan, 1941. www.nps.gov/parkhistory/online _books/james/index.htm.

Johnstone, Peter, ed. *Giants of the Earth: The California Redwoods*. Heyday Books, 2001.

Kerlin, Kat. "Discovery Uncovers a New Leaf for Redwoods." *UC Davis News*, March 16, 2022. www .ucdavis.edu/climate/news/discovery-uncovers-new-leaf-redwoods.

Libby, W. J. "Why Are Coast Redwood and Giant Sequoia Not Where They Are Not?" *Proceedings of* the *Coast Redwood Symposium*, 2016. www.fs.usda.gov/psw/publications/documents/psw_gtr258/psw_gtr258_423.pdf.

Ma, Jinshuang. "The Chronology of the 'Living Fossil' Metasequoia Glyptostroboides (Taxodiaceae): A Review (1943–2003)." *Harvard Papers in Botany* 8, no. 1 (June 2003): 9–18. http://flora.huh.harvard.edu/FOC/china/Harvard_Papers/Ma_8_1_009_018.pdf.

Muir, John. *Our National Parks*. Houghton, Mifflin, & Co., 1901.

Save the Redwoods League. "Interesting Facts about Redwood and Sequoia Genetic Diversity." Accessed May 5, 2024: www.savetheredwoods.org/project/redwood-genome-project/interesting-facts.

Schrepfer, Susan R. "Conflict in Preservation: The Sierra Club, Save-the-Redwoods League, and Redwood National Park." *Journal of Forestry History* 24, no. 2 (April 1980): 60–77.

"The Mammoth Trees of California." *Hutchings' California* magazine 3, no. 9 (March 1859): 385–397.

CASE FILE #6

What Happened to the Crew of the *Ghost Blimp*?

Growing up in the East Bay, across the water from San Francisco, I heard the story of the *Ghost Blimp* several times. Like other people, I took the tale for granted and eventually forgot about it. During a 2008 visit to the National Naval Aviation Museum in Pensacola, Florida, I saw the *L-8* control car and learned about its return to the skies as the *Goodyear Blimp*. Afterward, the story once again slipped from my mind until I began working on this book. Similarly, some visitors and locals forget how many beloved sites around what we simply call "the City" (a.k.a. S.F.) are part of an excellent NPS unit. When I confirmed how many of *L-8*'s movements happened around Golden Gate National Recreation Area, I realized it was a perfect mystery to reconstruct.

The opening scenes and subsequent movements of the *Ghost Blimp* come from a variety of historical news articles and secondary sources listed in this section. The professional background about airmen Adams and Cody, and key events from before and during World War II, come from Geoghegan (2016), Check-Six (accessed 2022), *Evening Star* (1935), and other sources. The radio reporter present at the *Hindenburg* disaster was Herbert Morrison, and his distressed quote and my descriptions come from the audio broadcast, film recordings, and photos of the horrific event.

I reconstructed the movements of the *Ghost Blimp* using most of the sources cited, and the quoted radio messages from *L-8* are reported repeatedly, including in Geoghegan (2016).

The witness accounts of the crash in Daly City, and descriptions of the blimp's final movements and collapse, come primarily from the *San Francisco Examiner* (August 17,

1942), which also provides the firefighter's quote and first responder observations. I closely examined photos from before and after the crash, which confirm many details in the story, including the envelope's comical landing atop Johnston's car.

The summary of the Navy inquiry comes primarily from the *San Francisco Examiner* (August 19, 1942) and Ross (1970). The conspiracy theories and rumors are from a wide variety of sources. A 2020 Facebook post by the Goodyear Tire & Rubber Company reported that *L-8* became the control car for the *Goodyear Blimps,* designated Ranger 46 and America 69, which allowed me to confirm that it was seen over sporting events that many readers and myself may have watched when we were kids.

Sources

"81 Safe as Macon Plunges into Sea." *Evening Star*, February 13, 1935.

"Blimp Mystery Baffles Navy." *Oakland Tribune*, August 17, 1942.

Daugherty, Greg. "The 80-Year Mystery of the U.S. Navy's 'Ghost Blimp.'" *Smithsonian* magazine, August 16, 2022. www.smithsonianmag.com/history/the-80-year-mystery-of-the-us-navys-ghost-blimp-180980531.

Geoghegan, John J. "The Mystery of the Navy's 'Ghost Blimp.'" HistoryNet. April 12, 2016. https://www.historynet.com/ghost-blimp-mystery-l-8.

Kamiya, Gary. "Ghost Blimp's Enduring Mystery: How Did Crew Vanish before Bay Area Crash?" *SF Chronicle*, September 29, 2018. www.sfchronicle.com/bayarea/article/Ghost-blimp-s-enduring-mystery-How-did-crew-13267309.php.

"Navy Hunts for Crew of Broken Blimp." *Sacramento Bee*, August 17, 1942.

"Navy Quiz Adds New Mystery to Blimp Crash." *San Francisco Examiner*, August 19, 1942.

Ross, Irwin. "The Mystery of the L-8." *Proceedings: United States Naval Institute* 96, no. 3 (March 1970). www.usni.org/magazines/proceedings/1970/march/mystery-l-8.

"The Crash of Navy Blimp L-8." Check-Six.com. Accessed December 30, 2022. www.check-six.com/Crash_Sites/L-8_crash_site.htm.

"U.S. Navy Blimp Falls in Daly City; Crew Missing." *San Francisco Examiner*, August 17, 1942.

CASE FILE #7

How Do the Sliding Stones Move Across Racetrack Playa?

My first visit to the Racetrack and Death Valley happened during spring of 2003 on a multiday field trip out of University of California, Davis. Yes, I was one of the laughing geology students wandering the playa and national park. Our teachers were correct in saying that we should be more serious. But they were hopelessly idealistic in the moment. Several later visits also inform the descriptions of Death Valley landscapes throughout the story. Plus, I consulted numerous historical and contemporary photos, maps, and satellite images.

The legend about Native American horse racing comes from Kirk (1953). I verified that the name "The Racetrack" appears on the USGS topographic map for the Ballarat, California, quadrangle published in 1913, prior to widespread awareness of the sliding stones. One interesting discovery was that the prior USGS quadrangle map reports that the playa and surrounding area to be "Unsurveyed" as of 1908.

The opening scene depicting Joseph and Cara Crook's visits comes from Stanley (1956), and I verified the family's lengthy presence in the region using obituaries. The more outlandish theories behind the sliding stones are taken from a variety of sources and my own experiences. (Yes, we were actually listening to our teachers on occasion.) The final scenes about the NASA-funded scientists solving the mystery come from Norris and from the *New York Times* (both 2014).

Sources

Fountain, Henry. "An Icy Answer to the Mystery of the Moving Death Valley Stones." *New York Times*, September 1, 2014. https://www.nytimes.com/2014/09/02/science/death-valley-mystery -why-rocks-move.html.

Kirk, Ruth E. "The Moving Rocks of Death Valley." *Natural History: The Magazine of the American Museum of Natural History,* September 1953.

Lorenz, Ralph D., et al. "Meteorological Conditions at Racetrack Playa, Death Valley National Park: Implications for Rock Production and Transport." *Journal of Applied Meteorology and Climatology* 50, no. 12 (December 2011): 2361–2375.

McCallister, J. F., and A. F. Agnew. "Playa Scrapers and Furrows on the Racetrack Playa, Inyo County, California." *Bulletin of the Geological Society of America* 59 (December 1948): 1307–1414.

Norris R. D., J. M. Norris, R. D. Lorenz, J. Ray, and B. Jackson. "Sliding Rocks on Racetrack Playa, Death Valley National Park: First Observation of Rocks in Motion." *Plos One* 9, no. 8 (2014).

O. Hanlon, Larry. "The Roving Rocks of Racetrack Playa." *Earth* 5, no. 1 (February 1996): 58–59.

Reid, J. B., E. P. Bucklin, L. Copenagle, J. Kidder, S. M. Pack, P. J. Polissar, and M. L. Williams. "Sliding Rocks at the Racetrack, Death Valley: What Makes Them Move?" *Geology* 23, no. 9 (September 1995): 819–822.

Sharp, Robert P., and Dwight L. Carey. "Sliding Stones, Racetrack Playa, California." *Geological Society of America Bulletin* 87 (December 1976): 1704–1717.

Shelton, John S. "Can Wind Move Rocks on Racetrack Playa?" *Science* 117, no. 3042 (April 1953): 438–439.

Stanley, George M. "Origin of Playa Stone Tracks, Racetrack Playa, Inyo County, California." *Bulletin of the Geological Society of America* 66 (November 1956): 1329–1350.

"The Case of the Skating Stones." *Life*, March 10, 1952.

CASE FILE #8

Did a 1950s Air Force Pilot Stage a Jet Crash?

Having spent so much time in the high country of the Sierra Nevadas, including hiking into the wilderness of Kings Canyon and summiting Mount Whitney via the Mountaineers Route, I knew there were a lot of mysteries in these mountains. With the adventurous mix of survival and troubling secrets, the mystery of David Steeves's crash was perfect for this book. Despite the intensive media attention during the late 1950s, the story has been mostly forgotten except for occasional retrospectives. Thus, I had to dive into newspaper archives to reconstruct this chapter. Even just the headlines cited here reveal the wild swings in the saga.

The opening scene where Steeves meets the fishing party, including the quotes attributed to him and later quotes attributed to Albert Ade, comes from the *Fresno Bee* (August 16, 1957). Details about his ejection, landing, exploits in Simpson Meadow, and Merced press conference—with attributed quote—come from a wide range of sources, including Hurley, *San Francisco Examiner*, *Oakland Tribune*, and *Stockton Record* (all July 2, 1957) and *Time* (July 15, 1957). Many details about Steeves's survival, state of mind, and several later quotes come from the *Redbook* profile by Peters (1958).

The reunion scene between Steeves and wife Rita, including dialogue attributed to her, comes from Gibson and *Fresno Bee* (July 4, 7, and 11, 1957). Descriptions of Steeves's return trip to Kings Canyon with Rita and Blair, the ensuing doubts about his honesty, and the confirmation of his ordeal by park service staff come from Hoffman, Molander, Robinson, Watry, and *Life* (all 1957), plus *Los Angeles Times* (August 15, 1957), *Time* (August 26, 1957) and *Fresno Bee* (July 11 and August 18, 1957). The troubling details of the Steeves's marital and family relationships, depicted throughout the chapter, come primarily from six articles in the *Fresno Bee* (August 12 and December 27, 1957; and February 27, March 18, April 9, and September 19, 1958).

The journalistic scandals surrounding Blair are confirmed in White (1973) and Goldstein (1998), and a legal settlement in Steeves's favor with the publishers related to Blair accusations is reported in *Fresno Bee* (October 1, 1963). Steeves's relocation to Fresno and his later years, including his stint in local theater and lingering public debate about him, and his death, comes from Reynolds (1959), *Ogden Standard* (1965), DeLacy (1987), and *Fresno Bee* (January 30, 1958; May 17, July 7, 1959; October 1, 1963; and October 17 and 18, 1965).

The discovery of Steeves's jet canopy by boy scouts comes from Paxton, from Rose, and from *Pantagraph* (each 1978), plus several retrospectives, including Harvey (2010) and *Plane & Pilot* (2018). In addition to the sources above, historical photos and maps, plus contemporary park maps and satellite imagery, were essential to depict Steeves's escape from the Kings Canyon wilderness.

Sources

"2nd Steeves Rift, S. F. Affair Told." *San Francisco Examiner*, December 27, 1957.

"Accident Claims Life of Pilot Who Survived 54-Day Ordeal in Wilds." *Ogden Standard*, October 18, 1965.

"Armed Forces: Certain Discrepancies." *Time*, August 26, 1957.

"Armed Forces: The Bad Earth." *Time*, July 15, 1957.

"Court Orders Steeves to Pay Child Support." *Fresno Bee*, April 9, 1958.

"'Dead' Flier Tells Ordeal in Sierra." *Oakland Tribune*, July 2, 1957.

DeLacy, Ron. "Jet Crash Still a Puzzle." *Fresno Bee*, May 9, 1987.

"Flier Survives 54 Days in High Sierra." *Stockton Record*, July 2, 1957.

"Fresno Theater Group Will Give Acting Awards." *Fresno Bee*, May 17, 1959.

"Fresno Woman, Steeves Disclose Wedding Plans." *Fresno Bee*, July 7, 1959.

"Funeral Rites Will Be Set for David Steeves." *Fresno Bee*, October 18, 1965.

Gibson, Wanda. "Mrs. Steeves Looks Forward to High Sierra Trip." *Fresno Bee*, July 11, 1957.

Goldstein, Richard. "Clay Blair, 73, Navy Veteran and an Expert on Submarines." *New York Times*, December 20, 1998. www.nytimes.com/1998/12/20/us/clay-blair-73-navy-veteran-and-an-expert-on-submarines.html.

Harvey, Steve. "Hero or Hoax? Public Doubted Pilot's Story of Survival." *Los Angeles Times*, October 17, 2010. www.latimes.com/archives/la-xpm-2010-oct-17-la-me-1017-then-20101017-story.html.

Hoffman, Fred S. "Lt. Steeves Sticks to Story of High Sierra." *Rocky Mount Telegram*, August 15, 1957.

Hurley, Charles S. "Airman Survives 54 Days in Sierra after Jet Crash." *Fresno Bee*, July 2, 1957.

"Idaho Crash Kills David Steeves." *Fresno Bee*, October 17, 1965.

"Jet Flyer, 'Dead' 2 Months, Walks Out of Sierra." *San Francisco Examiner*, July 2, 1957.

Molander, Robert P. "Park Aides Declare Evidence Backs Up Account by Steeves." *Fresno Bee*, August 14, 1957.

"Mrs. Steeves Denies Reconciliation Story." *Fresno Bee*, December 27, 1957.

"Packer Finding Steeves Defends Story of Ordeal." *Fresno Bee*, August 16, 1957.

"Park Ranger Backs Flier's Survival Epic." *Los Angeles Times*, August 15, 1957.

Paxton, John. "In Sierra Shangri-La, the Shattering of a Dream." *Los Angeles Times*, October 26, 1978.

Peters, William. "The Survival of Lt. Steeves." *Redbook*, January 1958.

Reynolds, Ray. "Theater Group Makes Brave Try at Saroyan's Dwellers." *Fresno Bee*, February 28, 1959.

Robinson, Grace, and Henry Lee. "High Sierras Hero Trips on the High Discrepancies." *New York Daily News*, August 15, 1957.

Rose, Gene. "Sierra Yields a Secret: Jet-Crash Find Vindicates Pilot." *Fresno Bee*, October 11, 1978.

"Steeves Again Is Ordered to Study Survival Training." *Fresno Bee*, August 21, 1957.

"Steeves Draws Alabama Duty." *Fresno Bee*, August 23, 1957.

"Steeves Returns to Hunt Piloting Job in Fresno." *Fresno Bee*, January 30, 1958.

"Steeves' Suits against Publishers Are Settled." *Fresno Bee*, October 1, 1963.

"Steeves' Wife Files Action for Divorce." *Fresno Bee*, March 18, 1958.

"Steeves' Wife May Obtain Divorce; Consults Lawyer." *Fresno Bee*, August 12, 1957.

"Steeves' Wife Wins Custody of Daughter." *Fresno Bee*, February 27, 1958.

"The Case of the Missing T-33." *Plane & Pilot* magazine, November 19, 2018. www.planeandpilotmag
.com/article/the-case-of-the-missing-t-33.

"The Strange Case of the Sierra Survivor." *Life*, September 2, 1957.

Watry, Richard. "Steeves Returns Minus Whiskers." *Fresno Bee*, July 25, 1957.

White, Gordon S. "Wally Butts, Ex-Georgia Coach, Dies." *New York Times*, December 18, 1973.

"Wife's Suit Says Steeves Beat Her, Flaunted Affair." *Fresno Bee*, September 19, 1958.

"Wife Welcomes Steeves, Finds Beard 'Horrible.'" *Fresno Bee*, July 4, 1957.

"Wreckage Clears Survivor's Name." *Pantagraph*, October 14, 1978.

"Writer Outlines 'Discrepancy' in Steeves' Story." *Fresno Bee*, August 18, 1957.

CASE FILE #9

Who Was the First to Climb Denali?

I learned about the convoluted and interwoven exploration history of Denali and the North Pole as a teenager while daydreaming about mountaineering and reading articles by outdoor authors like Jon Krakauer and David Roberts. However, the whole story was so convoluted that I retained little more than a feeling: *What a messy and disappointing history.* Decades later, when I began working on this book, I knew I wanted to include the bizarre story without getting bogged down by every minutia of the complicated controversy.

The opening scene and quoted telegram come from Bryce (2009), while the descriptions of Cook's polar claim come from numerous sources, including Roberts (2001). The celebrations in Copenhagen come from reviewing newsreel footage of Cook's arrival and examining contemporary articles like those cited from the *San Francisco Call* and *New York Times* (all 1909), which also inform the descriptions of Cook's return to New York, as does Bleyer (2014). Those sources also were helpful in describing Peary's competing claim, as was *Ogden Standard* (1909) and Roxburg (2016).

Descriptions of the worsening feud, the lampooning editorial cartoons, and the Denali hoax allegations against Cook come from numerous sources, including Robinson (2006), Henderson (2009), Hartman (2023), and Thorpe (2023). Details about Cook's true efforts and his summit hoax and photographs at Fake Peak come from several sources, particularly Bryce (1997) and Roberts (1999 and 2001). Scenes depicting the Sourdough Expedition come from Waterman (2017). The historical photograph showing that the sourdoughs reached at least 16,500 feet was rediscovered by Boyce (2022). The climb of Stuck comes from Brown (1991), plus a broad survey of the sources cited above, all of which were used to construct the epilogue events.

Sources

Berman, Eliza. "The Other Mount McKinley Controversy: Who Climbed Denali First." *Time*, August 31, 2015. https://time.com/4017660/mount-mckinley-denali-ascent-hoax.

Bleyer, Jennifer. "90°, N, 0°, W." *NYU* magazine, Spring 2014. https://alumnimagazine.nyu.edu /issue22/FEA_3.html.

Boyce, Rod. "Newly Found Photos Shed Light on 1910 Denai Climb." Geophysical Institute, University of Alaska Fairbanks. December 2, 2022. www.gi.alaska.edu/news/newly-found-photos -shed-light-1910-denali-climb.

Brown, William E. *A History of the Denali—Mount McKinley, Region, Alaska*. National Park Service, 1991. www.nps.gov/parkhistory/online_books/dena/hrs.htm.

Bryce, Robert M. "Dr. Cook-Mt. McKinley Controversy Closed." *Dio* 7, no. 203 (December 1997). http://www.dioi.org/vols/w73.pdf.

Bryce, Robert M. "One Man's Trash: The Recovery of Frederick A. Cook's Original Telegram Drafts Announcing His Attainment of the North Pole." *Polar Record* 45, no. 235 (2009): 351–359.

"Cook-Peary Dispute." *New York Daily Tribune*, September 12, 1909.

Hartman, Darrell. "The Artic Feud that Divided America." *Time*, July 15, 2023. https://time.com /6294794/robert-peary-frederick-cook-north-pole-feud/.

Henderson, Bruce. "Who Discovered the North Pole?" *Smithsonian* magazine, April 2009. www .smithsonianmag.com/history/who-discovered-the-north-pole-116633746.

"How Peary Reached the North Pole." *New York Times*, September 12, 1909.

"Nations Pay Tribute to Cook." *San Francisco Call*, September 3, 1909.

"Peary Discovers the North Pole after Eight Trials in 23 Years." *New York Times*, September 7, 1909.

"Question of Priority in the Discovery of the North Pole." *Ogden Standard*, September 7, 1909.

Roberts, David. "A Long and Brutal Assault." *Outside*, June 1999. www.outsideonline.com/outdoor -adventure/long-and-brutal-assault/.

Roberts, David. *Great Exploration Hoaxes*. New York: Modern Library, 2001.

Robinson, M. F. *The Coldest Crucible: Arctic Exploration and American Culture*. University of Chicago Press, 2006.

Roxburgh, Ellis. *Robert Peary vs. Frederick Cook: Race to the North Pole*. Gareth Stevens Publishing, 2016.

Thorpe, Vanessa. "Was 'The First Man to Reach the North Pole' a Fraud?" *Guardian*, May 28, 2023. www.theguardian.com/science/2023/may/28/was-the-first-man-to-reach-the-north-pole-a-.

Tierny, John. "Author Says Photo Confirms Mt. McKinley Hoax in 1908." *New York Times*, November 26, 1998. www.nytimes.com/1998/11/26/nyregion/author-says-photo-confirms-mt-mckinley -hoax-in-1908.html.

"University Finds That Cook's Papers Contain No Proof That He Reached the North Pole." *New York Times*, December 22, 1909.

Waterman, Jonathan. "The Sourdough Enigma." *Ascent*. 2017. https://jonathanwaterman.com/media /2020/7/sourdoughs.pdf.

CASE FILE #10 ═══════════════════════════════════════

Is Murder Legal in the Zone of Death?

I first heard about the zone of death from outdoor friends sometime before the COVID-19 pandemic. Then the mid-pandemic disappearance of Gabby Petito helped to re-popularize this modern myth. I was initially skeptical about the topic, thinking it would only be a short subchapter. Delving into the research revealed a wilder story than I had expected, and the mysterious question whether the zone of death exists (or more likely does not) seemed to mesh well with history I had previously learned. Not only did Yellowstone see a lawless era during the Wild West, but it's seen plenty of bad behavior ever since.

The opening scene, depicting the rangers discovering the poached elk carcass, comes primarily from the Yellowstone National Park press release (2006) and Ryan (2010). I also called upon my own experiences in the park and surrounding region, and I examined maps, satellite images, and roadway photos to describe the landscape in scenes throughout the chapter.

The scenes depicting Belderrain's experiences—from poaching the elk to fleeing and standing trial—come primarily from his podcast appearance with Longoria (2022), which provides his quoted thoughts and conflicted reactions. Also helpful were court records like Shumaker (2009), articles like Morton (2009), and Professor Brian Kalt's two scholarly law articles on the topic (2005 and 2008). The depictions of the investigation and court case call upon the sources above plus *Billings Gazette* (2009).

The description of Kalt's efforts to identify the zone of death, publicize his findings, and close the loophole come primarily from his two articles. His quoted monologue is printed in the 2008 publication, which also offers accounts and quotes from Belderrain's defense attorney and the presiding judge. The turbulent history of Yellowstone and the wider region comes mostly from Haines (1996), with the park stagecoach robberies informed by Haynes (1959) and Catharine & Galper (2020).

The viral media response to the zone of death comes from Kalt's two articles plus the three following sources, each from 2005: Kerr's blog post, articles by Morin and by Davis, and a radio broadcast by Seigel. The closing material about the lingering obsessions with the zone of death, and the media frenzy surrounding the murder of Gabby Petito by her fiancé Brian Laundrie, and his subsequent suicide, come from 2021 articles by Czopek, Graziosi, Morphet, and Briunno.

Sources

Briunno, J. B. "Read: Brian Laundrie's Notebook Confession, Message to Gabby Petito." *WFLA News*, June 24, 2022. www.wfla.com/news/sarasota-county/read-brian-laundries-notebook-confession-message-to-gabby-petito.

Catharine, Suzie, and Hailey Galper. "Stagecoach Robberies: Yellowstone's Archival Records to Tell an Alternative History." National Park Service. Accessed February 28, 2020. www.nps.gov/yell/blogs/stagecoach-robberies-yellowstone-s-archival-records-to-tell-an-alternative-history.htm.

Corbin, Clark. "Idaho Legislator Asks U.S. Congress to Close Yellowstone's 'Zone of Death' Loophole." *Idaho Capital Sun*, February 3, 2022. https://idahocapitalsun.com/2022/02/03/idaho-legislator-asks-u-s-congress-to-close-yellowstones-zone-of-death-loophole.

Czopek, Madison. "No, Murder Is Not Legal in a 'Zone of Death' in Yellowstone National Park." *Politifact*, June 4, 2021. www.politifact.com/factchecks/2021/jun/04/tiktok-posts/no-murder-not-legal-zone-death-yellowstone-nationa.

Davis, Matthew. "Loophole May Allow US Crime Spree." *BBC News*, May 9, 2005. http://news.bbc.co.uk/2/hi/americas/4529829.stm.

Graziosi, Graig. "Debunking Yellowstone's 'Zone of Death,' the Location Internet Sleuths Have Linked to Gabby Petito's Disappearance." *Independent*, September 17, 2021. www.independent.co.uk/news/world/americas/gabby-petito-brian-laundrie-zone-of-death-yellowstone-b1922432.html.

Haines, Aubrey. *The Yellowstone Story: A History of Our First National Park*. Vol. 1 & 2. University of Colorado Press, 1996.

Haynes, Jack Ellis. *Yellowstone Stage Holdups.* Haynes Studios, 1959.

Kalt, Brian C. "Tabloid Constitutionalism: How a Bill Doesn't Become a Law." *Georgetown Law Journal* 96, no. 6 (2008): 1971–1985.

Kalt, Brian C. "The Perfect Crime." *Georgetown Law Journal* 93, no. 2 (2005): 675–688.

Kerr, Orin. "Fun, Entertaining, Clever, and Short." Volokh Conspiracy. March 26, 2005. https://volokh.com/archives/archive_2005_03_20–2005_03_26.shtml.

Longoria, J., A. Melathe, K. Wells, and D. Herman. "The 50-Square-Mile Zone Where the Constitution Doesn't Apply." *The Experiment* podcast. May 26, 2022. www.theatlantic.com/podcasts/archive/2022/05/yellowstone-zone-of-death-murder-legal/638437.

"Man Loses Appeal in Yellowstone Elk Case." *Billings Gazette*, March 14, 2009. https://billingsgazette

.com/news/state-and-regional/wyoming/man-loses-appeal-in-yellowstone-elk-case/article
_72c0188b-09cc-5239-bf9f-b5981c9a4f98.html.

Morin, Richard. "Where Lawlessness May Roam." *Washington Post*, May 8, 2005. www
.washingtonpost.com/archive/opinions/2005/05/08/where-lawlessness-may-roam/6434c747–
4c21–43bc-8d9e-a729d557158b.

Morphet, Jack. "What Does Yellowstone's 'Zone of Death' Have to Do with Gabby Petito?" *New York
Post*, September 17, 2021. https://nypost.com/2021/09/17/zone-of-death-how-it-could-relate-to
-the-gabby-petito-case.

Morton, Tom. "Man Loses Appeal in Yellowstone Elk Case." *Casper Star-Tribune*, March 14, 2009.
https://billingsgazette.com/news/state-and-regional/wyoming/man-loses-appeal-in-yellowstone
-elk-case/article_72c0188b-09cc-5239-bf9f-b5981c9a4f98.html.

Morton, Tom. "Yellowstone Elk Shooter Heads to Prison." *Casper Star-Tribune*, March 12,
2009.   https://trib.com/news/state-regional/yellowstone-elk-shooter-heads-to-prison/article
_b546c3d6-c53e-56df-99ae-b6dc90dd360f.html.

Morton, Tom. "Yellowstone 'No Mans Land' Leaves Jurisdiction Question." *Casper Star-Tribune*.
March 12, 2009. https://billingsgazette.com/news/state-and-regional/wyoming/yellowstone-no
-mans-land-leaves-jurisdiction-question/article_f4caad4c-fd01–5e78-b2d9–1a0cf37b4855.html.

Ryan, Hannah. "Wildlife Forensics Sets Sights on Poachers." *Montana Kaimin*, November 9, 2010.
www.montanakaimin.com/wildlife-forensics-sets-sights-on-poachers/article_663ae3d0-a3c9–
5b01–8e35-e66641b489fa.html.

Shumaker, Elizabeth A., Clerk of the Court. "United States of America vs Michael David Bellderain."
January 29, 2009.

Siegel, Robert. "Is Yellowstone Ripe for a Crime Spree?" *All Things Considered* radio broadcast,
National Public Radio, May 10, 2005. www.npr.org/2005/05/10/4647041/is-yellowstone-ripe
-for-a-crime-spree.

Yellowstone National Park. "Bull Elk Poached in Yellowstone Park." *Pinedale Online!* January 8, 2006.
www.pinedaleonline.com/news/2006/01/BullElkPoachedinYell.htm.

CASE FILE #11

How Was *Heaven's Gate* Named One of the Worst *and* Best Films of All Time?

Being a big fan of Western films, I learned about the infamous *Heaven's Gate* long ago, but I
didn't watch it in full until sometime in the late 2000s. I was immediately struck by the fact
that the movie wasn't nearly as bad as people claimed. Yes, it did drag on at times. I could see
why many viewers found it challenging to sit through. But it was also beautifully shot with
many excellent scenes. Given my interest in epics, I quite enjoyed the film, despite it having

some pretty hokey moments. All part of its charms, I decided. A great film to appreciate *and* make jokes about. When I later watched Cimino's two prior motion pictures, I was equally impressed and bemused. These realizations piqued my interest in unraveling the hilarious and troubling mystery behind the split personality of *Heaven's Gate*.

The opening scenes and quotes from the New York City premiere come mostly from Winslow (2020) and also Bach (1999), with the latter book being used throughout the chapter. Negative reactions by critics, and the later shift toward acclaim, including quotes from published articles and reviews, come from Carroll, Canby, Kael, and Schreger (each from 1980), plus Burr (2012), Lim (2012), Dargis (2013), and Barber (2015). To describe the public opinions and backstory of *Heaven's Gate*, including reviews and details regarding Cimino's prior films, the sources used include Canby (1978), Kent (1978), Harmetz (1979), Laman (2022), and others.

The scenes depicting the controversial production in Montana and at Oxford come from a wide range of sources, including *Time*, Speelman, and Schreger (all 1979), which also provide details on the dispute with the park service, as does Gapay (1979). Also helpful for these scenes were Bach and the documentary by Epstein (2004), which includes on-screen interviews with the actors who describe Camp Cimino.

The quote attributed to Cimino about lunch is repeated in numerous sources, including Barber (2014). Many of the on-set concerns are raised in the letter to the *Great Falls Tribune* written by Carlyon (1979). The quote of an extra about interviewing horses comes from Gapay, as do much of the behind-the-scenes incidents and humorous moments. The scene depicting the screening for United Artists execs and Cimino's quote comes from Bach, as do the details about the re-release of the second cut, which is supplemented by Canby and by Thomas (both 1981). Finally, further details about the critical reappraisal, the quoted headline from the *New York Times*, and the scene depicting the standing ovation come from Lim (2012).

Sources

Bach, Steven. *Final Cut: Art, Money, and Ego in the Making of Heaven's Gate, the Film that Sank United Artists*. Newmarket Press, 1999.

Barber, Nicholas. "Heaven's Gate: From Hollywood Disaster to Masterpiece." *BBC Culture*, December 4, 2015. www.bbc.com/culture/article/20151120-heavens-gate-from-hollywood-disaster-to-masterpiece.

Burr, Ty. "Ty Burr Revisits 'Heaven's Gate.'" *Boston Globe*, November 24, 2012. www3.bostonglobe .com/arts/2012/11/24/burr-revisits-heaven-gate/km6gp1cBbxY75qxWrFs6tM/story.html.

Canby, Vincent. "Screen: Shorter 'Heaven's Gate,' with Voice-Overs, Tries Again." *New York Times*, April 24, 1981. www.nytimes.com/1981/04/24/movies/screen-shorter-heaven-s-gate-with-voice -overs-tries-again.html.

Canby, Vincent. "Screen: 'The Deer Hunter.'" *New York Times*, December 15, 1978. www.nytimes.com /1978/12/15/archives/screen-the-deer-hunter.html.

Carlyon, James M. "'Heaven's Gate' Extra Tells Why He Quit." *Great Falls Tribune*, June 15, 1979.

Carroll, Kathleen. "Heaven's No Help For 'Heaven's Gate.'" *New York Daily News*, November 20, 1980.

Dargis, Manohla. "Michael Cimino's 'Heaven's Gate' Returns to Film Forum." *New York Times*, March 17, 2013. www.nytimes.com/2013/03/17/movies/michael-ciminos-heavens-gate-returns-to-film -forum.html.

Davis, John W. "The Johnson County War: 1892 Invasion of Northern Wyoming." WyoHistory. November 8, 2014. www.wyohistory.org/encyclopedia/johnson-county-war-1892-invasion-northern -wyoming.

Epstein, Michael, dir. *Final Cut: The Making and Unmaking of Heaven's Gate.* Viewfinder Productions, 2004.

Gapay, Les. "Shoot-Out at 'Heaven's Gate.'" *Washington Post*, September 2, 1979. www.washingtonpost .com/archive/lifestyle/1979/09/02/shoot-out-at-heavens-gate/c9785a69–2f68–437b-852f- bec237f0afc8.

Harmetz, Aljean. "Oscar-Winning 'Deer Hunter' Is Under Attack as 'Racist' Film." *New York Times*, April 26, 1979. www.nytimes.com/1979/04/26/archives/oscarwinning-deer-hunter-is-under -attack-as-racist-film-among-the.html.

Kael, Pauline. "Poses." *New Yorker*, December 22, 1980. www.newyorker.com/magazine/1980/12/22 /poses-2.

Kent, Leticia. "Ready for Vietnam? A Talk with Michael Cimino." *New York Times*, December 10, 1978. www.nytimes.com/1978/12/10/archives/ready-for-vietnam-a-talk-with-michael-cimino -cimino.html.

Laman, Douglas. "The Wild and True Story of Making Michael Cimino's Epic Western 'Heaven's Gate.'" *Collider*, October 3, 2022. https://collider.com/heavens-gate-history-explained-michael -cimino.

Lim, Dennis. "Time Has Been Kind to 'Heaven's Gate.'" *New York Times*, September 21, 2012. www .nytimes.com/2012/09/23/movies/a-heavens-gate-revival.html.

Thomas, Kevin. "Shortened 'Heaven's Gate' Opens." *Los Angeles Times*, April 25, 1981.

Schreger, Charles. "Closing the 'Gate' after Premiere Fizzle." *Los Angeles Times*, November 20, 1980.

Schreger, Charles. "Shootout at the UA Corral: Artists vs. Accountants." *Los Angeles Times*, August 26, 1979.

Speelman, JoAnn. "'Mr. Iversen and His Park' Miffs Film Director." *Missoulian*, June 11, 1979.

"The Making of Apocalypse Next: Director Michael Cimino shoots a $30 million western." *Time* 114, no. 10 (1979): 64–65.

Winslow, Don. "Marquee Values & My Night at Heaven's Gate." *Deadline*, April 7, 2020. https:// deadline.com/2020/04/don-winslow-marquee-values-my-night-at-heavens-gate-premiere -1202901675.

CASE FILE #12

Why Did the Cliff Dwellers Abandon Their Stone Palaces?

My wife and I have been fascinated by the ancestral ruins of the Southwest since our first road trip together, which led us to Mesa Verde and other great sites and parks throughout the Southwest. During return trips, I've managed to explore many of the other archaeological parks throughout the region. The mystery of Mesa Verde's abandonment in the thirteenth century seemed like a perfect choice for this book, and I wanted to make sure that the wider controversy surrounding the first century of park archaeology was included in the chapter.

The opening scenes about the rediscovery and naming of the Cliff Palace and other ruins come from Mason (1917), Watson (1961), and Wenger (1991), with the dialogue attributed to Richard Wetherill and Acowitz appearing in several sources, but particularly in McNitt (1974). Descriptions of the relics rush and early artifacts found by the Wetherills come from a broad survey of the cited sources.

The correspondence between Ben Wetherill and the Smithsonian officials comes from mostly Harrell (1987) and also McNitt (1974). The section about Nordenskiöld's visit and legacy comes from his 1893 book and Lee (1970), Rothman (1989), and Smith (2002). The latter three books were also helpful for depicting the efforts of McClurg and the early decades of the park, including tensions with Native Americans. The details about Manitou Springs Cliff Dwellings come from Lovata (2012) and Griffis (2022).

Details about the controversy surrounding the word *Anasazi* come from Walters and Rogers (2001). The scene depicting the display of Esther and the effect on Navajo visitors in 1939, and the insensitive reactions by park staff come from McWhirt (1939) and Fine-Dare and Durkee (2011). The final scenes depicting Wetherill's excavation expeditions around the Southwest, and his final years at Chaco Canyon, including his death, come from Rothman (1989) and McNitt (1974), with the latter providing the dialogue attributed to Biyé.

Sources

Burns, Ken. "Mesa Verde National Park." PBS. Accessed May 31, 2024: www.pbs.org/kenburns/the-national-parks/mesa-verde.

Fine-Dare, Kathleen S., and Bryanna N. Durkee. "Interpreting an Absence: Esther's Legacy at Mesa Verde National Park." *Journal of the West* 50, no. 3 (Summer 2011).

Griffis, Miles W. "What's Wrong with the Manitou Cliff Dwellings Museum and Preserve?" *High Country News*, April 1, 2022. www.hcn.org/issues/54–4/archaeology-whats-wrong-with-the-manitou-cliff-dwellings-museum-and-preserve/.

Harrell, David. "We Contacted Smithsonian: The Wetherills at Mesa Verde." *New Mexico Historical Review* 62, no. 3 (1987). https://digitalrepository.unm.edu/nmhr/vol62/iss3/2.

Holmes, W. H. *A Notice of the Ancient Ruins of Southwestern Colorado, Examined During the Summer of 1875*. Washington, DC: U.S. Government Publications Office, 1875.

Lee, Ronald F. *The Antiquities Act of 1906*. Washington, DC: Office of History and Historic Architecture, 1970. http://npshistory.com/publications/antiquities-act-1906.pdf.

Lovata, Troy R. "Archaeology as Built for the Tourists: The Anasazi Cliff Dwellings of Manitou Springs, Colorado." *International Journal of Historical Archaeology* 15 (April 2011): 194–205.

Mason, Charles C. "The Story of the Discovery and Early Exploration of the Cliff Houses at the Mesa Verde." State Historical Society of Colorado, Denver, 1918. Reprinted in *Richard Wetherill: Anasazi* by Frank McNitt, 1974.

McNitt, Frank. *Richard Wetherill: Anasazi*. University of New Mexico Press, 1974.

McWhirt, Jean. "Esther." *Mesa Verde Notes* 9, no. 1 (December 1939). http://npshistory.com/nature_notes/meve/vol9-1d.htm.

National Park Service. "Important Events in the Development and Preservation of Mesa Verde National Park." Accessed May 20, 2024.

Noble, David Grant. *The Mesa Verde World: Explorations in Ancestral Puebloan Archaeology*. School of American Research, 2006.

Nordenskiöld, Gustav. *The Cliff Dwellers of the Mesa Verde*. P. A. Norstedt & Son, 1893.

Rothman, Hal. *America's National Monuments: The Politics of Preservation*. University of Illinois Press, 1989. Republished online: www.nps.gov/parkhistory/online_books/rothman/contents.htm.

Smith, Duane, A. *Mesa Verde National Park: Shadows of the Centuries*. University of Colorado Press, 2002.

Walters, Harry, and Hugh C. Rogers. "Anasazi and 'Anaasází: Two Words, Two Cultures." *Kiva* 66, no. 3 (Spring 2001): 317–326.

Watson, Don. *Indians of the Mesa Verde*. Mesa Verde Museum Association, 1961.

Wenger, Gilbert R. *The Story of Mesa Verde National Park*. Mesa Verde Museum of Association, revised 1991.

CASE FILE #13

What Was the Purpose of These Ancient Towers?

Hovenweep has been one of my favorite smaller NPS units ever since my wife and I stumbled across it during a road trip many years ago. I've been back several times to visit each of the ruin groups. The park service has chosen to leave Hovenweep in a mostly undeveloped state, with little interpretation, which allows for a particularly mysterious experience when visiting. Thus, I knew that I wanted to include the unit in this book, and my own impressions, notes, and photos from the area were essential in creating this chapter.

The scenes depicting the visit by the USGS photographic division come from the two National Park Service articles about Jackson (accessed 2024), plus a close examination of the photographs taken during the visit. Fewkes (1923) provides another historical impression of how the site looked in the late 1800s. Further details about the wet-plate process came from PBS (2024). Finally, interpretation about the site came from the Hovenweep article series by National Park Service (accessed 2024).

Sources

Fewkes, J. Walter. "The Hovenweep National Monument." *American Anthropologist* 25, no. 2 (1923): 145–155.

"History & Culture," "Geology," "Visitor Guide," "Little Ruin Trail Guide." Hovenweep National Monument. National Park Service. Accessed June 15, 2024. www.nps.gov/hove.

"Wet-Plate Photography." PBS American Experience. Accessed June 17, 2024. https://www.pbs.org /wgbh/americanexperience/features/eastman-wet-plate-photography/.

"William Henry Jackson." National Park Service. Accessed June 15, 2024. www.nps.gov/people /william-henry-jackson.htm.

"William Henry Jackson: Pioneer Photographer." National Park Service. Accessed June 15, 2024. www.nps.gov/museum/exhibits/whj/index.html.

CASE FILE #14 ═══════════════════════════════════

Who Was the Real Calamity Jane?

Though I watched it years later, I became a big fan of the *Deadwood* series that originally aired for three seasons on HBO during the early 2000s. The character of Calamity Jane played by Robin Weigert stole the show, and I wondered how accurate the portrayal and storylines were.

I had visited the region during several prior road trips, but a lengthy return trip during the early 2020s allowed me to explore most of the relevant sites from this story, including Laramie, Deadwood, Mount Moriah Cemetery, and the wider Black Hills. This further deepened my interest in unraveling the true story behind the mysterious Calamity Jane.

As it turns out, *Deadwood* got a decent part of the story correct, though much was left out or fictionalized for dramatic purposes. The dialogue seems to have been inspired by Quentin Tarantino, given they added about a million effing curse words. But all is bleeping forgiven. Once I realized how often Calamity's exploits ranged through later NPS units, it seemed like a perfect story to reconstruct in this book.

The chapter's opening quote, the contents of Calamity Jane's obituaries, and the legends about her life come from the *New York Times, The Sun, Courier Journal* (all 1903), and other sources.

The quote from the correspondent that closes the first section is from the *Milan Republic* (1903). Further details about Buffalo Bill's response, impressions of the general public, and disputed claims about Calamity Jane come from the *Pine Bluff Daily Graphic* (1903) and Etulain (2014). The latter book includes extensive research and informs much of my reconstructed story, particularly the early life of Martha Jane Canary, and the quote and information from the census ledger.

Canary's transformation into Calamity Jane during the Black Hills expedition mostly comes from John Hunton's diary, edited by Flannery (1956). The wagon party's arrival to Deadwood, and the article quote, come from a reprint of the original *Black Hills Pioneer* article found in *Cheyenne Daily Leader* (1876). The quote attributed to Calamity asking for a loan comes from Etulain, as do her actions surrounding the murder. The quote attributed to Jack McCall, and accounts of the murder of Wild Bill Hickok, are widely recorded in numerous sources that I consulted.

The legend-establishing quote attributed to the Montana man comes from Maguire (1877). The details that follow call upon my review of the works of the Deadwood Dick series by Wheeler.

Maguire's 1878 book also provides further details about Calamity's dismayed reactions to her growing infamy. The quotes from Calamity's dime show debut at the Palace Museum come from examining the historical poster, reprinted in Etulain, and a close reading of Canary's autobiography (circa 1896). The final scene, including quotes, comes from Lewis Freeman's *Sunset* article, reprinted in his cited 1922 book.

Sources

"Calamity Jane Is Dead: Mannish Border Woman Passed Away with the Real Wild West." *Pine Bluff Daily Graphic*, August 10, 1903.

"'Calamity Jane' Is Dead: Mrs. Burke Was Famous as an Army Scout and a Mail Carrier." *The Sun*, August 3, 1903.

"'Calamity Jane' Is Dead: Woman Who Became Famous as Indian Fighter." *New York Times*, August 2, 1903.

Canary, Martha J. *Life and Adventures of Calamity Jane by Herself*. Far West Travel Adventure, 1896.

"El Dorado Excerpts: 'Calamity Jane' Has Arrived." *Black Hills Pioneer*, July 12, 1876.

Etulain, Richard W. *The Life and Legends of Calamity Jane*. University of Oklahoma Press, 2014.

Flannery, L. G., ed. *John Hunton's Diary: Echoes from 1875*. Vol. 1. Guide Review, 1956.

Freeman, Lewis R. *Down the Yellowstone*. Dodd, Mead, and Company, 1922.

"Heroine of the Plains: Death of 'Calamity Jane,' a Missouri Woman Who Led a Wild Career." *St. Joseph Evening Express,* August 7, 1903.

Maguire, Horatio N. *The Black Hills and American Wonderland.* Donnely, Lloyd, and Company, 1877.

Maguire, Horatio N. *The Coming Empire.* Watkins & Smead, 1878.

"Many Men Fell Victim to Calamity Jane's Aim." *Courier Journal,* August 14, 1903.

Mattes, Merrill J. "Fort Laramie Park History 1834–1977." National Park Service. September 1980. www.nps.gov/fola/learn/historyculture/upload/FOLA_history.pdf.

CASE FILE #15

What Happened to Glen and Bessie Hyde on the Colorado River?

After joining a guided backpacking trip to the Grand Canyon in the early 2000s, I was inspired to become a wilderness and whitewater guide myself. During many trips with guests and fellow guides, mostly in the Sierras, what we just call *the Canyon* was a never-ending topic of conversation. I so wanted to get back there for a multiweek river trip. But after moving to St. Louis for grad school and staying around to teach, nearly fifteen years passed. During that time, I made it back to the West many times, but only managed a single hiking trip to the North Rim.

Thus, when I finally resumed exploring the Canyon in the mid-2010s, a string of return visits followed. I was lucky that this included rowing the river three times on private trips— one each in winter, spring, and summer. Through the experiences I describe here, plus exciting work on my book *Paddling the John Wesley Powell Route*, I became aware of several intriguing mysteries that happened within the confines of this rugged national park. If I ever get a chance to write a sequel to this book, I am ready to go with more Grand Canyon mysteries. I mean, I could use an excuse to run the river again—maybe this time in the fall.

Meanwhile, the biggest challenge became picking which story to include. With the blend of intrigue and whitewater adventure, the mystery of what happened to Glen and Bessie Hyde seemed like a perfect one to reconstruct in this book.

The opening conversation and quote attributed to Howland come from Marston (2014), who interviewed Howland's companion years later. That book was also critical in reconstructing the couple's progress and experiences on the river.

Another helpful source used throughout my reconstruction is Dimock (2007), which reprints many essential journal entries and letters written by the Hydes. This source also includes the historical photos taken with the Hydes' camera, which yield crucial details about clothing, demeanor, and progress through the canyon. Descriptions of the canyons, rivers, and rapids also come from considering my own experiences, and examining historical and contemporary maps.

The scene at Lees Ferry; the quoted letter by Glen; the sequence from Phantom Ranch to Sutro's departure, along with his attributed quote; and the campfire confession allegedly spoken in 1971 come from Myers (2001), from Dimock, and from Marston. The *Denver Post* reporter's story went out via the Associated Press and provides the quote attributed to Bessie during her visit to the South Rim. I found the article published in the *Daily Sentinel* (1928).

Sources

"Dares Rapids for Thrill: Idaho Woman on Perilous Journey in Boat." *Grand Junction Daily Sentinel,* December 2, 1928.

Dimock, Brad. *Sunk Without a Sound: The Tragic Colorado River Honeymoon of Glen and Bessie Hyde.* 2nd ed. Fretwater Press, 2007.

Marston, Otis Reed Dock. *From Powell to Power: A Recounting of the First 100 River Runners through the Grand Canyon.* Vishnu Temple Press, 2014.

Myers, Thomas M., and Michael P. Ghiglieri *Over the Edge: Death in Grand Canyon.* 2nd ed. Puma Press, 2001.

CASE FILE #16 ══

Who Left Behind the Forgotten Winchester?

I've been to Great Basin National Park several times, and I once spent a full day at the Buffalo Bill Center of the West. But I learned about this mystery the same way most people have: on the internet. Because so much from this story can be experienced in person—the rifle, the landscape where it was discovered, and the Wyoming museum—it was a perfect mystery to include.

The opening scene, and the dialogue attributed to Jensen and her unnamed team member, come primarily from Glionna (2015) and five Facebook posts made by the official profile of Great Basin National Park between January 9 and January 15, 2015. I closely examined photos from the NPS posts and other images published in the articles cited below for details used throughout the chapter.

The description of the road trip to the Firearms Museum comes from a Center of the West press release and McClure (both 2015). The rifle's return to the park was reported by the Associated Press (2019). The pandemic derailed my plans to visit in the early 2020s, but just like the rifle, I will return.

Sources

Associated Press. "137-Year-Old Winchester Rifle Found in Nevada Has New Home." May 26, 2019. https://apnews.com/article/ae5c9e87890a41f8af839c130b8addf6.

Buffalo Bill Center of the West. "Wyoming Museum Displays Forgotten Winchester from Great Basin National Park." Press Release. June 30, 2015. www.prweb.com/releases/wyoming_museum _displays_forgotten_winchester_from_great_basin_national_park/prweb12816925.htm.

Glionna, John. M. "Abandoned 1882 Rifle Sparks Archaeological Quest in Nevada." *Los Angeles Times*, January 15, 2015.

Griffith, Martin. "Researchers Puzzled by 1882 Rifle Find." *Reno Gazette*, January 21, 2015.

Izadi, Elahe. "The Mystery of the 132-Year-Old Winchester Rifle Found Propped against a National Park Tree." *Washington Post*, January 14, 2015. www.washingtonpost.com/news/morning-mix/wp/2015/01 /14/the-mystery-of-the-132-year-old-winchester-rifle-found-propped-against-a-national-park-tree.

McClure, Nancy. "Forgotten Winchester Visits the Center of the West's Cody Firearms Museum." Buffalo Bill Center of the West. July 2, 2015. https://centerofthewest.org/2015/07/02/forgotten -winchester-now-on-display-in-center-of-the-wests-cody-firearms-museum.

CASE FILE #17

Was Upheaval Dome Created by a Meteorite Impact?

By the time I hiked out to see Upheaval Dome, sometime in the mid-2010s, I'd spent several years studying photos and articles about its disputed origin. When I stood at the rim, looking at the feature, I was already leaning toward the impact arguments. Seeing it in person only further pushed me in that direction.

I have a fairly limited background in geology—an undergraduate degree and about three years working as a field researcher in surveying and sampling, plus some lab projects, but mostly on river and watershed projects. That doesn't make me any more qualified to solve this mystery, but the geology background did help me navigate the dense scientific papers that are essential to understanding this dizzying situation. As I delved deeper inside the research, and my head began to spin like an asteroid, I knew that the story was perfect for this book. I also discovered that the debate is less settled than many people realize.

I find that one of the biggest challenges with writing about science is turning it into a story that is accessible and interesting to a general audience. Thus, as I began to work on this chapter, and went searching for narrative content, I wondered about Edward Abbey. Given how much time he spent in the area, did he have any thoughts about Upheaval Dome? Re-reading *Desert Solitaire* didn't turn up much, so I began to broadly search for other connections between Abbey and Upheaval Dome. Entirely by chance, this led me to the two sources from the *Canyon Country Zephyr*, plus the name H. R. Joesting, which I'd noticed in some peer-reviewed research articles about Upheaval Dome. Slowly, the first half of this story fell together in such an unexpected and exciting way.

Then one day, I realized I'd spent several years doing research, but I hadn't written a damn thing. I'd been to Meteor Crater. I once cycled through Nördlinger Ries, for effing sake, on a bike trip from my wife's family home in Baden-Wurttemberg. But with my manuscript deadline approaching, and in true Abbey fashion, I still needed to compact this jumbled breccia of a story into a cohesive mass. Doing this would involve a frenetic week with a disturbing amount of coffee and an equal amount of beer.

The opening scenes, including all quotes attributed to Abbey, come mostly from *Desert Solitaire* (1968), Stiles (2014 and 2023), and Church (2006). Also helpful were Joesting (1958 and 1966).

My own experiences on the ground in these places, plus studying historical maps and satellite imagery, was essential to unraveling the movements of the figures involved.

The scenes depicting Eugene and Carol Shoemaker and their partner's experiences—from Meteor Crater to Australia—come from a variety of sources, including Grieve (1990), Levy (2002), Cokinos (2010), and Kieffer (2015). Descriptions of the formation of impact craters were informed by a broad survey of scholarly and secondary sources, including O'Dale (accessed 2024).

The details about Shoemaker and his colleagues' research efforts at Upheaval Dome come from Kriens (1999). Studying that paper's colorized geologic map and cross section were essential for grasping their arguments about Upheaval Dome. The competing salt dome theory comes from Jackson (1998), with other sources consulted to grasp the evolution of the debate. The discovery of shocked quartz grains comes from Buchner (2008). I'd like to think that Ed would have enjoyed this story, but he also might have laughed in my face, poured out my coffee, and taken my beer.

Sources

Abbey, Edward. *Desert Solitaire: A Season in the Wilderness.* Simon & Schuster, 1968.

Buchner, Elmar, and Thomas Kenkmann. "Upheaval Dome, Utah, USA: Impact Origin Confirmed." *Geology* 36, no. 3 (March 2008): 227–230.

Church, Lisa J. "Udall Returns, Savors His Legacy." *Salt Lake Tribune,* July 27, 2006. https://archive.sltrib.com/story.php?ref=/utah/ci_4100794.

Cokinos, Christopher. *The Fallen Sky: An Intimate History of Shooting Stars.* Penguin, 2010.

Grieve, Richard A. F. "Impact Cratering on the Earth." *Scientific American,* April 1990. www.scientificamerican.com/article/impact-cratering-on-the-earth/.

Jackson, M. P. A., D. D. Schultz-Ela, M. R. Hudec, I. A. Watson, and M. L. Porter. "Structure and Evolution of Upheaval Dome: A Pinched-Off Salt Diapir." *GSA Bulletin* 110, no. 12 (December 1998): 1547–1573.

Joesting, H. R., and Donald Plouff. "Geophysical Studies of the Upheaval Dome Area, San Juan

County, Utah." *Guidebook to the Geology of the Paradox Basin, Ninth Annual Field Conference*, 1958, 86–92.

Joesting, H. R., J. E. Case, and Donald Plouff. "Regional Geophysical Investigations of the Moab-Needles Area, Utah." *Department of the Interior, Geological Survey Professional Paper 516-C*, 1966.

Kieffer, Susan W. *Eugene M. Shoemaker 1928–1997: A Biographical Memoir*. National Academy of Sciences: 2015. http://nationalacademyofsciences.org/publications/biographical-memoirs/memoir-pdfs/shoemaker-eugene.pdf.

Kriens, Brian J., Eugene M. Shoemaker, and Ken E. Herkenhoff. "Geology of the Upheaval Dome Impact Structure Southeast Utah." *Journal of Geophysical Research* 104, no. E8 (August 1999): 18,867–18,887.

Levy, David H. *Shoemaker by Levy: The Man Who Made an Impact*. Princeton University Press: 2002.

O'Dale, Charles. "Crater Formation." Crater Explorer. Accessed March 21, 2024. https://craterexplorer.ca/crater-formation.

Stiles, Jim. "Bates Wilson: The 'Father of Canyonlands NP'... In His Own Words." *Canyon Country Zephyr*, October 1, 2014. www.canyoncountryzephyr.com/2014/10/01/bates-wilson-the-father-of-canyonlands-np-in-his-own-words/.

Stiles, Jim. "Rangers Lloyd Pierson & Lyle Jamison: Remembering Arches, Moab, & Ed Abbey in the 50s: from 1989 & 1992 Interviews." *Canyon Country Zephyr*, April 16, 2023. www.canyoncountryzephyr.com/2023/04/16/rangers-lloyd-pierson-lyle-jamison-remembering-arches-moab-ed-abbey-in-the-50s-from-1989–1992-interviews-w-jim-stiles-zx58/.

CASE FILE #18

Was Josie Bassett a Cattle Rustler, Bootlegger, and Murderer?

I've been exploring Utah since the mid-2000s, and I first visited Dinosaur National Monument toward the end of that decade. I can't recall when I first stepped inside Josie Bassett's homestead on Cub Creek. I do know that the first time, I was yet to grasp the significance of this legendary frontierswoman.

When I began to explore the rivers and reservoirs of the John Wesley Powell Route, I passed through Browns Park by boat. During a stop at the John Jarvie Historic Ranch on the Green River, I read museum displays about the area's violent past. Yet today, the remote mountain valley is mostly empty. Just irrigated fields, roaming wildlife, and a few decaying signs of the Old West.

This realization, and several further encounters with the so-called Outlaw Trail, put me on a path toward unraveling some of the most iconic true stories from the Wild West. Being a huge fan of Western films, I quickly realized how the pervasive fictions about that historic era overshadowed and obscured the underlying facts. The goals for me became to figure out what actually happened—and where.

Soon I was returning to these regions with new knowledge learned from source materials, comparing the history with my own experiences in these landscapes, to bring the stories to life on the page. Given the many myths and rumors surrounding Josie Bassett, unraveling the mysteries of her life seemed a perfect chapter for this book.

The opening scenes mostly come from Boren's interview (circa 1960), which provides all the quoted dialogue attributed to the young reporter and Bassett during their 1960 interview at Cub Creek. Additional lines of dialogue attributed to Bassett that appear throughout the chapter come from Messersmith (1960), including Bassett's appreciation of the beauty of Browns Park, her rebuttal of Charles Kelly's claims, and her desire "to be in the hills."

The quotes attributed to Bassett about her relationship with Butch Cassidy are printed in several sources, including Womack (2020), with that source also helpful throughout my reconstruction, including providing the later quote attributed to Wells, the quoted joke attributed to Morris, and quotes attributed to Bassett during her trial.

The scenes depicting Bassett's divorce from McKnight, plus other details about her life, come from McClure (1985), which also provides details used throughout my reconstruction, as do Kelly (1959), Burton (1990), and the Josie Bassett Morris resources file from the Regional History Center at the Uintah County Library, which I first visited in Vernal around 2016.

Sources

Boren, Kerry Ross. "A Personal Interview with Josie Bassett." Interviewed circa 1960, publication year unknown. Accessed December 28, 2022. https://uintahlibrary.org/GroupedWork/097f8443-9378-1b25-bbd9–9cda2b848aef-eng/.

Burton, Doris Karren. *Dinosaurs and Moonshine: Tales of Josie Morris Bassett and Jensen's Other Unique History and Folklore*. Vincent Brothers, 1990.

"Josie Bassett Morris." Dinosaur National Monument. National Park Service. August 1989. https://www.nps.gov/dino/learn/historyculture/josiebassettmorris.htm.

Kelly, Charles. *The Outlaw Trail: A History of Butch Cassidy & His Wild Bunch*. 2nd ed. Lincoln, NE: Bison Books, 1959.

"Life Visits Josie, Queen of the Cattle Rustlers." *Life* magazine 24, no. 1 (January 5, 1948).

McClure, Grace. *The Bassett Women*. Swallow Press, 1985.

Messersmith, Murl L. "Historic Interview: Josie Morris." Dinosaur National Monument. July 18, 1960.

"Morris, Josie Bassett." Resources File, Uintah County Library Regional History Center. Accessed December 28, 2022: https://uintahlibrary.org/GroupedWork/097f8443-9378-1b25-bbd9–9cda2b848aef-eng/Home?searchId=3872472&recordIndex=1&page=1&searchSource=local.

Wommack, Linda. *Growing Up with the Wild Bunch*. Twodot Books, 2020.

CASE FILE #19 ═══════════════════════════════════════

How Could a Sand Dune Swallow a Boy?

I was living in St. Louis when this burial incident occurred. I recall noticing a few reports at the time, but I didn't delve deeper until years later. Numerous sources were used to reconstruct this story, including news articles and broadcast reports from the days and years following the incident. The news broadcasts yielded essential details about the experiences of the victim, the family members, the searchers, and the hospital workers. Numerous photos, satellite images, and maps were also examined to create descriptions.

The opening scene at the lakefront beach and dune—including Nathan's disappearance and the dialogue from Greg Woessner and Colin—mostly comes from Mastony and Sabar (both 2014). These two sources were also called upon to depict the recovery efforts, the hospital scenes and dialogue, and the section depicting Professor Erin Argylian at the dunes and restaurant, including her dialogue and the quote attributed to Greg Woessner.

The details about the geology and human history at Mount Baldy, including dune migration and the resulting decomposition chimney theory, come from several sources, such as USGS (accessed 2022) and Argylian (2015). Prevailing scientific attitudes toward the phenomena were verified through a variety of sources, but especially from Sabar and from Smith (both 2014). The ranger who correctly theorized the cause of the burial was Bruce Rowe, interviewed by Owens for ABC News (2013). Research studies conducted at the dunes are described in Lavalley (2016) and NPS (accessed 2023).

Sources

Argyilan, E. P., P. G. Avis, M. P. S. Krekeler, and C. C. Morris. "The Origin of Collapse Features Appearing in a Migrating Parabolic Dune along the Southern Coast of Lake Michigan." *Aeolian Research* 19 (2015): 137–149.

Cortopassi, Ray. "Miracle on Mount Baldy." WGN News, May 16, 2023. https://wgntv.com/video/family-remembers-miracle-at-indiana-dunes-mount-baldy/8653815/.

"Family Vacation Turned Nightmare." *CNN New Day*, July 15, 2013. https://www.youtube.com/watch?v=pODmblE2KSM&t=96s.

Gmiter, Tanda. "Lake Michigan Beach Will Reopen, 4 Years after Boy Swallowed by Sand Dune." *MLive*, May 4, 2017. www.mlive.com/news/us-world/2017/05/lake_michigan_beach.

Lavalley, Amy. "Mount Baldy Remains Closed; Researchers Closer to Finding Sand Answers." *Chicago Tribune*, June 30, 2016. www.chicagotribune.com/2016/06/30/mount-baldy-remains-closed-researchers-closer-to-finding-sand-answers-2.

Mastony, Colleen. "Boy's Rescue Remembered as 'Miracle on Mount Baldy.'" *Chicago Tribune*, September 14, 2014. www.chicagotribune.com/2014/09/14/boys-rescue-remembered-as-miracle-on-mount-baldy.

"Mount Baldy Dune Investigation." National Park Service. Accessed March 26, 2023. www.nps.gov
/indu/learn/management/mount-baldy-dune-investigation.htm.

Owens, Ryan. "Buried in the Sand Dune." ABC News, July 15, 2013. https://www.youtube.com/watch
?v=np_pyn_Lst8.

Podesta, Laura. "Mount Baldy Beach Back Open for First Time Since 2013." ABC 7 Chicago, July 14,
2017. https://abc7chicago.com/mount-baldy-beach-indiana-dunes-boy-rescued/2216912.

Reynolds, Dean. "Buried Alive." *CBS This Morning*, July 16, 2013. https://www.youtube.com/watch?v
=_ETtl—IXOQ&t=3s.

Sabar, Ariel. "The Mystery of Why This Dangerous Sand Dune Swallowed a Boy." *Smithsonian*
magazine, December 2014. https://www.smithsonianmag.com/science-nature/mystery-why
-dangerous-sand-dune-swallowed-boy-180953404/.

Smith, Lindsey. "Baffling, Boy-Swallowing Holes Close an Indiana Dune." *All Things Considered*.
National Public Radio, May 8, 2014. www.npr.org/2014/05/08/310155197/baffling-boy
-swallowing-holes-close-an-indiana-dune.

United States Geological Survey. "Geology of Indiana Dunes National Park." Accessed June 22, 2022.
www.usgs.gov/geology-and-ecology-of-national-parks/geology-indiana-dunes-national-park.

CASE FILE #20

Did Hugh Glass Truly Survive a Grizzly Bear Attack?

Several events got me interested in unraveling the true story of Hugh Glass. Not long after
the 2015 release of *The Revenant,* a hit film that earned Leonardo DiCaprio an Oscar, I was
visiting the Museum of the Mountain Man in Pinedale, Wyoming, while working on my
book *Paddling the John Wesley Powell Route.*

During a fascinating tour with director Clint Gilchrist, I learned that a current topic
at the museum was separating fact from fiction in this entertaining film. I had yet to see the
movie, but once I did, I understood their points. As is the case with many motion pictures,
numerous elements are invented for dramatic and thematic effect. Not only are the action
sequences and violence exaggerated, but the settings are shifted to more mountainous landscapes. As I delved into the source materials, one goal became to unravel where the events
actually occurred. With the story passing through certainly one and most likely two modern-
day NPS units, it seemed perfect for this book.

To construct this chapter, I relied primarily upon a series of primary sources, plus
several secondary sources like hughglass.org and Myers (1976). The opening scene, and
the reactions of Allen, come primarily from Yount (1923), who claimed to have known
Glass.

The descriptions of the war on the plains also come from Myers, plus other sources, as do the attack scenes. The quote is from Potts's letter (accessed 2024).

The aftermath of the grizzly attack, including Glass's makeshift hospice, comes from numerous sources, with the debate of the kid's identity being particularly aided by hughglass.org. Details about the life history relayed by Glass come from Yount and from Myers, with those sources and others being helpful in reconstructing the flight of Fitzgerald and the kid.

Examining these sources and historical and contemporary maps leads me to theorize that the route of Henry's main party and the two trailing trappers passed through the modern-day boundaries of Theodore Roosevelt National Park. The sequence about Glass's survival, solo escape, and confrontation with the kid and Fitzgerald came from a broad survey of all cited sources, with the quoted lines of dialogue attributed to Glass coming from Yount (1923).

Sources

"An Unforgettable Man: Hugh Glass." The Museum of the Mountain Man. Accessed December 12, 2022. http://hughglass.org.

Chittenden, Hiram M. *The American Fur Trade of the Far West*. Vol. 2. Frances P. Harper, 1902.

Clyman, James. "The Adventures of Hugh Glass," written 1871. In *James Clyman, Frontiersman 1792–1881*, Charles L. Camp, ed. California Historical Society, 1923.

Cooke, Phillip St. George. "Some Incidents in the Life of Hugh Glass, a Hunter of the Missouri River." *St. Louis Beacon*, December 2 and 9, 1830. Reprinted in *Southern Literary Messenger*, 1842.

Flagg, Edmund. "Adventures at the Head Waters of the Missouri." *Southern Literary Messenger*, 1842.

Hall, James. "The Missouri Trapper." *The Port Folio* 19, no. 1 (1825).

"Hugh Glass Letter on Display at Cultural Heritage Center." South Dakota State Historical Society. January 21, 2016. https://history.sd.gov/archives/forms/news/2016/Hugh%20Glass%20Letter%20APPROVED.pdf.

Myers, John Myers. *The Saga of Hugh Glass: Pirate, Pawnee, and Mountain Man*. 2nd ed. Bison Books, 1976.

Neihardt, John G. *The Song of Hugh Glass*. The Macmillan Company, 1921.

Philipp, Maximilian Alexander. *Maximilian, Prince of Wied's, Travels in the Interior of North America*. Vol. 2 & 3. The Arthur H. Clark Company, 1906.

Potts, Daniel. "Daniel T. Potts Letter to Thomas Cochlan July 7, 1824." Montana State Library. Accessed August 2024. https://www.mtmemory.org/nodes/view/80132.

Sage, Rufus. *Scenes in the Rocky Mountains*. Carey & Hart, 1846.

Yount, George C. "The Adventures of Hugh Glass." Edited by Charles L. Camp. *California Historical Society Quarterly*, April 1923. http://hughglass.org/sources/cgcy-pg-30-edited-200-dpi/.

CASE FILE #21

Was the St. Louis Arch Designed to Control the Weather?

When I moved to St. Louis in 2006, I didn't know too much about the city. From a prior road trip, I knew there was an impressive shiny arch and an area to the south filled with rugged hills and rivers. I ended up spending more time exploring the Ozarks, while slowly learning about the polarized opinions and controversial backstory of the Gateway Arch.

Since I had moved from far away, I was untouched by the debate. With other transplanted or visiting friends, we enjoyed occasional visits to the Arch. However, I didn't spend much effort to understand the backstory until after the memorial was redesignated a national park in 2018. As a result, the so-called *Arch effect* received more attention as well. When I began to look closer, I suddenly realized how bizarre the Arch's history was—a perfect story for this book.

The opening scene comes from several sources, including watching documentary footage of the construction, plus Brown (1984) and Campbell (2013), with both books being consulted for project history throughout the chapter, including the civil rights issues and demonstration. Details about the mixed opinions toward the Arch come from surveying the sources cited in this section and others.

The St. Louis Municipal Parking Lot moniker was coined by the *Post-Dispatch* (1946). Descriptions of the design competition entries come mostly from Brown (1980) and Leonard (2014). The details about Mussolini's exhibition and planned arch come from Lathrop (2012) and other sources. The prescient artwork by Geneva Abbot, and the 1960s newspaper quote about her, come from "A Brief Bio..." (accessed 2024).

The daredevil exploits at the Arch come from *St. Petersburg Independent* (1980), Smith (1992), and Hahn (2016). Discussions of the Arch effect and St. Louis weather history come from Lynn (2023), CBS News (2022), and other sources.

Sources

"1967: A Chicago Man Is First in Line to Go to the Top of the Arch." *St. Louis Post-Dispatch*. www
.stltoday.com/news/archives/1967-a-chicago-man-is-first-in-line-to-go-the-top-of-the-arch
/article_6081db90-3386-5561-a57a-967ad2b0b71c.html.

"A Brief Bio of Geneva Patterson." Geneva H. Patterson. Accessed April 27, 2024. https://gpatterson.com/.

"Architectural Competition for the Jefferson National Expansion Monument." Yale University
Library. September 14, 2023. https://collections.library.yale.edu/catalog/10015733. www.govinfo
.gov/content/pkg/GOVPUB-I29-PURL-gpo82065/pdf/GOVPUB-I29-PURL-gpo82065.pdf.

Brown, Sharon. "Jefferson National Expansion Memorial: The 1947–1948 Competition." *Magazine of
the Missouri Historical Society* 1, no. 3 (Winter 1980): 40–48.

Campbell, Tracy. *The Gateway Arch: A Biography*. Yale University Press, 2013.

Corrigan, Patricia. "The Triumph of the Arch: 1965–1985." *St. Louis Post-Dispatch*. October 27, 1985.

Hahn, Valerie Schremp. "Identity of Pilot Who Flew through Arch in 1966 is No Mystery, Family Says." *St. Louis Post-Dispatch*, July 5, 2016. www.stltoday.com/news/local/identity-of-pilot-who-flew-through-arch-in-1966-is-no-mystery-family-says.

Kaplan, Fred. "The Twisted History of the Gateway Arch." *Smithsonian* magazine, October 2015. www.smithsonianmag.com/history/story-st-louis-gateway-arch-180956624.

Lathrop, Alan K. "The EUR: Mussolini's New Rome." Warfare History Network. Summer 2012. https://warfarehistorynetwork.com/article/the-eur-mussolinis-new-rome.

Leonard, Mary Delach. "Instead of the Arch, the St. Louis Riverfront Could Have Had...This." St. Louis Public Radio. August 26, 2014. www.stlpr.org/arts/2014-08-26/instead-of-the-arch-the-st-louis-riverfront-could-have-had-this.

Lynn, Stacy. "Arch Effect: Is it Real or St. Louis Lore?" Spectrum News, March 7, 2023. https://spectrumlocalnews.com/mo/st-louis/weather/2023/03/06/arch-effect--real-or-just-st--louis-lore-.

National Park Service. *Jefferson National Expansion Memorial: Cultural Landscape Report.* May 2010. http://npshistory.com/publications/jeff/clr-2010.pdf.

"Parachutist Dies after Landing on St. Louis Arch." *St. Petersburg Independent*, November 24, 1980.

"Record Rainfall Causes Widespread Flooding in St. Louis Area." CBS News, July 26, 2022. www.cbsnews.com/chicago/news/record-rainfall-causes-widespread-flooding-in-st-louis-area.

"Riverfront Memorial Area Now St. Louis Parking Lot." *St. Louis Post-Dispatch*, May 7, 1946.

Smith, Bill. "Climber Parachutes from Top of Arch." *St. Louis Post-Dispatch*, September 15, 1992.

CASE FILE #22

What Is the Full Length of Mammoth Cave?

My wife and I had heard about Mammoth Cave for years, but we didn't visit until the summer of 2023, when I was searching for places to take our new camper. While wandering through the visitor center exhibits, I came across two intriguing facts that hinted at an underground story worth unraveling. Mammoth Cave became known as the longest in the world in 1972, due to the underground expedition from Flint Ridge. However, the full length of the cave system remained unknown. As I began to research the efforts of the far-out cavers, I realized this was a perfect story for this book given the mix of mystery and adventure.

Most of the scenes and all of the dialogue in the chapter story come from closely studying Brucker (1987), with additional details coming from Wells (1973). Facts about the cave systems and the history of exploration and tourism come from all sources, but particularly from both National Park Service sources (accessed 2024), McGraw (2023), Tabler (2017), and Murray (1979), with the latter source contributing most of the details about Collins's entrapment.

Sources

Brucker, Roger W., and Richard A. Watson. *The Longest Cave*. 2nd ed. Southern Illinois University Press, 1987.

"Exploring the World's Longest Known Cave." National Park Service. Accessed March 14, 2024. www .nps.gov/articles/000/exploring-the-worlds-longest-known-cave.htm.

McGraw, Eliza. "How the Kentucky Cave Wars Reshaped the State's Tourism Industry." *Smithsonian* magazine, July 25, 2023. www.smithsonianmag.com/history/how-the-kentucky-cave-wars -reshaped-the-states-tourism-industry-180982585/.

Murray, Robert K., and Roger W. Brucker. *Trapped! The Story of Floyd Collins*. University of Kentucky Press, 1979.

Tabler, Dave. "The Kentucky Cave Wars." Appalachian History. April 19, 2017. www.appalachianhistory .net/2017/04/kentucky-cave-wars.html.

"The Kentucky Cave Wars." National Park Service. Accessed March 14, 2024. www.nps.gov/articles /000/the-kentucky-cave-wars.htm.

Wells, Steve G., and David J. DesMarais. "The Flint–Mammoth Connection." *National Speleological Society News* 31, no. 2 (February 1973).

CASE FILE #23 ———————————————————————

Did Al Capone Have an Outpost in the Everglades?

A trip with my wife to Everglades National Park and Big Cypress Swamp National Preserve during late fall of 2022 reinforced an impression I'd long formed from afar. The Everglades are a wild, ominous, and mysterious place. When I began to search through the area's many mysterious incidents for a single story to reconstruct, I encountered mostly myths, legends, and negative attitudes. There was little in the way of concrete mysteries worth recounting.

A thorough reading about Al Capone's escapades confirmed that any records about his alleged deeds in the Everglades could not be verified. Then I stumbled across articles about the final days of the Gator Hook Lodge and Pinecrest, which may be the place where the rumors began. Whether Capone truly had an outpost, speakeasy, or brothel in the Everglades will likely never be known.

The opening scenes, including quotes attributed to Allen and Douglas, and the latter author's explorations of the Everglades come from her cowritten autobiography (1987), which also provides the backstory and the direct quotes used in later scenes about her 1940s research for *River of Grass*. The attitudes toward the Everglades and various myths, violent events, and negative impressions that are mentioned throughout my reconstruction come from Kaye (2014), Ariza (2021), Finlay (2022), and the cited books by Douglas.

Descriptions of Al Capone, his life and crimes, the quotes attributed to him, and the Miami public attitudes toward him come from Bair (2016), Bousquet (1998), and Muir (1990). The latter author's book provides the details about Douglas's stage play based upon Capone. The summary of relevant history around Florida and the Everglades comes from a wide survey of secondary sources. The details about Ed Watson and Belle Starr come from Tebeau (1996) and Arnott (2006). Details about the Miami Jetport, and the resulting public outcry, come from Davis (2003) and Douglas.

The closing scenes at the Gator Hook Lodge and around Pinecrest come from English (1979), Klinkenberg (2012), Cooke (2016), and particularly Gore (1976), whose article provides the quotes attributed to Uncle Mac. I wish I could have met that guy.

Sources

Ariza, Mario. "Gruesome Secrets of the Florida Everglades." *Sun Sentinel*, March 3, 2021. www.sun-sentinel.com/2021/03/03/the-gruesome-secrets-of-the-florida-everglades-here-are-five-hideous-crimes-that-led-there.

Arnott, Richard D. "Belle Starr." HistoryNet. June 12, 2006. https://www.historynet.com/belle-starr.

Bair, Deirdre. *Al Capone: His Life, Legacy, and Legend.* Doubleday, 2016.

Bousquet, Stephen C. "The Gangster in Our Midst: Al Capone in South Florida, 1930–1947." *Florida Historical Quarterly* 76, no. 3 (Winter 1998): 297–309.

Cooke, Bill. "Remembering the Most Notorious Dive Bars in South Florida History." *Miami New Times*, January 27, 2016. www.miaminewtimes.com/music/remembering-the-most-notorious-dive-bars-in-south-florida-history-8207098.

Davis, Jack E. "'Conservation Is Now a Dead Word': Marjorie Stoneman Douglas and the Transformation of American Environmentalism." *Environmental History* 8, no. 1 (January 2003): 53–76.

Douglas, Marjory Stoneman. *The Everglades: River of Grass.* Rinehart, 1947.

Douglas, Marjory Stoneman with John Rothchild. *Voice of the River*. Pineapple Press, 1987.

English, Bella. "It's Come as You Are at Gator Hook Lodge." *Gulf Coast News*, January 21, 1979.

Finlay, T. L. "The History of the Florida Everglades Is a History of Crime and Mystery." Crime Reads. August 22, 2022. https://crimereads.com/the-history-of-the-florida-everglades-is-a-history-of-crime-and-mystery.

Gore, Rick. "Twilight Hope for Big Cypress." *National Geographic*, August 1976.

Kaye, Ken. "Finding Lost City: Everglades Site with Aura of Mystery Housed Capone Saloon, Indian Camp." *Sun Sentinel*, May 18, 2014. www.sun-sentinel.com/2014/05/18/solving-mystery-of-lost-city-in-everglades/.

Klinkenberg, Jeff. "The Gator Hook Bar Was as Wild as the Everglades Outside." *Tampa Bay Times*, March 15, 2012. www.tampabay.com/features/humaninterest/the-gator-hook-bar-was-as-wild-as -the-everglades-outside/1220032.

Muir, Helen. *Miami, U.S.A.* Rev. ed. Pickering Press, 1990.

Tebeau, Chalton W. *The Story of the Chokoloskee Bay Country.* 6th ed. Florida Flair Books, 1996.

CASE FILE #24

What Created the Appalachian Balds?

For years, I spent time around and on top of Appalachian balds before grasping their mysteriousness. Growing up out West, I was used to seeing bare summits rising above the tree line, which happens naturally at various higher elevations due to local conditions. So, when I began to encounter the Appalachian balds, I initially assumed something similar was happening in the Southeast, just at relatively lower elevations.

I don't recall exactly when I learned that the origin behind the balds is uncertain. Maybe it was while paddling rivers below them, mountain biking around them, or hiking and backpacking through them. However, I believe the topic came up during some sessions of "trail talk." When I began working on this book, I knew this was a worthy mystery to unravel.

The opening legend comes from Mooney, more specifically "Part VI: Notes and Parallels to Myths, section 13: The Great Yellow-Jacket," beginning on page 443 of my 1902 copy. Some observers have claimed the balds must have been created in modern times, since Bartram didn't explicitly mention them. However, a close examination of Bartram's 1794 book—which provides all quotes attributed to the explorer—suggests to me that they were present during his time. Perhaps Bartram took them for granted as normal features, like many people first do, including myself.

The quote attributed to Strother's diary comes from Owen (1898). Various historical theories about natural and human causes that attempted to explain the balds come from Wells (1937), Tabler (2019), and NPS (2023)—background details from these sources were also helpful throughout the chapter. Finally, the big-picture theory that continues to emerge comes from Weigl and Knowles (1995 and 2014).

Sources

Bartram, William. *Travels through North and South Carolina, Georgia, East and West Florida.* 2nd ed. J. Johnson, 1794.

"History of the Grassy Balds in Great Smoky Mountains National Park." National Park Service. Accessed February 14, 2023. www.nps.gov/parkhistory/online_books/grsm/4/intro.htm.

Mooney, James. *Myths of the Cherokee*. Government Printing Office, 1902.

Owen, Thomas McAdory. *William Strother, of Virginia, and His Descendants*. Harrisburg Publishing Co., 1898.

Tabler, Dave. "Bald Is Beautiful." Appalachian History. August 23, 2019. www.appalachianhistory.net /2019/08/bald-is-beautiful.html.

Weigl, Peter D., and Travis W. Knowles. "Megaherbivores and Southern Appalachian Grass Balds." *Growth and Change* 26 (Summer 1995): 365–382.

Weigl, Peter D., and Travis W. Knowles. "Temperate Mountain Grasslands: A Climate-Herbivore Hypothesis for Origins and Persistence." *Biological Reviews: Cambridge Philosophical Society* 89, no. 2 (May 2014): 466–476.

Wells, B. W. "Southern Appalachian Grass Balds." *Journal of the Elisha Mitchell Scientific Society* 53, no. 1 (July 1937): 1–26.

CASE FILE #25

How Did Murderer Bradford Bishop Escape?

When I began working on this book, I wanted to include several true crime chapters. However, most unsolved cases from NPS units involve missing persons or remote murders without much of a story to unravel. Typically, someone was hiking or camping, minding their own business. Later their mangled corpse was found in the woods. Other times, the visitor simply vanished without a trace. In most cases, no definitive suspect is ever identified.

Whoa, whoa, whoa—please stop running for the park exit! I don't want to scare anyone away from visiting our amazing National Park System, where the odds of something bad happening are much lower than in any highly populated region. Yes, strange and terrible things do *occasionally* happen in NPS units, but those are the exceptions. Just be careful and you should be fine.

So, with the goal of finding a few truly unique crime stories from NPS units, I settled upon the four in this book, including the saga of accused murderer Bradford Bishop, which starts in a swampy coastal state forest and ends in the Great Smoky Mountains. The morbid opening scene comes primarily from the reporting of Allegood (1976 and 2006) and McClees (1997), with the latter source consulted throughout my reconstruction. As the story shifts to Maryland and the scene of the crime, details come from the *Raleigh News & Observer* and *Durham Sun* (both March 9, 1976). The quote attributed to the family babysitter comes from *Time* (1976).

The background material about the family, and claims that Bradford Bishop may have been a spy, come from a wide survey of the cited sources, including *Durham Sun* (March 11,

1976), *Rocky Mount Telegram* (September 11 and 29, 1976), *News & Observer* (September 13 and 29, 1976), and Meyer (2013). Details about the press conference during which Bradford Bishop is named a suspect, the progressing investigation, and the quotes attributed to Edmisten come from Whittle (March 13, 1976).

The manhunt for Bishop—including witness accounts, alleged family tensions, psychiatric history, and his reported visit to a Spindale gun shop—comes from *News & Observer* (March 15, 16, 18, and 21, 1976), *Charlotte Observer* (March 16 and 23, 1976), and Phillips (1976), with the sources from March 21 and 23 providing the quoted dialogue. Also helpful was Thompson and Yarborough (2014). The scenes from Great Smoky Mountains National Park come from *Durham Morning Herald* (March 19, 1976), *Durham Sun* (March 30, 1976), and *Charlotte Observer* (April 28, 1976).

The theories and sightings after Bishop's disappearance from the national park come from numerous sources, including *Charlotte News* (September 27, 1976), McClees (1997), and Rasmussen (2006). The alleged encounter and dialogue attributed to Harrel come from James (1997), which also reveals how Sheriff Robert L. Keefer found Ken Bankston's 1976 letter to Bishop in the State Department Archives in 1992. I quote directly from a scanned version that I downloaded from Wikileaks.

The final developments, about Bishop's listing on the FBI most wanted list and his surprise daughter, come from the FBI (2014), *CBS News* (2014), and Yancy et al. (2021). Finally, I considered my own experience in the relevant areas, and I consulted numerous historical images found throughout my research, plus historical maps and trail maps to reconstruct this mystery.

Sources

Allegood, Jerry. "5 Burned Bodies Found in Tyrrell." *Raleigh News & Observer*, March 3, 1976.

Allegood, Jerry. "Authorities Press Nationwide Search for Bishop." *Raleigh News & Observer*, March 10, 1976.

Allegood, Jerry. "Bishop Still Wanted in Family's Death." *Raleigh News & Observer*, February 26, 2006.

Bankerton, Ken. Letter to Bradford Bishop, March 15, 1976. https://wikileaks.org/gifiles/attach/32 /32347_Bishop%20-%20Pen%20Letter.pdf.

"Bishop Believed Seen in Spindale." *Raleigh News & Observer,* March 21, 1976.

"Case of Accused Family Slayer Bradford Bishop Still a Mystery." *Rocky Mount Telegram*, September 29, 1976.

"Credit Card Receipt Yields Slayings Clue." *Raleigh News & Observer*, March 15, 1976.

"Edmisten Feels Sure Bradford Bishop Alive." *Durham Sun*, March 30, 1976.

"Edmisten Stymied by Missing Bradford Bishop." *Charlotte Observer*, April 28, 1976.

"Ex-U.S. Diplomat, Murder Suspect, Added to FBI's 'Most Wanted.'" CBS News, April 10, 2014. www
.cbsnews.com/news/ex-us-diplomat-murder-suspect-added-to-fbis-most-wanted.

"FBI Combing Western NC for Bradford Bishop Clues." *Charlotte Observer*, March 23, 1976.

"Jacksonville Shop Looks for Lead to 'Bishop.'" *Raleigh News & Observer*, March 16, 1976.

James, Michael. "Manhunt: The 21-Year-Old Search Continues for a Bethesda Man Who Murdered
His Family but Kept the Dog." *Baltimore Sun*, July 24, 1997. www.baltimoresun.com/1997/07/24
/getting-away-with-murder-manhunt-the-21-year-old-search-continues-for-a-bethesda-man
-who-murdered-his-family-but-kept-the-dog/.

"Maryland Family: Officials Identify 5 Burned Bodies." *Raleigh News & Observer*, March 9, 1976.

McClees, Ray, ed. "The Bradford Bishop Mystery." Tyrell County Genealogical & Historical Society.
October 1997. Reprinted in *Washington Daily News*, April 11, 2014. www.thewashingtondailynews
.com/2014/04/11/the-bradford-bishop-mystery.

"MD. Police Find Title to Car, Deem Sale by Bishop Difficult." *Raleigh News & Observer*, March 18, 1976.

Meyer, Eugene L. "The Man Who Got Away." *MoCo 360*, June 30, 2013. https://moco360.
media/2013/06/30/bradford-bishop-murders/.

"Missing Man in 5 Slaying Acted Like Spy, Friends Say." *Durham Sun*, March 11, 1976.

"Murder Suspect's Station Wagon Found in Tennessee." *Durham Morning Herald*, March 19, 1976.

Phillips, Pamela. "Friends Recall Bishop Differently." *Raleigh News & Observer*, March 29, 1976.

"Police Analyzing Bishop Signature." *Charlotte Observer*, March 16, 1976.

Rasmussen, Frederick N. "After 30 Years, Bishop Killings Still a Mystery." *Baltimore Sun*, October 14,
2006. https://web.archive.org/web/20130510142623/http://articles.baltimoresun.com/2006-10
-14/news/0610140093_1_brad-bishop-william-bradford-sledgehammer.

"The Bishop Murders." *Time* 107, no. 12 (March 22, 1976): 18–19.

Thompson, Tisha, and Rick Yarborough. "Inside the Evidence Room in the Hunt for William
Bradford Bishop." NBC Washington. www.nbcwashington.com/news/local/inside-the-evidence
-room-in-the-hunt-for-william-bradford-bishop/78473.

"U.S. Official Sought as 5 Found in NC Identified." *Durham Sun*, March 9, 1976.

"Was Bradford Bishop an Espionage Agent?" *Rocky Mount Telegram*, March 11, 1976.

"Where Is He? No Trace of Diplomat Bishop Six Months after Family Slayings." *Charlotte News*,
September 27, 1976.

Whittle, Richard. "Warrant on Bishop Issued." *Raleigh News & Observer*, March 13, 1976.

"William Bradford Bishop, Jr." Federal Bureau of Investigation: Most Wanted. Accessed August 2024.
https://www.fbi.gov/wanted/murders/william-bradford-bishop-jr/.

Yancy, S., R. Yarborough, and S. Jones. "FBI Confirms NC Woman Is Accused Killer William
Bradford Bishop's Daughter." NBC Washington, September 27, 2021. www.nbcwashington.com
/investigations/brad-bishop/fbi-confirms-nc-woman-is-accused-killer-william-bradford-bishops
-daughter/2807832.

CASE FILE #26

What Happened to the Lost Colony of Roanoke?

Growing up in Northern California, I was vaguely aware from history classes and textbooks that an English colony had disappeared from the East Coast during the sixteenth century. But I don't recall it being a big topic out West, where history emphasizes regional events. Meanwhile, western outdoor adventurers and national park enthusiasts are often focused on big mountain scenery and nature, so I hadn't yet considered exploring the forested islands and historic sites of the Outer Banks.

Then in 2016, my wife and I relocated to the edge of swampy Low Country in South Carolina, so she could teach at a university. As a result, I began to explore an entirely new set of parks and public lands. When I discovered that the Lost Colony site was now preserved by the National Park Service, I knew we had to visit. By then I had already made several visits to Lumbee country around the Lumber River, where I learned about a disputed theory that the lost English colonists may have integrated into the Native American population there.

Finally, we traveled through the Outer Banks from north to south during the fall of 2021. Our trip to Fort Raleigh National Historic Site not only piqued my interest to delve into this mystery, but it became the inspiration for this book. Shortly after visiting, I began to realize how many mysteries—both well-known and forgotten—I had stumbled across at NPS units over the years.

To reconstruct this mystery, I mostly relied upon the primary source materials created by John White in the 1580s and 1590s, including his two accounts and his watercolor paintings and map. To bolster my understanding of the mystery and develop the scenes, I read a wide range of secondary sources, including historical and contemporary discussions. These include the NPS essay series and other articles cited below.

The lone quote attributed to White comes from the end of his account of the fourth voyage, when he departed the colony in August 1587 on a resupply mission. The rumors surrounding the lost colonists' fate come from a survey of secondary sources plus visits to sites and museums mentioned at the end of chapter. My experiences exploring those sites and other coastal areas along the Southeast coast were particularly helpful in reconstructing this mystery.

Sources

"1584: The First English Voyage," "1585: The Military Colony," "1587: The Lost Colony," "1590 Voyage," "Navigating the Atlantic World," "Piracy and Privateering in the Elizabethan New World," "Ships of the Roanoke Voyages," "The Carolina Algonquin." National Park Service: Fort Raleigh. Accessed March 10, 2022. www.nps.gov/fora/learn/historyculture/stories.htm.

Bryant, William Cullen, and Sydney Howard Gay. *A Popular History of the United States from the First*

Discovery of the Western Hemisphere by the Northmen, to the End of the First Century of the Union of the States. Vol. 1. Scribner, Armstrong, and Company, 1876.

"John White (d. 1593)." Encyclopedia Virginia: Virginia Humanities. Accessed March 10, 2022. https://encyclopediavirginia.org/entries/white-john-d-1593.

White, John. Map of "Roanoac" and Outer Banks region. Circa 1584.

White, John. "The Fift Voyage of M. John White into the West Indies and Parts of America Called Virginia, in the Yeere 1590." Written circa 1593. Reprinted in *The Principal Navigations, Voyages, Traffiques, and Discoveries of the English Nation*. Vol. 13. Collected by Richard Hakluyt and edited by Edmund Goldsmid. E & G Goldsmith, 1889: 375–388.

White, John. "The Fourth Voyage Made to Virginia with Three Ships, in Yere 1587. Wherein Was Transported the Second Colony." February 4, 1593. Reprinted in *The Principal Navigations, Voyages, Traffiques, and Discoveries of the English Nation*. Vol. 13. Collected by Richard Hakluyt and edited by Edmund Goldsmid. E & G Goldsmith, 1889: 358–374.

White, John. Watercolor portraits and paintings of the Secotan people, their village, and Algonquin culture. Circa 1584.

"People: Manteo, Wanchese, John White, Virginia Dare (etc.)" National Park Service. Accessed March 10, 2002. www.nps.gov/fora/learn/historyculture/people.htm.

CASE FILE #27

Who Was Ned Simmons?

The first few years after my wife and I relocated to the Southeast coast, I wasn't excited about the move. I regularly traveled inland to places like the Appalachians, the Ozarks, and the Mountain West to continue work on outdoor articles and my books *Paddling the John Wesley Powell Route* and *Discovering the Outlaw Trail*. I admittedly didn't give my new area enough of a chance at first.

Then, one winter, a friend of mine who had moved back home to Iowa sent me an unexpected message. To this day, I imagine him bundled up in a full snowsuit, hunched over his computer while researching warmer destinations. He asked if I'd ever been to Cumberland Island National Seashore. Thing is, I'd heard about it. I'd seen it on maps. But I hadn't looked closely until receiving this message.

Within a few weeks, I was driving south with my pack raft and fat bike. The 2018 government shutdown had paused the ferry service, so I ended up paddling to the island and exploring it by bike over four days. There are ruins, sandy roads lined by saw palmettos, undeveloped beaches, tidal wetlands, and a northern wilderness of salt-pruned oaks draped in Spanish moss. I've been back several times.

After my first trip, at a bookstore in St. Marys, Georgia, I picked up my first book by Mary Bullard (2005) and began reading about the island's history. The most fascinating story I learned was about the British occupation during the War of 1812 and Ned Simmons's two escapes from slavery. I wrote about Ned Simmons for National Parks Magazine in March 2021, and parts of this chapter are adapted from that article. Because there is so little information available, the facts of his life remain shrouded in mystery. Thus, it's important to note that much of my reconstruction is based upon faint connections between scant sources and key assumptions made by Bullard, Smith (2013), and myself.

The opening scene and quoted British proclamation come from two of Bullard's books (2005 and 2008), plus my examination of historical and contemporary maps, tide charts, and moon phases to reconstruct the escape and likely route of the Florida refugees. Plus, I considered my own experiences on the waterways of that region. Also helpful was background information from "Forbes Bluff" (2020) and "A Brief History of Boatbuilding…" (accessed 2020). Summaries about U.S. events during the eighteenth and nineteenth centuries, and prevailing attitudes about slavery before, during, and after the War of 1812 mostly come from Wish (1937), Malcomson (2012), and Smith (2013).

Each of Bullard's three cited works and Smith's book were the most critical in reconstructing Ned Simmons's life. Bullard's 2007 article discusses how she connected the dots between the scant information in various sources to construct a hazy picture of who Simmons might have been, while acknowledging some assumptions may be incorrect. Bullard's 2008 book provides not just the quote from a family friend of Louisa Greene Shaw, but extensive documentation needed to describe the events during British occupation of Cumberland Island and the African Americans who were joining the invading force to escape slavery. Bullard's 2005 book includes the theory that the excavated cabin belonged to Simmons.

After watching a video recording of Smith speaking about his research on Simmons, I interviewed the historian by phone in 2020, during which he discussed his interviews with descendants of Simmons. Smith said the family's oral history reported that Simmons was given an older British redcoat uniform from 1808, and that his lingering grasp on the jacket ripped off the metal button, which he kept as a memento. The closing scenes from the last days of Simmons's life come from Bullard and from Moore (1889), with the latter source providing the final quote attributed to Simmons.

Sources

"A Brief History of Boatbuilding in Our Nation's Oldest Port." St. Augustine Lighthouse & Maritime Museum. Accessed June 26, 2020. www.staugustinelighthouse.org/wp-content/uploads/2019/03 /Boatbuilding-History-St.-Augustine-Craft.pdf.

Bullard, Mary R. *Black Liberation on Cumberland Island in 1815*. Published by the author, 2008.

Bullard, Mary R. *Cumberland Island: A History*. University of Georgia Press, 2005.

Bullard, Mary R. "Ned Simmons, American Slave: The Role of Imagination in Narrative History." The African Diaspora Archaeology Network. June 2007. https://scholarworks.umass.edu/entities /publication/114990d6-d434-40ba-ba4e-613e2ad00875.

"Forbes Bluff." Florida History Online. Accessed June 6, 2020. https://history.domains.unf.edu /floridahistoryonline/projects-proj-b-p-html/projects-plantations-html/hierarchy-of-plantation -pages/forbes-bluff/.

Malcomson, Thomas. "Freedom by Reaching the Wooden World: American Slaves and the British Navy during the War of 1812." *Northern Mariner* 22, no. 4 (October 2012): 361–392.

Moore, Frank, ed. *The Civil War in Song and Story: 1860–1865*. P.F. Collier, 1889.

Smith, Gene Allen. *The Slaves' Gamble: Choosing Sides in the War of 1812*. Palgrave Macmillan, 2013.

"Treaty of Ghent." National Archives. December 24, 1814. www.archives.gov/milestone-documents /treaty-of-ghent.

Wish, Harvey. "Slave Insurrections Before 1861." *The Journal of Negro History* 22, no. 3 (July 1937).

CASE FILE #28

Did Soldiers' Wounds Glow after a Civil War Battle?

While the angel's glow may very well be nothing more than a legend that arose after the battle, what intrigues me about this mystery is the enterprising high school student who demonstrated it could have been possible. The opening scene, depicting General Grant surveying the deadly aftermath at Shiloh, and the quoted line come from chapter 25 of his memoirs (1885–1886).

Background information on the battle and wider Civil War comes from years of reading and watching documentaries on the subject, plus consultation of two articles from American Civil War Story (accessed 2023). The depiction of the park visit and science project results by Martin and Curtis come from Durham (2001) and from Soniak (2012).

Sources

"Angel's Glow at the Battle of Shiloh." American Civil War Story. Accessed April 8, 2023. https://www .americancivilwarstory.com/angels-glow-shiloh.html.

"Battle of Shiloh." American Civil War Story. Accessed April 8, 2023. www.americancivilwarstory .com/battle-of-shiloh.html#google_vignette.

Durham, Sharon. "Students May Have Answer for Faster-Healing Civil War Wounds That Glowed." U.S. Department of Agriculture. May 29, 2001. www.ars.usda.gov/news-events/news/research -news/2001/students-may-have-answer-for-faster-healing-civil-war-wounds-that-glowed.

Grant, Ulysses S. *Personal Memoirs of U.S. Grant.* Charles L. Webster & Company, 1885 and 1886.

Soniak, Matt. "Why Some Civil War Soldiers Glowed in the Dark." *Mental Floss*, April 5, 2012. www
.mentalfloss.com/article/30380/why-some-civil-war-soldiers-glowed-dark.

CASE FILE #29

Iron in the Mud?

I finally got a chance to see an ironclad in person during 2022, when my wife and I stopped by the USS *Cairo* Museum at Vicksburg National Military Park. To reconstruct this story, I called upon my notes and photos from that visit, plus several key sources. Background information came from a variety of history and culture essays by NPS (accessed 2024). The scenes depicting the search, the direct quote, and the salvage operation come mostly from Bearrs (1980), plus Chambers (1964). I also studied historical photos of the USS *Cairo* and other ironclads, and I examined historical maps and satellite images of the Yazoo River.

Sources

Chambers, Elsie May. "A Slow Job: Cairo Will Be Surfacing Soon." *Clarion-Ledger*, September 26, 1964.

Bearss, Edwin C. *Hardluck Ironclad: The Sinking and Salvaging of the Cairo.* 2nd ed. Louisiana State
University Press, June 1980.

"USS Cairo Gunboat and Museum," "Campaign for Vicksburg," etc. History & Culture Essays
by National Park Service. Accessed March 10, 2024. www.nps.gov/vick/learn/historyculture
/index.htm.

CASE FILE #30

Is a 1980s Treasure Buried Near the Oldest Stone Fortress in the United States?

I learned about *The Secret* around the mid-2010s, when I began researching the Forrest Fenn treasure hunt. Eventually, my friends and I searched for the Fenn treasure in the Colorado Rockies, using kayaks and a raft, and I wrote about the topic for *Canoe & Kayak* and *Men's Journal.* We had a fun trip, and it inspired me to research several of the puzzles in *The Secret* that were theorized to be in areas I visited regularly. My interest is less about actual searching, which I've yet to do, and more about unraveling the multidecade story. Given that at least two casques may be in or near NPS units, it seemed like a perfect story to include in this book.

The opening scenes and interview quotes attributed to Preiss come from 1982 newspaper articles by Archibald, Carroll, Holt, and Zorn—these sources also report early critical reactions to the book. Summaries about the history of *The Secret*, the broader nationwide search, theorized locations of the remaining casques, and descriptions of online discussion forums come from sources like Scott (2018), and from examining the major websites devoted to *The Secret*, including http://quest4treasure.co.uk, http://thesecret.pbworks.com, https://12treasures.com, and others.

The Chicago discovery scenes come mostly from Zorn (1983) plus other sources. The Cleveland discovery comes from Evans (2004). Brian Zinn's descriptions of meeting Preiss, and quotes attributed to Zinn and Preiss, come from "Cleveland Pictures from Egbert" (2012). The death of Byron Preiss was reported by the *New York Times* (2005). The final email message attributed to Preiss is quoted from a post by user *wilhouse* on Tuesday, May 18, 2004, to the topic thread "Huge Discovery ?!?!?!?" (2004–2012). The scenes depicting the casque recovered due to the efforts of Krupat come from Baker and from White (both 2019). The history of Florida is culled from a wide variety of sources, as is the section about a casque possibly being buried in St. Augustine. All verses are quoted directly from *The Secret* (1982). A wide range of historical photos, maps, and personal experiences at relevant sites was considered to reconstruct this mystery.

Sources

Archibald, John J. "Elves and Trolls Bury Treasures, Get in Some Digs." *St. Louis Post-Dispatch*, October 25, 1982.

Baker, Billy. "Hidden Treasure, a Family's Quest, and 'The Secret.'" *Boston Globe*, October 25, 2019. https://www.bostonglobe.com/metro/2019/10/25/hidden-treasure-family-quest-and-the-secret/RkYsVbk5DoSD6ReMCN9JJJ/story.html.

"Byron Preiss, 52, Digital Publishing Pioneer, Dies." *New York Times*, July 11, 2005. www.nytimes.com/2005/07/11/nyregion/byron-preiss-52-digital-publishing-pioneer-dies.html.

Carroll, Jerry. "A Modern Guide to Buried Treasure." *San Francisco Chronicle*, November 2, 1982.

"Cleveland Pictures from Egbert." Quest4Treasure Discussion Forum, February 23–28, 2012. Accessed April 6, 2024. http://quest4treasure.co.uk/phpbb3/viewtopic.php?f=32&t=1816&start=15.

Evans, Christopher. "The Secret Garden." *Plain Dealer Sunday* magazine, June 13, 2004.

Holt, Patricia. "Emperor Norton Returns in Spirit." *San Francisco Chronicle*, May 31, 1982.

"Huge Discovery ?!?!?!?" Quest4Treasure Discussion Forum. April 15, 2014 to October 16, 2012. http://quest4treasure.co.uk/phpbb3/viewtopic.php?f=32&t=1081&hilit=huge+discovery.

MacDonald, Heidi. "Byron Preiss Assets on the Block for $150K." *Comics Beat*, October 2, 2006. www.comicsbeat.com/byron-preiss-assets-on-the-block-for-150k.

Merrick, George E. "Moonlight in Old St. Augustine," from *Songs of the Wind on a Southern Shore, and other Poems of Florida*. Four Seas Publishing Co., 1920.

Preiss, Byron, ed. *The Secret: A Treasure Hunt*. Bantam, 1982.

Scott, Sam. "Can This Puzzle Be Solved?" *Stanford* magazine, July 16, 2018. https://medium.com/stanford-magazine/a-treasure-hunt-for-the-ages-440c823fc019.

"The Complete History of The Secret." 12 Treasures. Accessed April 5, 2024. https://12treasures.com/history-of-the-secret.

"The History Behind *The Secret*." The Secret (a Treasure Hunt). Accessed April 5, 2024. http://thesecret.pbworks.com/w/page/87278728/History.

"Very Sad News." Quest4Treasure Discussion Forum, July 11, 2005. Accessed April 6, 2024. http://quest4treasure.co.uk/phpbb3/viewtopic.php?f=32&t=1849&p=23141#p23118.

White, Dustin. "Found Treasure: The Boston Casque of the Secret Armchair Treasure Hunt." Mysterious Writings, October 31, 2019. https://mysteriouswritings.com/found-treasure-the-boston-casque-of-the-secret-armchair-treasure-hunt.

Zorn, Eric. "Chicago Pals Unearth 'Secret' Treasure." *Chicago Tribune*, August 9, 1983.

Zorn, Eric. "Fantasy Tale Sparks Treasure Hunt." *Chicago Tribune*, November 16, 1982.

CASE FILE #31

Who Carved the *Mona Lisa* of the Mountains?

I learned about the mysterious face sometime after it received attention from regional journalists during the early 2020s, which roughly coincided with New River Gorge National River being redesignated as a national park and preserve. Details about Gene Kistler's discovery of the face were originally reported by David Silbray in *West Virginia Explorer* magazine. Silbray's 2022 article provides the quote attributed to Kistler and his interpretations of the face. Su Clauson-Wicker's 2020 article offers additional details. The opening scene with Kistler following the trail and spotting the face, plus descriptions of the surrounding landscape and landmarks, were taken from the source material and my own experiences while visiting the stone face and relevant park sites during 2023.

Sources

Clauson-Wicker, Su. "'Mona Lisa of the Mountains?' The Stone Face of the New River Gorge." *Blue Ridge Country*, Jan/Feb 2020.

Silbray, David. "Remarkable Stone Face Attracting Curious in New River Gorge." *West Virginia Explorer*, August 20, 2022. https://wvexplorer.com/2022/08/20/mystery-stone-face-new-river-gorge-fayetteville-wv/.

CASE FILE #32 ═══

The Second-Oldest River in the World—and the "Northiest"?

I've been visiting the New River area since the fall of 2009, when I first whitewater kayaked the lower gorge. I later returned several times to kayak and raft the nearby Gauley. During a visit with my wife to the region in 2023, a display in the visitor center museum at New River State Park reminded me of the various sayings I had encountered about the river's age and flow direction. Fortunately, geographers Morgan and Mayfield (1994) have expertly unraveled the backstory behind the age claim, which was supplemented with geological details from NPS (accessed 2024). The history behind the New River's name comes from Johnston (1906). Debunking the "northiest" claim was simply a matter of examining maps.

Sources

Errick, Jennifer. "The Oldest River in North America?" National Parks Conservation Organization blog. August 2, 2021. www.npca.org/articles/1990-the-oldest-river-in-north-america.

"Geology of New River Gorge." National Park Service. Accessed March 6, 2024. www.nps.gov/neri /learn/nature/geology.htm.

Johnston, David E. *A History of Middle New River Settlements and Contiguous Territory*. Standard Printing & Publishing Company, 1906. www.loc.gov/item/06026016/.

Morgan, John T., and Michael W. Mayfield. "The Second Oldest River in the World?" *Southern Geographer* 34, no. 2 (November 1994): 138–144.

CASE FILE #33 ═══

Did Pocahontas Save John Smith's Life?

In the fall of 2021, my wife and I visited the excellent National Museum of the American Indian on the National Mall in Washington, DC. A fascinating display about Pocahontas, in the *Americans* exhibition, piqued my interest in learning more about her life. During a summer 2023 road trip, we went to Historic Jamestowne and Colonial National Historic Park in Virginia to further grasp the locales and events of the early 1600s that gave rise to the legend of Pocahontas saving John Smith's life.

To reconstruct this mystery, I primarily relied upon a close reading of the limited primary source materials, while consulting a wide range of secondary sources to grasp the various debates surrounding the original events and subsequent legends. Of particular help was consulting the Pocahontas Archive website from Lehigh University.

The opening scene and quote come from the 1617 stage play for *The Vision of Delight* by

Jonson (1640). The description of a typical masque and audience comes from several contemporary sources, including "The Masque…" (accessed 2024). The clothing Pocahontas wore is approximated based upon the 1616 engraving by Simon van de Passe (1616), which also provides the given names of Pocahontas, and other details.

The scenes depicting Pocahontas and her party visiting England come from the 1600s letters of John Chamberlain (reprinted 1939), Selman (2016), Dismore (2016), and Smith (1624), with the latter source providing his 1617 letter to the queen.

Accounts of the Virginia Colony during the early 1600s come from numerous sources, including Smith (1608, 1612, 1624), Wingfield (1608), Symonds (1612), Purchas (1614), Rolfe (1614), and others.

The reunion between Pocahontas and Smith, including the quoted dialogue, comes from Smith (1624). The final scene comes from several sources, with the quoted dialogue attributed to Pocahontas recorded by Rolfe (1617).

Sources

Chamberlain, John. *The Letters of John Chamberlain.* Vol. 1. Edited by Norman Egbert McClure. American Philosophical Society, 1939.

Dismore, Jane. "Pocahontas in England." History Today. May 24, 2016. www.historytoday.com /pocahontas-england.

Jonson, Ben. *The Vision of Delight: Presented at Court in Christmas, 1617.* University of Virginia Library. Accessed August 2024. https://xtf.lib.virginia.edu/xtf/view?docId=chadwyck_evd/uvaGenText /tei/chevd_V1.0044.xml.

Purchas, Samuel. *Purchas His Pilgrimage: Or Relations of the World and the Religions Observed in All Ages and Places Discovered, From the Creation Unto This Present in Foure Parts.* 1614. Republished by James MacLehose and Sons, 1906.

Rolfe, John. Letter to Sir Edwin Sandys. 1617. Reprinted in *Virginia Magazine of History and Biography* 10, no. 2 (October 1902): 130–138.

Rolfe, John. Letter to Sir Thomas Dale. 1614. Reprinted in *Narratives of Early Virginia, 1606–1625,* ed. Lyon Gardiner Tyler. Charles Scribner's Sons, 1907.

Selman, Ruth. "Pocahontas in London, 1616–17." The National Archives Blog. June 28, 2016. https:// blog.nationalarchives.gov.uk/pocahontas-london-1616–1617/.

Smith, John. *A Map of Virginia with a Description of the Countrey, the Commodities, People, Government and Religion.* Joseph Barnes, 1612.

Smith, John. *A True Relation of Such Occurrences of Noate as Hath Happened in Virginia.* John Tappe, 1608.

Smith, John. *The Generall Historie of Virginia, New-England, and the Summer Isles.* Michael Sparkes, 1624.

Symonds, William. *The Proceedings of the English Colonie in Virginia*. 1612. Repr. in *The Complete Works of Captain John Smith*. Philip L. Barbour, ed. Vol. 1. University of North Carolina Press, 1986.

"The Masque: A Fabulously Extravagant, Early 17th Century Court Entertainment." Historic Royal Palaces. Accessed February 26, 2024. from https://www.hrp.org.uk/banqueting-house/history-and-stories/the-masque.

The Pocahontas Archive. Lehigh University. Accessed February 2024. https://history-on-trial.lib.lehigh.edu/trial/pocahontas.

Van de Passe, Simon. Engraved portrait of "Matoaka als Rebecka," 1616. National Portrait Gallery. Smithsonian Institution.

Wingfield, Edward Maria. "A Discourse of Virginia." 1608. Reprinted in *Archaeologica Americana: Transactions and Collections of the American Antiquarian Society* 4. Charles Deane, ed. 1860.

CASE FILE #34

Who Was Involved in the Conspiracy to Assassinate Abraham Lincoln?

For years, I didn't think too much about the Lincoln assassination beyond the basic details regarding Booth and his accomplices that are commonly repeated in history classes or retellings of the event. I was aware, generally, that many dramatizations take wide license with the facts. Frankly, I often found the full story hard to grasp due to the many debates, disagreements, and gaps in the record.

Then a visit to Ford's Theatre with my wife in fall of 2021 piqued my interest in unraveling a true shortform story surrounding the conspiracy. This chapter—plus Mesa Verde and Upheaval Dome—became perhaps the most challenging mysteries to reconstruct in this book. Let's just say, I went down some fascinating rabbit holes so that you don't have to. Unless you want to, of course. In that case, may I recommend, and inquire with the powers that be, that intravenous coffee become a thing. Okay, let's do this.

Given the mountain of primary source material available, I sought guidance for my reconstruction from several compilations and secondary sources, including Holzer's compilation (2015), Linder (accessed 2024), and others. One goal was to understand the various points of debate within the historical record.

All references in the chapter to tribunal testimony, including quotes, were verified through transcripts in books like Poore (1865) and online like Lincoln Conspirators (accessed 2024), which were also immensely helpful in depicting the scenes.

The opening execution scene calls upon several sources including the *New York Times* (1865), "Prock's Last Letters..." (reprinted 1939), and others. The final words of Powell, Atzerodt, and Surratt are reported with slight variation in phrasing and speaking order in numerous sources, and the version here is a condensed approximation that tries to accurately render the scene. Also helpful were the execution photographs by Gardner.

Descriptions of the grand illumination of Washington, DC, and public opinions of Booth—before and after the assassination—are culled from a variety of historical newspaper articles and later secondary sources. The quoted line attributed to President Lincoln is from the transcript of his last public address (1865). The quoted response attributed to Booth comes from the 1867 congressional testimony of Major Thomas T. Eckert (Holzer 2015), who claimed it was told to him by Lewis Powell during an interrogation.

The backstories of the various conspirators, and the meetings at the Surratt boardinghouse, come mostly from witness testimony offered during the military tribunal and from a survey of secondary sources, as do the movements and actions of Booth and his accomplices throughout the day of the assassination. The quoted note Booth left for the vice president is now in the National Archives. The quoted dialogue attributed to Harry Hawk comes from the stage play for Our American Cousin.

Events in the theater, including the quote attributed to Booth, come from numerous accounts, with particular clarity afforded by the following sources reprinted in Holzer (2014): an Associated Press dispatch written by Lawrence Gobright; four telegrams sent by Edwin Stanton; an affidavit from Henry Rathbone; and letters by Harry Hawk and Helen DuBarry. The shifting mood in the streets of Washington comes from James Tanner's letter plus examining the painting "Lincoln Borne by Loving Hands" by witness Carl Bersch, with helpful discussion by Taylor (2016).

Lincoln's final hours after being shot come from the report of doctors Charles Leale and Charles Taft (Holzer, 2015). The quote attributed to Stanton is printed in a wide range of sources, though the veracity of this epitaph is debated. Some scholars believe he actually said the word "angels" not "ages," while others claim that either quote was invented by later historians.

The movements of Booth and Herold, during their flight from the capital and leading to Herold's surrender and Booth's death, come from tribunal testimony and National Park Service (accessed 2024). The descriptions related to Booth's corpse come mostly from Spiegel (1998). The quotes attributed to Bates come from trial testimony. The quoted lines from MacBeth, are, of course, Shakespeare's. I actually enjoyed reading the play this time around, given that unraveling a historic murder was involved.

Regarding the issue of spies and ciphers, Atzerodt's confession was recorded by McPhail (1865.). An excellent discussion of the alleged spy Sarah Slater is found in Brooks (2013). And the cipher discovered among Booth's effects comes from Taylor (2019).

Phew. How about some more intravenous coffee?

Sources

Brooks, Rebecca Beatrice. "The Disappearance of Sarah Slater: Confederate Spy and Lincoln Conspirator." Civil War Saga. May 14, 2013. https://civilwarsaga.com/the-disappearance-of-sarah -slater-confederate-spy-and-lincoln-conspirator/.

Burnett, Henry Lawrence. "Assassination of President Lincoln and the Trial of the Assassins." In *History of the Ohio Society of New York, 1885–1905,* edited by James H. Kennedy. Grafton Press, 1906.

Edwards, William. "The Confession of Samuel Arnold." UMKC School of Law. April 18, 1865. http:// law2.umkc.edu/faculty/projects/ftrials/lincolnconspiracy/Arnoldconfession.html.

"End of the Assassins." *New York Times,* July 8, 1865.

Gardner, Alexander. "Execution of the Conspirators—the Drop." Photos. Library of Congress. Accessed August 2024. https://www.loc.gov/item/2008680151/.

Holzer, Harold, comp. *President Lincoln Assassinated! The Firsthand Story of the Murder, Manhunt, Trial, and Mourning.* Library of America, 2014.

Holzer, Harold. "What the Newspapers Said When Lincoln Was Killed." *Smithsonian* magazine, March 2015. www.smithsonianmag.com/history/what-the-newspapers-said-when-lincoln-was -killed-180954325.

Lincoln, Abraham. "The President's Last Public Address." American Presidency Project. Accessed August 2024. www.presidency.ucsb.edu/documents/the-presidents-last-public-address.

Linder, Douglas O. "The Trial of the Lincoln Assassination Conspirators: An Account." UMKC School of Law: Famous Trials. Accessed April 17, 2024. www.famous-trials.com/lincoln/2163-home.

McPhail, James. "The Confession of George Atzerodt." UMKC School of Law: Famous Trials. May 1, 1865. https://famous-trials.com/lincoln/2145-atzerodtconfession.

Poore, Ben Perley. *The Conspiracy Trial for the Murder of the President.* J.E. Tilton and Company, 1865.

"'Prock's' Last Letters to the Vincennes Western Sun." *Indiana Magazine of History* 35, no. 1 (March 1939): 76–94.

Spiegel, Allen D. "Dr. John Frederick May and the Identification of John Wilkes Booth's Body." *Journal of Community Health* 23, no. 5 (October 1998): 383–405.

Taylor, Dave. "John Wilkes Booth's 'Confederate' Cipher." Lincoln Conspirators. July 26, 2019. https://lincolnconspirators.com/2019/07/26/john-wilkes-booths-confederate-cipher/.

Taylor, Dave. "Lincoln Borne by Loving Hands on the Fatal Night of April 14, 1865." Lincoln Conspirators. March 2016. https://lincolnconspirators.com/2016/03/22/lincoln-borne-by -loving-hands-on-the-fatal-night-of-april-14–1865.

"The Assassin's Escape: Following John Wilkes Booth." National Park Service. Accessed April 18, 2024. www.nps.gov/foth/learn/historyculture/the-assassin-s-escape.htm.

"The Conspiracy Trial: Day by Day." Lincoln Conspirators. Accessed March and April 2024. https:// lincolnconspirators.com/the-trial.

"Thoughts from an Assassin: The Journal of John Wilkes Booth." National Park Service. Accessed April 17, 2004. www.nps.gov/foth/learn/historyculture/thoughts-from-an-assassin-the-journal -of-john-wilkes-booth.htm.

CASE FILE #35

Could a Kayaker Survive Niagara Falls?

As a young kayaker in the mid-2000s, I learned about the legend of a paddler running Niagara Falls several times, particularly during my visits to the Ocoee River in Tennessee. As the years passed, I heard the story less often. But one memorable detail about almost every retelling was the claim, often accompanied by a sly grin, that since Jesse Sharp's body was never found, he might have faked his own death. While this sounds like a tall tale from the campfire, I wanted to unravel the story behind the myth.

The opening scene and descriptions of Sharp's actions throughout the day of his disappearance, plus the reactions of local officials and people gathering on shore, come from witness accounts reported in the news articles listed in this section. I also closely examined photos and still images taken from video footage that documented the event, which can be found online, and I considered my own experience and knowledge of whitewater paddling.

The account of Sharp's aborted 1979 desire to run Niagara comes from two articles in which photojournalist Eric Demme was interviewed, UPI and Warner (both 1990). The latter article provides the quote attributed to officer Hollidge. Details about Sharp's life, from high school to his Niagara attempt, come from *The Tennessean* (1990) and various reported interviews with Sharp's paddling friends and acquaintances at the Ocoee. Descriptions of Sharp's boat and the condition of his recovered equipment come from witness accounts and my observations of the official photographs that were released.

The history of Niagara Falls daredevils, including Annie Edson Taylor and Robert Overacker, comes from historical news articles. The alleged sightings of Sharp after Niagara come from a humor article by Carlson (1990), who claimed Sharp's survival was already being turned into a myth in the whitewater community.

And the final detail about rusty boater vehicles seen near the rivers of the Southeast? That comes from me. I spotted those bumper stickers a few times before I even realized what they referred to. Eventually, most of the regional references that *Jesse Lives* also vanished.

Sources

"Accident Database: Report ID #74." American Whitewater. June 6, 2017. Accessed December 31, 2022. https://www.americanwhitewater.org/content/Accident/detail/accidentid/74.

Baker, David R. "Californian Killed in Niagara Falls Stunt." *Los Angeles Times*, October 2, 1995. www
.latimes.com/archives/la-xpm-1995-10-02-mn-52471-story.html.

Brown, Barry, and David Y. Cooper. "Ontario Hikes the Fines for Falls Stunts." *Buffalo News*,
December 17, 1989. https://buffalonews.com/news/ontario-hikes-the-fines-for-falls-stunts
-daredevil-penalty-rises-from-500-to-10–000/article_ca06f7d0-ffe9–5ebd-893c-9574216389f3.
html.

Buckham, Tom. "Falls Daredevils Have Officials over a Barrel." *Buffalo News*, July 17, 1990. https://
buffalonews.com/news/falls-daredevils-have-officials-over-a-barrel-stiffer-fines-fail-to-halt
-stunts/article_f832ea56-2037-5c31-bd80–261cc6d83ca5.html.

Carlson, Gary. "A Modern-Day Kayaking Myth: Jesse Lives!" *American Whitewater Journal*,
September/October 1990.

"Daredevil Not One of Bodies at Falls." *The Sun Times*, June 29, 1990.

"Jesse Sharp Rites Slated Tomorrow." *The Tennessean*, June 12, 1990.

"Kayaker So Sure He'd Succeed He Had Reservations for Dinner." *Tampa Tribune*, June 7, 1990.

"Man Apparently Killed in Niagara Falls Kayak Stunt." United Press International, June 6, 1990.
www.upi.com/Archives/1990/06/06/Man-apparently-killed-in-Niagara-Falls-kayak-stunt
/2749644644800.

"Over Horseshoe Fall in a Barrel." *Buffalo Commercial*, October 25, 1901.

"Search for Stuntman Called Off." *The Gazette*, June 7, 1990.

"Tennessee Kayaker Still Missing." *The Leaf Chronicle*, June 7, 1990.

Warner, Gene. "Kayaker Died Pursuing Dream He Could Conquer the Falls." *Buffalo News*, June 7,
1990. https://buffalonews.com/news/kayaker-died-pursuing-dream-he-could-conquer-the-falls
-white-water-bum-brought-friends-to/article_e9ece7e6–48c7–53ca-9392-daec1e2f6b80.html.

ACKNOWLEDGMENTS

A big thank-you to my wife, Ina Seethaler, for joining me on so many visits to NPS units and listening to me rant about how all the clues point to us hiking every trail.

Thank you to all the great people I've met in and around our national parks, including rangers, staff, researchers, and fellow visitors who shared insights and adventure tips that pointed me toward many of the mysteries in this book.

And thank you to Anna Michels and her excellent team at Sourcebooks, including Jillian Rahn, Emily Proano, Kayleigh George, and Madeleine Brown, for believing in this book and pointing it toward the shelves.

ABOUT THE AUTHOR

© Ina Seethaler

Mike Bezemek is an award-winning of stories and books with an adventurous spin. A former whitewater rafting and wilderness backpacking guide, he remains an avid paddler, mountain biker, skier, and hiker. His writing and photography can be found in publications like *Outside, Smithsonian* magazine, *National Parks* magazine, *Blue Ridge Outdoors, Terrain, Duct Tape Diaries, Paddling Magazine,* and more.

Three of his books combine storytelling, photos, and travel guides:

* *Discovering the Outlaw Trail: Routes, Hideouts, and Stories from the Wild West*
* *Space Age Adventures: Over 100 Terrestrial Sites and Out of This World Stories*
* *Paddling the John Wesley Powell Route: Exploring the Green and Colorado Rivers*

Check out his work or connect with the author at https://mikebezemek.com. Over the past two decades, the author has explored widely across America. He's lived and worked on both coasts and in the middle. He's done the road life thing during long projects in the field. Along the way, he's made hundreds of visits to units of the National Park System. In *Mysteries of the National Parks*, the author shares the strangest and most baffling tales he's discovered during his travels.